MULTIMEDIA MATERIALS FOR AFRO-AMERICAN STUDIES

MULTIMEDIA MATERIALS FOR AFRO-AMERICAN STUDIES

A CURRICULUM ORIENTATION AND ANNOTATED BIBLIOGRAPHY OF RESOURCES

**Edited and Compiled by
Dr. Harry Alleyn Johnson**

144671

**R. R. BOWKER COMPANY
New York & London, 1971**

Published by R. R. Bowker Company (A XEROX COMPANY)
1180 Avenue of the Americas, New York, N.Y. 10036

Copyright © 1971 Xerox Corporation
Internatonal Standard Book Number: 0–8352–0404–9

Library of Congress Catalog Card Number: 75–126009

Manufactured in the United States of America

COVER PHOTO BY TRINA LIPTON

I DEDICATE THIS VOLUME TO MY WIFE, MAE, who over the years has been my most valuable proofreader and critic of the highest order, and to my friend and teacher Dr. Paul W. F. Witt, Professor of Education, Michigan State University, who in his own inimitable way has lived "some of my best friends are Negroes" without ever having uttered the words.

Harry Alleyn Johnson

Contents

PART THREE: Multimedia Materials on the Peoples of Africa, Their Cultures, and Contributions to Mankind.

Preface

The treatment of the American Negro as the "invisible man" has been a long standing practice in the recording of American history. The past few years have witnessed much concern for this blatant omission. A constant stream of inquiries has come from teachers and others concerned with creating curriculum designs for suitable and relevant materials for teaching black studies and current social issues. This demand for introducing or expanding ethnically-oriented curricula is a concern of critical importance in American education as we approach the twenty-first century. The issue first emerged to public attention from college campuses and has spread to secondary and elementary schools of all levels, to government, and to business. It has, in fact, made its way to the conscience of the American people. However, with this impetus, we discovered that there was no single source one could turn to for a compilation of materials and resources relevant for designing a meaningful and realistic curriculum which incorporated black studies content.

School systems and colleges throughout the country are groping with the task of including in their educational programs curriculum materials relevant to non-white children and young adults. Our great concern is that of providing minority children and youth with an educational environment in which they can identify, and a secure and comfortable atmosphere in which they can continue to identify and learn; an atmosphere in which they value themselves as persons and take pride in their own ethnic heritage. This is an urgent need for all minorities: Mexican-Americans, Puerto Ricans, Hawaiians, Indians, Negroes, indigent whites and others.

We felt that a standard source book would greatly assist educators in planning and executing necessary curriculum changes. Many publications have been made available which list suitable print materials for teaching about minorities, but no completely documented bibliography has produced information on non-print resources, addressing itself to the fast changing curriculum needs. This document sets out to develop a broadly based rationale in well designed position papers by distinguished black professionals now on the American scene. In the first paper, I focus on the new technology and educational media as related to the special educational problems and characteristics of ghetto youth. Dr. Jacquelyne Jackson, Psychiatric-Sociologist at the Duke University Medical School, focuses on the sociological and psychological needs of ghetto youth. Dr. Deborah Wolfe, Professor of Education at New York's Queens College, concentrates her paper on the integration of black studies into today's curriculum. The eminent historian, Dr. Charles Wesley, former Wilberforce University president and now Executive Director, Association for the Study of Negro Life and History, writes from the historian's vantage point of the need for integrating Negro history into the mainstream of world history. Sections two and three, which annotate the accumulated and selected items, were researched from every source known or available. In bits and pieces from university collections, educational TV stations, publishing firms, libraries, and other sources, the final document was created. It was not possible to get all information about each entry. All entries do, however, provide the user with enough data for further exploration. Although this volume concentrates on one of America's racial minorities, the blacks, it is certainly well established by now that the same kind of research is needed on other groups. Perhaps forthcoming sequels will concentrate on these ethnic groups.

For their assistance as researchers, advisors, and consultants, I wish to extend my very deep appreciation to the following persons: Mrs. Catherine V. Bland, Library Director, Virginia State College, Petersburg, Virginia; Mr. Kenneth M. McIntyre, Director, Bureau of Audiovisual Education, University of North Carolina, Chapel Hill, North Carolina; Mr. James E. Parker, Director, Audiovisual Center, North Carolina Central University, Durham, North Carolina; and Dr. Ralph L. Wooden, Director, Audiovisual Center, North Carolina A & T University, Greensboro, North Carolina.

Harry Alleyn Johnson
Virginia State College
July, 1970

MULTIMEDIA MATERIALS FOR AFRO-AMERICAN STUDIES

PART ONE: POSITION PAPERS

A black educator relates the new technology and educational media to the special educational problems and characteristics of ghetto youth

Dr. HARRY ALLEYN JOHNSON
Associate Dean and Director, Learning Resources Center,
Virginia State College, Petersburg, Va.

Designing a curriculum in a changing society is a task that educators must face squarely as we approach the twenty-first century. This need has reached crisis proportion for the economically deprived youth of this land and especially the black youth in the rural pockets and congested urban slums. The verbatim transfer of suburban middle class curriculum to black children and the poor and socially deprived has proven time and again a failure. The purpose of this paper and those which follow is an attempt to spell out the pressing need for black youth to find his identity, his history and his manhood among the bits and pieces now fragmented by a Western culture which included only its own heritage with the development of human history through the past centuries.

To begin with, children from slum environments and disadvantaged backgrounds, especially black children, possess certain characteristics which seem consistent as they tackle a curriculum not designed for them at all.

The ghetto youth is academically and intellectually behind his suburban-majority counterpart; short of skills, verbal self-expressions, training and refinements, and all the other attributes which lend themselves to learning. He is, however, well aware of certain measures of self protection; he has grown up and matured rapidly, formulated many mistrusts and survived the wear and tear of the ghetto and the fated hand of prejudice and discrimination when venturing from its confines. He sees the enemies—the police, the rent collector, the teacher, a drunken father, a grocery store boss—and they all dispute his passage. When he comes to school—if he comes to school—he comes with more of a complexity of burdens than any children anywhere in the world. He's concerned with being drafted for the Vietnam War, he's eighteen and plagued with an ignorance and fear of venereal diseases surrounding him, usually hungry or never quite full, dressed in clothes which he long ago learned to despise and he is already tired from the long walk to school from a tenement house where babies cried all through the long night, and equally frustrated parents fought either verbally or physically in an interminable conflict. He gets to school just on time, but most likely late, to get the abuses of a battery of middle class rules and regulations from middle class school personnel with middle class values and an obsolete middle class curriculum planned around a scheduled set of time blocks that won't move an inch. At 9:00 A.M. he is greeted with a talking face, the same one he left yesterday, droning on and on about the dates, location and details of the Hundred Years' War between France and England. And really, who gives a damn? Not even the teacher, who fifty-three times out of a hundred grew up in the same neighborhood, finished the local high school and a city teachers college, all to come back to teach about a subject she knows little about and cares less about. Her meager, dull, uninspired "teaching" is all she can bring forth from an impoverished social, economic and academic past. So it goes on and on, cycle repeating itself, getting worse as the world around them moves into the age of technology and space. That is a part of the picture of a ghetto child and the school he goes to and the home he comes from. Wherein this picture may prove to be the rule in some locations and exception in others, the mere fact that it exists at all should foster a disquieting and repugnant feeling to all Americans.

The survey known as the Coleman Report[1] sounds a ringing rebuke to the failure of contemporary American education to meet the needs of low status minority poor of this land. The survey represented a massive effort involving many quantitative measures. Complete sets of information were collected from more than 3,000 schools representing about 650,000 students in five grades of public school. More than 60,000 teachers, several thousand principals and several hundred superintendents in school districts also responded to this research. These data were analyzed in 1966 and the 737 page Coleman Report, *Equality of Educational Opportunity*, was published by the U.S. Office of Education in the summer of 1966. Deep as it is in statistics, facts and fallacies, it is accurate enough to sound warnings of the presence of social and political dynamite ready to be ignited into the greatest social explosion since the French Revolution. Enough generalizations may be drawn from these massive statistics to get the message about the unequal opportunities in American education.

By and large, ghetto children dislike or hate the school curriculum. Their greatest joy at school is often a denied opportunity to relate and react to each other. They have every right to this feeling. What they are required to do in the planned curriculum is irrelevant in both content and method. Kenneth Clark describes it succinctly:

> What I believe I know about the nature of this crisis I think can be summarized in one sentence or, more accurately, one anguished explana-

---

[1] James S. Coleman and others. *Equality of Educational Opportunity*. Washington, D.C.: Office of Education, U.S. Department of Health, Education, and Welfare, 1966.

tion—namely, contemporary American education, urban public education, is a national disaster. A calamity. A catastrophic, inefficient situation. A social and political powder keg, awaiting just a capricious spark to set off a tremendous social explosion.

The chief victims of this calamity are clearly low-status minority-group children and other children from low-income families. The public educational system has broken down in terms of fulfilling the responsibility of preparing these children for a meaningful role in our society . . . Specifically, these children, literally abandoned by our public schools, in terms of any meaningful definition of the term education, are suffering from a pattern of unsolved educational problems.

. . . But the data that are available support without question the calamitous, catastrophic, criminally inefficient level of public education in deprived areas. These data support the fact that the retardation is cumulative; that the longer the children remain in school, the further behind they fall in the basic subjects when compared with more privileged children. Drop-outs are excessive, and analysis of the drop-outs leaves at least this observer to believe that these children are probably the more intelligent, in that they escape from a dehumanized and intolerable situation.[2]

In his address for the Educational Media Council on Television as an Educational Tool, Dr. Clark goes on to further state:

First, develop a parallel educational program on television. And, I'm suggesting, outside of the control of the present educational bureaucracy. A parallel educational program in basic skills of reading, arithmetic, communication—oral *and* written, etc.[3]

One may not agree with all of Dr. Clark's recommendations, but certainly must agree that ghetto schools and minority groups must shake off the shackles of the whole middle class aura that prevails from preschool to college. We have mimicked and aped and copied middle class values to such an extent that it has destroyed the very fabric of the educational system for minority groups.

Deprived minorities include not only the nation's blacks but Mexicans, Puerto Ricans, Indians, migrant workers, and a larger portion of whites than most Americans realize. Learning characteristics of the deprived are not inherent but result from the hopeless poverty cycle of rural or urban slum existence. This analysis is neither all inclusive, nor does it apply equally to all minority youth. At the risk of further stereotyping, however, here are some identifications and characteristics recognizable among children from deprived backgrounds:

Language deficiency and damaging personal restraints. Because his speech patterns follow a restricted linguistic code, he cannot cope with the standard English communication of his classroom. Limited opportunities to

[2] Kenneth B. Clark. "Unstructuring Education," *New Relationships in ITV*. Washington, D.C.: Educational Media Council, Inc., 1967.
[3] *Ibid.*

develop language skills at home deny him the development of an extensive vocabulary and thought itself is kept at a low level.

Weak perception discrimination, concentration difficulty, and limited attention span, combined with unimaginative and irrelevant curriculum materials, make it difficult for him to give attention to abstractions.

Orientation to present fulfillment and a nebulous perspective of the future. The pressures of existing from day to day and meal to meal prohibit the luxury of long range goals and daydreaming of the future.

Low self-esteem and low educational aspiration. Generations of poverty and discrimination deny him an identity with the middle class life his school emulates. The police, the grocer, the rent collector, the teacher represent the authority he bitterly resents, and reflect a defensive, hostile, and negative behavior toward authority.

Disoriented to intelligence and standarized tests. If one believes that intellect is developed rather than inherited, then there is validity in classifying standardized tests as representing the middle class child's capacity to learn. Low scores on such tests have caused deprived youth to confront such tests with a defeatist attitude. This condition, together with an inability to decode standard English, convinces him that his performance will be interpreted as low mental ability.

Slow learning as a way of learning. Many children among the disadvantaged are limited by genetic endowment, but educators make a mistake when they identify all slow learners in this category. Some are slow learners in a very different way. With more appropriate tactics, they can be taught to improve their rate of learning.

A unique learning style. A teacher who fails to detect varying learning styles and fails to make her instructional strategies flexible will also fail to discover some students' potential for success and achievement.

One of the most important reasons for the multi-media or technological approach to instruction for the economically deprived lies in what Frank Riessman calls "style of learning." In planning strategies of learning for youngsters who have been disadvantaged, the fact that these patterns do exist should be a guiding factor. In individualizing instruction, each child's strengths and weaknesses should be diagnosed and treated through the most effective strategies available. Says Frank Riessman:

> One index of style relates to whether you learn things most easily through reading or through hearing, or whether you learn through doing things physically; whether you learn things slowly, or quickly; whether you learn things in a one track way or whether you are very flexible in your learning. The examples just cited are not to be seen as separate from one another. There can be combinations such as a visual-physical learner who learns in a slow one-track fashion.[4]

An expressive, visually creative role player. Economically deprived children tend to be expressive in a spontaneous manner, eager to relate to others

---

[4] Frank Riessman. "The Strategy of Style," *Education of the Disadvantaged*, A. Harry Passow, et al, eds. New York: Holt, Rinehart and Winston, Inc., 1967. p. 327.

through role playing. The fantasy world appeals to them, and they learn through these motivating techniques. Allied closely is their ability to see artistically, which they often possess to a degree far above their talents to learn through other methods.

Lack of familiarity with middle class standards prevents him from identifying with the school environment which includes the teacher, her standard English, the prevailing taboos, and conventional textbooks and resource materials.

Achievement is likely to be highly motivated and influenced by teacher expectations. Research has proven that slum children who are not expected to achieve by their teachers achieve very little indeed. Perhaps more than his middle class counterpart he needs and constantly seeks affection and approval from his teacher. Some teachers of slum children, ill-prepared and reluctant to teach in the ghetto, have too often displayed their real feelings and prejudices, thus contributing to the lack of achievement.

The status of American education today inflicted on economically deprived minorities is influenced by many factors which prevent change. Outmoded curricula not meeting the current needs of learners is evidenced everywhere. Irrelevant instructional materials and traditional strategies within this curriculum complicate further its effectiveness. There is a crying need for changing both the content and the organization of the learning environment if the growing gap between youth and the establishment is to be lessened. The Commission on Instructional Technology, recently reporting to the President and Congress, states succinctly:

> But today, we observed, learning in our schools and colleges is increasingly impeded by such troubles as the growing gap between education's income and needs, and the shortage of good teachers in the right places. Formal education is not responsive enough: the organization of schools and colleges takes too little account of even what is now known about the process of human learning, particularly of the range of individual differences among students. This condition makes schools particularly unresponsive to the needs of disadvantaged and minority-group children. Moreover, formal education is in an important sense outmoded —students learn outside schools in ways which differ radically from the ways they learn inside school. Educational institutions make scant use of the potent means of communication that modern society finds indispensable and that occupy so much of young people's out-of-school time.[5]

In pressing home the point that there is great evidence for a need to individualize instruction because all children are different, the Commission further states:

> Researchers in human learning agree that individuals differ markedly in the ways they learn, in the speed at which they learn, in their motivation to learn, and in what they desire to learn. But educa-

[5] Commission on Instructional Technology. *To Improve Learning: A Report to the President and the Congress of the United States (The McMurrin Report)*. Washington, D.C.: U.S. Government Printing Office, March 1970. p. 6.

tional institutions cater only fractionally to these individual differences. Even in the best schools, where students' achievements in the three R's and the standard subjects are well above grade, and resounding percentages graduate from high school to enter college, many thoughtful educators and outside observers believe that institutions have lost touch with the individual student.

Most schools and colleges are still locked into conventional patterns of grade structure, time span, and subject-matter division that fail to exploit each student's individual capacities, interests, and personality. Conventional practice is geared to some abstract "average" or "norm" that penalizes both the unusually gifted and the seemingly backward students as well as the spectrum that lies between.[6]

Hilda Taba underscores this need in what she calls new focus on nature of teaching. She, too, makes a plea for conditions which provide for inventive and creative minds and an opportunity for developing methods of inquiry:

> Considerable attention has been devoted recently to studies of what is variously referred to as productive, creative or autonomous thinking. The result of this attention has been a new focus on the ability and the necessity for independent formulation of concepts and generalizations and the facility to put these concepts and generalizations to work to create new knowledge. This process of learning is often characterized as discovery learning, and it capitalizes on developing methods of inquiry which can be transformed from one situation to the next.
>
> This is a far cry from what now happens in schools. To provide conditions for the development of such an inventive and creative mind, it would be necessary to reorganize the curriculum so as to rid it of conformity pressures both in the content that is offered and in the reactions to content that are expected. That conformity and uniformity are far more potent than is indicated even by the similarity of topics and subjects taught has been shown by some recent studies of teacher acts in the classroom. These investigations indicated that not only do all students in many classrooms study precisely the same content, they also are expected to find similar answers and to find them in a similar manner. In short, the major portion of teachers' acts is directed to controlling both the nature of the answer and the manner of arriving at it. The result is not only systematic failure to develop autonomy and individuality but also systematic pressure of conformity and an erosion of whatever autonomy and creativity children possess. This conclusion is supported by countless observations regarding the increased stereotyping of thought and feeling and deletion of spontaneity that comes as children advance in grade levels.[7]

In our zeal to encourage innovation and the use of educational technology in ghetto schools, we often risk misinterpretation of the importance of the

[6] *Ibid.*, p. 15.
[7] Hilda Taba. "Education for Independent Valuing," *New Insights and the Curriculum.* Alexander Frazier, ed. Washington, D.C.: Association for Supervision and Curriculum Development, 1963. pp. 237–238.

teacher. We pause here to stress the point that the classroom teacher is the *essential factor* in setting up objectives, in guiding instruction, managing the learning environment, and assessing outcomes. The teacher needs all the help she can get, for nothing suggested in this article has any possibility for success without an urgent need to develop programs for retraining teachers and providing adequate funds for many new inservice experiences for these teachers. This also means that some administrators must change their attitude on the importance of inservice training.

Now that psychology is providing us with much better understanding of the learning process, technology must furnish the instructional tools to enable educators to capitalize on these findings.

Programming the learning Environment to learner characteristics. Modern educational technology can be the greatest boon to bridging the cultural and educational gap for ghetto youth in this century. The complexity of educational problems requires redesigning the curriculum, retraining educational personnel, and proper utilization of educational media experts and supporting staff—all within an instructional systems approach to educating ghetto youth.

When functioning in a systems approach, media will take its rightful place in the instructional process. The whole array of television and videotape packages, slides and filmstrips, motion pictures, realia, audio teaching tapes, telelectures, graphic materials, mock-ups, simulations, and other more traditional audiovisual resources should be built into and claim a portion of the whole curriculum—not used in isolation, nor at whim. Coupled with such other innovations as team teaching, individualized instruction, relevant courses, flexible facilities, and above all, a school-wide philosophy that believes in and encourages the permissiveness necessary to arrive at the objectives of such a dramatic new venture, pupil achievement is certain.

Such a system must recognize first of all, not lastly, the necessity for stating goals and setting up specific and unequivocally stated behavioral objectives. Robert F. Mager states:

> When clearly defined goals are lacking, it is impossible to evaluate a course or program efficiently, and there is no sound basis for selecting appropriate materials, content, or instructional methods. After all, the machinist does not select a tool until he knows what operation he intends to perform. Neither does a composer orchestrate a score until he knows what effects he wished to achieve. Similarly, a builder does not select his materials or specify a schedule for construction until he has his blueprints (objectives) before him. Too often, however, one hears teachers arguing the relative merits of textbooks or other aids of the classroom versus the laboratory, without ever specifying just what goal the aid or method is to assist in achieving. I cannot emphasize too strongly the point that an instructor will function in a fog of his own making until he knows just what he wants his students to be able to do at the end of the instruction.[8]

[8] Robert F. Mager. *Preparing Instructional Objectives.* California: Fearon Publishers, Inc., 1962. p. 3.

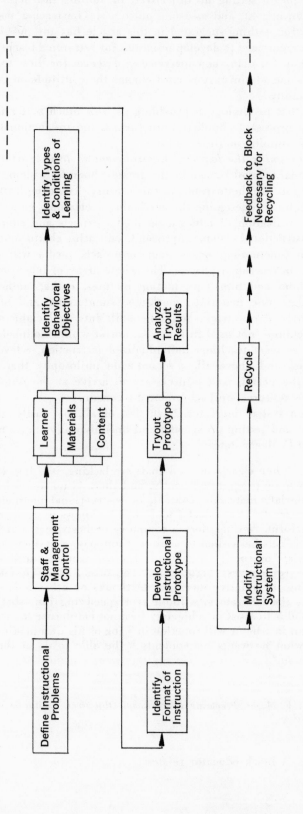

A MODIFIED SYSTEMS APPROACH
FOR DEVELOPING INSTRUCTIONAL SYSTEMS FOR GHETTO SCHOOLS

Define Instructional Problems → Staff & Management Control → Learner / Materials / Content → Identify Behavioral Objectives → Identify Types & Conditions of Learning

Identify Format of Instruction → Develop Instructional Prototype → Tryout Prototype → Analyze Tryout Results

Modify Instructional System → ReCycle

Feedback to Block Necessary for Recycling

In most schools teaching and testing combine into one long guessing game for students. What will they be tested for? How should they say it like the teacher wants it said? Clear, precise objectives, stated and understood by teachers and learners alike, will eliminate a lot of uncertainty.

Some schools and colleges are already programing the learning environment and are using educational technology to enhance learning for the children of the poor. They are experimenting with instructional technology as they put students in active independent learning roles. Technology is being used intelligently, comprehensively, and is being coordinated intensively and evaluated. Alva R. Rittrick, Research Council, Great Cities Program on School Improvement, points out several successful efforts:

> In the St. Louis school system emphasis is being placed on speech improvement in inner-city schools through the use of tapes, tape recordings, and radio lessons.

> The Baltimore school system has developed closed-circuit television instruction in math for selected children in junior highs with large concentrations of disadvantaged children. Longitudinal studies are made to determine effectiveness of this technique over conventional approaches. A similar study is being conducted in senior highs with experimental and control groups.

> The Los Angeles public school system has developed and is evaluating instructional programs designed to improve oral English of Negro and Mexican-American children, using various media including recorders and auto-tutors.

> In San Diego junior high schools, electronic classrooms have been organized to teach foreign languages. Closed-circuit television is being used to transmit 75 systematically prepared tape lessons to facilitate teaching English as a second language.

> The Cleveland public schools are studying the effects of programed instructional materials on development of basic reading skills, in an attempt to identify successful approaches with children in six inner-city schools.

> The New York public schools' "More Effective Schools Program" has made abundant quantities of equipment and instructional materials available to teachers. The effects of mechanical facilities such as overhead projectors, film cartridges, film libraries, and teaching machines are being studied.

> The Philadelphia schools have developed a Language Arts Communication Media Program. Students are provided with opportunities to employ communication media such as motion pictures, still photograpy, and tape recorders to extend their understanding and appreciation of literature and competence in spoken and written expression. Teachers are trained in techniques necessary to implement the program. Teachers and students work with various types of equipment. Much individualized instruction is required.

The Boston school system has developed an Interdisciplinary Slide/Film Program. This material was created by ninth-grade students. *The Concept of the Hero* was developed in an interdisciplinary context making use of a slide-tape presentation.[9]

The tragic need for technological resources, individualized facilities, and new instructional strategies beyond those now available to most slum teachers is reflected in the Coleman Report. "Fifty-three percent of the teachers have lived in the same locality most of their lives."[10] What this really means is that these teachers have grown up in the same slum neighborhood, finished the same ghetto schools and most likely have had college training in predominantly Negro colleges which are below the national ratings of institutions of higher education in almost everything. As an additional insult to ghetto youth the Coleman Report further states that only forty-six out of a hundred teachers in ghetto schools would not care to move if given the opportunity. Of these forty-six, it would be indeed interesting to know what percentage would prefer to stay because of their own insecurity and tragic shortcomings that would be glaring in a more demanding school district.

The answer then is technology. The ghetto teacher must be retrained to play a more important role in management of the learning environment and less of a role as presenter of information. The risk is too high to have it any other way. The systematic use of technology is going to prove even more upgrading in pupil achievement in ghetto schools than the predominantly white suburban schools. This assumption is indicated in the Coleman Report:

> The school of the minority pupil will increase his achievement more than will improving the school of the white child increase his. Similarly, the average minority pupil's achievement will suffer more in a school of low quality than will the average white pupils. In short, whites, and to a lesser extent, oriental Americans are less affected one way or the other by the quality of their schools than are minority pupils.[11]

What this is really saying is that our minority youth must look more to the school than other youth in preparing them totally for the society in which they are to enter. "The deficiency in achievement," states the Coleman Report in referring to minority groups, "is progressively greater for minority pupils at progressively higher grade levels."[12] Now let's look at some of the promises of technology in schools for minority groups which promise new directions toward achievement.

Dial access and information retrieval systems would utilize materials designed for the ghetto youth. In a study of civics, he learns respect for police and how to get a job by learning something about taking examinations for police work, learning behind the scene responsibilities of police, hearing audio tapes

---

[9] Commission on Instuctional Technology, *op. cit.*, p. 98.
[10] Coleman, *op. cit.*
[11] *Ibid.*
[12] *Ibid.*

by police and city officials regarding preparations for job requirements. Girls, in the privacy of a dial access system, learn about protection from pregnancies and venereal diseases and the dangers of abortions. Through multi-high school tie-ups dial access youngsters learn typing and shorthand skills, see examples of everyday economics for developing a perspective on consumer buying, see examples of the three branches of the federal government as explained on videotapes by Ralph Bunche or Senator Edward Brooke.

Programed materials allow a youngster to learn at his own rate of speed. He builds his limited vocabulary with programed materials, solves simple mathematical problems, learns the principles of combustion engines, or the process of local city government all at his own pace—and with no frustrating failures, no competition, no sarcasm from a teacher tired of repeating, and no threats of failure. Properly programed materials paint for him a total picture in sequences small enough for him to handle. Immediate feedback gives him a sense of confidence and accomplishment.

Study carrels and independent learning facilities equipped with single concept 8mm film, record players, filmstrips, and color slides with earphones, lend a person-to-person excitement to learning. These materials can reinforce an inspiring teacher's introduction to carpentry, typing, or music. A system employing self-study facilities has vast resources for repetitive, stimulating, and creative activities.

Harold Wigren synthesizes the case for individualized instruction:

> Individualized instruction is a major focus in educational research today. How can educational technology help with this need?
>
> At the heart of individualization of instruction is programmed learning—materials organized in a logical manner with frequent testing of the concept presented. The greatest breakthrough in the technology for individual learning is the computer. CAI (computer-assisted instruction) has now moved from concept to classroom in public schools. The computerized classroom is simply an extension of programmed learning in textbooks; the computer is, in fact, the most sophisticated of all the teaching machines.
>
> The showcase example of instructional uses of computers in the elementary schools of our nation is in the first grade in Brentwood School in East Palo Alto, California. There, as part of a program being conducted by a Stanford University group directed by Patrick Suppes and Richard Atkinson, 170 first-graders are using a classroom computer to learn to read and to work arithmetic problems. They spend 20 minutes a day with the computer, and one commentator reports that, "Teachers have to peel them off the machines to get them back to other classroom work."
>
> Results are already quite promising. After less than a year of work, those pupils who had been taught reading by the combination of computer and classroom teacher were several months ahead of their peers in reading ability. They achieved higher marks in recognition and pronunciation of words, in phonetics, and in vocabulary. Paragraph comprehension was the only skill in which they were not superior, and even there the difference was slight. Brentwood is a slum area with an 80

percent Negro enrollment; hence, the experiment may have vital significance for many other schools.[13]

Even black children of the slums are deluged by electronic media and multi-media communications, such as movies and television. Transistor radios are constant companions of these children as the outpour pounds at their ears with rock and roll rhythms and lyrics which they understand and to which they react on a personal and intimate basis. Tape recorders and the telephone and paper bound books and phonograph records—all are already shaping the ways children and young adults think and feel. These media help determine whom they admire and reject, what and how they feel about life and death, love and war, and about school and college.

Tape teaching, programing for flexible groupings, redeploying the teacher for more personal assistance, and programing learners into sequences utilizing audiotapes could be one of the most profitable features of educational technology. A well-developed library of audiotapes such as "Let's Look at Jobs" and "Getting Ready for Your Job" set forth interesting and helpful points on how to land a job. Such tapes, used individually in a tutorial arrangement, are often better planned and sequenced than many live lectures. A classroom or a laboratory wired to a tape recorder frees youngsters to move about as instructions are given. For example, for such activities as learning how to use a dictionary or how to read a map, the youngster puts on the tape and the tape patiently and slowly sequences the learning experience.

Arthur Lalime, educational media specialist in Connecticut public schools, has spearheaded the development of tape teaching in that area. Norwalk has developed decentralized libraries of tape packages in each school. Each package includes the audio portion of the prerecorded lesson, along with correlated printed materials to accompany the lesson, teacher guides, student worksheets, and a diagnostic cross-index catalog of the materials available. Study carrels, with earphones and tape playback units, have been set up in each participating school. The plan is less expensive than dial access, provides for decentralized libraries of tapes, and provides the teacher with essential information he must have in order to prescribe specific uses of the recorded materials for students.

Mr. Lalime has experimented with and found excellent results in tape teaching. He states:

> Taped lessons can be instructional and they can be fun. For example, stories may be recorded on tape and the students can be "read to" via the tape playback and earphones. Students usually have a greater degree of comprehension through listening than when the student reads the selection silently. With book in hand, the student can read silently as the teacher on the tape recording reads the story. The earphone creates the sensation that the teacher is talking directly to the child. This type of

---

[13] Harold E. Wigren. "What Is Here in Educational Technology." *A Curriculum for Children.* Alexander Frazier, ed. Washington, D.C.: Association for Supervision and Curriculum Development, 1969. pp. 46–47.

tape lesson is also being used to help slow readers master the social studies and science material that may be too difficult to read without help. This is a "read with me" situation in which the teacher can make reference to new words, and explain illustrations. Once these taped materials are prepared by the teacher, they can be used at any time with one or many students.

Pre-recorded instruction makes possible the initial teaching of phonetic and word analysis skills as well as providing many opportunities for review of these phonetic skills as the need arises. Tape recorded lessons dealing with these specific skills are prepared in a planned sequence to insure continuity.

Commercially prepared records can also be linked to the tape tables and earphone system. Many teachers believe that the earphones add a new dimension to listening. Teachers have indicated that recorded programs played to the entire class were not effective, but when used with earphones the recorded programs were a "great success."[14]

Television can do much towards helping minority youngsters identify and develop a pride in race and cultural heritage. Educational television has not begun to tap the potential it has for minority and slum children. Commercial television has recently made a start. All three commercial networks and NET initiated special series defining, exploring, and explaining the plight of the black man in America. The most ambitious of these projects was the CBS entry, *Of Black America,* a seven-part series dealing with the history, heritage, and significance of the black American.

Educational television has a potential more than any other media for helping to equalize the quality of instruction. A teacher in a rural section of a Southern state was recently asked, "What important effect has educational television made on you?" She replied, "It has been the most thoroughly effective course in educational methodology I have had. My classroom teaching has improved from watching TV teachers. This includes everything from attitude towards children to skill-developing activities." This, and other concomitant potentials of educational television should not be underestimated.

Television resources give slow children an opportunity to deal with the vast, never-ending flow of information. Unlike his middle class suburban brothers, the ghetto youth, in order to even survive in the mainstream competition, must play catch up! Children of lower economic families in developing countries are profiting greatly by the technological revolution.

Telephone teaching is another resource that is coming into focus. Harold Wigren states:

> In our country, in addition to TV and radio, teaching by telephone seems to be expanding rapidly. In Topeka, Kansas, teachers have found a way to be in three separate classrooms at the same time through the telelecture system. This technique brings the teacher to the classroom audience via regular telephone lines, enabling the speaker to participate

---

[14] Arthur W. Lalime. "Tape Teaching." A Report prepared for the Norwalk Board of Education, February 1967.

with several classes simultaneously at different locations. The system enables questions to be answered through the use of microphones in the classrooms that are connected to the telelecture network. A telewriting device provides the visual link between the teacher using telelecture and his students. Written notes, formulas, or drawings are transmitted "live" from the teacher's location and projected on a screen in each classroom for his audience.[15]

Computer-assisted instruction in the systems approach for minority youth can help catapult them into the mainstream of our society. The limitless promise of computers seems to offer a portion of the solution. The ignorance of educators concerning the wide range of potentials of computers in education must be eliminated. A ghetto school with limited resources, poorly prepared teachers, and a low level of achievement can turn to computers to make quick decisions based on assessments of student performance, and then match available resources to individual student needs. One such decision might be for the computer to present lesson materials directly to the student in a tutorial mode.

The computer is capable of serving a large group of learners simultaneously, dealing with the same problems. It therefore becomes a tool for problem solving, far more resourceful than a teacher in much shorter time. Before the student can make the computer solve his mathematical problem, he must analyze the problem and explicitly formulate its solution as a series of discrete, operationally defined steps corresponding to the computer's repertoire of operations. This type of high level experience quickly removes the bright slum child out of the restrictions and limitations of a mediocre ghetto teacher. Repeatedly, I refer to the poor quality of ghetto teachers. It must be remembered that just a few years ago, before any serious thought was given to racial ghetto education, few whites knew and most couldn't care less about the training of teachers for and the quality of teaching in ghetto schools. The products of these schools are mainly our ghetto teachers of today.

Let us explore such a system which has infinite potentials in upgrading the achievement of ghetto youth. The system is a multi-purpose computer-assisted instruction system designed to provide highly individualized daily instruction for up to 6000 students during classroom hours, and also to perform special after-hours instructional functions, a broad variety of educational services, and the administrative data-processing requirements of a large city school district, multi-campus university or other major educational activity.

The system utilizes a computer which drives up to 192 remotely located student instructional terminals simultaneously, each terminal presenting curriculum materials continuously adjusted to the learning rate and capability of the individual student working at it. System response time at each terminal, all terminals operating simultaneously, is approximately half a second. Curriculum materials for use with the system are offered directly to system users by leading textbook publishers. Subject matter available includes elementary arithmetic, elementary language arts, and elementary science. Large city school systems with

---

[15] Wigren, *op. cit.*, p. 42.

a majority or high percentage of black children would do well to seriously consider this type of innovative resource.

In an experiment at the BOCES Demonstration Center in Westchester County, a New York project directed by Walter Goodman, efforts were made to try a computer system through the use of simulated techniques. The three economics games which were used in this project represent one kind of tactic in the broad startegy of simulation. Simulation, or the "simulated environment mode," is a methodological technique designed to provide individual students with substitutions for the significant features of a natural or conventional learning situation realized by the delivery of a teacher-made instructional program through the resources of a computer system.[16]

This type of computer use has great potentials for ghetto youth, too. They could have invented simulation. They know all about it. They use it daily to survive. The computer has so much potential that the limit of its use is equaled only by the stretch of the imagination.

Teachers, supervisors, school boards, administrators, trainers of teachers, researchers, and the resources of the community, backed up by well-organized, well-staffed and well-equipped regional and district instructional materials centers, must engage in a partnership never before known.

Robert J. Havighurst turns to the potentials of a learning center for big city youth:

> Often, in a big city, the local neighborhood is segregated economically or racially, or both, and there seems to be nothing that can or should be done to change this situation in the near future. In other words, this is a typical situation for the vast majority of schools in the big city. The teachers and administrators, as well as some, at least, of the parent leaders, recognize that their neighborhood school is too simple for their children to encounter much of the complexity of the city.
>
> Consequently, they use a Learning Center in their section of the city for a good part of the school week. The Learning Center is a building with a variety of facilities for learning that may not be in the neighborhood school. It has a stage for dramatics, a room for language and speech instruction with tape recorders, a good school library, a variety of teaching machines, and an array of learning programs. It has a large recreation area, and several buses to bring children to the Center and to take them on trips in the metropolitan area. It has a small permanent staff, and the teachers of the neighborhood school have learned to use some of the equipment in the Center.
>
> The Center is scheduled so as to bring children of various social and ethnic groups together and to encourage them to associate in many of the activities. Also, the Center encourages a limited amount of competition between neighborhood schools, in athletics and academic "games." The relation between the neighborhood school and the Learning Center is somewhat like that of a homeroom to the other classrooms of a large

---

[16] Richard L. Wing. "The Relation of Computer-Based Instruction and Other Media to Individualized Education." DAVI Conference, Atlantic City, N.J., April 4, 1967.

departmentalized school. The neighborhood school is a kind of home-room, which specializes in teaching the skill subjects of reading, writing, and arithmetic.[17]

Many educators can point to failures in the attempted use of educational technology in schools. What many fail to realize is that no sincere effort to change the curriculum was made but technology was pressed into the old traditional framework of an already dying curriculum. This has happened as educators approached the use of team teaching, classroom television, independent study and inquiry techniques, but rarely did educators provide what David Engler calls the "mechanism for changing the ecological balance between teachers and learners." He states:

> In the past, many attempts to change education, particularly those attempts to individualize instruction and to develop skills of independent inquiry, have failed because they did not include any mechanism for changing the ecological balance between teachers and learners. Usually, these changes were imposed on the existing ecology in which the teacher leads a group-based lockstep progression through the course of study. This ecology is inevitably characterized by a high degree of active involvement on the part of the teacher and a comparably high degree of passive involvement on the part of the learner.
>
> Only a new instructional technology can change the existing ecological balance in education. The state of the art in instructional technology is such today that many of the tools and techniques needed to effect such change are available and feasible. We can, for example, by individual, specific diagnosis and instruction eliminate the practice of teaching youngsters what they already know or of teaching them what they are not prepared to learn. We can devise the means and organize the instructional environment to permit individuals to master the basic skills and acquire the basic information that are necessary ingredients of analytical or problem-solving work in most subjects. We can leave to the teacher the functions of diagnosis, evaluation, decision making, and direct, individual interaction with the learner on the level of the higher order intellectual, esthetic, and ethical objectives that are the essential ingredients of a humanistic curriculum.[18]

One might ask, what does research say about technology and learning? Not nearly enough is known or tested through research. There are sufficient enough research results substantiating the need for the serious incorporation of technology into the teaching-learning process. Several publications are worthy of note here as listed by John Moldstad, professor of education, Indiana University:

Allen, William H., "Audio-Visual Communications," *Encyclopedia of Educational Research*, edited by Chester W. Harris, The Macmillan Co., New York, 1960. pp. 115–137.

[17] Robert J. Havighurst. "The Neighborhood School: Status and Prospects." *A Curriculum for Children*. Alexander Frazier, ed. Washington, D.C.: Association for Supervision and Curriculum Development, 1969. pp. 80–81.
[18] David Engler. "Instructional Technology and the Curriculum." *Phi Delta Kappan*, Vol. 51, No. 7, March 1970. p. 381.

Reviews the research in audiovisual communication during the last decade under five major headings: (a) effectiveness of audiovisual materials, (b) audience-learner characteristics, (c) characteristics of the learning environment, (d) use of audiovisual materials, and (e) administration of audiovisual programs. Includes a 320 item bibliography of research studies.

Chu, Godwin C. and Schramm, Wilbur, *Learning from Television*: *What The Research Says* (U.S. Office of Education, Contract 2 EFC 70894). Institute for Communication Research, Stanford University, 1967.
Restricted to review of instructional television and includes the following six areas concerning the conditions of effective learning from television: (a) how much pupils learn from instructional television, (b) efficient use of the medium in a school system, (c) treatment, situation, and pupil variables, (d) attitudes toward instructional television, (e) television in developing regions, and (f) learning from television compared with learning from other media.

Finn, James D., and Allen, William H., Co-Chairmen, "Instructional Materials: Educational Media and Technology." *Review of Educational Research*, 32: 115–221, April, 1962. (American Educational Research Association, 1201 Sixteenth Street, N.W. Washington, D.C.)
Reviews the research literature from 1956 to 1962 under the following headings: (a) theoretical formulations in audiovisual communications, (b) textbooks and other printed materials, (c) audiovisual materials, (d) learning from instructional television, (e) language laboratories, (f) self-teaching devices and programmed materials, and (g) administration of instructional materials.

Godfrey, Eleanor P., *The State of Audiovisual Technology: 1961–1966 Monograph #3*. Department of Audiovisual Instruction of the National Education Association, Washington, D.C., 1967.
Examines three surveys of national scope in audiovisual technology conducted during a six-year period from 1961–1966. Identifies the audiovisual resources available in the individual schools, describes the extent to which these resources are used by teachers in different grade levels and subject specialists, and considers factors that encourage or inhibit use.

Kumata, Hideya, *An Inventory of Instructional Television Research*. Educational Television and Radio Center, Michigan State University, Ann Arbor, 1956.
Restricted to studies of the teaching of formal courses by television and includes (a) a review of research findings and (b) a collection of abstracts of pertinent articles. Intended as a guide to those interested in further study of the use of television in formal instruction situations.

Lumsdaine, Arthur A., "Instruments and Media in Instruction," *Handbook of Research on Teaching*. American Educational Research Association, Rand McNally and Co., Chicago, 1963. pp. 583–682.
Part 1: Theoretical Orientations also include valuable background for the researcher.

1. Historic Exemplars of Teaching Method
2. Logic and Scientific Method in Research on Teaching
3. Paradigms for Research on Teaching

Reid, J. Christopher, and MacLennan, Donald W., *Research in Instructional Television and Film*. U.S. Department of Health, Education, and Welfare, Washington, D.C., 1967. (Superintendent of Documents, U.S. Government Printing Office, Washington, D.C. 20402.)
Presents a summarization of 333 research studies concerned with instructional films and instructional television in the period 1950 to 1964. The introductory review points out the direction in which the research has been going, the present status of the research, and some possible future directions.

Wendt, Paul R., *Audiovisual Instruction*. Department of Classroom Teachers of the National Education Association and the American Educational Research Association, Washington, D.C. 1964.
Discusses the nature of communication and the role of audiovisual materials in classroom instruction. Presents research material on audiovisual instruction which promises to be of most help to classroom teachers, identifies factors affecting the value of audiovisual instruction, and considers what audiovisual materials can and cannot do.

Summaries of the research papers presented at the annual Department of Audiovisual Instruction's national convention have been included in the following issues of *AV Instruction:*

Moldstad, John, "Summary of A-V Research." *AV Instruction*, September, 1964, pp. 492–497.
"Highlights of 1965 Research Reports." *AV Instruction*, June–July, 1965, pp. 528–531.
"1966 Research Reports Feature the Controlled Experiment." *AV Instruction*, June–July, 1966.
"1967 Research Studies Stress Stimulus Variables and Technology." *AV Instruction*, June–July, 1967, pp. 638–642.

Godwin C. Chu and Wilbur Schramm point up some encouraging and exciting research findings on the use of media, several of which are listed below. Each of these headings constitute an umbrella for a number of successful studies on the respective subjects. They are:

Given favorable conditions, pupils can learn from any instructional media that are now available.

Television and radio have certain advantages over films in flexibility and deliverability.

More complete control of film by the classroom teacher gives it a potential advantage over television.

There is some evidence to suggest that moving visual images will improve learning if the continuity of action is an essential part of the learning task.

Student response is effectively controlled by programmed methods, regardless of the instructional medium.[19]

There is no longer any real doubt that children learn a great deal from technology—whether educational or not—so long as the experience seems relevant to them. It is now the major task of educators to provide the favorable conditions under which technology can be used.

The emotional content of meaning, such an essential ingredient in motivating our actions, is particularly difficult to get through to slum children through verbalizing and reading. The kind of training teachers colleges have afforded teachers is partly responsible for ignorance of these facts. The training of teachers to work with slum children must get out of the doldrums of the conservative content of liberal arts courses and the abstract binds of professional education courses and into involvement with people.

Failure of teacher preparation to use the fast-growing resources of educational technology is reflected in a report on the results of a teacher-opinion poll published in the December, 1963 issue of the *NEA Journal*. The NEA Research Division asked "a scientifically selected cross-section of the nation's one and a half million public school teachers" how their college preparation had fitted them for teaching. Every teacher education faculty concerned with change should have the results of that survey: over sixty percent of the teachers reported too little preparation in the use of audiovisual equipment and techniques; over forty percent, too little teaching methods; and only twenty-seven percent, too little in subject knowledge.

A well-designed teacher education curriculum will provide teachers with preservice and inservice experience in many new techniques—whether in audiovisual courses or portions of methods courses is not important as long as it is related to the development of theory and practice.

A retraining of teachers in the imaginative uses of multi-media and the newer techniques is a prerequisite to understanding and solving the learning problems of children of the poor. But most important is attitude change. Old stereotypes and prejudices picked up from middle class American standards must be re-examined. Teachers must learn that, although poverty and racial discrimination may force many people to live in the slums, there can yet be found among them higher standards of conduct and family life, better manners, and higher life goals than are to be found in many middle class suburban families. This fact again points to the great diversity among ghetto youth and the need for individualized learning. Trainers of teachers must help them to develop the skills necessary for finding solutions to the many-faceted problems of the poor.

During the period of reflecting and researching for this paper, the writer went into several schools to observe and talk with teachers, children, and administrators. It is probably safe to generalize that many ghetto teachers are

---

[19] Godwin C. Chu and Wilbur Schramm. *Learning from Television: What the Research Says*. Washington, D.C.: National Association of Educational Broadcasters, 1967. pp. 84–95.

working against surprising odds. Class sizes from thirty-eight to forty and often forty-five children seem the rule rather than exception. Outmoded architectural arrangements pour as many as 1500 humans in one or two small corridors at once. There was evidence of little organization and administration of non-print materials, making mediated instruction almost impossible. The absence of a media specialist seems to be one of the most obvious personnel weaknesses in each school. Overcrowdedness in general is one of the most serious problems. Classes meet in cafeterias each hour of the day excluding the three-shift services. The lack of opportunity for some privacy, small group instruction, individual study, team teaching facilities, instructional materials—all defy innovation.

On the other hand, to see three teachers, with a huge overhead screen and a public address system, working with over 150 children in a cafeteria at the Jacox Junior High School in Norfolk, Virginia, was a wonderful sight. Students seemed enthusiastic and they coordinated in a rhythmic fashion their typing lesson to the loud and clear instructions and music from a disc played by a typing teacher at the Booker T. Washington High School in Norfolk, Virginia. A language laboratory, or rather an electronic classroom, built to the specifications and needs of the school, created by the industrial arts teacher, was a sight worthy to be seen at the Norfolk, Virginia Lindenwood Elementary School. These and other efforts are bright spots to watch.

Black Studies and the Curriculum—a challenge to reorganizing for technological advances. For too long, all American children have shared an illusion that the history of civilization from the Middle Ages to the twentieth century was the history of Europe and its offsprings in pockets of settlements throughout the world. We have felt that the Western experience was one to be interpreted and worn by all humans considered civilized and learned. This misconception of history has come to an end almost abruptly in the last few years. The new world of nations and the non-whites of the world have sought their place in the sun. So it is with the American of African descent. We are asking that the history of Africa and America be written as it was and is. Move out Daniel Boone, make room for Nat Turner! There is a time, place and appreciation in our history for both the great Washingtons—George and Booker T.

This volume of resources, media and materials, will help acquaint the American educator, from the kindergarten teacher to the university professor, with the wide range of resources about black Americans and Africans now available for curriculum integration and enrichment. Charles V. Hamilton, a black professor at Columbia University, speaks for Black Studies in Higher Education:

> The black students and the black studies demands have a valid *political* point. If this is generally accepted, as very many thoughtful people have conceded, it would appear that the next step would be to begin to work out the kinds of *academic* changes those demands call for. Clearly, the students who have served as the catalyst for this should not be expected to come up with the final answers. Those people who style themselves scholars have the burden of proceeding to try to develop new knowledge consistent with a new orientation.

Much of the empirical work has yet to be done, because the questions have never been asked. What is the feasibility of massive economic cooperative ventures in rural and urban black communities? What is the nature of and significance of the black culture vis-à-vis new forms and styles of political action in the black community? Is it possible to talk about a peculiar "black experience" that has relevance to the way black Americans organize themselves and conduct their lives? What is the impact of the oral tradition on social, economic, and political phenomena? Black Americans have a heritage, a black experience of abrupt cultural transformation to traumatized conditions of slavery in a distant, alien land with a different language and different life styles; to legal freedom from legal slavery in the same place and economic position; to an urban, atomized, technological environment from a rural, intimate, agrarian environment. What is the meaning of this heritage and experience in terms of new adaptive cultural characteristics, characteristics that can sustain black Americans as a viable people? What are the implications of all this for enlightened public policy? What does it mean for the kinds of effort made to bridge tradition and modernity in the black community? What is meant by the "crisis-oriented" nature of the black political experience? What is meant by "political traumatization" (as opposed to "political apathy") that makes this distinction relevant to one trying to understand and deal with the problems of black community development?

These are some of the kinds of questions that their proponents want black studies to deal with. Are these "soul courses?" Are they "separatist," "violent advocacy of revolution," "catharsis-serving" courses? Do they take one *out* of "higher education?"[20]

Let us make it clear however that "Black Studies" also means introducing Frederick Douglass and Sojourner Truth into the list of men and women who stood tall in the making of this nation. "Black Studies" means fifth graders studying the contributions of Benjamin Franklin and Benjamin Banneker. As our children individualize their learning and enquiry becomes a pivot, one child will have at his fingertip the resources for an in-depth study of contemporaries which might include John F. Kennedy, Martin Luther King, Dwight Eisenhower, Ralph Bunche, Adlai Stevenson and Edward Brooke.

The inextricable involvement of both black and white Americans in the making of America is a fact of our history. It is past time that we catch up with the black Americans' contributions. That is what this book is all about.

BIBLIOGRAPHY

Chu, Godwin C., and Schramm, Wilbur, *Learning from Television: What the Research Says.* Washington, D.C.: National Association of Educational Broadcasters, 1967.
Clark, Kenneth B., "Unstructuring Education," *New Relationships in ITV.* Washington, D.C.: Educational Media Council, Inc., 1967.

[20] Charles V. Hamilton. "The Question of Black Studies." *Phi Delta Kappan,* Vol. 51, No. 7, March 1970. p. 363.

Coleman, James B., et al, *Equality of Educational Opportunity*. Washington, D.C.: Office of Education, U.S. Department of Health, Education, and Welfare, 1966.

Commission on Instructional Technology, *To Improve Learning: A Report to the President and the Congress of the United States* (The McMurrin Report). Washington, D.C.: U.S. Government Printing Office, March 1970.

Engler, David, "Instructional Technology and the Curriculum." *Phi Delta Kappan*, Vol. 51, No. 7, March 1970.

Hamilton, Charles V., "The Question of Black Studies." *Phi Delta Kappan*, Vol. 51, No. 7, March 1970.

Havighurst, Robert J., "The Neighborhood School: Status and Prospects." *A Curriculum for Children*. Alexander Frazier, ed. Washington, D.C.: Association for Supervision and Curriculum Development, 1969.

Lalime, Arthur W., "Tape Teaching." A report prepared for the Norwalk Board of Education, February 1967.

Mager, Robert F., *Preparing Instructional Objectives*. California: Fearon Publishers, Inc., 1962.

Riessman, Frank, "The Strategy of Style," *Education of the Disadvantaged*, A. Harry Passow, et al, eds. New York: Holt, Rinehart and Winston, Inc., 1967.

Taba, Hilda, "Education for Independent Valuing," *New Insights and the Curriculum*. Alexander Frazier, ed. Washington, D.C.: Association for Supervision and Curriculum Development, 1963.

Wigren, Harold E., "What Is Here in Educational Technology." *A Curriculum for Children*. Alexander Frazier, ed. Washington, D.C.: Association for Supervision and Curriculum Development, 1969.

Wing, Richard L., "The Relation of Computer-Based Instruction and Other Media to Individualized Education." DAVI Conference, Atlantic City, N.J., April 4, 1967.

A black sociologist crystallizes social and psychological needs to the characteristics and special problems of ghetto youth

Dr. JACQUELYNE JACKSON
Assistant Professor of Medical Sociology,
Department of Psychiatry,
Duke University Medical Center,
Durham, North Carolina.

Perhaps one appropriate way of commencing is that of admitting clearly that the title attached to that which follows ("A black sociologist crystallizes social and psychological needs to the characteristics and special problems of ghetto youth") contains, at the very least, an element of untruth, a nebulous concept, and, without doubt, an indictment upon democracy in *these* United States.

Although some may find an element of untruth in "black sociologist," given the variety of operational definitions of "black" currently in vogue, the element of untruth referred to is "crystallizes." The current status of our educational, psychological, and sociological knowledge about social and psychological needs as they relate to the characteristics and special problems of ghetto youth prohibits such crystallization at this time.

This available knowledge, generally limited in scope, polemical in nature, and bound by the "truths" lucid to and adhered to by middle-class producers, agents, and consumers of such knowledge is, in fact, fragmentary. A basic and regrettable cause of such fragmentation is, quite simply, a failure (in *will* and *deed*) to settle the ethical and practical issue of distinguishing sufficiently between those characteristics and special problems of "ghetto youth" properly attributable to human nature *and* those characteristics and special problems of "ghetto youth" properly attributable to racism, classism, and even sexism.

The crystallization of social and psychological needs to the characteristics and special problems of ghetto youth yet awaits an overwhelmingly positive and *will*-committed response to McWorter's inquiry:

The question is this: Is it possible in this great country that a few million dollars—which is *not* a lot of money—could be made available to black social scientists to investigate the whole question of the black experience and the body of knowledge that must be amassed, knowledge that is authentically an extension and reflection of the black experience?[1]

Is it possible? And, if so, and funded adequately (and in excess of a few million dollars!), is it not possible that certain "ghetto youth" exposed to such multimedia materials as those suggested herein by Dr. Harry A. Johnson might not be stimulated—even driven—to participate actively in amassing such knowledge?

The crystallization of social and psychological needs to the characteristics and special problems of ghetto youth yet awaits, as well, an overwhelmingly positive and *will*-committed response to make unintelligible to any American youth of tomorrow an adequate interpretation of

> Once riding in old Baltimore,
>   Heart-filled, head-filled with glee,
> I saw a Baltimorean
>   Keep looking straight at me.
>
> Now I was eight and very small,
>   And he was no whit bigger,
> And so I smiled, but he poked out
>   His tongue, and called me, "Nigger."
>
> I saw the whole of Baltimore
>   From May until December;
> Of all the things that happened there
>   That's all that I remember.[2]

without having studied (i.e., having acquired cognitive as opposed to experiential knowledge of) the *past* history of these United States.

In short, no transparent or clear mineral, such as ice, appears below. Instead, this "premature crystallization" is still freezing; it is presently a sphinx: the solvable riddle remains unresolved.

But, some unraveling of this riddle can occur, I think, through use of the multimedia materials suggested, again, in this work, *provided that* such usage is accompanied by sincere efforts and actions to reduce the special problems of "ghetto youth" and to meet (and attend to) their manifested social and psychological needs, at least, and by well-designed, well-controlled, and well-financed research undertaken to specify and evaluate the net effects of these materials in such reduction and need-satisfaction. In short, use of these materials should be predicated upon responsibility and accountability both on the part of the user (i.e., teacher, shower, etc.) and the usee (i.e., "ghetto youth," viewer, etc.) for "telling and understanding it like it is" *and* for individual and collective social involvement to effect change so that "it will not be like it is."

---

[1] Gerald A. McWorter: "Deck the Ivy Racist Halls: The Case of Black Studies." A. L. Robinson, C. C. Foster, and D. H. Ogilvie (eds.), *Black Studies in the University*. New Haven: Yale University Press, p. 71.
[2] Countee Cullen, "Incident: Baltimore." Arna Bontemps (compiler), *Golden Slippers: An Anthology of Negro Poetry for Young Readers*. New York: Harper & Brothers Publishers, 1941. p. 138.

Although there is substantial agreement, certainly, that the term "youth" refers to that period between childhood and adulthood (irrespective of any variation in chronological or other criteria utilized to mark the end of the former and the onset of the latter), the term "ghetto" is nebulously employed in many contemporary quarters, and, on occasion, is sneakily employed to avoid, perhaps, calling a rose a rose.

Historically, of course, sociologists have generally defined a "ghetto" as a

(1) Place outside the walls of a town where Jews: (a) voluntarily live; (b) are compelled or legally required to dwell. (2) a natural area of the city, where a minority, not necessarily Jewish, settles.[3]

If one substitutes "blacks" for "Jews" in (1) above, then a literal transference to "Black Ghetto" is unwarranted.

In (2) above, where a "natural area" has referred, in general sociological context, to

Any particular extent of surface that has become differentiated as the result of unplanned ecological and/or social processes rather than as the result of conscious planning and/or administrative control.[4]

then, once more, a literal transference to "Black Ghetto" is not possible.

Obviously, increasing application of the term "ghetto" to blacks has been accompanied by modification, whereby but not exhaustively, the term "ghetto" may be used to refer to (1) *all blacks* (Negroes, Afro-Americans, reader's choice); (2) *only blacks living in urban slum areas* (typically characterized by such variables as high rates of crime, delinquency, poverty, welfare, unemployment, female-headed households, deteriorated housing, "non-standard English," infant and maternal mortality, births and deaths, sexual immorality, "low morals," absence of structured organizations, apathy, alienation, fatalism, and rats and roaches; and, unfortunately, much less often by exploitation such as underemployed and underpaid and overworked workers, exorbitant rents for "rats in the cribs," and disproportionate victims of crimes against persons, by structured social organization, by stable female-headed families who "make it," by individuals communicating with others and each other, and by individuals and groups concerned—and hence not apathetic, or indifferent or unemotional—about and involved in—and hence not alienated or estranged from-living and the conditions under which they live, but who

> Hold fast to dreams
> For when dreams go
> Life is a barren field
> Frozen with snow.[5]

and who, despite the odds, maintain high educational aspirations for their children); (3) *blacks living within and on the peripheries of urban slum areas;*

---

[3] Henry P. Fairchild (ed.): *Dictionary of Sociology*. Totowa, N.J.: Littlefield, Adams & Company, 1968, pp. 180–181.
[4] *Ibid.*, p. 14.
[5] Langston Hughes, "Dreams" (second verse). Bontemps, *op. cit.*, p. 194.

and (4) *all blacks with the exception of the "exceptional" blacks* (e.g., Ralph Bunche, Marian Anderson, John Hope Franklin, Kenneth Clark, Sammie Davis, Jr., Thurgood Marshall, Andrew Brimmer, Robert Weaver, John H. Johnson, Jr., Sidney Poitier, and Shirley A. Chisholm—all of whom, incidentally, but importantly, are not merely "exceptional" blacks, but "exceptional" humans, black or white).

A recent (and apparently hastily assembled) work, *Life Styles in the Black Ghetto*,[6] exemplifies the increasingly popular and academic tendency to use the terms "black(s)" and "ghetto" interchangeably (notwithstanding the explicit use of "black ghetto" in the title), thus negating thereby any need for an operational definition of "ghetto." One searches in vain for an index reference to "ghetto" in this work.

The work's "Introduction"[7] contains the following references to "ghetto":

[6] William McCord, *et al.*, *Life Styles in the Black Ghetto*. New York: W. W. Norton & Company, 1969.

[7] *Ibid.*, pp. 9–12. In addition to the failure to "crystallize" their usage of "ghetto," the authors, who are at least verbally committed to anti-racism ("There is only one lasting solution to the racial dilemma: that whites and Negroes work together to improve their common lot as Americans." p. 294) and pessimistic about the outcome if the racial dilemma is not resolved ("The spirit of reconciliation and good will seems moribund. If this spirit cannot be revived, *we face a new civil war*," p. 294, italics added), in their "Introduction" commit several serious "sins" of omission and commission, such as those of: (1) asserting *without sufficient qualification* that "housing segregation has actually increased *because* of [black] urban migration," (italics added), which, in effect, places unfairly the cause of residential segregation by race upon black urban migrants whose shoulders are already sagging heavily under other undue blames, and thus failing to recognize that "Specifically, in the case of Chicago [*and certainly generalizable elsewhere*], it was found that, as a result of the selection and segregation incident to the expansion of population, the Negro community had assumed a definite spatial pattern" (E. Franklin Frazier: "Negro Harlem: An Ecological Study," 1937. G. Franklin Edwards, ed.: *E. Franklin Frazier on Race Relations*, The University of Chicago Press, Chicago, 1968, p. 142, with bracketed statement added); (2) crediting Lee Rainwater (white), and not such predecessors as, e.g., E. Franklin Fraizer (black; see his *The Negro Family in the United States*, The University of Chicago Press, Chicago, 1939, and, for that matter, earlier articles on black families and urbanization, or his *The Negro Family in Chicago*, The University of Chicago Press, Chicago, 1932) or, although not a central concern, W. E. B. DuBois (black; see, e.g., brief comments related to family responsibility in "Education and Work," *The J. of Negro Education*, 1:60–74, 1932) for having "pointed out" that "the move to the cities . . . may well have contributed to the break-up of Negro families;" Rainwater should, of course, not be held responsible (in fact, cannot be) for that citation, and, as Andrew Billingsley (*Black Families in White America*, Prentice-Hall, Inc., Englewood Cliffs, N.J., 1968, p. 207) noted, Rainwater has been an outstanding contributor to the emergence of "a small but growing literature on Negro families which takes these families seriously in their own right and does not treat them essentially as deviants from white norms;" and (3) their apparent denial of earlier riots (such as the 1900 New York City, the 1906 Atlanta, the 1908 Springfield, Illinois, the 1917 East St. Louis, the 1919 Chicago, Washington, D.C., and Phillips County, Arkansas, the 1942 and 1943 Detroit, and the 1948 Columbia, Tennessee race riots, e.g.) which could be inferred (although they cautiously employ the term "apparently") from their statement that "And then, of course, there are the riots—that apparently distinctive characteristic of American cities in the 1960's" (p. 9). Inasmuch as several questionnaire items (pp. 304–325) referred specifically to riots, and the authors indicate that "Several of us have had the instructive, frightening experience of directly observing the riots in Watts (1965), Houston, Oakland, Newark, and Detroit (1967), and Orangeburg, South Carolina (1968)" (p. 10), and especially since, as the authors again observe, "Some of us are Negro," (p. 12), it is extremely disconcerting to witness either this apparent denial of earlier

(1) "Why . . . should we issue . . . opinions about the ghetto Negro?"; (2) "These interviews were conducted . . . in the . . . streets of the ghetto"; (3) "Americans should know the temper of the ghetto—now"; (4) ". . . to gain a less ephemeral knowledge of the ghetto, we have . . . interviewed . . . people who represent different responses to ghetto life"; (5) "Anyone acquainted with . . . *Black Bourgeosie* and *Black Metropolis*[8] will recognize some of these people, for the historical constraints of the ghetto allow only a limited number of ways to survive"; and (6) "Here we . . . based our comments on interviews with indigenous leaders of the Negro ghetto. . . ."

Again, for emphasis, and as can be deduced quite readily from the above, the term "ghetto" remains, in this work, undefined in any precise manner. A plausible—and, in this case, probably valid—inference is that "black ghetto" as used in the title and in the work itself refers to urban blacks (i.e., rural blacks were excluded, but it was not clear as to whether they were excluded because they were without the "ghetto," or simply because the focus was limited "to an analysis of the urban Negro"[9]).

Yet, the formula of "black ghetto"="urban, black ghetto" in *Life Styles in the Black Ghetto* is not an isolated genre. Generally, traditional usage of both the terms "ghetto" and "slum" has been restricted to urban or urban-peripheral areas.[10] Both terms have had, and currently have, negative connotations (as is historically true of the term "black," as well): restricted centralization of "undesirables" in the first instance, e.g., physical and human decadence in the second instance.

Hence, it could be argued that the present tendency to refer to urban blacks as "ghetto blacks" represents progress: "career-ladder" progression from "slum Negroes." In either instance, nevertheless, insidious derogation is intrinsic within the concept, and within the conceptions surrounding the concept. Therefore, a useful definition of a "ghetto" (at least for present purposes) ought be one which "calls a spade, a spade." One such definition is at hand.

Weaver[11] has indicated that the *coincidence* of the flight of white middle

---

riots, as previously indicated, or this apparent lack of knowledge about earlier riots— although, of course, the riots of the 1960's were not mere replicas of earlier ones.

Such omissions and commissions, however trivial or minor they may be judged, point, nevertheless, toward at least the authors' responsibility for having defined clearly their conception of the "ghetto;" reemphasis upon McWorter's (*op. cit.*) plea for "knowledge that is authentically an extension and reflection of the black experience;" *and, above all, the necessity for teachers and other purveyors of knowledge about blacks to assess and, where proper, to modify and correct such knowledge.*

[8] E. Franklin Frazier, *Black Bourgeoisie*. Glencoe, Ill.: Free Press, 1957; and St. Clair Drake and Horace R. Cayton, *Black Metropolis; A Study of Negro Life in a Northern City*. New York: Harcourt, Brace and Company, 1945.

[9] McCord, *et al., op. cit.*, p. 9.

[10] One exception is the employment of the term "rural slum" in *The People Left Behind*, Report by the President's National Advisory Commission on Rural Poverty, Washington, D.C.: U.S. Government Printing Office, September, 1967 (e.g., p. ix).

[11] Robert C. Weaver, "Non-white population movements and urban ghettos," *Phylon*, 20: 235–241, 1959. Also see his *The Negro Ghetto*, New York: Harcourt, Brace and Company, 1948. In the article cited, Weaver also, and correctly, emphasizes that open occupancy of housing "is the best possible insurance against further ghettoization of our

and upper-income groups to suburbia and black, urban migration has been misinterpreted by those who regard the latter as being *the* cause of the former:

> Had there been no migration of non-whites to urban communities, large-scale expansion of suburbia would have occurred in the post-World War II period (p. 236).

What is particularistic about the black, urban migration, however, is that "widespread enforced racial residential segregation has given a unique cast to a recurring phenomenon" (p. 236). This

> Enforced residential segregation is a relatively recent phenomenon in American industrial centers. Its true beginnings coincide with the rise of suburbia. . . . more and more emphasis has been placed upon single-class, all-white and otherwise homogeneous neighborhoods in new developments. Resulting extreme color consciousness in housing spread inward to the central cities. Soon it was institutionalized into racial ghettos which today represent a serious threat to surrounding downtown businesses (p. 238).

In a nutshell, the "black ghetto"= (at least) the spatial area(s) of black, residential clusters enforced by racial segregation. Or, more simply, black ghettoes are parcels and products of racial segregation. I agree.

(To return for a moment to *Life Styles in the Black Ghetto*: would they agree? If they do, and using Harwood's Chapter 1[12] as the basis for evaluation, they fail to produce an unequivocal consensus. The tone of that chapter is set within the phrase "To understand the problems encountered *in* the urban Negro ghettos," which is followed, *inter alia*, by emphasis upon "the important relation between Negro unemployment and the incidence of Negro family desertion," black family disorganization, and other weaknesses and strengths of blacks, largely in comparison with European immigrants. Conspicuously absent, however, is any overt mention of residential segregation by race. Instead, urban renewal—a baby, as compared with the aged adult of housing segregation by race—is elevated as the principal villain:

> The renewal of transitional neighborhoods in the central cities has prevented some Negroes from acquiring housing of fairly good quality that they would have obtained in the *normal course of events* (p. 28, *italics added*).[13]

---

central cities," that it would "do much to take the prestige out of racial exclusiveness," and that it would facilitate more rapid renewal of some of the worst slums, since existing occupants could be relocated more easily and quickly," and that "Under such conditions, the geographic expansion of black belts would be slowed down" (pp. 239–240). In view of increased residential segregation by race in certain major—and less major—cities since 1959, he was, on hindsight, overencouraging in asserting that "The most encouraging sign is the tendency of those dedicated to the preservation of our great cities to approach the problem of residential segregation with a new realism" (p. 241).

[12] Edwin Harwood, "Urbanism as a Way of Negro Life." McCord, *et al., op. cit.*, Chapter 1, pp. 19–35.

[13] In this chapter, and throughout *Life Styles in the Black Ghetto*, use of the term "Black" occurs with extreme infrequency; the predominant term appearing is that of "Negro."

Without comment, one final quote depicting Harwood's conception of the ghetto: "I think the increasingly explosive tensions of the ghetto are in part the result of a *growing political alienation* of their lower-class residents" (p. 30, *italics added*).

As, in essence, previously indicated, Weaver's definition of a black ghetto is the "spade" definition. While it also connotes insidious derogation, the cast is changed: blacks are not held accountable for the existence of black ghettoes, for they have not been and are not the leading heroes and heroines, and, thus, deserve no Oscars; those, in truth, who are derogatory are those who enforce (and "the silent majority" are "silent enforcers," as well) residential segregation by race. Hence, it may not be too far afield to label such ghettoes not by the racial nomenclature of their inhabitants, but by that of their producers and enforcers: to wit, "white ghettoes" or "white-made ghettoes."

The nutshell definition of "black ghetto" provided earlier permits one now to return to the historical definition of a "ghetto" (1-b). While, again, a literal transference from the latter to the former is yet unwarranted, slight modification can provide an adaptable transference. Hence, in the present context, the term "ghetto" refers, in the narrow sense, to any urban area containing a minority compelled to dwell there (or in other ghettoes) through racial, religious, economic, or legal segregation and discrimination by a dominant group; in the broader sense, the term "ghetto" refers to any individual or group subject to (or victims of) such segregation and discrimination.

A "ghetto youth," therefore, may be either (1) a youth living in the ghetto area, or (2) a youth belonging to a group experiencing segregation and discrimination.

Some justification for this somewhat extensive discussion of the term "ghetto" is probably in order. More important than, perhaps, my usual tendency toward verbosity are at least the following justifications: (1) the discussion may have prompted you, the reader, to examine critically what you really mean when you say or think "ghetto;" and (2) upon completion of that critical examination, you, the reader, may examine critically how your perception of "ghetto" affects or may affect your interaction with a ghetto (a ghetto child, a ghetto drug addict—does he elicit the sympathy, if any, evoked in you by a drug addict who happens to also be the teenage son of a state governor? A ghetto female household head on welfare, or a ghetto high school senior who wants to attend Harvard and who—perhaps through "benign neglect"—usually "axes" instead of "asking" you). Finally, the discussion may be justified if it provokes you, the reader, to increase your knowledge and awareness of ghettoes, and of the individuals living within the ghettoes (if you do not already live within one and have no prior experience in such living, go "slumming" for course credit in independent or small-group work in sensitivity training[14]).

---

[14] Lest anyone consider that suggestion in jest, it is serious. An urban, black minister attended a training conference in Chicago several years ago, and, as a part of the training, was allowed only several dollars to go and "make it" in the Bowery for three days. He indicated to me that, despite cold soup and hard floors shared with alcoholics and other Bowery inhabitants, he benefitted tremendously, as exhibited, e.g., by his improved understanding and counseling in his pastoral work (alcoholics, e.g., no longer "turn him off").

The indictment upon democracy in *these* United States is merely that no real democracy would permit the existence of any ghetto, for ghettoes are anathemas to democracy.

Bearing in mind the element of untruth, the nebulous concept, and the indictment upon democracy contained within the title of "A black sociologist crystallizes social and psychological needs to the characteristics and special problems of ghetto youth," the remainder of this paper now focuses more specifically upon the task at hand: setting forth certain social and psychological needs as they relate to the characteristics and special problems of ghetto youth, with the predominant (if not sole) emphasis upon black, ghetto youth, and commenting upon "black studies" as a mechanism to meet such needs of these youth.

The task at hand is set forth in four parts: (1) characteristics and special problems of ghetto youth; (2) social and psychological needs of ghetto youth; (3) relationships between (1) and (2); and (4) "black studies" as related to (1), (2), and (3). The most important general conclusion emerging below is not a novel one: "black studies" cannot serve as a basic or fundamental mechanism in alleviating or reducing the special problems and social and psychological needs of black, ghetto youth; they can, however, heighten the awareness of such problems and needs, and increase individual and group motivation and action to reduce such problems and needs, provided there is a fundamental and basic commitment to do so from the controlling power sectors of this country.

Characteristics and special problems of ghetto youth. In general, the two most overwhelming characteristics of black, ghetto youth are their "blackness" and their low-income status. In turn, their most overwhelming special problems are inevitably linked to these two characteristics of race and poverty.

A recent census description of blacks in the United States[15] may be useful in pinpointing major demographic characteristics of the group in which ghetto youth, too, hold membership. In 1969, the more than 22 million blacks counted by the Census comprised approximately 11% of the total United States population. Most lived in the South (52%) or the North (41%), but an increasing number were in the West (from 1% in 1940 to 7% in 1969), and, as is well-known, blacks were more urbanized than were whites: 55% of all blacks were in central cities (as compared with only 26% of all whites). In 1969, Washington, D.C. was already more black than white, and other major cities tending to follow that trend certainly included such ones as Baltimore, Maryland; New Orleans, Louisiana; Memphis, Tennessee; Atlanta, Georgia; and Newark, New Jersey.

The black population was younger than the white population (median age of 19.8 for black and 28.2 for white males, and of 22.4 for black and 30.3 for white females), and almost 3 million of these blacks were 14 through 19 years of age in 1969.

These youths were, no doubt, members of black families whose annual

---

[15] *The Social and Economic Status of Negroes in the United States, 1969.* BLS Report No. 375, Current Population Reports, Series P–23, No. 29, Washington, D.C.: U.S. Government Printing Office, 1969.

family incomes, on the average, were considerably below that of whites. In 1968, the median white family income in the United States was $8,936; the median black family income was only $5,359, or a difference of $3,577. This difference becomes even more alarming when one considers the fact that the black family was, on the average, larger than the white family, and likely to have had *more* breadwinners contributing toward the total family income. For example, in 1968, a black family with only one earner had a median income of $4,151, as compared with a white counterpart of $7,724; with two earners, the black family's income increased to $7,181, as compared with an increase in a white family's income with two earners to a median of $10,000.

If quantity of education received is used as an index, income discrepancies still appear: e.g., black males, 25–44 years of age, with eight years of education, had a median 1968 income of $4,499, as compared with $6,452 for their white counterparts, and those with high school education averaged $5,801, as compared with an average of $8,154 for their white counterparts.

These census data did indicate that "the proportion of both whites and Negroes below the poverty level decreased between 1959 and 1968"; *nevertheless,* "the decline was greater for whites than for Negroes."[16] In fact, about "39 percent of all poor children in 1968 were Negro,"[17] which means, of course, that black children are, by far, grossly overrepresented among the poor.

The black unemployment rate, a rate which *excludes* many of the ones who are actually unemployed,[18] was "still about double the white rate" in 1969, and, for nonwhite teenagers between 16 and 19 years of age, was quite high: one out of every four was unemployed; in short, "Workers of Negro and other races are twice as likely as white workers to be unemployed and among the long term unemployed."[19]

Even when employed, "a larger than proportionate share of the lower-paid, less-skilled jobs were still held by" blacks in 1969, and "A larger proportion of mothers of young children" among nonwhites had "jobs or were looking for work than white mothers in 1969."[20]

The educational data reveal an increasing trend toward a greater percentage of blacks receiving more formal education, in terms of years, than formerly, of course. There is also an educational statistic of great importance in the context of this paper: "In 1968, 97 percent of Negroes in elementary school were in public school."[21] Although comparable data for secondary schools were not available, the vast majority of blacks so enrolled are also in public, rather than private schools. In addition, in 1969, "42 percent of the Negro 20 and 21 year olds had not completed high school."[22]

16 *Ibid.*, p. 24.
17 *Ibid.*, p. 25.
18 By definition, "The unemployed are persons who did not work or have a job during the survey week, and who had looked for work within the past 4 weeks, and were currently available for work. Also included are those waiting to be called back to a job from which they had been laid off or waiting to report to a new job." *Ibid.*, p. 28.
19 *Ibid.*, p. 37.
20 *Ibid.*, pp. 43, 46.
21 *Ibid.*, p. 49.
22 *Ibid.*, p. 50.

In addition to the fact that, in 1968, 24% of all nonwhites resided in substandard housing; that, in general, nonwhites have lower life expectancy and higher maternal and infant mortality rates than do whites, and less access to adequate health care services; it is also the case that "The proportion of female-headed families of 'nonwhites' has increased since 1950." Thus, in 1969, 27.3% of nonwhite families were headed by a female (as compared with 17.6% in 1950).[23] Yet, as is obvious but, on occasion, overlooked, almost 70% of nonwhite families, in 1969, were headed by a husband with his spouse present. Additionally, as family income increases, so does the likelihood of a husband-wife headed family (e.g., 56% of all black families with incomes under $3,000, in 1968, were female-headed, whereas only 7% of such families with incomes of $15,000+ were female-headed[24]). Finally, in this connection, in 1969,

> At family income levels $7,000 and above, about 90 percent of Negro children are living with both parents. At the other end of the economic scale, only about one-fourth of Negro children in families with incomes below $3,000 are living with both parents.[25]

Thus, these census data cited above provide a "typical" picture or profile of blacks. From a relative standpoint, as compared with whites, the dominant picture is that of a group disadvantaged in every major area: employment, income, health care, housing, and education. Their life-chances, therefore, are considerably more likely to be programmed, from Day One, for "failure" than for "success," as measured by the usual accomplishments embodied within the "American Dream."

These census characteristics do not, of course, describe any given individual, for there is, in reality, no individual who equals the "typical" individual projected by demographic data. Any number of qualitative descriptions of the ghetto and of ghetto youth abound, but doubt can also be raised about the extent to which they, too, reflect accurately any given individual.

One work, *Poverty in America*,[26] is useful in portraying some of these qualitative characteristics, and even more useful in that it contains articles which tend to be in disagreement about some of these characteristics.

Some characteristics contained in this work with which, I think, most, if not all of us, would find ourselves in substantial agreement are such ones as:

> . . . there is now a hard core of the specially disadvantaged—because of age, *race*, environment, physical or mental defects, etc.—that would not be significantly reduced by general prosperity.[27] (italics added)
> Being non-white makes for a very high risk of poverty. Since 1954 the risk of poverty has increased for all non-whites. The general improvement in business conditions which took place after 1954 and after 1957 was not

[23] *Ibid.*, p. 70.
[24] *Ibid.*, p. 73.
[25] *Ibid.*, p. 75.
[26] Louis A. Ferman, Joyce L. Kornbluh, and Alan Haber (eds.) : *Poverty in America: A Book of Readings.* Ann Arbor: The University of Michigan Press, 1965.
[27] Dwight Macdonald, "Our Invisible Poor," Ferman, *et al., op. cit.,* p. 23.

felt by the non-white families living below subsistence and below adequacy. Following the 1958 recession, improvement was not apparent until 1960.[28]

The poor do not usually have only one problem and many poor families are classified as "multi-problem" families. Available data point clearly to low education and shrinking occupational mobility as one of the major causes of poverty. Here the increased requirements in education for employment are one of the major causes of poverty. In addition, bad physical and mental health contribute to poverty to an undetermined but clearly significant degree.[29]

. . . poverty breeds poverty.[30]

A high rate of chronic unemployment is only one of many socioeconomic characteristics signaling distress in an area. A stagnating population, deterioriation in the quality of available labor resources, declining labor force participation rates, low wages and income, inadequate investment in capital outlay, and substandard housing are associated with chronic labor surplus areas.[31]

. . . social and economic conditions of Negroes are most responsive to changes in unemployment rates.[32]

(Comparisons of black and white incomes) implicitly assume the Negro's $3,000 buys as much as the white's $3,000. It does not.[33]

. . . non-white poverty, far more than white, is associated with families headed by women. American Negro women have always borne exceptionally heavy family responsibility.[34]

Batchelder pinpoints "some six forces afoot today that enrich the affluent members of society and even poor whites while injuring poor Negroes." These forces are urban renewal, rising education norms, agricultural mechanization and change ("Poor Negroes are already committed to the city."), manufacturing migration, increased manufacturing technology, and "the rising social minimum wage and the able-bodied unemployed."[35] He then concludes by noting that

Because of discrimination in education and employment, there is one last important difference between the Negro and white poor. Logic rather than statistics suggests its existence and its implications. . . . It follows that poor whites are the least able whites, but that poor Negroes include those least able as well as many of middling to superior ability. These able Negroes are poor because of racial discrimination; society denied them access to the channels in which their earning ability could be developed and used.[36]

---

28 Oscar Ornati, "Poverty in America," Ferman, *et al., op. cit.*, p. 23.
29 *Ibid.*, pp. 34–35.
30 Ferman, *et al., op. cit.*, p. 86.
31 Sar A. Levitan, "Characteristics of Urban Depressed Areas," Ferman, *et al., op. cit.*, p. 90.
32 Alan Batchelder, "Poverty: The Special Case of the Negro," Ferman, *et al., op. cit.*, p. 113.
33 *Ibid.*
34 *Ibid.*, p. 115.
35 *Ibid.*, pp. 115–118.
36 *Ibid.*, p. 118.

The characteristics showing greater divergence are largely cultural and/or psychological in nature. The editors of *Poverty in America*, who offer several cogent criticisms of the "culture of poverty" thesis (that "the cycle of poverty may refer to the intergenerational exposure to certain kinds of economic problems rather than exposure to a particular set of values and beliefs," that its utility "as an explanatory variable in the behavior of the poor" is open to question, and certain implications derived from the thesis inevitably raising "the question of the utility and worthiness of lower-class values in solving the poverty problem"),[37] garnered, in this collection, several articles which, in my judgment, ought to be read with profit by potential users of the multimedia materials related to Afro-American studies suggested here or elsewhere.

These articles are Rodman's "The Lower-Class Value Stretch,"[38] and Miller, Riessman, and Seagull's "Poverty and Self-Indulgence: A Critique of the Non-Deferred Gratification Pattern."[39] Essentially, Rodman takes issue with those writers who "assert that the basic values of a society are common to all social classes within that society" and with those who "assert that the values differ from class to class." The value stretch, by which

> I mean that the lower-class person, without abandoning the general values of the society, develops an alternative set of values. Without abandoning the values placed upon success, such as high income and high educational and occupational attainment, he stretches the values so that lesser degrees of success also become desirable. . . . The result is that the members of the lower class, in many areas, have a wider range of values than others within the society. They share the general values of the society with members of other classes, but in addition, they have stretched these values, or developed alternative values, which help them to adjust to their deprived circumstances.[40]

This stretch is Rodman's mechanism of reconciling the apparent contradictions existing in the two extreme positions of common values shared by all or of different values peculiar to each class.

His application of this stretch to Rosen's[41] is of particular importance, inasmuch as the latter tended to conclude that blacks had lower educational aspirations than did whites. Rodman, in commenting upon Rosen, wrote:

> He studied the occupational aspirations of different ethnic and class groups and showed that certain ethnic groups and also the lower classes are characterized by a lower level of aspiration. This is because he follows

[37] Ferman, *et al., op. cit.,* pp. 259–261.
[38] Hyman Rodman, "The Lower-Class Value Stretch," Ferman, *et al., op. cit.,* pp. 270–285.
[39] S. M. Miller, Frank Riessman, and Arthur A. Seagull, "Poverty and Self-indulgence: A Critique of the Non-Deferred Gratification Pattern," Ferman, *et al., op. cit.,* pp. 285–302.
[40] Rodman, *op. cit.,* p. 277.
[41] Bernard C. Rosen, "Race, ethnicity, and the achievement syndrome." *American Sociological Review,* 24: 47–60, 1959. My reading of Rosen's findings tended to emphasize more nearly his emphasis upon "lower" aspirational levels for blacks than for his other comparative groups, and his tendency to justify certain statements by a "relative" measure of "high aspiration."

the common and in some ways unfortunate habit of reducing his data to single aspiration scores. Nevertheless he correctly points out that "it is misleading to speak of the 'height' of vocational aspirations. . . . If we examine his data on ethnic group differences closely, we can see that certain ethnic groups have a wider range of aspirations, and we can safely infer that members of the lower class also have a wider range of aspirations—they express satisfaction rather than dissatisfaction over a wide range of occupational goals. Rosen's study, therefore, in an indirect way, demonstrates the existence of the lower-class value stretch in the area of occupational aspiration. . . ."[42]

What is of particular importance here is that, for our purposes, various characteristics ascribed to ghetto youth should probably be *greater* in number and range than those the average middle-class ghetto teacher would normally perceive; and, quite importantly, characteristics which represent "stretches" of the usual middle-class characteristics should not be perceived as pejorative traits. As discussed in greater detail below, the educational curriculum for black ghetto youth ought be "stretched" or expanded to include black studies as an integral part of the entire curriculum, as, in truth, the traditional "white studies" for while youth also ought be expanded to include "black studies" as well, or, more simply, present educational curriculum should be stretched so as to approach closer and closer to a more exact approximation of truth.

Miller, Riessman, and Seagull provided, in their aforementioned article, an excellent critique of the usual ploy that lower class (including black ghetto youth) persons are unable to defer gratification. Important conclusions reached by them are those that:

> . . . many lower-income people have a shorter time perspective than do many middle-income persons. The shorter time outlook may handicap many of the poor. But we are not sure that the shorter time perspective is *always* linked with an inability to defer gratification. More importantly, we do not view all those who seem to be unable to defer gratification as so psychodynamically constrained that the ability to delay is unavailable to them. . . .
>
> The experimental studies on the importance of trust underline the significance of situational rather than psychodynamic variables . . . by emphasizing nonpersonality variables, we have the possibilities of helping individuals to *learn* the kinds of patterns that may be important for their well-being. . . .
>
> Many studies show that educational level is the major variable explaining different social class behavioral/attitudinal patterns. This conclusion suggests that we are not dealing with outlooks that have an immutable quality; rather, they are affected by knowledge, and understanding. They are subject, consequently, to influences and change.[43]

Any number of other instances might be cited, but all would point toward the fact that there is considerable doubt about the specific qualitative character-

[42] Rodman, *op. cit.*, pp. 281–282.
[43] Miller, *et al.*, *op. cit.*, p. 301.

istics of any given ghetto youth: that one must approach such a youth as an individual who is unique, despite the fact that, in some respects, as the couplet goes, he is as "some others," and, in some respects, he is as "all others."

The general characteristics of ghetto youth, largely those of or those linked to their "blackness" and poverty and relative deprivation, create special problems for such youth. These special problems can be categorized in a variety of ways, but, in the final analysis, they are the old, familiar ones of:

1. Search for identity and the need for "respect".
2. Prejudice and discrimination, especially in
   a. Housing
   b. Employment
   c. Income
   d. Education
   e. Health-care services
   f. Legal and judiciary procedures (including police contacts, other forms of law enforcement)
   g. Religion (and especially certain "Christian" forms of reinforcement of prejudice and discrimination)
   h. Welfare (especially as it has operated traditionally in maintaining, rather than reducing, welfare, and, thereby, maintained massive employment for "middle-class welfare professionals").
3. Development of response mechanisms to (1) and (2) above which provide constructive channeling of energies and produce visible and desired results in the direction of improving significantly the status of blacks in America, and, thereby, reducing prejudice and discrimination, and becoming a part of the power structure.

Inasmuch as these special problems overlap the social and psychological needs of ghetto youth, they are subsumed in the following section.

Social and psychological needs of ghetto youth. Perhaps one of the most important of the social and psychological needs of ghetto youth at this decisive point in our current history is that of the need for more informed and more courageous social and behavioral scientists who (usually federally funded) continue to amass datum after datum, interpretation after interpretation, conclusion after conclusion, implication after implication about them.

The four most widely circulated and controversial documents or works focusing upon blacks produced in the decade of the 1960's were, without a doubt, "The Moynihan Report," "The Coleman Report," "The Kerner Report," (all published by the U.S. Government Printing Office, Washington, D.C.), and *the* Jensen article.[44] All of them can be regarded as "political" reports, in the sense that they were intended to have, or have had, implications for social

---

[44] Daniel P. Moynihan, *The Negro Family: The Case for National Action*, United States Department of Labor, Washington, D.C.: U.S. Government Printing Office, 1965; James S. Coleman, *et al., Equality of Educational Opportunity*, U.S. Department of Health, Education, and Welfare, Washington, D.C.: U.S. Government Printing Office, 1966; Otto Kerner (Chairman), *Report of the National Advisory Commission on Civil Disorders*, Washington, D.C.: U.S. Government Printing Office, 1968; and Arthur R. Jensen, "How much can we boost IQ and scholastic achievement?", *Harvard Education Review*, 39:1–123, 1969.

policies as they relate especially to blacks and black families, blacks and education (including Project Headstart), and blacks as victims of racism. All have produced controversy, but all bear careful examination, and none can be simply dismissed without "throwing away the baby with the bath."

"The Moynihan Report," which is largely a rehash of E. Franklin Frazier,[45] bears especial attention not because of his emphasis placed upon black family disorganization or a need to strengthen its structure, but because, although rarely noted by its critics, it did indicate that:

> The impact of unemployment on the Negro family, and particularly on the Negro male, is the least understood of all the developments that have contributed to the present crisis. There is little analysis because there has been almost no inquiry.[46]
>
> The fundamental, overwhelming fact is that *Negro unemployment . . . has continued at disaster levels for 35 years.*[47]
>
> The most conspicuous failure of the American social system in the past 10 years has been its inadequacy in providing jobs for Negro youth. . . . This problem will now become steadily more serious.[48]

and, quite important, emphasized that

> . . . the emergence and increasing visibility of a Negro middle-class may beguile the nation into supposing that the circumstances of the remainder of the Negro community are equally prosperous, whereas just the opposite is true at present, and is likely to continue so.[49]

"The Coleman Report," irrespective of various criticisms leveled against it, has served an extremely useful function in at least stressing anew the what-ought-be-obvious factor that the quality of education received ought not be

---

[45] Moynihan referred specifically to E. Franklin Frazier, *The Negro Family in the United States*, Chicago: The University of Chicago Press, 1939; "Problems and Needs of Negro Children and Youth Resulting from Family Disorganization," *Journal of Negro Education*, Summer, 1950, pp. 276–277; and his *Black Bourgeoisie*, New York: Collier Books, 1962.

[46] Moynihan, *op. cit.*, p. 19.

[47] *Ibid.*, p. 20.

[48] *Ibid.*, p. 26.

[49] *Ibid.*, p. 6. An intellectual heir to whom Moynihan might well have referred here could certainly have included Ernest E. Neal, "Two Negro Problems Instead of One: A Challenge to Negro Colleges." *Journal of Negro Education*, 21:161–166, 1952, whose article is especially recommended for serious study. Neal noted therein that there were "two Negro problems instead of one." The first is that of middle-class Negroes who had acquired the trappings entitling them to integration, with the vital exception of the proper color. The second is that of the masses of Negroes, almost forgotten since "The spokesmen for the Negro people have become so preoccupied with the frustration of the middle-class group that they have lost sight of the fact that the concern of many Negroes is a job—any kind of a job that pays wages—a house—anywhere, but one that is dry and warm,—and enough food and clothing for them and their too many children" (pp. 161–162). Too often, today, there is still a tendency for persons (including teachers) to deny the fact that black masses can—and increasingly do—articulate for themselves, and that blacks are composed of heterogeneous subgroups, so that, in reality, there can be no single black spokesman, nor a cadre of elite spokesmen. Robert Penn Warren's answer to *Who Speaks for the Negro?* (New York: Vintage Books, 1966) bears serious consideration: ". . . there is, in one sense, no Negro leader. There are, merely, a number of Negroes who happen to occupy positions of leadership" (p. 405; also see especially pp. 405–423).

measured solely on the basis of such quantitative factors as the age of the school building, the presence of a gymnatorium, and the average pupil expenditure, but must, in the case of lower-class pupils, at least, consider also the quality of the teacher-pupil relationship.[50]

"The Kerner Report," I think, is probably most useful in demonstrating (as has been observed by a number of persons, including Kenneth Clark) that (to use a rhyme recalled from my own childhood) "sticks and stones may break my bones, but words will never harm (nor help) me." Such reports are as useless as a week *set aside* for Negro History Week, National Brotherhood Week, or taking the perennial basket of used clothing and canned foods to a needy family for Thanksgiving or Christmas (why in the hell must such baskets be given, when the need is not for baskets, but for jobs or for income so that such families can buy their own clothing and their own food—as do the persons contributing to such crummy baskets?). Unfortunately, I think this Report helped to "cool things" for awhile, as so many became elated with the sound of "racism," "racism," "racism," and, belatedly (or, in some instances, not yet at all) realized that while the Report indicted white racism, it provided no concrete mechanism to reduce racism.

The Jensen article stresses several important points. One of the most important, to me, is the need for a redefinition of the functions of black studies (as they are presently being developed in a number of prestigious universities today) so that they develop black ghetto youth into able and competent geneticists, psychologists, child development specialists, statistical and methodological specialists, etc., all capable of refuting, where necessary, and on the basis of sound empirical investigations and logical inferences and theories, the sophisticated formulations of "trash" contained in such articles.

The Jensen article also provoked a comment from Martin Deutsch[51] that might well serve as a model for social and behavioral scientists who publish study after study after study about blacks. In his own words, listen:

> Some years ago, I wrote an article on the concept of social courage, which I defined as an act ". . . taking place in a context of overt or covert social intimidation. . . . The hypothesis was advanced that the manifestation of social courage would depend on the relationship between inner conviction (with respect to the issue around which the act would take place) and the punishment potential which the act would invoke." It would be in the social and scientific interest if Arthur Jensen would summon the social courage necessary to repudiate the positions which have been taken in his name; and to reexamine his thinking, reevaluate his sources of information, reassess his argument, and retract his genetic conclusions in the light of data about and understanding of environmental factors with which he was apparently not familiar at the time he

---

[50] Although there is some emphasis on comparative monetary expenditures, see Charles S. Johnson, "Patterns of Segregation," *Negro Digest,* 5:75–82, 1943, on "Educational Institutions," and his indictment of racially segregated schools as disadvantageous for black youth especially.

[51] Martin Deutsch, "Happenings on the Way Back to the Forum." *Harvard Educational Review,* 39:523–557, 1969, p. 552.

wrote the article. In times of serious social crisis, when the barriers to social change are so enormous and when young people are venting such frustration, a senior social scientist's manifestation of the courage to reformulate a well-publicized opinion would be a positive example of the conquering of discomfort by the inner conviction of the necessity for scientific objectivity. It would be a positive act, too, because in the immense task which social scientists have with respect to our changing social structure, gifted experimentalists like Jensen can play important roles in generating new knowledge about the environment and the interactions individuals have with it.

A basic social and psychological need, once again, is for the development of more black, ghetto youth as competent social and behavioral scientists, who, given sufficient insights into and experiences in the black ghetto, and provided with sufficient scientific and humanistic training, will help close the present gaps in our knowledge of and our understanding of the black ghetto in general, and ghetto youth in particular.

The other major social needs, as indicated previously, are those of social acceptance as first-class citizens and first-class human beings; of immediate access to a guaranteed annual income sufficient for at least a moderate (and not, therefore, a minimum) standard-of-living; of immediate access to improved employment, at higher wages, with adequate retirement and other fringe benefits, and with adequate education and provision for occupational mobility in an upward direction (and not, as is presently the case, federal and other programs "dead-ending" blacks through such programs as "New Careers"[52]); for adequate health-care, and on and on and on. You know the needs as well as I—if not better!

There is a particular need for drastic educational reforms, so that black ghetto youth will learn and will be motivated to continue to learn. This cannot be done best, I think, by using such a model as James Brown and his "Don't Be No Fool, Stay In School" rock-'n'-roll message. It is, indeed, ironic that one who did *not* stay in school and who has, as measured by economic "success," "made it," is utilized to urge youth to remain in school!

More nearly, there is a need for teachers to assume responsibility for that which they are paid to do: to teach their pupils. Consequently, those teachers

[52] For example, while there is an admitted need for increased development of paraprofessionals, subprofessionals, nonprofessionals (select any term), it is also the case that too much emphasis is currently being spent upon training blacks for such positions, and too little emphasis upon training blacks for professional positions. If there is, e.g., a critical shortage of nurses, why are blacks being "pushed into" training programs as nurses' aides or LPN's, rather than a heavier emphasis being placed upon "pushing" ghetto youth into training programs as registered nurses, nurses with bachelor degrees, etc.? It is also of interest to note that, as already alluded to earlier, professional welfare workers seem to maintain vested interest in maintaining welfare clients and in perpetuating generational family welfare. In addition, to the best of my knowledge, no anti-poverty agency in this country has, since 1964, apparently developed any poverty-level individual to the extent that he or she was "career-laddered" through progressive stages to occupy such positions as those of executive directors of such agencies, or even top-level executive and/or managerial positions immediately below that of an executive director. In some sense, many of these programs have become bureaucratized in support of maintaining the vested interests of the middle-class poverty professionals.

who continue to shift their responsibilities upon the heads of parents whose shoulders are already bending heavily and whose heads may be sagging are not really worthy of the title of teachers; rather, they should bear the title of "parent-blamers."

Article after article, demonstration project after demonstration project, orator after orator, for decade after decade has shown clearly the need for an individual to feel that "I am somebody!" Black ghetto youth are no exception. Their basic psychological needs include those of developing positive self-images or identities, of having adequate models available for behavioral patterning, of being able to realize rewards for their efforts, of receiving further motivation and encouragement to enhance their growth and development, or, in short, receiving a "pay-off" for conformity to the basic social and cultural norms and for constructive deviation from such norms.[53]

One recent work (i.e., Deutsch, Katz, and Jensen, eds., *Social Class, Race, and Psychological Development,* 1968[54]) which, incidentally, is "dedicated to the memory of Dr. Martin Luther King, Jr."[55] may be especially recommended to those interested in a partial review and critique of recent literature pertaining to such factors as those of intercorrelations among social and individual background, achievement, and measures of ability, black self-images, effects of deprivation upon perception, environmental intervention in early childhood, attention sets, development of logical thinking, and, in particular, certain effects of segregation as they relate to the development of self-images and self-identities.

This work emphasizes at the outset that

> . . . basic assumptions about class and race differences in psychological development continue to rest more upon conjecture and subjective impressions than upon the findings of scientific research.[56]

Yet, it also emphasizes, and rightly so, that

> . . . discrimination tends to create in its victims those very traits of "inferiority" that are mentioned to rationalize its practice. . . . Thus the belief that Negroes are intellectually incompetent can cause both whites and Negroes to behave in such manner as to yield confirmatory evidence.[57]

If I were to isolate a single section for required reading for teachers and other professionals involved in programs related to black studies, it would,

---

[53] In addition to some suggested works contained in the bibliography, an interested reader who is already familiar with (or if not so familiar, who explores) findings, generalizations, principles, and theories in the area of small groups (see, e.g., the voluminous and excellent set of readings contained in A. Paul Hare, *Handbook of Small Group Research.* The Free Press, New York, 1962, pp. 416–492) may find such information extremely helpful in furthering his understanding—and, thereby interpretations—of much of the dynamics of group processes involved in the everyday or ordinary lives of black ghetto youth. Charles Cooley's "looking-glass self," George H. Mead's "generalized other," and W. I. Thomas' "definition of the situation" are also useful constructs in analyzing and understanding such behavior.

[54] Martin Deutsch, Irwin Katz, Arthur R. Jensen, *Social Class, Race, and Psychological Development.* New York: Holt, Rinehart & Winston, Inc., 1968.

[55] *Ibid.*

[56] *Ibid.,* p. 1.

[57] *Ibid.,* pp. 3–4.

without a doubt, be "Part Three: Social and Psychological Perspectives" (pp. 175–290). If any further restriction were necessary, then I would opt for Harold Proshansky and Peggy Newton, "The Nature and Meaning of Negro Self-Identity" (pp. 178–218).

Finally, this work contains, at the end of each chapter, references which tend to highlight the gamut of research available on major psychological variables as they relate to deprivation.

Relationships between characteristics and special problems of ghetto youth and their social and psychological needs. Any number of alternatives of treating this subsection came to mind, as, no doubt, will be true of an informed and a not-so-informed reader of any hue. One extreme position, e.g., is certainly that the characteristics and special problems of ghetto youth which may exist would disappear if the "honkie" or "The Man" took his feet off their (our) necks!

From the standpoint of many whites, an accompanying (or companion) position to that stated above is that such characteristics and problems would simply disappear if—and only if—ghetto youth would behave as if they were white—and white middle class at that!

Either such position is not only extreme, but absolutely abasing and absurd.

What ought to be emphasized most is that, from an adaptive viewpoint, the various social and psychological needs manifested by ghetto youth and their characteristics and special problems are linked or bridged by coping mechanisms which they have learned, modified, and developed within the special confines of their environment. In short, their varying coping mechanisms, whether in such forms as those of dope addiction, delinquent gang behavior, dropping out of school, *und so weiter*, or in such forms as maintaining full employment at slave wages, emphasizing their blackness, *et cetera*, are functional for most of them. It can even be argued, and succintly so, that becoming and remaining mentally ill represent functional mechanisms of coping for particular individuals within particular environments.

Therefore, the relationships between characteristics and special problems of ghetto youth and their social and psychological needs are, in essence, the same as those relationships between heredity and environment, and between and among the individual, his culture, and his society. There is absolutely no point, no point whatsoever!, in dealing with the special or specific social and psychological needs of ghetto youth unless those adverse factors affecting heredity (including inadequate prenatal and postnatal diets) and the sociocultural environment (including overcrowded housing and bad public school teachers) are significantly reduced.

It is, as variously explicated by such writers as Kardimer and Ovesey, Grier and Cobbs, and Hendin,[58] quite true that the oppression, the repression, and the suppression thrust upon blacks especially scars drastically and perma-

---

[58] Abram Kardiner and Lionel Ovesey, *The Mark of Oppression*, Cleveland: Meridian Books, The World Publishing Company, 1962 (first published in 1951); William H. Grier and Price M. Cobbs, *Black Rage*, New York: Basic Books, Inc., Publishers, 1968; and Herbert Hendin, *Black Suicide*, New York: Basic Books, Inc., Publishers, 1969.

nently black personalities. The healthiest ones are certainly those who reduce, control, and/or eliminate self-hatred or hatred of one's own racial group, and turn outward their hatred. A sign of directing hatred outward (i.e., projecting it upon whites or upon the oppressors, the repressors, and the suppressors) is a healthy sign. Thus, one could well argue that the most devastating relationship between the aforementioned variables is that which has induced black self- and group-hatred among blacks, as may, no doubt, be the case among other minority groups (e.g., Mexican-Americans and Indians), and that, therefore, one of the major objectives of any program in black studies ought to be that of helping to direct hostility and hatred in the appropriate directions.

Such redirection of hostility and hatred should tend to reduce many of the critical social and psychological needs now characteristic of many youth in the ghetto, for when such hatred is redirected in appropriate channels, the responses from many of the oppressors tend, at least in recent years, to be channeled toward the direction of reducing the conditions which make such hatred possible. On the other hand, of course, there is always the ever-present danger (as has also occurred during recent years) that these oppressors will increase their oppression, and, thereby, increase the devastating social and psychological needs of those who are oppressed.

Black Studies as related to characteristics, special problems, and social and psychological needs of ghetto youth. As Freeman[59] noted elsewhere, although in a different context nevertheless applicable to current and emergent Black Studies Programs,

> Campaigns for curriculum revision are not new. They have always followed in the wake of times of stress or strain resulting finally not in a complete revision of the curriculum, but an improvement of emphasis on some points and de-emphasis of others (p. 130).

And so it is with black studies!

The Association for the Study of Negro Life and History, organized by the late black historian, Carter G. Woodson, in Chicago, on 9 September 1915, had among its chief purposes those of collecting "sociological and historical data bearing on the Negro," publishing "books on Negro Life and History," promoting "the study of the Negro through clubs and schools," and, most lofty of all, bringing "about harmony between the races by interpreting the one to the other."[60]

In addition to initiating publication of *The Journal of Negro History* (January, 1916), the Association established a Department of Research in 1922, with the assistance of a Laura Spelman Rockefeller Memorial, and, in 1926, began "the celebration of Negro History Week," an

> occasion for public exercises inviting special attention to the achievements of the Negro. . . . Negro History Week has helped to arouse the

---

[59] James N. Freeman, "The Negro and the Teaching of Agricultural Vocations." *Negro College Quarterly*, 3:126–132, 1945.
[60] "History of the Association for the Study of Negro Life and History." *The Negro History Bulletin*, 1:14, 1938.

people to a keener appreciation of the contribution of the Negro to civilization. Men are now learning to think of civilization as the heritage of the centuries to which all races have made some contribution.[61]

And so declared *The Negro History Bulletin* in 1938! In light of current events and developments, alas, this optimism appeared highly unwarranted.

Also, over three decades ago, in the very first volume (1932) of *The Journal of Negro Education* (pp. 289–290), great stress was placed upon the need for "provision for instruction in the history and achievements of the Negro race" for the education of the Negro. It was

> maintained that every American child needs to know the complete history and life of this country, and the history and life of the Negro people are a part of this history. Whereas history was formerly expected to teach blind obedience to the principles and practices of one's country, the modern social studies program of today includes a critical approach to the merits and deficiencies of American civilization. For example, *this would admit of a critical treatment of the race problem in American life, the contributions of the races to the nation's achievements and the proper attitude of all citizens in improving undesirable conditions that make the matter a problem* . . . this attitude is one of understanding and tolerance which are based upon thorough knowledge of the group to be studied. . . . There are instances where units of work on the Negro and his achievements are conducted in schools for white pupils only. The contention summarized is that a basic understanding and appreciation of the history and achievements of the Negro race are just as desirable content for the elementary curriculum of the white child as it is for the Negro child (*italics added*).

Yet today, adequate provision for the inclusion of instruction about blacks and about other minority groups is still usually absent in the vast majority of educational curricula. Therefore, the history of the United States, as taught in such curricula is also inadequate, and must remain inadequate until such time as the histories and cultural materials of the United States of America are revised to approach a more precise approximation of reality—of truth.

In 1942, noting that the study of American history had recently been introduced in the secondary schools of Great Britain, Harcourt Tynes urged that

> If the British in their desire for solidarity find it necessary to understand the American people through the study of American history, *it should be doubly necessary for the American public to study the history of the Negro. Such a study is long overdue.* Many of the social and economic proscriptions of the Negro are due to ignorance of his past, his worth as a man, his longings and his aspirations. We are long and loud in professing the democratic way of life. But we deny to one-tenth of our citizens the principles enunciated in the great American documents. . . .
>
> The Association for the Study of Negro Life and History, which will celebrate Negro History Week from February 8–15, has been trying

[61] *Ibid.*

to resolve all doubts concerning the contributions of the Negro to civilization and his services to the American nation. In its stress upon this phase of history *it desires to call the attention of the public to what the schools have failed to do.* It aims to open up avenues for study and research relation to the Negro's past. It attempts to have the American public understand the aspirations of this group which is devoting its energies and resources to the furtherance of truth. It desires to disabuse the minds of those who form their opinions of the Negro solely through the caricatures and stereotypes of the press, the radio and the movies.[62] (*Italics added.*)

A proliferation of statements could be amassed over the years, all of which have as their central theme the necessity to include black studies as an integral component of educational curricula, in order to benefit both blacks and whites, and to improve, in general, race relations in the United States. One contemporary statement, full of suggestions useful for any ghetto teacher, policeman, community relations worker, *et cetera*, warrants special mention: Sidney Trubowitz, *A Handbook for Teaching in the Ghetto School* (Quadrangle Books, Chicago, 1968).

In this work, Trubowitz, stressing the fact that "Those teachers who do accept positions in ghetto schools are often ill equipped to deal with the situations they meet," indicates quite emphatically that such teachers must 1) "understand the values of his students"; 2) "examine his own responses to those values"; 3) "know about curriculum approaches that make contact with the children, about instructional materials that have within them the sense of reality that can make for pupil growth"; 4) "needs ideas about how to set up relationships with the children that will create an atmosphere most conducive to learning"; 5) "must be prepared to deal effectively with deviations from normal behavior"; 6) "needs a deep knowledge of the community from which underprivileged children come, of the parents, and of the pupils themselves"; and 7) "needs especially sensitive supervision, so that he can get support in times of stress and be guided toward the self-knowledge that is so essential for the teacher of ghetto children."[63]

Trubowitz, as I interpret him, would place far more value upon an educational curriculum which integrated black studies into its content in a meaningful way, rather than upon any curriculum which merely included a unit or two, for a week or two, or even a month or a year or two, on black studies. He stated quite clearly that:

> although it is the job of the total society to lift the crushing burden of prejudice and discrimination that contributes to self-deprecation, the teacher can do *something* to improve the image of the Negro child by helping to dissipate the notion that the Negro has made a negligible contribution to the cultural heritage of America,[64]

---

[62] Harcourt A. Tynes, "Negro History Week." *The Negro Quarterly*, 1:5–6, 1942.
[63] Sidney Trubowitz, *A Handbook for Teaching in the Ghetto School*. Chicago: Quadrangle Books, 1968. This is, again, an excellent source for aid.
[64] *Ibid.*, p. 97.

that

Since greater emphasis needs to be given to the role of the Negro in American cultural development, it is incumbent upon the teacher to become knowledgeable in this area. The teacher who recognizes the impact of the Negro upon American culture can help his pupils gain a more complete picture of American historical development,[65]

and that

When children learn that members of the Negro race have made and are making important contributions to the development of American culture, they can begin to attach a sense of value to their group.[66]

Trubowitz specifies what some of the relationships between black studies and characteristics, special problems, and social and psychological needs of ghetto youth ought to be, while, at the same time, he raises (usually implicitly) some very serious issues concerning these relationships.

The basic, or most fundamental relationship between any black studies program and these characteristics, problems, and needs is simply that of improving self-images and group images of ghetto youth. Such a program ought to make the ghetto youth feel and know that they are important and valued as individuals and that the racial group to which they belong is also an important and valued group.

Yet, as Trubowitz himself (and many others, for that matter) is quite aware, simply "saying that you are somebody will not make it so!"

Consequently, the critical issue must be raised: can a black studies program really help to enhance those characteristics which are regarded as desirable, reduce those special problems which are present, and meet the various social and psychological needs of ghetto youth? No unequivocal answer can be given, for the issue is entirely too complex, depending, as it does, upon a multitude of variables.

But, we know that earlier efforts to emphasize Negro History Week or to inculcate "Negro studies" into the curricula of various educational institutions have not produced the desired results with any rapidity of all deliberate speed.

In commenting especially upon black studies at institutions of higher education, Clark[67] makes an exceptionally good case for teaching black studies to integrated, rather than segregated groups. Earlier provision for instruction of "Negro studies" catered largely, if not exclusively, to separate groupings of whites and of blacks. That may, in fact, have been one of the fundamental weaknesses. Hence, any current black studies program may have a greater potential of success in helping to meet the problems and needs of ghetto youth if they serviced a desegregated clientele. In order to accomplish this goal, of course, the schools themselves must be desegregated.

[65] *Ibid.*, p. 90.
[66] *Ibid.*, p. 100.
[67] Kenneth B. Clark, "A Charade of Power: Black Students at White Colleges." *Antioch Review*, 29:145–148, 1969.

Pickens[68] has asked: "Teaching Negro Culture in High Schools—Is It Worthwhile?" His answer is that yes, it is worthwhile, provided that it is done properly. In his own words,

> Our basic premise is that the proper teaching of Negro culture and history is one of the few effective ways to motivate Negro students to higher levels of achievement, and at the same time help whites to remove some of their false values, based on ungrounded concepts of their racial superiority. It is one of the few ways of helping both groups toward a greater appreciation of the Negro as a human being, and toward a better understanding of themselves and each other. . . .
> Curriculum changes should be encouraged that would simply teach the truth. Then students, Negro and white, would learn the facts about the Negro in the arts in general, and American culture, in general and American history. . . .
> If teachers will teach more of the truth, the solution is perhaps in sight, for this may lead to a corresponding rise in the Negro's self-esteem. With greater self-esteem the Negro secondary school youth may become more teachable, the white youth more understanding and appreciative. This is not guaranteed, but is it worth a try?[69]

Pickens obviously sees the relationship as one remedy which must be utilized in order to improve substantially the lives and life opportunities of blacks, and one which cannot be done in isolation. Rather, as a constant thread running through his work, this paper, and, in fact, throughout the writings of most of those seriously concerned about the fate of American society (and not just about blacks), it is quite true that there must be positive changes occurring within the very fabric of American society, changes to reduce significantly discrimination and prejudice against blacks and against other minority groups. Otherwise, and in the case of blacks, in particular, there is the great possibility that black studies programs may well serve as a catalyst to ignite "the fire next time." Even that, however, may not be disastrous, for if the appropriate racial climate, one respecting the dignity and inherent value of each and every human being, is not reached, and reached fairly quickly within this country, "the fire next time" may leave this earth free to generate a new kind of man, a man to supersede man as we know him today, a man who will exist free of racial prejudices, free of racial discrimination, free of unwarranted and ugly hatred for his fellowman.

Thus it is that the relationships between black studies and these critical characteristics, special problems, social and psychological needs of ghetto youth cannot be singled out by any given writer for anyone else, but I would contend that of those main purposes "for the development of materials on the Negro" singled out by Cuban[70] (i.e., a more balanced picture of American history and its past, the improvement of race relations, and improved self-concept of low-

---

68 William G. Pickens, "Teaching Negro Culture in High Schools—Is It Worthwhile?" *The Journal of Negro Education*, 34:106–113, 1965.
69 *Ibid.*, pp. 106–110.
70 Larry Cuban, "Not 'Whether?' But 'Why? and How?'—Instructional Materials on the Negro in the Public Schools." *The Journal of Negro Education*, 36:434–436, 1967.

income Negro children), the most important is that of improving significantly the self-concept of low-income Negro children, to which one must add improving significantly the self-concept of all black children, to which one must add improving significantly the self-concept of all whites. In other words, whites must not base their feelings of positive self-concepts upon their distorted and deliberate and racist conceptions of blacks. If whites could have positive self-concepts without having to depend upon "being better than a black," then we would have come a long way indeed.

In any case, although the crystallization of social and psychological needs to the characteristics and special problems of ghetto youth yet awaits a more definitive answer, which is, in turn, dependent upon much needed research and many socioeconomic changes within the United States, it is still the case that any teacher genuinely concerned about ghetto youth can learn to teach them effectively, as suggested earlier, if he or she enters into a contract—a contract which cannot be broken—to teach them. Ghetto children are eager to learn until they are "turned off" by the "outside world!" The question is not so much, then, what are their characteristics, what are their special problems, what are their needs, but *are you willing to work with them, are you willing to teach them about themselves and their past, are you willing to help them "make it out of the ghetto," even if it means that you must inevitably share some of the "goodies" you now have with them?*

BIBLIOGRAPHY

Batchelder, Alan. "Poverty: The Special Case of the Negro," Louis A. Ferman, Joyce L. Kornbluh, and Alan Haber (eds.), *Poverty in America: A Book of Readings.* Ann Arbor: The University of Michigan Press, 1965.

Bontemps, Arna. *Golden Slippers: An Anthology of Negro Poetry for Young Readers.* New York: Harper & Brothers, 1941.

Billingsley, Andrew. *Black Families in White America.* Englewood Cliffs, N.J.: Prentice-Hall, Inc., 1968.

Clark, Kenneth B. "A Charade of Power: Black Students at White Colleges." *Antioch Review,* 29:145–148, 1969.

Coleman, James S., et al. *Equality of Educational Opportunity.* U.S. Department of Health, Education, and Welfare, Washington, D.C.: U.S. Government Printing Office, 1966.

Cuban, Larry. "Not 'Whether', But 'Why? and How?'—Instructional Materials on the Negro in the Public Schools." *The Journal of Negro Education,* 36:434–436, 1967.

Deutsch, Martin. "Happenings on the Way Back to the Forum." *Harvard Educational Review,* 39:523–557, 1969.

Drake, St. Clair and Horace Cayton. *Black Metropolis; A Study of Negro Life in a Northern City.* New York: Harcourt, Brace and Company, 1945.

DuBois, William E. B. "Education and Work." *The Journal of Negro Education,* 1:60–74, 1932.

Edwards, G. Franklin, ed. *E. Franklin Frazier on Race Relations.* Chicago: The University of Chicago Press, 1968.

Fairchild, Henry P. (ed.). *Dictionary of Sociology.* Totowa, New Jersey: Littlefield, Adams and Company, 1968.

Ferman, Louis A., Joyce L. Kornbluh, and Alan Haber (eds.). *Poverty in America: A Book of Readings.* Ann Arbor: The University of Michigan Press, 1965.

Frazier, E. Franklin. *Black Bourgeoisie.* Glencoe, Ill.: The Free Press, 1957.

Frazier, E. Franklin. *The Negro Family in Chicago.* Chicago: The University of Chicago Press, 1932.

Frazier, E. Franklin. *The Negro Family in the United States.* Chicago: The University of Chicago Press, 1939.

Frazier, E. Franklin. "Problems and Needs of Negro Children and Youth Resulting From Family Disorganization." *The Journal of Negro Education,* Summer, 1950, pp. 276–277.

Freeman, James N. "The Negro and the Teaching of Agricultural Vocations." *The Negro College Quarterly,* 3:126–132, 1945.

Grier, William H. and Price M. Cobbs. *Black Rage.* New York: Basic Books Inc., Publishers, 1968.

Hendin, Herbert. *Black Suicide.* New York: Basic Books., Inc., Publishers, 1969.

"History of the Association for the Study of Negro Life and History." *The Negro History Bulletin,* 1:14, 1938.

Jensen, Arthur R. "How Much Can We Boost IQ and Scholastic Achievement?" *Harvard Educational Review,* 39:1–123, 1969.

Johnson, Charles S. "Patterns of Segregation." *The Negro Digest,* 5:75–82, 1943.

Kardiner, Abram and Lionel Ovesey. *The Mark of Oppression.* Cleveland: Meridian Books, The World Publishing Company, 1962 (originally published in 1951).

Kerner, Otto (Chairman). *Report of the National Advisory Commission on Civil Disorders.* Washington, D.C.: U.S. Government Printing Office, 1968.

McCord, William, et al, *Life Styles in the Black Ghetto.* New York: W. W. Norton and Company, 1969.

Moynihan, Daniel P. *The Negro Family: The Case for National Action.* United States Department of Labor, Washington, D.C.: U.S. Government Printing Office, 1965.

Neal, Ernest E. "Two Negro Problems Instead of One: A Challenge to Negro Colleges." *The Journal of Negro Education,* 21:161–166, 1952.

Pickens, William G. "Teaching Negro Culture in High Schools—Is It Worthwhile?" *The Journal of Negro Education,* 34:106–113, 1965.

Robinson, A. L., et al, eds. *Black Studies in the University.* New Haven: Yale University Press, 1969.

Rosen, Bernard C. "Race, Ethnicity, and the Achievement Syndrome." *American Sociological Review,* 24:47–60, 1959.

The People Left Behind. Report by the President's National Advisory Commission on Rural Poverty. Washington, D.C.: U.S. Government Printing Office, 1967.

The Social and Economic Status of Negroes in the United States, 1969. BLS Report No. 375, Current Population Reports, Series P-23, No. 29, Washington, D.C.: U.S. Government Printing Office, 1969.

Trubowitz, Sidney. *A Handbook for Teaching in the Ghetto School.* Chicago: Quadrangle Books, 1968.

Tynes, Harcourt A. "Negro History Week." *The Negro Quarterly,* 1:5–6, 1942.

Warren, Robert P. *Who Speaks For the Negro?* New York: Vintage Books, 1966.

Weaver, Robert C. "Non-White Population Movements and Urban Ghettos." *Phylon,* 20:235–241, 1959.

Weaver, Robert C. *The Negro Ghetto.* New York: Harcourt, Brace and Company, 1948.

A Recommended Bibliography of Relevant Works

The following selections, constitute only a partial (and an extremely partial, at that) listing of many available works useful in focusing upon some of the problems, issues, and, in general, content of various black studies programs and upon blacks in the United States. Those listed below were chosen primarily because they tend to be overlooked or ignored in many listings focusing upon blacks, but not compiled by blacks (just as, e.g., many Sociology Departments in southern institutions especially ignore the work of Oliver C. Cox in race relations or analyses pertaining to blacks and to the class-caste controversy), and because some of them, although not the produce of the past several decades (or precisely because they were produced much earlier) remind us emphatically that many of the current issues are "old" issues—they contain many ideas and proposals, criticisms and complaints yet with us, re-emphasizing, therefore, that any black studies program must be accompanied by nothing less than a fundamental commitment to reduce prejudice and discrimination against blacks and other minority groups, and, therefore, to do nothing less than eliminate "the ghetto." Some of the works listed, of course, fall without the above categories, but they can be of prime value in focusing upon problems, characteristics, and social and psychological needs.

The four categories listed (i.e., I. Predominant emphasis upon social needs and/or social conditions; II. Predominant emphasis upon psychological needs, factors, and/or variables; III. Predominant emphasis upon interaction of social and psychological needs, factors, and/or variables; and IV. General emphasis related to Blacks) are not, in fact, mutually exclusive, but the predominant theme of each reference under each category, for present purposes, tended to fit best where given.

I. Predominant emphasis upon social needs and/or conditions.

Amos, William E. and Jane Perry. "Negro Youth and Employment Opportunities." *The Journal of Negro Education,* 32:358–366, 1963.

Anderson, Jourdan (dictated on August 7, 1865). "A Letter From a Freedman to His Old Master." *The Negro Quarterly,* 1:72–74, 1942.

Arnez, Nancy L. "A Thoughtful Look at Placement Policies in a New Era." *Journal of Negro Education,* 35:48–54, 1966.

Bland, Edward. "Social Forces Shaping the Negro Novel." *The Negro Quarterly,* 1:241–248, 1942.

Butcher, Phillip. "Breaking the Ground." *The Negro Quarterly,* 1:186–187, 1942.

Daniel, Walter G. "Editorial Comment—A Memorandum on the Education of Negroes." *The Journal of Negro Education,* 33:97–102, 1964.

Daniel, Walter G. "The Time is Now: Some Educational Imperatives for 1964." *The Journal of Negro Education,* 33:1–5, 1964.

Determan, Dean W. and Gilbert Ware. "New Dimensions in Education: Title VI of the Civil Rights Act of 1964." *The Journal of Negro Education,* 35:5–10, 1960.

Doddy, Hurley H. "The Progress of the Negro in Higher Education." *The Journal of Negro Education,* 32:485–492, 1963.

Dodson, Dan. W. "The Role of the Community in Social Studies." *Journal of Educational Sociology,* 33:85–92, 1959.

Edwards, G. Franklin. "Marriage and Family Life Among Negroes." *The Journal of Negro Education,* 32:451–465, 1963.

Gosnell, Harold F. and Robert E. Martin. "The Negro as a Voter and Officeholder." *The Journal of Negro Education,* 32:415–425, 1963.

Guzman, Jessie P. "Twenty Years of Court Decisions Affecting Higher Education in the South, 1938–1958." *Journal of Educational Sociology,* 32:247–253, 1959.

Herndon, Angelo. "Voice of Freedom." Book review of Richard Wright's *Twelve Million Black Voices. The Negro Quarterly,* 1:85–87, 1942.

Hoffman, Marvin. "The Lord, He Works in Mysterious Ways . . ." *New South,* 24:2–27, 1969.

Hughes, Langston. "The Bitter River." *The Negro Quarterly,* 1:249, 1942.

Humboldt, Charles. Book review of A. Locke and B. J. Stern, *When Peoples Meet. The Negro Quarterly,* 1:184–186, 1942.

Huyck, Earl E. "Faculty in Predominantly White and Predominantly Negro Higher Institutions." *The Journal of Negro Education,* 35:381–391, 1966.

Jackson, Augusta V. "One Unhappy Slave." Book review of Kate Pickard, *The Kidnapped and the Ransomed. The Negro Quarterly,* 1:75–78, 1942.

Jackson, Jacquelyne J. "An Exploration of Attitudes Toward Faculty Desegregation at Negro Colleges." *Phylon*, 28:338–352, 1967.

Jones, Clara A. and Frank A. De Costa. "The Negro's Contribution to the Beginning of Public Education in South Carolina." *Negro Educational Review*, 2:129–134, 1951.

Rauch, Jerome S. "Area Institute Programs and African Studies." *The Journal of Negro Education*, 24:409–425, 1955.

Stembridge, Barbara P. "A Student's Appraisal of the Adequacy of Higher Education for Black Americans." *The Journal of Negro Education*, 37:316–322, 1968.

Wolff, Max. "The Role of the Sociologist as a Community Consultant." *Journal of Educational Sociology*, 24:146–250, 1955.

II. Predominant emphasis upon psychological needs, factors, and/or variables.

Baldwin, James. *Nobody Knows My Name*. New York: Dial Press, 1969.

Brink, William J. and Louis Harris. *Black and White: A Study of the United States' Racial Attitudes*. New York: Simon & Schuster, 1967.

Bullough, Bonnie. "Alienation in the Ghetto." *American Journal of Sociology*, 72:469–478, 1967.

Cameron, Howard K. "Nonintellectual Correlates of Academic Achievement." *The Journal of Negro Education*, 37:252–257, 1968.

Clarizio, Harvey F. "Maternal Attitude Change Associated with Involvement in Project Headstart." *The Journal of Negro Education*, 37:106–113, 1968.

Cleaver, Eldridge. *Soul On Ice*. New York: McGraw-Hill Book Company, 1968.

Clinard, Marshall and Donald L. Noel. "Role Behavior of Students From Negro Colleges in a Non-Segregated University Situation." *The Journal of Negro Education*, 27:182–188, 1958.

Coles, Robert. *Children of Crisis*. Boston: Little, Brown, and Company, 1967.

Dwyer, Robert J. "Reactions of White Teachers in Desegregated Schools." *Sociology and Social Research*, 44:348–351, 1960.

Editorial comment. "Is There an Oversupply of Negro Teachers?" *The Journal of Negro Education*, 1:343–347, 1932.

Fishman, Jacob R. and Frederic Solomon. "Youth and Social Action: Perspectives on the Student Sit in Movement." *American Journal of Orthopsychiatry*, 33:400–411, 1963.

Goldberg, Albert. "The Effects of Two Types of Sound Motion Pictures on the Attitudes of Adults Toward Minorities." *Journal of Educational Sociology*, 29:386–390, 1956.

Gordon, Daniel N. "A Note on Negro Alienation." *American Journal of Sociology*, 70:477–478, 1965.

Gottlieb, David. "Some Comments on Comments—Negro Alienation." *American Journal of Sociology*, 70:478–479, 1965.

Gregory, Dick: *Nigger: An Autobiography*. New York: Dutton, 1964.

Grossack, Martin M. "Psychological Considerations Essential to Effective Educational Integration." *The Journal of Negro Education*, 34:278–279, 1965.

Harris, Edward E. "Upward Social Mobility as an Escape: The Cases of Negroes and Whites." *The Journal of Negro Education*, 36:420–423.

Hines, Ralph H. "Social Distance Components in Integration Attitudes of Negro College Students." *The Journal of Negro Education*, 37:23–30, 1968.

Koenig, Frederick W. and Morton B. King, Jr. "Cognitive Simplicity and Prejudice." *Social Forces*, 40:220–221, 1962.

Middleton, Russell. "Alienation, Race, and Education." *American Sociological Review*, 28:973–977, 1963.

Pettigrew, Thomas F. "Negro American Intelligence: A New Look at an Old Controversy." *The Journal of Negro Education*, 33:6–25, 1964.

Reddick, L. D. "Anti-Semitism Among Negroes." *The Negro Quarterly*, 1:112–121, 1942.

Rowland, Monroe K. and Phillip DelCampo. "The Values of the Educationally Disadvantaged: How Different Are They?" *The Journal of Negro Education*, 37:86–89, 1968.

Smith, Alan P., Jr. "The Role of Psychoanalytic Psychology and Psychopathology in the Practice of Teaching." *The Negro Educational Review*, 3:3–12, 1952.

Vittenson, Lillian K. "Areas of Concern to Negro College Students as Indicated by Their Responses to the Mooney Problem Checklist." *The Journal of Negro Education,* 3:51–57, 1967.

Weinburg, Carl. "Social Attitudes of Negro and White Student Leaders." *The Journal of Negro Education,* 35:161–167, 1966.

Wright, Richard. "Men in the Making." *The Negro Quarterly,* 1:123–127, 1942.

III. Predominant emphasis upon interaction of social and psychological needs, factors, and/or variables.

Aiken, Michael and Louis A. Ferman. "The Social and Political Reactions of Older Negroes to Unemployment." *Phylon,* 27:333–346, 1966.

Baldwin, James. *The Fire Next Time,* New York: Dial Press, 1967.

Blake, Elias, Jr. Book review of Charles Silberman, *Crisis in Black and White. The Journal of Negro Education,* 34:79–81, 1965.

Blake, Elias, Jr. "Color Prejudice and the Education of Low-Income Negroes in the North and West." *The Journal of Negro Education,* 32:173–178, 1963.

Blood, Robert O. *Northern Breakthrough.* Belmont, Calif.: Wadsworth Publishing Company, 1968.

Bolden, Wiley S. "Tasks for the Negro Teacher in Improving Academic Achievement of Negro Pupils in the South." *The Journal of Negro Education,* 32:173–178, 1963.

Boskin, Joseph. "The Revolt of the Urban Ghettos, 1964–1967." *The Annals of the American Academy,* 382:1–14, 1969.

Bragg, Emma W. "Changes and Challenges in the '60's." *The Journal of Negro Education,* 32:25–33, 1963.

Brazziel, William F. and Margaret Gordon. "Replications of Some Aspects of the Higher Horizons Program in a Southern Junior High School." *The Journal of Negro Education,* 32:107–113, 1967.

Brown, H. Rap. *Die, Nigger, Die!* New York: Dial Press, 1969.

Carawan, Guy and Candie. *Ain't You Got a Right to the Tree of Life?* New York: Simon and Schuster, 1967.

Clark, Kenneth B. *The Negro Protest.* Boston: Beacon Press, 1963.

Clarke, Jacquelyne J. "Standard Operational Procedures in Tragic Situations." *Phylon,* 22:318–328, 1961.

Clift, Virgil A., A. W. Anderson, and H. G. Hullfish. *Negro Education in America: Its Adequacy, Problems, and Needs.* New York: Harper & Row, 1962.

Codwell, John E. "The Education Improvement Project of the Southern Association of Colleges and Schools—A Focus on Improving the Educational Performance of Disadvantaged Pupils." *The Journal of Negro Education,* 36:326–333, 1967.

Cruse, Harold. *Rebellion or Revolution?* New York: Morrow, 1968.

Curry, Jesse E. and Glen D. King. *Race Tensions and the Police.* Spingfield, Illinois: Thomas, 1962.

Davis, Allison, B. Gardner, and M. Gardner. *Deep South.* Chicago: University of Chicago Press, 1965.

Deutsch, Martin, I. Katz, and A. Jensen (eds.). *Social Class, Race and Psychological Development.* New York: Holt, Rinehart and Winston, Inc., 1968.

DuBois, William E. B. "The American Negro Press." *The Negro Digest,* 1:33–36, 1943.

DuBois, William E. B. *The Philadelphia Negro.* Philadelphia: University of Pennsylvania Press, 1899.

DuBois, William E. B. *The Souls of Black Folk.* New York: Blue Heron Press, 1953.

Dwyer, Robert J. "The Negro Teacher and Desegregation." *Sociology and Social Research,* 42:26–30, 1957–1958.

Dyer, Henry S. "Summary and Evaluation of Contributions of the Yearbook: Race and Equality in American Education." *The Journal of Negro Education,* 37:340–361, 1968.

Edwards, Harry. *Black Students.* New York: Free Press, 1970.

Essien–Udom, Essien U. *Black Nationalism.* Chicago: University Press, 1962.

Fauset, Arthur H. *Black Gods of the Metropolis.* Philadelphia: University of Pennsylvania Press, 1944.

Finney, Joseph C. (ed.). *Culture Change, Mental Health, and Poverty.* Lexington: University of Kentucky Press, 1969.

Freeman, Donald, Rollie Kimbrough, and Brother Zolili. "The Meaning of Education." *The Journal of Negro Education,* 37:432–434, 1968.

Geisman, Ludwig and Ursula C. Gerhart. "Social Class, Ethnicity, and Family Functioning: Exploring Some Issues Raised by the 'Moynihan Report.'" *Journal of Marriage and the Family,* 30:480–487, 1968.

Ginzberg, Eli. *The Negro Potential.* New York: Columbia University Press, 1956.

Ginzberg, Eli. *The Middle-Class Negro in the White Man's World.* New York: Columbia Uni-niversity Press, 1967.

Grier, William H. and Price M. Cobbs. *Black Race.* New York: Bantam Books, Inc., 1968.

Grossack, Martin M. *Mental Health and Segregation.* New York: Springer Publishing Company, 1963.

Grossack, Martin M. Book review of Thomas F. Pettigrew, *A Profile of the Negro American. The Journal of Negro Education,* 34:78–79, 1965.

Gustafson, Lucille. "Relationships Between Ethnic Group Membership and the Retention of Selected Facts Pertaining to American History and Culture." *Journal of Educational Sociology,* 31:49–56, 1957.

Hager, Don J. "Social and Psychological Factors in Integration." *The Journal of Educational Sociology,* 31:57–63, 1958.

Hamilton, Homer. "They Spoke of Their Futures With Hope." *The Journal of Negro Education,* 34:184–187, 1965.

Handlin, Oscar. *Fire-Bell in the Night: The Crisis in Civil Rights.* Boston: Little, Brown, and Company, 1964.

Harrison, E. C. "Working at Improving the Motivational and Achievement Levels of the Deprived." *The Journal of Negro Education,* 32:301–307, 1963.

Hayes, Charles F. "Institutional Appraisal and Planning for Equal Educational Opportunity." *The Journal of Negro Education,* 37:323–329, 1968.

Hill, Beatrice M. and Nelson S. Burke. "Some Disadvantaged Youths Look at Their Schools." *The Journal of Negro Education,* 37:135–139, 1968.

Hill, Mozell C. and Thelma D. Ackiss. "Some Ideological Confusion Among Negro College Students." *The Journal of Negro Education,* 12:600–606, 1943.

Holmes, Eugene C. "The American Negro: Three Views." Book reviews of E. R. Embree, *American Negroes,* P. S. Buck, *American Unity and Asia,* and M. J. Herskovits, *The Myth of the Negro Past. The Negro Quarterly,* 1:277–282, 1942.

Lee, Frank F. "A Cross-Institutional Comparison of Northern and Southern Race Relations." *Sociology and Social Research,* 42:185–191, 1957–1958.

Lee, Wallace. "Is Civil Disobedience Practical to Win Full Rights for Negroes?" *The Negro Digest,* 1:25–26, 1943.

Millard, Thomas. "The Negro and Social Protest." *The Journal of Negro Education,* 32:92–98, 1963.

Miller, Carroll L. "Issues and Problems in the Higher Education of Negro Americans." *The Journal of Negro Education,* 35:485–493, 1966.

Nelson, Harold A. "A Note on Education and the Negro Revolt." *The Journal of Negro Education,* 34:99–102, 1965.

Parker, Seymour and Robert J. Kleiner. *Mental Illness in the Urban Negro Community.* New York: Free Press, 1966.

Pettigrew, Thomas F. "Actual Gains and Psychological Losses: The Negro American Protest." *The Journal of Negro Education,* 32:493–506, 1963.

Radin, Norma and Constance K. Kamii. "The Child-Rearing Attitudes of Disadvantaged Negro Mothers and Some Educational Implications." *The Journal of Negro Education,* 34:138–145, 1965.

Randolph, A. Phillip. "Is Civil Disobedience Practical?" *The Negro Digest,* 1:27–29, 1943.

Ransford, H. Edward. "Isolation, Powerlessness, and Violence: A Study of Attitudes and Participation in the Watts Riot." *American Journal of Sociology,* 73:581–591, 1968.

Record, Wilson. "Negro Intellectuals and Negro Movements: Some Methodological Notes." *The Journal of Negro Education*, 24:106–112, 1955.

Repke, Arthur. "Sociology for High Schools." *Sociology and Social Research*, 44:37–41, 1959–1960.

Riessman, Frank. "The Overlooked Positives of Disadvantaged Groups." *The Journal of Negro Education*, 34:160–166, 1965.

Scott, J. Irving. "Academic Preparation of Negroes Above the Master's Degree." *The Negro Educational Review*, 2:135–140, 1951.

Searles, Ruth and J. A. Williams, Jr. "Negro College Students' Participation in Sit-ins." *Social Forces*, 40:215–220, 1962.

Singleton, Robert and Paul Bullock. "Some Problems in Minority Group Education in the Los Angeles Public Schools." *Journal of Negro Education*, 32:137–145, 1963.

Thompson, Charles H. "The Higher Education of Negro Americans: Prospects and Programs— A Critical Summary." *The Journal of Negro Education*, 36:295–313, 1967.

Townsend, Willard S. "Leadership in the Economy of Living." *The Negro College Quarterly*, 3:166–180, 1945.

Turner, Ralph H. "Needed Research in Collective Behavior." *Sociology and Social Research*, 42:461–465, 1957–1958.

Vontress, Clemmont E. "The Negro Against Himself." *The Journal of Negro Education*, 32:237, 1963.

Ware, Gilbert. "Lobbying as a Means of Protest: The NAACP as an Agent of Equality." *The Journal of Negro Education*, 33:103–110, 1964.

Willie, Charles V. "Education, Deprivation, and Alienation." *The Journal of Negro Education*, 34:209–219, 1965.

Wright, Nathan, Jr. *Black Power and Urban Unrest.* New York: Hawthorne Books, Inc., 1967.

IV. General emphasis related to blacks

Alexis, Marcus. "Pathways to the Negro Market." *The Journal of Negro Education*, 28:114–128, 1959.

Allen, William F., Charles P. Ware, and L. Garrison (eds.). *Slave Songs of the United States.* New York: Oak Publications, 1965.

Banton, Michael. *Race Relations.* New York: Basic Books, Inc., 1967.

Barbour, Floyd B. *The Black Power Revolt: A Collection of Essays.* Boston: P. Sargeant, 1968.

Bardolph, Richard. *The Negro Vanguard.* New York: Holt, Rinehart, and Winston, 1959.

Bennett, Lerone. *Before the Mayflower: A History of Black America.* Chicago: Johnson Publishing Company, 1969.

Blake, J. Herman. "Black Nationalism." *Annals of the American Academy*, 382:15–25, 1969.

Bluford, Lucile H. "The Lloyd Gaines Story." *Journal of Educational Sociology*, 32:242–246, 1959.

Bontemps, Arna W. *Famous Athletes.* New York: Dodd, Mead, 1964.

Bressler, Marvin. "White Colleges and Negro Higher Education." *The Journal of Negro Education*, 36:258–265, 1967.

Broderick, Francis L. and August Meier. *Negro Protest Thought in the Twentieth Century.* Indianapolis: Bobbs-Merrill Co., 1965.

Butcher, Margaret J. *The Negro in American Culture.* New York: Knopf, 1956.

Clarke, Jacquelyne J. *These Rights They Seek.* Washington, D.C.: Public Affairs Press, 1962.

Cox, Olive C. "The Modern Caste School of Race Relations." *Social Forces*, 21:218–226, 1942.

DuBois, William E. B. "Moton of Hampton and Tuskegee." *Phylon*, 1:344–351, 1940.

DuBois, William E. B. "Pushkin." *Phylon*, 1:265–269, 1940.

Edwards, Harry. *The Revolt of the Black Athlete.* New York: Free Press, 1969.

Fisher, Miles M. *Negro Slave Songs in the United States.* Ithaca, N.Y.: Cornell University Press, 1953.

Glenn, Norval D. and Charles M. Bonjean (eds.). *Blacks in the United States.* San Francisco: Chandler Publishing Co., 1969.

Grant, Joanne. *Black Protest.* New York: Fawcett World Library, 1968.

Greenberg, Jack. *Race Relations and American Law.* New York: Columbia University Press, 1959.

Handling, Oscar. *The Newcomers: Negroes and Puerto Ricans in a Changing Metropolis.* Cambridge: Harvard University Press, 1959.

Henderson, A. D. "Educators of Tomorrow." *The Negro College Quarterly,* 3:108–116, 1945.

Henderson, Vivian W. "The Role of the Predominantly Negro Institutions." *The Journal of Negro Education,* 36:266–273, 1967.

Hope, John, II. "Rochdale Cooperation Among Negroes." *Phylon,* 1:39–52, 1940.

Jenkins, Joseph H., Jr. "A Chronicle of Race Relations." *Phylon,* 1:175–200, 1940.

Katz, Irwin and Patricia Gurin. *Race and the Social Sciences.* New York: Basic Books, Inc., 1969.

Killian, Lewis and C. Grigg. *Racial Crisis in America: Leadership in Conflict.* Englewood Cliffs, N.J.: Prentice-Hall, Inc., 1965.

Lacy, Leslie A. *Cheer the Lonesome Traveler: The Life of W. E. DuBois.* New York: Dial Press, 1970.

Lane, Russell A. "The Legal Trend Toward Increased Provisions for Negro Education in the United States Between 1920 and 1930." *The Journal of Negro Education,* 1:396–397, 1932.

Lee, Harold F. "Educating Negro Teachers For a Democratic Society." *Negro College Quarterly,* 3:117–125, 1945.

Lowe, Gilbert A., Jr. "Howard University Students and the Community Service Project." *The Journal of Negro Education,* 36:368–376, 1967.

Meeth, L. Richard. "The Transition of the Predominantly Negro College." *The Journal of Negro Education,* 35:494–505, 1966.

Meier, August. "Early Boycotts of Segregated Schools: The Alton, Illinois Case, 1897–1908." *The Journal of Negro Education,* 36:394–402, 1967.

Meier, August. "Negro Protest Movements and Organizations." *The Journal of Negro Education,* 32:437–450, 1963.

Moore, Carman. *Somebody's Angel Child: The Story of Bessie Smith.* New York: Crowell, 1970.

Osofsky, Gilbert. "Race Riot, 1900: A Study of Ethnic Violence." *The Journal of Negro Education,* 32:16–24, 1963.

Reid, Ira DeA. "A Chronicle of Race Relations." *Phylon,* 1:270–300, 1940.

Rose, Harold M. "An Appraisal of the Negro Educator's Situation in the Academic Marketplace." *The Journal of Negro Education,* 35:18–26, 1966.

Smythe, H. and L. Chase. "Current Research on the Negro: A Critique." *Sociology and Social Research,* 42:199–202, 1957–1958.

Stuhardt, J. Gunther and S. V. LeGrange. "Coloured Folk of South Africa." *Phylon,* 1:352–363, 1940.

Valien, Preston. "The Brotherhood of Sleeping Car Porters." *Phylon,* 1:224–238, 1940.

Valien, Preston. "Sociological Contributions of Charles S. Johnson." *Sociology and Social Research,* 43:243–248, 1958–1959.

Walker, Jack L. "The Functions of Disunity: Negro Leadership in a Southern City." *The Journal of Negro Education,* 32:227–236, 1963.

Weaver, Robert C. "Racial Policy in Public Housing." *Phylon,* 1:149–156, 1940.

Williams, John A. *The Most Native of Sons: A Biography of Richard Wright.* New York: Doubleday and Company, Inc., 1970.

Yoshino, I. Roger. "The Stereotype of the Negro and His High-Priced Car." *Sociology and Social Research,* 44:112–117, 1959.

Young, Harding B. "Negro Participation in American Business." *The Journal of Negro Education,* 32:390–401, 1963.

Useful Bibliographies:

Miller, Elizabeth W. *The Negro in America: A Bibliography,* 1966.

Porter, Dorothy B. *A Selected List of Books By and About the Negro,* 1936.

Salk, Erwin A. *A Layman's Guide to Negro History*, 1966.
Welsch, Erwin K. *The Negro in the United States, A Research Guide*, 1965.
Work, Monroe N. *A Bibliography of the Negro in Africa and America*, 1928.

Some Useful Black Periodicals or Journals

The Crisis (Organ of the National Association for the Advancement of Colored People)
The Journal of Negro Education
Freedomways
The Black Scholar
The Black Politician
The Journal of Social and Behavioral Sciences
Afro-American Studies, An Interdisciplinary Journal
Phylon
The Negro Digest
The Journal of Negro History
The Negro American Literature Forum
The Negro History Bulletin
Jet
Ebony
Muhammed Speaks
The Black Liberator

Some Useful Black Newspapers

The Chicago Defender
The Afro-American
The Pittsburgh Courier

Integrating black studies into the curriculum of today's schools

Dr. DEBORAH PARTRIDGE WOLFE
Professor of Education, Queens College of the
City University of New York

Of one blood God created all men to dwell on the face of the earth.

Acts 17:26

Our Hebraic-Christian tradition has bound us to a faith in our fellowman. We have enunciated in all of our basic documents of American history our belief in "the equality of man." We have proudly pointed to the fact that the United States of America has a multi-pluralistic culture of people from every nation in the world, from every creed and every color. And yet, as we enter the seventies, we must admit that we have not given to every man the equality we espouse. It is no wonder that in planning for a Black Studies Program the faculty of the State University of New York at Buffalo wrote in its prelude:

It is widely admitted that the most serious crisis the nation faces is urban disorders and racial conflicts caused by long and pervasive white racism. Throughout most of this nation's history the black man has been de-graded, brutalized, exploited, segregated, and debarred from opportuni-ties to achieving human dignity. Yet, against almost insuperable odds, the black man has fought long, hard, sometimes desperately, but mostly peacefully to become an integral and respected part of American society. Since 1964, his frustration, stemming from his deteriorating position in the crowded inner cities, in the face of the marked and growing affluence of white suburban America, has led to unprecedented urban violence. It was in particular the costly disorders of the summer of 1967 which im-pressed upon Americans the gravity of the crisis in black and white, and on the part of the enlightened the need to take urgent and concerted steps to confront and attempt to solve the problem. As a result of the crisis, President Johnson appointed a Commission on Civil Disorders on 27 July 1967. The Commission's Report, issued in March 1968, made history by unequivocally attributing the urban disorders and the plight of Afro-Americans to white racism. It stated that "White racism is essen-tially responsible for the explosive mixture which has been accumulating in our cities. . . ." (p. 203); and again: "What white Americans have never fully understood—but what the Negro cannot forget—is that white society is deeply implicated in the ghetto. White institutions created it, white institutions maintain it, and white society condones it." The Report conveyed the need for urgent action on the part of all responsible

Americans. "The tragic waste of human spirit and resources, the unrecoverable loss to the nation which this denial [of freedom and equality of opportunity] has already caused—and continues to produce no longer can be ignored or afforded" (p. 34). It called for "an American commitment to confront those conditions and eliminate them—a commitment so clear that Negro citizens will know its truth and accept its goal."

The violent and untimely death early April last of Dr. Martin Luther King (1929–1968), a black champion of interracial harmony and of freedom and justice to all men, dramatized and further reinforced the need for measures to end urban violence and racial conflicts.

Our University was quick to recognize this need. This was reflected in the following statement of President Meyerson at SUNYAB's memorial service for Dr. King. "We in the University must begin now to do everything that is in our power to help create a society in which dialogue and constructive, tangible achievement will replace the violence and prejudice that threaten to tear our society apart if we do not act boldly and effectively." Action followed. In late April 1968 the President established the Select Committee and the Office of Equal Opportunity. With the encouragement of the Committee the Black Student's Association drew up a proposal for a Black Studies Program" designed to promote an understanding of Black American Life and History as well as equip students to be able to both study and practically improve the socio-economic condition of the Black Man in America." The University administrators and faculty responded positively to the idea.[1]

Similar action must be taken by schools all over the nation to remove the blight of the ghetto and its concomitant problems. We must develop relevant curricula which are perceived by the learner as having meaning in his present life and the expectation that it will have utility in future learning or coping situations. According to Jablonsky, such a curriculum "implies a dissolution of the dichotomy between cognitive and affective factors, between content and feeling. There (would be) no set ratio between these factors since a dynamic interaction is required in order to accommodate the vacillation in needs for each individual.[2]

Such changes should not be limited to ghetto schools but *all* schools on *all* levels must turn their attention to the development of meaningful curricula. Indeed, Black Studies must be integrated into the entire curriculum of today's schools—pre-schools, elementary and secondary schools, and colleges and universities.

WHAT DO WE MEAN BY "BLACK STUDIES"?

"Black Studies" has been defined in many different ways by many different people. For many persons concerned, "Black Studies" is the study of

---

[1] Faculty-Student Committee, State University of New York at Buffalo, "Proposal for a Black Studies Program Offering an Undergraduate Major." Mimeographed report, 1969, p. 1–2.
[2] Adelaide Jablonsky, "Toward Curriculum Relevance for Minority Group Children." *IRCD Bulletin*, Vol. V, No. 3, Summer 1959, p. 5.

the past, present and future of people of African descent. According to Lawrence C. Howard, such an experience would begin with "the explication of the
life experiences of the average black man's deep and mysterious African's
experience in America and it will assess the black man's outreach to the peoples
of the Third World. . . . (It) will also go beyond the African derivatives. To be
black also means to be colored by European and white American influences. It
involves interaction with cultural forces, like class, which are not Afro-American
in origin. And, most important, being black is coming to celebrate in the legacy
of the black experience."[3]

In clarifying the meaning of "Afro-American Studies" Bethune first
defines Afro-American to mean "the people of African ancestry living in the
United States. It also means people of African ancestry living within the continental complex that includes North, South, Central America, and the Caribbean."[4] He further indicates that, in spite of certain diversities of language and
cultural traits, they (the Afro-Americans thus defined) share a common historical experience in the New World and a set of common cultural antecedents—
African in origin. Fundamentally, they have shared a common concrete aspiration for that full freedom, which they have not been heir to as long as they've
been in the New World.

> It may be useful to metaphorically represent the Afro-American experi-
> ence by picturing a set of three continuous rings, with Africa as the outer-
> most ring, the New World as the second, and the United States as
> the innermost. We must consider these as related, in the sense of a dy-
> namic and continuous unit spiralling inward and outward backward and
> forward. And it is the history of that spiral metaphor, the dynamics of its
> movement, the nature of its composition and the consideration of its
> contemporary attributes and problems which constitute the Afro-Ameri-
> can experience and must, therefore, be reflected in Afro-American
> Studies.[5]

In summary, "Black Studies" is the organizing of knowledge around the
experiences of people of Africa and African descent. It is both historical and
contemporary since it *must* deal with the experience itself with its *real issues*
and problems as lived in the past and present. It utilizes the content, methodology, and skills of the separate disciplines of history, sociology, anthropology,
psychology, literature, language, linguistics, political science, biology, geography, social welfare, economics, law, theology, music, art, and drama but is also
interdisciplinary since the Black Experience is interdisciplinary. Certainly,
there is sufficient evidence to demonstrate that the traditional disciplines have
not been adequate to the task of understanding blacks. Hence "Black Studies"
cannot afford the luxury of "hardening the categories" if it is to have the
dynamic quality it must possess to meet the following purposes:

---

[3] Lawrence C. Howard, "Comments on a paper by W. Todd Furniss on Racial Minorites
and Curriculum Change." Mimeographed paper presented at 52nd Annual Meeting of
American Council on Education, October 9, 1969, p. 2.
[4] Lebert Bethune, "Afro-American Studies: Perspectives Toward a Definition," *IRCD Bulletin*, Vol. V, No. 3, Summer 1969, p. 9.
[5] *Ibid.*

1. To build an understanding of the history of Africa and its development with special emphasis upon Black Africa, including a study of government, family and community structure, art, literature and language, music, drama, laws, education, customs, religion, occupations, and every aspect of the culture of the people.
2. To heighten awareness of the effect of the migration of black Africans to the Western Hemisphere, especially to the United States.
3. To deepen the appreciation for the contributions of black people to the entire development of civilization.
4. To foster an understanding of the unique "black experience" in America as it is reflected in:
   a) Afro-American modes of cultural expression;
   b) Afro-American social and political institutions;
   c) historical developments within the cultural, social, political, and economic contexts of American life as a whole.
5. To study the problems which Afro-Americans face in American communities today and, wherever possible, actively cooperate with individuals and organizations of the black community in their solution.

WHAT SHOULD WE TEACH?

With goals of such magnitude, what shall we teach? As indicated earlier, Black Studies must be integrated into the curriculum at all levels, for all ages, for all learners. Let us look first at needed experiences in the nursery school and kindergarten and primary years.

Experiences for Early Childhood

We like to think of the public school as the meeting place for the American masses with their cultural differences. In order to develop a positive self-image for the child, the schools must begin by accepting every child and helping him realize that his everyday experiences are important to others as well as to himself. The curriculum must embrace experiences that will develop the child's basic mental abilities to analyze and organize his experiences, to draw inferences and develop creativity and inventiveness. This can only be accomplished in an atmosphere where there is an appreciation of the worth of each individual. The young child should be encouraged to share freely incidents which provide understanding of his home and community life. Not only will such sharing help him to feel better about himself, but will provide an opportunity for the entire group to be enriched through knowledge of the cultural differences present in their group.

Development of a positive self-image may be reinforced by use of black, white, and oriental dolls. As the black child plays with the black doll, not only will she obtain a more realistic image of herself as a "mother," but she will feel an identification with all black mothers and all black people in a very positive and acceptable way. The white child will also have an opportunity to know and "love" a black "baby." In an atmosphere of love and acceptance all are appreciated.

Every teacher should use a camera in the classroom. No pictures will stimulate conversation like pictures of ourselves. When the pictures are thrown on the screen with an opaque projector or mounted on a chart, children will begin to talk, not only about themselves but about their families and neighborhoods. Such discussions can form the beginning of an "Our Community" book to which can be added pictures of people of the community and stories of class field trips. It is fascinating to see how the John Day Folio or the Shaftel Picture Series (which deliberately portray mixed groups) can stimulate discussion among young children and begin a serious study of black people and their heroes.

Holidays provide a wonderful and natural way to introduce children to the concept of the pluralistic nature of our society. Celebration of George Washington Carver Day, Martin Luther King Day, Malcolm X Day as well as Negro History Week may supplement the normal emphasis given to understanding blacks throughout the total school curriculum.

Music and rhythms may be used not only for developing auditory discrimination skills but may provide excellent opportunities to note the contributions of the black man to music. Children may be introduced to the instruments used for accompanying the song and dance. Stories about black composers and musicians may be used as a part of the story hour. Pictures of black performing artists may adorn the room.

Every aspect of the curriculum can build understanding of the cultural differences in our classrooms and in the society at large. Puppetry and choral speaking can help to free children who seem hesitant and afraid. Puppets can speak for them if they are too shy to speak for themselves. In choral speaking, everyone can take part so no one needs feel that he is different. Young children would enjoy learning Paul Laurence Dunbar's "Dawn" or David W. Cannon's "Pigment" and there are many poems written by black poets especially for young children. Anthologies of children's writings such as *The Me Nobody Knows*, edited by Stephen M. Joseph, provides material which young and old enjoy. Certainly young children can identify with Langston Hughes' *Black Misery* when he says:

"Misery is when you start to play a game and someone
begins to count out: 'Eenie, Meenie, Mini, Mo."
or
"Misery is when the kid next door has a party and
invites all the neighborhood but you."

It should be evident that schools for young children are organized to serve many needs. The flexibility and breadth of a good nursery or kindergarten curriculum provide for these needs without distorting the life style of the young child. Though flexible, it is well planned. It provides for:

1. Strengthening the physical powers of the child;
2. Expressing their ideas and feelings creatively through art, music, language, and movement;
3. Extending interests and understanding of the world about them by observation, experiments, etc.;
4. Playing well with other children, acquiring responsibility and some independence, and expanding their understanding of their social world;
5. Extending and enriching their language (this often means developing standard speech);

6. Growing in some understanding of space, time, number, and size relationships, measuring, counting, etc.;
7. Deepening and extending their emotions, expressing ideas spontaneously and creatively, learning to respond to new situations with satisfaction, and to be at ease and confident in the group.

If a teacher is to accomplish these goals and, at the same time, deliberately integrate "Black Studies" in the curriculum, she must develop a program, schedule, and interest centers sufficiently diverse to meet these needs. The classroom should provide arts and crafts center, dramatic play center, block building center, manipulative materials center, library center, music center, display center and other centers such as areas for sand and water play or for apparatus in support of large muscle activity or a woodworking area. In each, attention must be given to be certain that wherever natural and possible the black experience will be included.

The Elementary Curriculum

If one believes that the schools must develop a better understanding of the implications of the social and psychological dynamics of cultural differences and translate this understanding into educational programs, then the teacher planning for elementary children must reflect this in her curriculum development. While all children learn better when the content of the curriculum is tuned to their own experience as a point of departure for black children this is a *sine qua non* if any motivation is to be generated.

Just as stress on the development of skill in language and concept formation and the development of an adequate self image has been recommended for young children, teachers of older children must also place emphasis upon language skills. Every possible effort should be made to provide good classroom and school libraries with books by and about the black man. No subject in the school's curriculum can lend more to the development of good human relations and an understanding of our democratic goals than reading. Reading may enlarge the child's sensitivities so that he may be equipped to live in an expanding world. Biographies of black Africans and Americans should be an integral part of the reading program. Poetry by such blacks as Margaret Williams, Countee Cullen, Phyllis Wheatley, LeRoi Jones, James Weldon Johnson, Claude McKay and others should be included.

Through reading and the discussions and socio-drama which may follow, children may learn about America's cultural diversity, destroy stereotyped thinking about the black man, develop their own self-image and generally develop an understanding of our society.

Since oral communication is a medium for sharing thoughts and ideas, children should be given opportunity to speak before the class or a group using poetry and/or prose. Children should be encouraged to write their own stories and poems for sharing orally. Story telling should be continued with older children. They may tell stories using flannel boards, puppets, dramatizations and other media.

The teacher should strive to enable her students to think critically so that they will be able to spot racist propaganda and deal with it. She should strive to use facts to destroy the misinformation which her students may have. This should include using textbooks and visual aid materials which stress the contributions each culture has made to our heritage. This is true not only in social studies when discussing the history of our country but in science, mathematics, music, art, and every area of the curriculum.

At the elementary level, Black Studies consist of a general cultural orientation and the social studies may form a core around which many understandings may be developed. An average white American when asked how he felt about putting the black man into the pages of United States history replied quickly and unhesitantly, "American history without the Negro is only a partial American history." Congressman James H. Scheuer, feeling that partial American history has been the bill of fare in the nation's schools since the first school bell rang, introduced a bill into Congress which would create a Presidential Commission on Negro History and Culture. He said, as he began hearings on that bill, "If American history had been written as it happened in the first place we probably wouldn't have today's black-white confrontation."

The following is a brief illustration of a unit which could be used in a fifth or sixth grade by using the study of black Americans as the basis for the development:

Language Arts: Langston Hughes, Paul Laurence Dunbar, Countee Cullen, Phyllis Wheatley, Gwendolyn Brooks, Arna Bontemps, Shirley Graham, Willard Motley

Social Studies: Booker T. Washington, Mary McLeod Bethune, Harriet Tubman, Sojourner Truth, Frederick Douglass, Crispus Attucks, Benjamin Banneker, John Henry, Ralph Bunche, Carter G. Woodson, Paul Cuffee, Robert Smalls, William Carney, Henry Johnson, Matthew A. Henson, Robert Smalls, Martin Luther King

Science: George Washington Carver (Chemurgy), Charles Henry Turner (Marine Biology), Percy Julian (Botany), William Hinton (Bio-Chemistry), Charles Drew (Hematology), Jan E. Matzeliger (Invention), Daniel Hale Williams (Surgery)

Arts and Crafts: George Washington Carver, Henry O. Tanner (painting), E. Simms Campbell (cartoons), Augusta Savage, (sculptor).

Physical Activities and Sports: Willis Read, Arthur Ashe, Gill Russell, Jesse Owens, Althea Gibson, Jackie Robinson, Roy Campanella, Bill Robinson, Pearl Primus, Carmen deLavallade, Henry Aaron, Joe Louis, Willie Mays, Wilt Chamberlain, Emmett Ashford, Oscar Robinson, O. J. Simpson

Music: W. C. Handy, R. Nathaniel Dett, Harry I. Burleigh, William Grant Still, Count Basie, Louis Armstrong, Pearl Bailey, Duke Ellington, Marian Anderson, Charity Bailey, Josh White, Leontyne Price, Odetta, Harry Belafonte, Sammy Davis, Lena Horne, Ella Fitzgerald, Aretha Franklin

Theatre: Sidney Poitier, Ossie Davis, Ruby Dee, Claudia McNeill, Paul Robeson, Ira Aldridge, Bill Cosby

These are but a few of the names of persons who might be studied as a background to understanding the contributions of the black American.

Another approach may be found in the study of the black man in American history by beginning with the present situation and its problems and tracing backwards to the coming of the black man to America. The Encyclopaedia Britannica Educational Corporation in its development has presented a three volume study:

I. Black Americans 1928–1968
      Showdown for Nonviolence (1966–1968)
      The Civil Rights Movement (1961–1965)
      The Supreme Court and the Schools (1954–1960)
      Discrimination in War and Peace (1941–1953)
      The Cost of Prejudice (1928–1941)

II. A Taste of Freedom 1854–1927
      Militancy and Racism (1905–1927)
      The Color Line (1883–1905)
      Civil Rights and Reconstruction (1886–1833)
      Emancipation (1882–1865)
      John Brown's Body (1854–1861)

III. Slaves and Masters 1567–1854
      The Great Compromise (1850–1854)
      Slavery as It Is (1839–1849)
      The Abolitionists (1832–1839)
      A Firebell in the Night (1820–1831)
      The New Nation (1777–1819)
      Traffic in Men's Bodies (1567–1758)

Through a series of articles written by persons living at the time of the event, students are helped to understand the history of the black man in America. The teacher using this series may supplement the materials presented by choosing appropriate music, poems, art work, films and other visual and auditory aids so that a full picture of the times and the people are presented. Such an outline would best fit the upper grades, even though many of the ideas may be introduced earlier.

In working with younger children in grades one and two, the teacher may wish to approach the study through the use of an Afro-American Calendar:

JANUARY: Benjamin Lundy (4); Paul Cuffee (17); Dr. Daniel Hale Williams (18)

FEBRUARY: Langston Hughes (1); Dr. Charles Henry Turner (3); Richard Allen (14); Frederick Douglass (14); Dr. W. E. B. DuBois (23); Marian Anderson (27)

MARCH: Col. Charles Young (12); Norbert Rillieux (18); Crispus Attucks (died on March 5, 1770); Harriet Tubman (10); Jan Matzelinger (20)

APRIL: Cpt. Robert Smalls (5); Booker T. Washington (5); Paul Robeson (9); Granville T. Woods (23); James Beckwith (26); Duke Ellington (29); John James Audubon (26)

MAY: Elijah McCoy (2); Nannie H. Burrough (2); Major Martin

<table>
<tr><td></td><td>Delany (6); William Grant Still (11); Joe Louis (13); Countee Cullen (30)</td></tr>
<tr><td>JUNE:</td><td>Dr. Charles R. Drew (3); Roland Hayes (3); Dr. Charlotte Hawkins Brown (11); James Weldon Johnson (17); Charles W. Chestnut (20); Henry O. Tanner (21); Paul Laurence Dunbar (27)</td></tr>
<tr><td>JULY:</td><td>Mary McLeod Bethune (11); Ira Aldridge (24); Charles S. Johnson (24)</td></tr>
<tr><td>AUGUST:</td><td>Robert Purvis (4); Dr. Ralph J. Bunche (7); Matthew A. Henson (8); Clarence Cameron White (10); Ernest Everett Just (14); Peter Salem (16)</td></tr>
<tr><td>SEPTEMBER:</td><td>Hiram R. Revels (1); James Forten (2); Prince Hall (12); Jesse Owens (12); Alain Leroy Locke (13);</td></tr>
<tr><td>OCTOBER:</td><td>R. Nathaniel Dett (10)</td></tr>
<tr><td>NOVEMBER:</td><td>Benjamin Banneker (9); W. C. Handy (16); J. Ernest Wilkins (27)</td></tr>
<tr><td>DECEMBER:</td><td>William A. Hinton (15); Dr. Carter G. Woodson (19)</td></tr>
</table>

Many other dates may be added, especially of contemporary black achievers. The students would not only study about the particular person but would spend some time learning about the period in which they lived, the place they were born and reared and educated, and the problems they faced. They could read about them, write about them, sing about them, draw them, and construct dioramas and other visual aids.

Still another approach might be found in the development of "The Story of Black Americans—Yesterday and Today." The following outline might be employed:

I. The Black Man in Africa
II. The Slave Trade
III. Slavery in America
    A. In Colonial Times
    B. After the Revolutionary War
    C. Growth of Slavery
    D. Free Negroes
IV. Changing Status of the Negro
    A. The Abolition Movement
    B. Emancipation
    C. After Reconstruction
    D. Through the World Wars
V. The Civil Rights Movement
    A. The Legal Battle
    B. The "Negro Revolution"
    C. New Civil Rights Acts
    D. Violence and Racial Tension
VI. Black Militancy
    A. Unrest in the Cities
    B. Black Power
    C. Racism and its Problems
VII. The Black Man Today
    A. In Politics

B. In the Total American Life
C. His Relations with Colored Peoples of the World

One of the most comprehensive curriculum guides which have been developed in the United States was conducted by the school district of the city of Pontiac, Michigan.[6] By official action of the Board of Education, the outline of content and concepts for teaching the contributions and participation of Afro-Americans in the elementary grades became an integral part of the instructional program of the school district. All teachers were expected to utilize the materials developed by the curriculum committee. Teaching ideas and suggestions were made for kindergarten through grade six giving concepts to be developed in social studies, health, reading, writing, arithmetic, science, spelling as well as a list of reading materials, songs, films, filmstrips and records, tapes, study prints and posters. Possible activities are given and a complete outline is presented which may be followed. Areas recommended for each grade are:

Kindergarten—All Around Me
First Grade—People at Home
Second Grade—Families and Social Needs
Third Grade—Communities and Social Needs
Fourth Grade—Regions and Social Needs
Fifth Grade—This Is Our Land
Sixth Grade—The Changing World

Children were expected to grow in their comprehension of the black man as he studied all men. Each grade capitalized upon the learnings of the previous grades and concepts broadened and extended as children delved more deeply into the problems of the black man.

The Secondary School

At the high school level, where students are more accustomed to studying specific courses in history, political science, and sociology, there should be opportunity given to delve into the history of the black people in the United States and Africa. In "Problems of American Democracy" extensive attention should be given to comprehensive treatment of the life and contemporary problems of black America. Courses and/or integrated experiences may be offered in African and/or Afro-American music, art, and drama and provision should be made for students to study the black community and become acquainted with the resource people available. Since facts, while they are important, are not enough to change attitudes, the teacher must plan experiences which will involve her students emotionally with different cultures. Face-to-face contact with a perceptive person encourages dialogue and often leads to continuing interest in and awareness of the world.

[6] School District of the City of Pontiac, Michigan. *An Outline of Content and Concepts for Teaching the Contributions and Participation of Afro-Americans in the Elementary Grades.* Pontiac, Michigan, 1968. (Mimeographed)

Throughout the United States, increasing numbers of school districts, particularly the big cities, are endeavoring to make every text in every subject reflect, where possible, our pluralistic society. Among the states encouraging curriculum and textbook changes to provide inclusion of Black Studies are: Alaska, California, Colorado, Connecticut, Florida, Iowa, Illinois, Indiana, Kentucky, Maryland, Michigan, New Jersey, New York, North Carolina, Ohio, Oregon, Pennsylvania, Rhode Island, South Carolina, Tennessee, Texas, Virginia, Washington, and Wisconsin.[7]

At Atlantic City High School, a team of teachers who believed it important that the Afro-American would be integrated in the American History course, revitalized the syllabus, calling it "Solutions to History in Crisis: American History in the High School." The stated objectives were:

1. To appreciate the role, significant contributions, and achievements of minority groups in the making of America.
2. To develop a sense of belonging so that each student will know who he is, where he came from, and where he is going. Each student has a responsibility to correct the wrongs of the past.
3. To provide a meaningful course of study for terminal students, a course that relates to the present and prepares for the future.
4. To enable each student to develop an understanding that the basis of a truly democratic America lies in the recognition of the dignity and worth of the individual.[8]

In the process of restructuring the course, the team related past history to present on-going events and involved the community in the development of the experience. The students shared in the curriculum redesigning and together they developed seven units: 1) Origins of the American People, 2) The American Constitution, 3) Living in America, 4) Labor and the American Economy, 5) American Culture, 6) America's Wars, and 7) American Protest Movements. In studying about the origins of the American people, such topics were included: American Minority Groups; Myths of Prejudice; Hate Words for Minority Groups; African, European, Asian and American (Mayas, Incas, Aztecs, American Indians) Backgrounds of American Citizens; History of World Slavery and the Process of Colonization. Likewise in each of the other units attention was given to the role and problems of black Americans. Students were expected to know not only about Booker T. Washington but Malcolm X and Claude Brown as well. They talked about the Brotherhood of Sleeping Car Porters as they studied the development of labor unions in America. They raised such questions as: Which type of worker is most likely to lose his job? How does prejudice effect job opportunities?

In examining the American protest movements they concerned themselves with an investigation of the slave revolts; the role of the abolitionists;

---

[7] Charles H. Harrison, "The Negro in America." *Education News*, Vol. 3, No. 6. October 21, 1968, pp. 14–16.

[8] Norman Gasberro et al, *Solutions to History in Crisis: American History in the High School*. Mimeographed by Atlantic City Public Schools, Atlantic City, New Jersey, August 2, 1968.

world documents of human rights; American documents such as the Declaration of Independence and Constitution; major judicial decisions such as the Dred Scott Decision, Plessy v. Ferguson, and Brown v. Board of Education; legislative action such as amendments to the Constitution, Black Codes, and the Civil Rights Acts. The biographies of many leaders were to be studied, including Toussaint L'Ouverture, Gabriel Prosser, Denmark Vessey, Nat Turner, John Brown, William Lloyd Garrison, Frederick Douglass, David Walker, Wendell Phillips, John Murray Forbes, Theodore Weld, Walt Whitman, Martin Luther King, Elijah Muhammad, and Roy Wilkins. Various techniques of protests were examined and attention was called to the civil rights organizations and commissions developed to study the nature of riots and civil disorder. All in all, an attempt was made to include the entire history of American protest from the Revolutionary War to the present day.

In Pontiac Michigan, several units were recommended for their high school curriculum: a semester elective course on Afro-American History;[9] a unit for American Problems entitled, "The Vicious Circle"; a twelfth grade program on African Studies; a twelfth grade World History supplement on "The History of Africa"; a unit for study for seventh grade social studies on "Man in His Environment: The Brotherhood of Man"; Civics supplement for grades seven through twelve on "Recognizing Minority Contributions—Civil and Human Rights"; "Man in the World," a program for junior high school social studies; and a supplement to ninth grade units on "Racism, the Slave Trade, and the Development of America." Concepts and basic understandings to be developed are clearly enunciated in each of the several curriculum guides. Comprehensive lists of materials including music, art works, slides, records, and other media were given. Questions to be used as motivation were suggested and additional information for the teacher's use was included.

In the unit for American Problems on the Crisis in Race Relations, "The Vicious Circle," five major areas are considered: The Search for Identity; The Negro in America Today; Income and Jobs; Housing, and Education. Following a general content outline in which four questions are raised: What is the "Vicious Circle"? What are the basic human needs? What are prejudice and discrimination? and, What efforts have been undertaken to alleviate the problems of the Negro American? The teacher was provided with a statement of the purposes, concepts to be developed, basic understandings, motivation, inquiry procedure, methods and activities, evaluation process, background materials and bibliography.

Other working ideas may be drawn from the Association for the Study of Negro Life and History which is the oldest organization devoted to the study of black Americans and their heritage. The National Association for the Advancement of Colored People has an Education Department which has developed many worthwhile suggestions for use in schools on all levels. Professional organizations in education such as the National Education Association, the American Federation of Teachers, the Association for Supervision and Curriculum De-

---

[9] John F. Perdue, Wesley Mass., William Lacy, and Dana P. Whitmer, et al, Board of Education, School District of the City of Pontiac, Pontiac, Michigan, Mimeographed, 1968.

velopment, the Anti-Defamation League of B'Nai B'rith, and the Civil Rights Commission are engaged in the development of materials for use in today's schools. Likewise, increasing numbers of textbook publishers have become aware of their responsibility in the production of materials of all kinds which will aid the teacher and other interested persons in the process of integrating Black Studies into the entire school curriculum.

Even the Far West Laboratory for Education Research and Development at Berkeley, California, has published a handbook for educators on "Afro-Americans in the Far West." This handbook contains information on: The Significance of the Afro-American People; We are All Africans; West's Afro-American Heritage; American Negro Cultural Characteristics; and Problems of Segregation and Integration.

The College and University

On the collegiate level many trends emerge. Recent demands for Black and "Third World" Studies and for black and third world control of these departments in American universities have been supported by arguments ranging from the compelling to the ridiculous. Faculty and administrative responses have likewise ranged over a wide spectrum from inexcusable inaction to the development of majors in Black Studies provided through newly developed departments and colleges. The importance of this issue is reflected in the fact that two of the most prestigious organizations in higher education chose related topics as the theme of their annual conferences in 1969–1970.[10]

In discussing "Racial Minorities and Curriculum Change" at the American Council on Education annual meeting, W. Todd Furniss indicated that "most academics would agree that colleges and universities in the United States have not met their obligations to all students who need advanced education and particularly to those of minority racial groups." He further asserts that the recommendations or demands for Black Studies programs have been motivated by the following considerations:

Correcting American history by a more adequate recognition of the past and present experience of 25 million black citizens.

Hastening integration by improving the understanding of blacks by non-blacks.

Hastening integration by preparing black students to take part in American society with pride and self-confidence.

Preparing black students to understand and work for a black community.

Providing black students with a sense of "power."[11]

[10] The 52nd Annual Meeting of the American Council on Education which met October 8–10, 1969 in Washington, D.C. had for its theme "The Campus and Racial Crisis," and the 25th National Conference on Higher Education of the American Association for Higher Education which met March 1–4, 1970 in Chicago, Illinois had the theme "The Troubled Campus: Mandate for Change."

[11] American Council on Education, *The Campus and the Racial Crisis: Background Papers*. The Council, Washington, D.C., 1969. p. 1.

It is not surprising that the study of Africans and Afro-Americans had its beginning in the predominantly black colleges. More than fifty years ago Carter G. Woodson, who founded the Association for the Study of Negro Life and History, urged the inclusion of Negro History in the schools and colleges of America. He wrote one of the first texts in this area and predicated his actions on the fact that race prejudice was a result of poor historical insights and teachings which either ignored the Negro achievements or said they were nonexistent. He believed that race prejudice in America was a result of miseducation of both races. He early introduced college courses in Negro History at Howard University. When Hanes Walton, Jr. made a survey of black colleges which offered African and Afro-American courses, he reported that during the year 1967–68 forty-three colleges offered Negro History courses and twenty-two had courses on Africa. One college listed Negro History as a requirement for all students. Three colleges offered full-fledged African Studies Programs and one program led to an M.A. in that field.[12]

In response to an informal survey which I conducted in the fall of 1969, Annette H. Eaton, Associate Dean at Howard University, indicated that both a major and minor are offered in the area of Afro-American Studies. Thirty semester hours are required for a major, fifteen for a minor. In the major area five courses are required: Introduction to Afro-American Studies I and II; Survey of Negro Literature; and the Negro in the United States I and II. Majors in the department must complete all the general education requirements of the college (approximately 60 semester hours), including distribution in the humanities, social sciences, natural sciences, English, foreign language, philosophy, and physical education. There are also many other related courses offered to students at Howard University, both those who are concentrating in Afro-American Studies and the general student body, including such courses as "The Economics of Black Manpower," "Black Nationalism in Contemporary American Life," and "African Languages." The list of courses follows:

Course Offered in the Department of Afro-American Studies
First Semester 1969–1970
Introduction to Afro-American Studies I
Survey of Negro Literature
Economics of Black Manpower
The Negro in the United States to the Civil War (Dept. of History)
The Negro in the New World to 1800
Major Negro Poets

Related Courses
The Economics of Housing and Urban Renewal (Economics Dept.)
The Economics of Poverty and Manpower (Economics Dept.)
American Prose and Poetry of Negro Life (English Dept.)
The Sociology of Power (Sociology Dept.)

---

[12] Hanes Walton, Jr. "African and Afro-American Courses in Negro Colleges." *The Quarterly Review of Higher Education Among Negroes*, Vol. 36, No. 4, October, 1968. pp. 188–189.

The Negro in America (Sociology Dept.)
Intergroup Relations (Sociology Dept.)
Black Rhetoric I (Speech Dept.)
Business, Government, and the Ghetto (Business Administration Dept.)

Second Semester 1969–1970
Introduction to Afro-American Studies I
Introduction to Afro-American Studies II
Negro Social and Political Thought from Frederick Douglass to
  Malcolm X
Introduction to Afro-American Music
Black Nationalism in Contemporary American Life
The Negro in the New World to 1800
Major Negro Poets
Economics of Black Manpower
Survey of Negro Literature
The Negro in the United States since 1865

Related Courses
Afro-American Art (College of Fine Arts)
Business, Government, and the Ghetto
Economics of Housing and Urban Renewal
American Literature of Negro Life (English Dept.)
Negro Politics: Electoral and Non-Electoral (Government Dept.)
Africans and Afro-Americans (History Dept.)
The Negro in America
Black Rhetoric since 1850 (Speech Dept.)
The Language of the Ghetto (Speech Dept.)

In reviewing Black Studies programs on predominantly white campuses, ninety-nine programs were examined. Of these, twenty-one programs indicated that the black people desired to be identified as Afro-Americans; eleven that they desired to be identified as black; and one program indicated that the black people desired to be identified as African. The stated goals on these campuses varied from pluralism to assimilation to separatism. The following courses indicate the wide variety of courses offered by the various programs on white campuses:

History: History of Colonialism; The Harlem Renaissance; The History of Apartheid; History of the West Indies; Reconstruction; Slavery; History of the Third World; Black Involvement in Scientific Development; African History; History of the Civil Rights Struggle.
Sociology: Individual and Family Health Problems Among Afro-Americans; Black Communities and Suburbia: A Comparative Analysis; Poverty and Public Policy; Demography of Black Communities; The Structure of Colonial Society; African Sociology; Dynamics of Racism: Including Apartheid and Colonialism; Social Control and the Black Community; Black Social Movement; Urban Problems; Black Statistics: Survey and Method; Afro-American Family; Black Church.
Anthropology: Pre-Colonial Africa: Africa South of the Sahara; West Africa; East Africa; Black Africa: Its Past, Present and Future; Religions of Africa; Afro-American Linguistics: Including African Languages

other than Swahili; Comparative Black Anthropology; Black Non-Verbal Communication; Black Physical Anthropology; Social and Communal Life in African Societies; Afro-American Culture.

Political Science: Racial and Ethnic Politics in America; Theories of Nation Builders; Theories of Pan-African Nationalists; Black Nationalism and the International Community; The Third World Concept; Politics of Liberation; Black Political Leaders; Black Power; African Political Development.

Economics: Afro-American Economic Development; History of Economic Philosophy; Economic Problems of Black Americans; Communalism in Black Business; Economic Relationships of Africa to the U.S.; Economic Experience of the Afro-American; The Economics of Racism and Poverty; The Economics of the Ghetto; Economic Geography of Africa.

Literature and English: Afro-American Folklore; Contemporary African Novels; Ancient African Literature; Black Perspectives of Composition and Reading; Black Oratory; Black Journalism; Contemporary Black Poetry; History of Black Poetry; Some Black American Writers; Literature of Racial Protest.

Aesthetics (Dance, Drama, Art, Music): Afro-American Music; Afro-American Art; Art and Architecture of Africa; History of African Music; Contemporary Afro-American Theater, African Dance; Afro-American Dance; Revolutionary Black Art.

Psychology: Testing and Evaluating the Black Child; Black Counseling; Social Psychology of the Black Community: Culture and Personality; Black or Afro-American Psychology; Social Psychology of Prejudice.

Education: Educational Problems of Black Americans Curriculum Development for the Urban Poor; Teaching Black Children; Teaching Black Art, Literature, and History; Centralization, Decentralization and Community Control; Black Curriculum: Problem, Design, Role and Responsibilities of the Teacher in the Black Community.

Philosophy: 19th and 20th Century Afro-American Philosophies; Philosophical Movements of Black Americans; Major Philosophies of Africa: Past and Present; Black Existentialism; Theories of Men of Resistance.

In examining the program structure which exists on the ninety-nine campuses reporting programs, there were eleven categories or methods of organizing the Black Studies Programs: School of Black Studies; Departments; Programs; Instructional Center; Coordinating Center; and Ethnic Studies. In all of the preceding structural categories, the emphasis was on Black Studies as an autonomous area of study. The following categories represent structural arrangements which would merge Black Studies with other traditional areas of concentration: Urban Studies; Special Majors; "Random Offerings" (which indicates a willingness to allow the inclusion of the black experience without any special effort to establish a special program).

In regard to granting of degrees, twenty-one public and sixteen private institutions have chosen to sanctify their commitment to Black Studies by granting degrees. Fifteen public institutions are funding the B. S. programs through their own resources. Eleven private institutions were planning to fund the Black Studies programs through their own resources. Two colleges reported external funding.

Thus it may be clearly noted that the program and structure varies greatly. The major goal must be a commitment to the need. Establishment of Black Studies presents the moral crisis for our colleges and universities.

An illustration of an interdisciplinary program where Afro-American Studies is offered as a minor is seen in the program at Oberlin College. The purposes stated for this program are similar to those already given:

"1) To foster an understanding of the unique 'black experience' in America; . . . 2) To enrich the educational offerings of Oberlin College by providing all students with the opportunity for extensive work in this vital area, and thus raising the concerns and contributions of black Americans into their rightful prominence; 3) To increase the relevance of an Oberlin education to the black community and the larger society of which it is a part; (and) 4) To heighten awareness and appreciation of African history and cultures." In order to reach these goals students participating in the program must fulfill the following requirements: 1) at least six hours in any combination of the Core Courses: Images of the Black Man in African and Western Civilizations and Research Workshop in Afro-American studies; and four courses from at least three of the following areas: a) history (History of Afro-Americans); b) behavioral sciences—5 courses are offered (African Cultures, Racial and Cultural Minorities, Seminar in the Psychology of Afro-American Experience, Urban Political Analysis, and Comparative Government and Politics: Africa); c) humanities—3 courses offered (The Heritage of Afro-American Literature, Modern Afro-American Literature, Topics in French Literature: African Literature of French Expression); d) education (education in the Black Community); and e) music (Afro-American Music). Other courses offered which present substantial emphasis upon Afro-American life include: Poverty and Affluence; Labor and Management Relations; Politics of Modernization; Proseminar in European History: British African Policy 1663–1966; Social Psychology; Urban Sociology; Society, Culture, and Personality; Anthropology-Race Relations Seminar; and Seminar in Sociology: Conflict and Violence.[13]

At San Francisco City College the program in Black Studies is included in a program in Ethnic Studies. Through the Program in Ethnic Studies, the college seeks to develop both on campus and in the community an awareness and appreciation of the culture, historical and contemporary importance, special problems, and unique contributions of Afro, Chinese, and Latin Americans. The college thus seeks to help remove barriers preventing the full participation of these groups in the mainstream of American life, and to help students belonging to them develop increasing pride in their origins and heritage. The Curriculum in Afro-American Studies, offered by the Department of Afro-American Studies, comprises the following courses: Independent Study in Afro-American Studies, Afro-American Culture in the United States, Ethnic Biology, Introduction to Black Theater, the Afro-American Poet, Contemporary Afro-American Novelists, the South in American History, the Afro-American in the United States, African

[13] Oberlin College Bulletin, 1969–70, May 1969.

Civilization, Musical Traditions of the Afro-American, Co-educational Physical Education—Primitive Dance, Political Problems of Afro-Americans, Government and Politics of Africa, the Psychology of Minority Groups, Social Change in Contemporary Africa, and Swahili. In addition, examples of black drama are produced periodically by the college drama department and credit for performance in these is given toward completion of the major in Afro-American studies.[14]

The program at the State University of New York at Buffalo aims at combining training in a discipline or closely related disciplines with supplying correct information about and an understanding of the Afro-American experience. As a general principle, the program will encourage experimentation and innovation in learning. According to the Student-Faculty Committee responsible for the educational design, the program will have two major divisions: The Social Sciences and the Humanities. The first will comprise of Economics, Geography, Political Science, Psychology and Sociology; the second of Literature, Art, Music and Drama. Education, History and Law can gain credit in either division.

Students entering the program will have to elect to major either in Black Studies Social Sciences or in Black Studies Humanities. Within each division, a student must have a disciplinary base. For example, a student majoring in Black Studies Social Sciences might elect sociology (or any one of the other social sciences) as his disciplinary base. The student will take at least three advanced (junior and/or senior level) courses in the subject constituting his disciplinary base of which one must be a Black Studies subject. Under the new four-course load, a minimum of eight advanced Black Studies division courses will constitute a major. Of these two might be drawn from the Black Studies division other than the one in which the student is majoring. Each Black Studies major must take at least one advanced interdisciplinary seminar in his division.[15]

Normally students wishing to major in Black Studies at Buffalo will enter in their junior year and take one of the following courses: The African Background—An Introduction to the History and Culture of Traditional Africa; The Afro-American Today: Problems and Prospects; or African and Afro-American Social Thinkers.

For persons majoring in Black Studies Social Sciences, the following courses would constitute the curriculum:

1. The Economics of Poverty and the Afro-American: Causes, Effects and Possible Remedies.
2. Urban Geography: The Function and Arrangements of the Inner City.
3. Negro Politics: The Search for Liberation.
4. The Psychology of the Negro: Attitudes and Patterns of Behavior Resulting from Discrimination and Inequality of Opportunity.
5. The Sociology of Poverty and Segregation:
   a. The Sub-culture of the Black American
   b. The Sociology of Race Relations

---

[14] City College of San Francisco *General Catalogue*, 1969-70.
[15] Faculty-Student Committee, *op. cit.*, p. 4.

6. The Afro-American
   a. Afro-American History 1619 to the Present
   b. Modern Africa and Afro-America: Their Interaction and Influence Upon Each Other
7. Law:
   a. A History of Civil Rights Litigation and Legislation
   b. Law and the Black Ghetto
8. Problems of Education in the Black Ghetto

For those majoring in Black Studies Humanities, the core courses besides the education, history and law courses listed above, are:

1. Literature:
   a. African Literature and the Theme of Negritude
   b. Afro-American Literature
2. Art:
   a. African Art
   b. Afro-American Art
3. Music:
   a. Jazz and the Black Man
   b. Blues: Rural and Urban
4. Black Drama: A Workshop on Drama and Humor deriving from the black experience; and the study and staging of black plays by outstanding black playwrights

And so, as we have seen the development of Black Studies programs on college and university campuses has varied greatly from a few courses, to minor fields of concentration, to majors in Black Studies. But Black Studies is more than an academic pursuit in the college and university community—it must embrace the psychological aspects of life as well. Thus it may be concluded that a Black Studies program should include: a psychological home for black students with special emphasis upon counseling services and congenial recreational and housing facilities; presentation of black writers, artists and musicians as a part of the total college cultural program; consideration by the entire college of the major issues in black-white relationships; increased enrollment of black students in predominantly white universities; additional black faculty and resource personnel; infusion of the black man in courses in history, sociology, etc. which are not specifically identified as Black Studies, and sensitivity training.

Teacher Education: A Specific Need
In order to execute the recommended programs for pre-school, elementary, secondary and collegiate education, there must be instituted a new teacher education program which will produce teachers* on all levels who not

---

* Here "teacher" is used to refer to all teachers on all levels. Unfortunately, the preparation of college teachers has often been neglected due to the common belief that "knowing the subject" prepares one to teach in college. The suggestions for teacher education, then, refer to all teachers.

only have the necessary content orientation to deal with Black Studies but will also have the positive attitudes necessary for dealing with such an important and sensitive issue. The teacher's preparation should be interdisciplinary. If they are to integrate the understanding of blacks into the entire curriculum they must draw on knowledge from any different fields. It is particularly important that these teachers have a solid grounding in anthropology and sociology as well as history, language and the arts. It is essential to their effective teaching, that instructors get to know the value system of their learners and understand their life styles and the way the world they live in operates. Also sorely needed is a good understanding on the part of the teacher of psychology. To cope with the actual problems they will find, the teacher will need to understand urban problems and those of the "ghetto" communities from which most black Americans come. Along with all these subjects must come an intensive preparation in the actual skill of pedagogy. During their pre-service and/or in-service education, teachers should have close relationship with social workers, anthropologists, urban planners, members of social welfare agencies, faculty of predominantly black colleges, and others who can provide the full development of a sound educational philosophy and understanding of the black experience.

To really gain an understanding of the black experience the teacher education program cannot be conducted only in a classroom or on a campus. Those who are to give meaningful instruction in Black Studies must go out into the field, into the community and among the people about whom they will teach. Their field experiences should include sensitivity training. Over and above the formal training and experiences, there must be a sincere concern and interest in black people. The teacher must realize that there are many nonverbal ways of insulting a person. These may be simply a look or a gesture but frequently they are more damaging than a verbalized insult.

Finally, above all, and at the heart of all these training programs, must be the instilling of a feeling of dedication and hope to replace feelings of discouragement and despair; of love rather than hate; and of respect rather than cynicism. Without a change in attitude I do not think any training program can produce teachers who will be truly effective in one of America's most important jobs.

Working with the Community
The crisis in race that exists on the school and college campuses of our nation is only a reflection of a large, more serious crisis in the country, and indeed, throughout the world. Any curriculum change which consciously and directly focuses upon the black experience will require the cooperation of the community—both the academic and general communities. If the school is to achieve its goal, it must become a center for the study of how to make man behave in a truly civilized manner (with respect for the dignity of all men and willingness to set limits on personal freedom when such freedom impinges on the rights of others) rather than a center for the study of why man behaves as he does. Hence, at all levels, the people of the community served by the school and/or geographically related to the school must be involved in the dynamic program being evolved by the school community.

BIBLIOGRAPHY

American Council on Education, *The Campus and the Racial Crisis: Background Papers.* The Council, Washington, D.C., 1969. p. 1.

Bethune, Lebert. "Afro-American Studies: Perspectives Toward a Definition." *IRCD Bulletin,* Vol. V, No. 3, Summer 1969. p. 9.

City College of San Francisco *General Catalogue,* 1969–70.

Faculty-Student Committee, State University of New York at Buffalo, "Proposal for a Black Studies Program Offering an Undergraduate Major." Mimeographed report, 1969. pp. 1–2.

Gasberro et al., *Solutions to History in Crisis: American History in the High School.* Mimeographed by Atlantic City Public Schools, Atlantic City, New Jersey, August 2, 1968.

Harrison, Charles H. "The Negro in America." *Education News,* Vol. 3, No. 6, October 21, 1968. pp. 14–16.

Howard, Lawrence C. "Comments on a paper by W. Todd Furniss on Racial Minorities and Curriculum Change." Mimeographed paper presented at 52nd Annual Meeting of American Council on Education, October 9, 1969. p. 2.

Jablonsky, Adelaide. "Toward Curriculum Relevance for Minority Group Children." *IRED Bulletin,* Vol. V. No. 3, Summer 1969. p. 5.

Oberlin College *Bulletin,* 1969–70, May 1969.

Perdue, John F., William Lacy, Dana P. Whitmer, et al., "History of American Protest." Board of Education, School District of the City of Pontiac, Michigan, Mimeographed, 1968.

School District of the City of Pontiac, Michigan. *An Outline of Content and Concepts for Teaching the Contributions and Participation of Afro-Americans in the Elementary Grades.* Pontiac, Michigan, 1968 (Mimeographed).

Walton, Hanes, Jr. "African and Afro-American Courses in Negro Colleges." *The Quarterly Review of Higher Education Among Negroes,* Vol. 36, No. 4, October 1968. pp. 188–189.

A black historian sets forth needs in negro history for integration

Dr. CHARLES WESLEY
Executive Director The Association for the Study of
Negro Life and History (ASNLH)

There are two ways of approaching the research and instruction in Black History, one is to have the perspective, the method, and the process of a separate subject, and to pursue a continued single development of the subject. The second is to regard it from the beginning as a part of total history, to see it in relationships and to integrate it in research and writing. Both methods have advantages and limitations.

The first way is the one which has been used in the writing of Negro History in the past, and it has been followed currently. Negro History has been written and published as a separate book, and a separate paper. The first black authors writing in this field have employed this process, James W. C. Pennington in 1841, R. B. Lewis in 1844, William C. Nell in 1851, William Wells Brown in 1863, George W. Williams in 1882 and Edward A. Johnson in 1891.[1]

The second way was undertaken in its beginnings by W. E. B. Du Bois who departed from this view after several years. Trained in Economic Philosophy and History at Harvard University, Du Bois completed his doctoral dissertation in 1896, *The Suppression of the African Slave Trade to the United States of America, 1638–1870*.[2] This work was drawn from colonial history and sources, later history and its sources, and was integrated with related historical events in its field.

---

[1] James W. C. Pennington, *A Textbook of the Origin and History of the Colored Race.* Hartford H. Skinner, 1841; R. H. Lewis, *Light and Truth, Collected from the Bible and Ancient and Modern History Containing the Universal History of the Colored and Indian Races.* Moses M. Taylor, 1844; William C. Nell, *Services of Colored Americans in the Wars of 1776 and 1812.* Philadelphia: Prentiss & Sawyer, 1851; William Wells Brown, *The Black Man, His Antecedents, His Genius and His Achievements.* New York: Thomas Hamilton, 1863; George Washington Williams, *History of the Negro Race in America from 1619 to 1880. Negroes as Slaves, Soldiers and Citizens, Together with a Preliminary Consideration of the Unity of the Human Family, An Historical Sketch of Africa and an Account of the Negro Government of Sierra Leone and Liberia,* New York: Putnam's Sons. 1882.

[2] W. E. B. Du Bois, *The Suppression of the African Slave Trade to the United States of America.* New York: Longmans, Green & Company, 1896.

Books were published in the years immediately prior to the organization of the Association for the Study of Negro Life and History. Two of them were Benjamin G. Brawley, *A Short History of the American Negro* (1913) and John Wesley Cromwell, *The Negro in American History* (1914).[3] Both of these were separate histories and prepared with only occasional references to general events in American history.

An historical landmark in American history was made when the Association for the Study of Negro Life and History was organized. Five black persons formed this group of organizers: Carter G. Woodson and W. B. Hartgrove of Washington, D.C., George Cleveland Hall, Physician, James E. Stamps and Alexander L. Jackson of Chicago. The meeting assembled at the Wabash Avenue Colored Y.M.C.A., on September 9, 1915. A constitution was adopted and the following officers were elected: George Cleveland Hall, President; J. E. Moorland, Custodian of Funds, Secretary-Treasurer; and Carter G. Woodson, Editor. Woodson described his reasons for this type of beginning, which contrasted with the public convention movement of other years:

> At first, it was thought best to call a national meeting to form an organization. This plan was abandoned, however, for the reason that it was not believed that a large number of persons would pay any attention to the movement until an actual demonstration as to the possibilities of the field had been made. The Director, therefore, had these few persons to join him in organizing, so to speak, in a corner and proceeded at once to bring out *The Journal of Negro History*.

The Journal of Negro History with its beginning in 1916, *Negro History Week* with its beginning in 1924, and *The Negro History Bulletin* were launched in 1935. In launching these efforts Woodson called attention to other efforts which had not continued "long enough to accomplish definite results." He stated that "three Negroes of vision, William C. Nell, William Wells Brown and George W. Williams, had endeavored to record the salient facts of Negro History, but there was nothing in their experience to encourage the coworker in this cause to believe that the program of the founder could be carried out."[4]

In 1922, Woodson published his first edition of *The Negro in Our History*. The Preface stated that it was issued to meet "the need of schools long since desiring such a work in handy form with adequate references for those stimulated to more advanced study."

This book in its title gives the impression that it was integrated because it used the word "our." While references are to whites and pictures of them were included in the volume, it was directed primarily to and about black folk in Africa and the United States. He and the Association were setting the record

---

[3] Benjamin G. Brawley, *A Short History of the American Negro*. New York: Macmillan 1913; John Wesley Cromwell, *The Negro In American History*, Washington, D.C.: The Negro Academy, 1914.

[4] Carter G. Woodson, "Ten Years of Collecting and Publishing the Records of the Negro," *The Journal of Negro History*, X, No. 4, October, 1925, pp. 598–606; Charles H. Wesley, "Carter G. Woodson—As A Scholar," *The Journal of Negro History*, XXXVI, No. 1, January, 1951, pp. 12–24.

straight, correcting the misconceptions and destroying the myths of those who have written them into American history.

The Association came to birth in 1915 (during a period of low esteem for black people in American history). It was the year when Griffith's *Birth of a Nation* in its unadulterated form was shown and the NAACP could not stop it. North Carolina adopted its white primary excluding blacks. In this year, Dr. Du Bois issued his book *The Negro,* an historical account of Africa and the United States in relation to Negroes. Then too, Oklahoma required separate telephone booths, and bills for segregation were introduced in the House of Representatives. The separation of the races was being increased as the Wilson administration came into power. This condition continued and became a characteristic of the first half of the Twentieth Century. Trends of the fifties seemed to be easing the divisions between white and black, as the Supreme Court made its famed decision in 1954, bridging the gap between Plessy V. Ferguson in 1896, a classic segregation case, and the Brown v. Board of Education's unanimous decision.

For more than three centuries racism has been a part of American life, and during this long period, Americans of dark color have been forced into inferiority in status and in education. During the last decade legal enforcement of equal opportunity has been making headway but forms of racism remain and affect the curriculum of the schools. Black folk continue to be denied their equal entrance to predominantly white schools, and their control over the schools to which they are assigned, so as to improve them. When the National Advisory Commission on Civil Disorders reported March 1, 1968, it declared:

"Our Nation is moving toward two societies,
one black, one white—separate and unequal."[5]

This separation had been descriptive of the prior history of the United States. The continued division into white and black has been shown in the lack of the realization of the dream of "one nation indivisible with liberty and justice for all." This equalitarian concept of the founders of the nation has been delayed across the years. The Declaration of Independence and the Fourteenth Amendment asserted the equality of rights and of treatment for all from the time of birth. Declarations in the states, cities, and nation have often made assertions of the equal privileges of equality, liberty, and justice for all. And then there was the neglect and the opposition which gave opportunity and license for some of the white majority to nullify these declarations in law and in fact. Property rights became more important to the majority than human rights. This was demonstrated in the growth of all white neighborhoods and in separate population neighborhoods based on color. Education was soon controlled by this concept of division and the separate school was as common as the divided neighborhoods, despite the court decisions.

At the same periods, the American people were divided into various minorities, religious and racial groups, each of whom had been contributing through the years to the development of American life and history. These

[5] Report of the National Advisory Commission on Civil Disorders, Washington, D.C., 1968, p. 1.

peoples came from various lands in Europe, but it must not be overlooked that they came from Africa, Asia and islands of the seas. Each group brought with them their own traditions and cultures, settled in areas, sometimes ghettoes, where their backgrounds could be maintained for a period, and their children adjusted to American life more fully than their parents and ultimately they were integrated into the American scene.

This problem of variety in peoples has become complicated for white and black because of the rapid growth of city population, through the migrations from rural sections to urban ones, and the shifts of peoples from South to North and from state to state. These trends have become an outstanding dramatic urban change in the mid-twentieth century. In ten of the largest cities the black population had increased from 1950 to 1960 to 1.6 million or 55 percent, while whites declined 1.4 million. Twelve of the largest cities had almost one third of the Negro population in 1960, while the white population decreased continually in these urban centers. By 1970 these concentrations were in 207 of the largest cities and the average segregation index was 86.2 percent.[6] Residential segregation had developed in all these urban areas, more as regards blacks than for other minorities. This segregation was the result of the attitudes of whites toward blacks, and this attitude had become known as white racism.

Backed by this strong resentment to black pupils, the inner schools of the cities have continued to be segregated. The report of the U.S. Commission on Civil Rights in its report on "Racial Isolation in the Public Schools," found that 75 percent of all black students in 75 of the major cities were in schools with enrollments of 90 percent or more of blacks. This isolation was the result of racial segregation, and operated to create a defective educational program. This fact was demonstrated when re-enforcement was given to old attitudes, old behavior and belief about black Americans and the deadly silence of the school books.

Three-fifths of the black school children, sixteen years after 1954, attend all black schools. This division is greater in the South but it is also widespread in the North and West. In every 20 students in the North and West, nine go to schools that are 95 percent black, and 40 percent of the white pupils go to schools that are 99 percent white. These divisions follow the neighborhood patterns.

The teaching in these schools has had to reflect their population division. Negro History Week has had large celebrations, and textbooks and library books have dealt directly with black life, history, and literature. Then too, some blacks have demanded that their schools become neighborhood schools and under their controls. Whites have often asked for the same.

With these school divisions the neglect is more evident as the contributions and personalities in white America were portrayed in the books used in the classrooms, while on the basis of race distinction and different color, blacks were omitted in the teaching and the reading in integrated schools.

The neglects of black people in history came not only from the ignorant and the unlearned, but from persons in higher places, from the educated or the

---

[6] U.S. Department of Commerce, Bureau of the Census, No. 322.

miseducated persons in the arts and the sciences, and particularly in the field of history. Two examples are selected: Charles C. Josey, then a Dartmouth College professor, wrote a book on *Race and National Solidarity,* in which appeared the following sentences:

> The white race dominated mankind. They are rulers *par excellence.* In the white man, the evolutionary process seems to have reached its highest point. He is the culminating achievement.

Later on the floor of the Senate of the United States Congress, a Senator said the following which so many white Americans have said or thought:

> I have no prejudice in my heart; but the white race is a superior race and the Negro race is an inferior race and the races must be kept apart by law.

Many other persons, who have not used any such specific words about this superiority, nevertheless, have fostered the same ideas, and believed in white supremacy. Exaggeration, false assumptions, and egoistic declarations have made many white persons believe in their superiority and conversely have influenced Negroes to believe in their inferiority. This build-up has been continued through the years until a type of segregation doctrine and a separation code have been created. Schools, colleges, universities have promoted these ideas and continued the neglect and avoidance of even the mention of black people in their textbooks, classrooms and lecture halls. Despite the gaining of court decisions which have been victories for democracy, the chains that bind have continued.

The presentation of black Americans in an important textbook has been continued in *The Growth of the American Republic* by Samuel Morrison of Harvard University and Henry S. Commager, formerly of Columbia University and Amherst College. These authors wrote the following in the 1950 edition:

> As for Sambo, whose wrongs moved the abolitionists to wrath and tears, there is some reason to believe that he suffered less than any other class in the south from its "peculiar institution";

and they refer to

> "The average childlike improvident, humorous, prevaricating and superstitious Negro."

These comments do not appear in a 1962 edition, but these noted historians continued the references to how Southern slaveowners "understood and loved him as a slave" and "loved him 'in his place' " as well as his "great success as a slave."

In 1968 Thomas Bailey in a paper before the organization of American Historians entitled "The Mythmakers of American History" stated in referring to the publication of the supplements on Negro History in New York City and Detroit:

> This belated recognition, though praise worthy in many respects, is fraught with danger. Most non-militant Negroes would probably like to think of themselves as dark-skinned Americans, and this self imposed Jim-

Crowism can be self-defeating. Pressure group history of any kind is deplorable especially when significant white men are bumped out to make room for much less significant black men in the interest of social harmony.

In instances such as these, neglects give way to false assertions, corrupt images and concepts about Negro Americans. As long as they are portrayed in such roles, the division will be encouraged, differences will increase, and Black Studies will be used as foundations to buttress and support false opinions unless there is serious research for truth.

How stupid and misinformed can such research historians become! They would research and write from middle-class backgrounds about middle-class whites—forgetful of lower class whites and blacks, and have the black excluded. This too, is now "fraught with danger," unless it is changed.

The acknowledgment of the power of the mind in the division of man throughout the world is recognized in the Constitution of UNESCO which declared:

> Since wars begin in the minds of men, it is in the minds of men that the defenses of peace must be constructed; that ignorance of each other's ways and lives has been a common cause throughout the history of mankind of that superstition and mistrust between the people of the world through which the differences have too often broken into war.

The integration of subject matter is as important as the integration of persons. In a country with a history as complex as ours and as various as its people are, it is imperative that education should give a composite picture in the process of the search for truth. There was no one stock to create the colonies which were widely separated along the coast, each with its own institutions, religion and public leaders and followers. Each of these has a history of its own. These differences must be merged in order to give opportunity and consideration for federated institutions. Integration takes place all along the lines of study of our history, as it is told of one nation of peoples.

There should be no study of American history without the inclusion of all of its varied peoples and nations. The background of Europe is no more important than the background of Africa and Asia. When the background of one is omitted, there is an error in presentation. When time is spent on the records of presidents and statesmen who are white, and in the details of their administrations and services, while the underdogs are forgotten and neglected, history so taught and published is an error. When authentic records are ignored because they relate to dark Americans, something is wrong with the pursuit of truth, and integration is again on the scaffold.

A long line of students, black and white, gave reality to black history through a series of researchers, many of which have been published in the *Journal of Negro History*, which is almost alone among scholarly magazines in this field. Despite these monumental endeavors in pursuit of truth, some historians and educators would not believe that there is any record of blacks worthy of presentation beside the record of whites. When such persons—even in the administration of schools, colleges and universities—are told of such historical events, they receive them without serious comprehension and little sympathy.

White students need to know their history in its reality and not in its falseness. They need to know what the forefathers of our nation have done to the ancestors of Negro-Americans in our history. They should know of the contributions, achievements, and personalities with black and brown skins who were in activities of public concern in state and national affairs. They should know more than the white ones, when they are going to be associated with black as well as white persons in their own careers. They will not develop into rounded whole and well functioning individuals unless they can have an integrated view of the practices of history.

Eldridge Cleaver saw this when he wrote of "The White Race and Its Heroes" in his *Soul on Ice:*

> The great white statesmen whom school children are taught to revere are revealed as the architects of systems of human exploitation and slavery. The new generation of whites, appalled by the sanguine and despicable record carved over the face of the globe by their race in the last five hundred years, are respecting the panoply of white heroes, whose heroism consisted in erecting the inglorious edifice of colonialism and imperialism; heroes whose careers rested on a system of foreign and domestic exploitation rooted in the myth of white supremacy and the manifest destiny of the white race.

There is need for this point of view which is present and active in youth, black and white, today, who are developing opposition to those in power who would preserve white supremacy. There is a growing body of youth who have learned Negro History and are participating in demonstrations for Black Studies programs for all students so that the truth of history shall not be hidden from youth but known by them.

Philadelphia, Pennsylvania has a textbook in use, *America—Red, White, Black, Yellow* (copyrighted 1969), which has been adopted for use in the schools. The authors are two blacks, Arthur Huff Fauset and Nellie Rathbone Bright. The Preface states:

> This history of America will tell you many surprising things— curious things about America's Indians in Peru, Mexico and the United States.
>
> You are going to be surprised at some things you will read about other wonderful people, called "minority groups"—such as Chinese, Japanese, Jews, East Europeans, and especially the Blacks (Afro-Americans).
>
> You will be surprised at things even Presidents and educated men thought and did as they tried to make our nation more powerful, rich and important.
>
> You will learn more about all these people, than you ever knew before.
>
> If this history surprises you, then read other books that tell you still more about America's vast variety of peoples—red, white, black and yellow.
>
> We hope you will do just that!

The book is prepared in units, but not one entire unit is exclusively on blacks or any other minority, for its purpose is the integration of history. It is illustrated with drawings by Shirley Whitman. A section in Unit II is on *Africa and the Blacks*. Short biographies of distinguished Negro-Americans among whom was Carter G. Woodson, are in the appendix section, followed by reference books and a list of intergroup organizations, and in this list is the Association for the Study of Negro Life and History. This is a new effort in this direction and it may be followed by others. History and social studies can be a curriculum through which majority and minority youth get to know one another and their backgrounds; class instruction can present programs which can become intergroup communications beyond the conference stage on differences, for intergroup relations are a matter of doing rather than talking, performance rather than big service.

The Flint, Michigan, community schools began to integrate their curriculum before the state law of 1966 was adopted for private, parochial and public schools to use books on the achievements of ethnic groups. The board also required that emphasis should be on an integrated curriculum and not on separate courses in Black Studies. A curriculum guide of 238 pages was issued and a new guide was published for the eleventh grade United States History course.

Robert W. Blackburn, Director of Intergroup Relations in Philadelphia, Pennsylvania says that "guidelines should be developed for teachers in all twelve grade levels so Black Studies materials can be woven into the entire kindergarten to twelve curriculum, not just into social studies. It is now better known that separate Black Studies courses help students to cover more widely the subject and make up for the neglect of earlier years in school."

Thornton Townsly High School, Harvey, Illinois, was a pioneer in the development of an integrated American history course in an integrated high school. There was an integrated guide, supplementary reading, audio-visual materials, monthly inservice seminars, and cooperation between departments. The course guide urged that the black man be kept in focus as a constant and natural participant in American history. The guide includes class reading and topics for further study. It gives importance to "a proper proportion of integrated history questions on all quizzes and tests," and that "if only a lick and a promise are given, this is what the students will accord the integrated material." Another step now in process is to find out how the use of this integrated material has affected changes in student attitudes after taking the course.

Another school district, San Mateo, California has the Union High School district with less than 10 percent black enrollment. In the fall of 1968, instruction in black history was begun for all students in history. It was reported that parents, teachers and other citizens were favorably disposed toward it. Two additional courses were added, due to demands, in Chinese and Japanese history in 1969–1970. When black history was undertaken it was in a pilot course in two schools and then in five of the seven high schools. There was a summer course in 1968 for students and a workshop for eight teachers of social sciences.

The course was described "to give students an understanding of the contributions of black people to American culture and civilization." Sections on literature and the arts were also parts of the course.

The statement of the board in 1969 was, "The Board of Trustees of the San Mateo Union High School District believes that an education of the highest quality can be achieved best in an integrated setting providing a multi-racial student body and faculty and an educational program designed to develop understanding of diverse cultures and ethnic backgrounds."

A story is told of an event in a theological school where there had been tolerance but no real performance of that which was being taught. A white boy said to a black boy as he looked backward to an earlier year:

> "Now I can smile about it because I think this was part of that year you were hating us and hating the institution. You were one of the first blacks I really encountered. The day I could say to you 'hey, black boy,' and you could say to me, 'what do you want, you white bastard,' meant something, I was not scared of you anymore."

While the teaching of history has expanded to include the treatment of nations and peoples other than white Americans, minority groups of black, brown, and red in the United States have asserted that they have not been treated fairly by American historians. They have seen the field of history expand so as to include nationalities, but they have also seen smaller nationalities and minorities within national boundaries given inadequate treatment. This neglect has been due both to a conscious and an unconscious bias or a lack of consideration. In order to correct this error of omission and to establish the truth, historical societies on the racial basis have arisen. With the support of these societies, scholars and teachers have reconstructed the past so that the presentations have been more complete. Manifestly, it is possible to overstate the case for a particular group and to overemphasize the unimportant, but when these result in a renewed stimulation for the suppressed and neglected group, it is far better than the neglect so common to the past. Into the field there have come the Irish Historical Society, known as the American-Irish Historical Society, the German-American Historical Society, the American-Jewish Historical Society, the Huguenot Society of America, the Scotch-Irish Society of America, and the Holland Society of New York.

In a citizenship which is composed of various groups, it was inevitable that there would be teachers and writers who consciously and unconsciously neglect and ignore other contributions than their own and those of their group to American life. Michael J. O'Brien, Chief Historiographer for the American-Irish Historical Society, in a volume entitled, *A Hidden Phase of American History*, set forth the contributions of the Irish to American History. *The Irish World* in reviewing this book stated, "All the Anglo-Saxon writers from Bancroft on suppressed, ridiculed where they could not suppress, mutilated where they could neither suppress nor ridicule, everywhere Irish in American History." Few Irish-Americans could read this book without a sense of pride. As for this comment on the work, with the substitution of the word "Negro" for the word "Irish," this sentence would be equally true, if not more so, in relation to the black American.

Albert B. Faust has prepared a volume under the title, *The German Element in the United States*. He stated that many historians have made "a blanket indictment" against the Germans in the United States. He writes, "That race (the Germans) comprises upward to twenty-five per cent of the American people and has been a stalwart factor in American life since the middle of the seventeenth century." It was the expressed purpose of the author to present this book to the Germans of the United States so as to insure to them "a proper pride of ancestry." The Jews have experienced a similar neglect. Numerous books have endeavored to supply the historical data to give the Jews their place in American life. Their Old Testament and ours made them a chosen people and yet they were slaves deprived and dispersed.

All of these societies have been engaged in the reconstruction of their histories. Our Association for the Study of Negro Life and History has also expanded the field of history so as to include the Negro people. This organization has pursued the truth concerning the black people in Africa, the West Indies and the United States and has lifted them into view so that all who read may learn.

History is not the story of men and women of one group or one color and the neglect and omission of the men and women of another group or color. It is neither the glorification of white people nor black people, but it is the integrated story of all our people irrespective of race or color. It deals with people in all times and places and should represent the contribution of all the people to civilization. When a part of the people has been neglected or given subordinate places, history, in order to be truthful, must be integrated in its research, preparation and teaching.

In contrast to integration there is the separatist demand for Black Studies taught by black teachers to black students alone and in a black classroom. This is so unlike the life which has been lived on the integrated school and college campus that its lasting value may be questioned and doubted. It may be temporary as an expedient which emphasizes the need for these studies and the denial that they can be taught by those who are self servers. The full answer is not in separate study and teaching. It is in integrated study and teaching and to be in the company of whites with each black and white accepting the other. Grier and Cobbs believe that "the black masses will rise with a simple and eloquent demand to which new leaders will give tongue." They will say to America simply: "Get off our backs." This needs to be said again and again, louder, not only by the masses but by intellectuals who too often join the oppressors and traducers in their thought and action and stay on the backs of other less fortunate blacks. These blacks are militantly demanding that Black Studies be separate, and they have much in their arguments.

In the integrated school and the separate one, a fact of the program would be to give the opportunity to blacks to achieve an identity with the past. A most pressing need is for them to develop pride, for all around them there is structured the opposite conclusion, the loss of pride, and regard for whiteness. Thus they even find it impossible to relate themselves to middle class persons, some of whom have risen from lower classes in the context of American life, but seem to have forgotten the masses. Nevertheless, with integration, it might be harder for the teacher to present black images for there would be those youth who would ask for Jewish, Italian or Mexican or other minority images. But the way must be opened for the light of knowledge to shine for both black and white.

Alexander once met Diogenes, who had looked with a lantern for an honest man. He was asked as he stood, "what service can I render you?" Diogenes replied "That you stand a little aside that the sun may come to me." Black Americans said to white Americans surrounded by their racism in textbooks and in their thinking, "Stand aside, Whitey, that the sun may see us also."

History should be integrated so that Africa—the home of the darker race—shall become a part of world history. Africa was once known as a continent without a history or a civilization. Its study was left to anthropology and ethnology. Traditions of inferiority concerning this land developed and were kept alive by travelers and missionaries. The eleventh edition of the *Encyclopedia Brittanica* could then say almost without contradiction that, "Africa, with the exception of the lower Nile Valley and what is known as Roman Africa, so far as its native inhabitants are concerned, is a continent practically without a history and possessing no records from which such a history might be constructed." Subsequent editions of this work have had to change this view, due largely to the research and publications of our Association for the Study of Negro Life and History and other circles of scholars thus interested. We now know that there were kingdoms and governments in Africa as well organized as those of the Goths, the Vandals, the Huns, the Angles, the Saxons, the Jutes and other European tribes of the North prior to their acquisition of the civilizations of Greece and Rome. Africa had no opportunity of profiting by such contracts, but without them, there was an indigenous civilization, at periods blended with Arabic culture, which compared favorably with any civilization in Europe. There were organized governments, laws, roads, buildings, artistic manifestations which challenge the admiration of students of our time. The contacts of Greece and Rome with Africa are shown in their art.

Civilizations flourished in west and central Africa, from which a majority of the American slaves came. Benin, Yoruba, Nupe, Melle, Songhay, Mossi and other kingdoms had civilizations worthy of commendation. Europe had its Charlemagne, its Charles the Great; Africa had its Askia Mohammed, its Askia the Great. When European tribal life was primitive in large areas, Africa organized kingdoms, spread over the west and central parts of that continent. These civilizations declined and were strengthened also through the Mohammedan conquests but were followed by the rise of the slave trade. Some few smaller kingdoms were advanced to greater activity by the Mohammedan influences, but the slave trade east and west proved to be a blight upon civilizing developments. Whole villages were depopulated, and kings turned to the easier ways of living provided by the trade in men rather than to the slower processes of permanent state building.

With the facts which have come to light concerning African history, the traditions of its past will have to be changed. Africa, then, must be given a place in history with other people as has been recently done for Japan, China, and

India. It will be found that America has not only a European background but also an African background, and that this history should be woven into its history because a large part of its population has a background in the African continent of worthy connection.

It should be a privilege to engage in the democratic opportunity to help unify history and to create appreciation and understanding among peoples of different creeds, races, and nationalities. We should continue to integrate the school by entrance, but we should also integrate the subject-matter of history. They are parts of one whole. We should continue to criticize the curriculum, learn about the teaching, and protest the neglects so that our schools shall be learning places for all of our population, and so that no group of people shall be slandered by history nor committed to oblivion, nor become a neglected factor in our current life because of omissions in our past life. As Americans, we should present and make available the history with facts and correct the falseness of the myths, seek to destroy the sterotypes and help to uproot the negative traditional opinions about black Americans.

Let us support the organizations, the schools, the churches, and the institutions, white and black, which continue to advocate the teaching of the truth so that the treatment of history on the basis of the superiority or inferiority of color can be terminated in our time. Let us continue our insistence that history's teaching about black Americans shall be truthful and that it shall become a part of the history of the nation's expressed goal of freedom and opportunity, although we may belong to different population groups.

Our purpose and objective should center around the declaration which we would have all Americans say with pride, "I too have a goodly heritage." This heritage is a living, changing, spiritually vital thing, and is not enshrined in historical documents—the Declaration of Independence, the Constitution of the United States, the Emancipation Proclamation, and the Civil Rights Act—merely to be revered. This heritage is to be transmitted not only by what is said in these documents but by what is done about them, and primarily by us.

Our heritage is a continuously functioning process which needs to be relearned in the schools and revitalized by each generation of youths. The textbooks must be criticized continuously, the intercultural programs increased, the teachers supplied with supplementary materials and the citizen leaders should know the truth now so active in the minds of men. Basic to the success and attainment of freedom and the extension of democratic practices through the current Revolution is the freedom of all minds through history's study, reading and teaching. In this respect:

> We are the music-makers
> And we are the dreamers of dreams
> Wandering by lone sea-breakers;
> And sitting by desolate streams—
> World losers and world-forsakers,
> On whom the pale moon gleams;
> Yet we are the movers and shakers
> Of the world for-ever it seems:
> We, in the ages lying

In the buried past of the earth
Built Nineveh with our sighing,
And Babel itself in our mirth;
And o'erthrew them with prophesying
To the old of the new world's worth:
For each age is a dream that is dying
Or one that is coming to birth.

In history, what shall it be through us—a dream of acting together forgetful of color *dying,* or a dream being apart conscious of color difference that is coming to *birth?* The answer is ours!

PART TWO: MULTIMEDIA MATERIALS IN THIS SECTION ARE DESIGNED TO PROVIDE AN UNDERSTANDING AND APPRECIATION OF THE AFRO-AMERICAN, HIS CULTURE, HERITAGE, AND CONTRIBUTIONS TO THE GROWTH AND DEVELOPMENT OF THE UNITED STATES OF AMERICA.

Films (16mm)

The Accident. Producer/Distributor: KETCTV/IU, 1957. Grade Level: Sr. H.S.
through Adult. Running Time: 30 min. Rental: $6.75. Purchase: $125.
B&W.

Presents two versions of an automobile-pedestrian accident from which a
law action develops. Shows first the accident as seen through the eyes of the
victim, 11-year-old Judy Martin; then the version remembered by the driver of
the car, Alfred Sharp. Explains and demonstrates how the girl's parents seek
legal counsel when her injury does not heal properly. Dramatizes how a suit is
filed and the serving of a summons on the defendant, Alfred Sharp. A film from
The Action at Law Series.

Action Against the Law. Producer/Distributor: TFC, 1959. Grade Level: Jr. &
Sr. H.S. Running Time: 30 min. Rental: $105. B&W.

Discusses an aggravated situation with interracial frictions resulting in
mob violence that almost costs the life of an innocent boy. This film is a series of
minor incidents in a small California town.

Afro-American Music: Its Heritage. Producer/Distributor: CGW. Grade Level:
H.S. through Adult. Running Time: 16 min. Color.

From the talking drums of West Africa to contemporary "rhythm and
blues," 250 years of Black America's contributions to the history and culture of
the United States are vividly portrayed in this film. Noted jazz composer Calvin
Jackson traces the history and evolution of this unique musical style from tribal
communications through plantation life origins of spiritual and gospel music to
the eras of the "blues," "ragtime," "dixieland," "jazz," and "swing," climaxing
with the Afro-Cuban music and the "rhythm and blues" of today.

An Afro-American Thing. Producer/Distributor: FRITH, 1968. Grade Level: Sr.
H.S. through College. Running Time: 25 min. Rental: $20. Purchase:
$150. B&W.

Soul music and primitive dances provide the principal background for a
picture which expresses the similarities and contrasts of African and American
cultures. Created and performed primarily by black people, the picture is an
outgrowth of a neighborhood arts exchange program. It is based on the idea that
the performing arts are an important part of black culture.

Agnes Varda's Black Panthers: A Report. Producer/Distributor: GROVE. Running Time: 26 min. Rental: $60. Purchase: $375. Color.

This report articulates the main goals; focuses on a rally to free Huey

Newton from prison; allows Bill Brandt, Bobby Seale, Stokely Carmichael and Mrs. Eldridge Cleaver to speak freely; takes no sides.

Aid to Families With Dependent Children: Intake Interview. Producer/Distributor: USC. Running Time: 18 min. Rental: $3.80.

Explains how interviewer's skills affect the interviewee and determine the success of the interview. Designed specifically for training social workers. Available in 5 parts.

Al Stacey Hayes. Producer/Distributor: JAS, 1969. Grade Level: Jr. H.S. through College. Running Time: 25 min. Purchase: $300. Color.

A cinema portrait of a black teenager who lives in the Delta area of Mississippi. The film portrays Al's frustration at the slow pace of progress for the blacks in the South, and shows the almost unbridgeable gap between the young and old in the black community.

All My Babies. Producer/Distributor: CMC, 1953. Grade Level: College, Adult. Running Time: 55 min. Purchase: $330. B&W.

This film shows simply and clearly the methods a midwife should follow from the time she takes a case until the baby is taken to its first Well Baby Clinic. The film was photographed in Georgia and features a certified midwife, her patients and the doctors and nurses who supervise the local midwife training program. Restricted to use by professional audiences and cinema courses. Directed by George C. Stoney.

All the Way Home. Producer/Distributor: FR, 1964. Grade Level: Jr. H.S. through Adult. Running Time: 28 min. Rental: $3.50. Purchase: $150. B&W.

This film portrays what happens in a typical suburban community when a Negro couple comes to look at a house marked "for sale." This is a fictionalized drama that explodes the myth of "falling property values" and explores the human resources that can ease the transition to integrated neighborhoods. The film shows the whole range of ordinary black people at work, while on the sound track, "white" voices are heard shouting all the possible degrading slang terms.

Almost Neighbors. Producer/Distributor: NCC, 1965. Grade Level: Adult. Running Time: 34 min. Rental: $10. Purchase: $155. B&W.

Two neighboring communities are depicted as separate communities with economic and social barriers. One is a suburban community where the Harleys live, and the other is the sprawling community of Easthill. The former is affluent and pleasant; the latter is a place of poverty, despair and unemployment resulting from modern automation. A proposed merger of the two communities causes the Harleys to consider their total responsibilities.

The Alphabet. Producer/Distributor: UB/IU, 1958. Grade Level: College, Adult. Running Time: 29 min. Rental: $6.75. Purchase: $125. B&W.

This film analyzes the English writing system and traces the origin, development, and spread of the alphabet. It shows and explains various writing systems including Sanskrit, Chinese, and Arabic, and discusses the significance of hieroglyphics in the development of written language.

America, Home of the Free, Land of the Brave. Producer/Distributor: CFS, 1969. Grade Level: Sr. H.S. through Adult. Running Time: 7 min. Rental: $10. Purchase: $125. Color.

This is a satirical underground film modeled after the famous *Oh Dem Watermelons.* The film shows scenes of violence, crime and lust from old Hollywood movies, and scenes of black people being beaten and repeatedly arrested. Some brief nudity.

An American Girl. Producer/Distributor: ADL, 1958. Running Time: 29½ min. Rental: $7.50. Purchase: $150. B&W.

This film tells the story of an American teenager who is mistakenly believed to be Jewish by her friends and neighbors. The particular incident, based on an actual event, revolves around anti-Semitism, but the story is basically concerned with the irrational prejudice.

American Music: From Folk to Jazz and Pop. Producer/Distributor: MGH, 1966. Grade Level: Intermediate through College. Running Time: 51 min. Rental: $29. Purchase: $325. B&W.

The origin and development of popular American music is traced in this film. It includes jazz, square dance, hoedown, hillbilly songs, gospel hymns and funeral marches. Originally, the film was an ABC-TV project.

American Negro: The Economic Straightjacket. Producer/Distributor: UM, 1964. Grade Level: Sr. H.S. through Adult. Running Time: 30 min. Rental: $7. Purchase: $90. B&W.

Herbert Hill, National Labor Secretary of the NAACP, analyzes the problems of Negro unemployment and discusses several solutions. Professor Albert Wheeler of the University of Michigan is the interviewer.

The American Negro Sings. Producer/Distributor: MLA, 1968. Grade Level: Jr. H.S. through Adult. Running Time: 24 min. Rental: $10. Purchase: $275. Color.

With music and song, the film traces the progress of the Negro from Africa, through the hardship of slavery to his place as neighbor and co-worker, working side-by-side with the members of other races and ethnic groups of this country.

American Revolution. The Civil War. The Negro Soldier. Producer/Distributor: VDEF, 1969. Grade Level: Elementary through College. Rental: $19.83. Purchase: $48.17. B&W.

This series of film clips includes paintings of Crispus Attucks, monuments of James Caldwell at Howard University, varied shots of Negroes helping to rebuild America, Negroes participating in the fight against British soldiers in the Boston Massacre, and other short sequences affecting Negroes in American history.

American Revolution of '63. Producer/Distributor: NBC, 1963. Grade Level: H.S. & College. Running Time: 180 min. Color.

Examines the origins, philosophy and impact of the American Negro's struggle for equality. Describes the goals of the civil rights movement in different parts of the country, voter registration in the South, equal job opportunities and open housing in the North, and everywhere, the fight for school desegration. Includes scenes of demonstrations and violence in numerous cities.

Anacostia: Museum in the Ghetto. Producer/Distributor: NET/IU. Rental: $5.00. Purchase: $100.00. Grade Level: H.S. & College. Running Time: 17 min. B&W.

Describes how a neighborhood museum, a branch of the Smithsonian Institute, located in a Washington, D.C. ghetto, is bringing beauty, creativity, and joy to the children there. Candid scenes depict the museum's policy of involving children in its activities. The Smithsonian's secretary and patrons of the local museum present the rationale for the museum. A youth explains why exhibits are not vandalized. Scenes of the museum's surroundings emphasize a plea for more institutions to enter the ghetto.

The Anderson Platoon. Producer/Distributor: MGH, 1968. Grade Level: Sr. H.S. through Adult. Rental: $50. Purchase: $450.

This film depicts Lieutenant Joseph B. Anderson, a Negro graduate of West Point, through six weeks in the Central Highlands of Vietnam.

Angry Negro. Producer/Distributor: NET/IU, 1966. Grade Level: Sr. H.S. through Adult. Running Time: 30 min. Rental: $6.75. Purchase: $125. B&W.

Leaders of the Negro community, such as Elijah Muhammad of the Black Muslims, editor Daniel Watts of the *Liberator* magazine, Jimmy Garrett of the Congress of Racial Equality, Fannie Lou Hamer of the Mississippi Freedom Democratic Party, Julian Bond and John Lewis of the Student Non-Violent Coordinating Committee, Andrew Young of the Southern Christian Leadership Conference, and Bill Epton of the Progressive Labor Party presented various opinions concerning Negro problems. "Freedom now!" is the one ideal on which all are agreed.

Appalachia: Rich Land, Poor People. Producer/Distributor: NET/IU, 1969. Grade Level: Sr. H.S. through Adult. Running Time: 59 min. Rental: $13. Purchase: $200. B&W.

An in-depth study of the failure of federal programs in the war on poverty in Appalachia, emphasizing the local resistance from middle-class townspeople and industry owners toward those from outside Appalachia who have come to help the poor.

Applying for a Job. Producer/Distributor: DEROCH, 1967. Grade Level: Jr. & Sr. H.S. Running Time: 11¼ min. Purchase: $66.30. Color.

This film highlights the things many young people say and do during an interview which impair their chances of getting jobs. Youthful viewers can identify with the various roles and situations shown; see the mistakes which are commonly made and how to correct them. This is followed by a sequence demonstrating the right way to apply for a job.

Approaches to Early Childhood Curriculum. Producer/Distributor: ADL, 1967. Running Time: 25 min. Rental: $7. Purchase: $75. B&W.

Three short sequences filmed at a pre-kindergarten class in a ghetto school are used to explain that Institute for Developmental Studies' methods for teaching abstract concepts, self-image development, and how games can be adapted to reinforce learning. After each sequence, members of the staff examine the teacher's techniques and assess where she has succeeded in reaching the children or explain how she has failed. Following each discussion sequence the film projector is stopped to give the teacher-viewing audience an opportunity for its own evaluation.

Aretha Franklin, Soul Singer. Producer/Distributor: MGH/CON, 1968. Grade Level: Jr. H.S. through Adult. Running Time: 25 min. Rental: $25. Purchase: $325. Color.

The film shows Aretha Franklin in rehearsals, during intimate "skull sessions" with her friends and advisors, at home relaxing and, finally, at center-stage beneath the spotlights, singing to a roaring crowd. During the course of the film, Miss Franklin discusses her musical influences and talks of her own feelings about her music.

Arrowsmith. Producer/Distributor: TFC, 1952. Grade Level: Sr. H.S. through College. Running Time: 13 min. Rental: $35. B&W.

This film presents problems of social and medical ethics involved in the emergency administration of an unproved serum to provide immunity to bubonic plague. West Indies authorities refuse to allow people to be used as "guinea pigs." This film is based on the novel by Sinclair Lewis, and pictures a Negro doctor and his efforts to enlist the aid of his people in a village of the interior. Despite conflicts of opinions, scientific testing is encouraged.

Ask Me, Don't Tell Me. Producer/Distributor: CON, 1961. Grade Level: Sr. H.S. through College. Running Time: 22 min. Rental: $10. Purchase: $95. B&W.

The film explores the causes and remedies for juvenile delinquency. It portrays the unsatisfactory and frustrating world of today's youth. The film attempts to set forth the dilemma of a community with groups of young, restless, unemployed teenagers.

Autumn Comes to the City. Producer/Distributor: CORF, 1970. Grade Level: Primary through Elementary. Running Time: 11 min. Purchase: Color, $140; B&W, $70.

This film deals with seasonal colors, sounds and activities in the city. It is dramatically presented, without narration, and in a racially integrated manner. It shows changing weather, clothing, food, animals, children's fun at Halloween and a family Thanksgiving. Children of different backgrounds are shown sharing common experiences.

The Awakening. Producer/Distributor: MGH. Grade Level: Sr. H.S. through College. Running Time: 28 min. Purchase: $160. B&W.

This film is about the relationship of poverty to ignorance. Shows the importance of educational development.

The Background of the Civil War. Producer/Distributor: BFA, 1959. Grade Level: Jr. H.S. through Adult. Running Time: 21 min. Rental: $15. Purchase: Color, $220; B&W, $110.

The beginnings of the American Civil War lie buried in the differences between the North and the South. The South had developed into a great agricultural region dependent upon the growing and selling of cotton. The North had developed into a great commercial region, dependent upon the manufacture and sale of products and their rapid transportation across the country. By compromise and arguments, each section tried to control the Federal government for its own benefit.

Bargaining Collectively. Producer/Distributor: TFC, 1952. Grade Level: Sr. H.S. through College. Running Time: 9 min. Rental: $35. B&W.

This film presents arguments of labor and management for and against union recognition as a committee of workers meets with plant directors to mediate conditions of employment. The setting is in the early 1930's, and the film is an excerpt from the MGM feature motion picture, *An American Romance.*

Battle of Algiers. Producer/Distributor: ADF, 1964. Grade Level: College through Adult. Running Time: 123 min. Rental: $75.

This film depicts the guerrilla struggle for independence within the city of Algiers. It is a realistic re-enactment of the rebellion against the French between 1954 and 1957. Sense of authenticity achieved through the use of non-professional actors and undramatic camera work. Pontecorvo's sympathy for the rebels is apparent, yet he maintains a good balance in this account of the terrorism and atrocities perpetrated by both sides in the conflict. Pontecorvo begins his story in 1954 when the rebel organization starts its drive for independence with a terror campaign against the European community in Algiers. An epilogue summarizes the events of the years following 1957, concluding on July 3, 1962, when the Algerians win independence. The film is a winner of eleven international awards.

The Battle of East St. Louis. Producer/Distributor: CAROUF, 1969. Grade Level: Adult. Running Time: 46 min. Purchase: $250. B&W.

In the spring of 1969, East St. Louis was a racial bomb waiting to detonate. Fear prompted the city to get opposing groups together to discuss their grievances before mass violence erupted. The catalyst used was an encounter and sensitivity training marathon with black militants and white policemen. The results provide hope for all the cities of this country now involved in a volatile racial situation. (Highly recommended for use by police-community action groups, management-personnel relations, church and other adult organizations.)

The Battle of Newburgh. Producer/Distributor: MGH, 1962. Grade Level: College. Running Time: 54 min. Rental: $25. Purchase: $250. B&W.

This film shows the community's response to a proposal for a tightened relief code for Newburgh, New York. The code is outlined, and its relation to taxation, housing, employment, and business growth is shown. The presentation includes interviews with families on relief, ministers, businessmen, and other town people. From the White Paper series.

Big City—1980. Producer/Distributor: CAROUF, 1960. Running Time: 52 min. Purchase: $250. B&W.

Experts present statistics to support the theory that 95% of the nation's population will live in big cities by 1980. Problems and solutions attendant on huge concentrations of populations are explored. This film was narrated by Garry Moore and produced by CBS News.

The Bill of Rights in Action: Equal Opportunity. Producer/Distributor: BFA, 1970. Grade Level: Elementary through Adult. Running Time: 22 min. Rental: $15. Purchase: $265. Color.

In this film, a black factory worker has been promoted over a white, even though the white has seniority. The company feels it must have blacks in supervisory positions and also wants to make up for past discrimination. The white protests, saying that, in fact, he is the one being discriminated against. The case is argued in depth before an arbitrator and the film is left open ended—the viewers are asked to decide the issue.

The Bill of Rights in Action: Freedom of Speech. Producer/Distributor: BFA. Grade Level: Elementary through Adult. Running Time: 21 min. Rental: $15. Purchase: Color, $260; B&W, $135.

The Bill of Rights guarantees us freedom of speech. But are there limits to this freedom? Is it necessary to balance an individual's freedom of expression against the community's need for law-and-order? This film follows the case of an unpopular speaker who is convicted of disturbing the peace. Lawyers argue the Constitutional issues to a Court of Appeals. We learn, from this in-depth study, of the importance and complexity of the issues involved in free speech. The viewers are asked to be the judges.

Billabong. Producer/Distributor: CFS, 1969. Grade Level: Adult. Running Time: 9 min. Rental: $18. Color.

This film is a poetic study of the tensions in an integrated boys' camp.

Birth of a Union. Producer/Distributor: NET/IU, 1966. Grade Level: Jr. H.S. through Adult. Running Time: 30 min. Rental: $6.75. Purchase: $125. B&W.

The story of how the National Farm Workers Association, a new labor union, came into existence, this film documents the unique problems of picketing nearly 4000 acres of vineyards, the mundane problems of keeping the small band of union workers fed and clothed, repairing the automobiles and other equipment needed, and recruiting more members. Interviews are presented with people behind the union movement as well as the representatives of the growers, the local police, and several of the local clergy.

Black Athletes. Producer/Distributor: CI, 1970. Grade Level: Sr. H.S. Running Time: 40 min. Purchase: $55. B&W.

This film presents portraits and action shots of black athletes in football, basketball, baseball, track, boxing, wrestling. Audio tape accompanies film.

The Black Cop. Producer/Distributor: NET/IU, 1969. Grade Level: Sr. H.S. through Adults. Running Time: 16 min. Rental: $5. Purchase: $100. B&W.

The relationship of the black policeman to other blacks is explored by interviewing those on both sides in New York City and Los Angeles.

Black Determination: Crisis at Cornell. Producer/Distributor: ADF, 1969. Grade Level: College through Adult. Running Time: 15 min. Rental: $25. Purchase: $115. B&W.

    A black leader at Cornell explains the situation at the University when black students decided that it had to respond to their demands for a black studies program. He explains each phase of the negotiations with the University, the move to demonstrations, and the final decision of the black students to arm themselves. He also is cognizant of the part played by white students after they allied themselves with the blacks, and the irony of the University's response after the white students became involved in the struggle.

Black Entertainers. Producer/Distributor: CI, 1970. Grade Level: Sr. H.S. Running Time: 40 min. Purchase: $55. B&W.

    This film presents black singers, dancers, and musicians from the present and the past. Audio tape lecture with film.

The Black Experience. Producer/Distributor: UM, 1970. Grade Level: Sr. H.S. through Adult. Rental: $7. Purchase: $90. B&W.

    The co-hosts in this series are Ronald Edmonds, Human Relations Director, Ann Arbor Public Schools, and William Toll, Lecturer in Black History, University of Michigan History Department. The ten programs are: Humanity Defiled; A Dream Deferred; The Politics of Resistance; A System to Destroy; The Black Migration. Culture in Crisis; A Cry of Defiance; The Barriers; The Black Caucus; The Black Experience and American Education.

Black Heritage: A History of Afro-Americans. Producer/Distributor: HRW, 1969. Grade Level: Elementary through College. Running Time: 27 min. each. Purchase: $165 each. B&W.

    This series of 108 filmed lectures, supplemented with visual effects, is a comprehensive and professionally compiled film study of Black History. All the material was developed by a Black Heritage Advisory Board. Leading black scholars, writers, artists, and activists, including Lerone Bennett, Charles Hamilton, St. Clair Drake, James Farmer, Staughton Lynd, James Boggs, and Leroi Jones, examine in detail the Afro-American experience from its beginnings in Africa to 1969.

Black Heroes of American History. Producer/Distributor: CI, 1970. Grade Level: Sr. H.S. Running Time: 40 min. Purchase: $55. B&W.

    This film recreates the lives and activities of black people prominent in American history. Audio tape lecture accompanies film.

Black History. Producer/Distributor: ADF, 1971. Grade Level: Sr. H.S. through Adult. Running Time: 120 min. Color.

    The history of Black America is presented, from Africa through the years of slavery to the Civil War, Black Reconstruction, the Civil Rights Movement, Black Power, Black Liberation, the Black Panther Party and the Third World Revolution. Four parts; in production.

Black Men and Iron Horses. Producer/Distributor: NYT/ARNO, 1969. Grade Level: Intermediate through Sr. H.S. Running Time: 18 min. Purchase: $200. Color.

This film discusses the contributions of black inventors to American railroading, focusing on such figures as Elijah McCoy, who developed lubricators to solve engine overheating; Andrew Beard, who invented automatic car-coupling; and Granville T. Woods, who devised a telegraph warning system. This film shows how railroading benefited from these contributions while restricting most black workers to menial jobs and segregating black passengers in Jim Crow coaches. An interview with A. Philip Randolph is also included.

Black on Black. Producer/Distributor: TIMELI, 1970. Grade Level: Jr. H.S. through College. Running Time: 60 min. Rental: $7.50 each. Purchase: $50 each; $600 set. Color.

A series of 20 four-minute color sequences presenting positions of 20 prominent blacks as they discuss race in America. The 20 contemporary figures are: Ralph Abernathy, Julian Bond, H. Rap Brown, Jim Brown, Shirley Chisholm, Eldridge Cleaver, Coretta King, Sidney Poitier, Jackie Robinson, Bayard Rustin, Harry Belafonte, Edward Brooke, James Brown, Stokely Carmichael, Mohammed Ali, Dick Gregory, Martin Luther King, Adam Clayton Powell, Carl Stokes, and Malcolm X.

Black Scientists. Producer/Distributor: CI, 1970. Grade Level: Sr. H.S. Running Time: 40 min. Purchase: $55. B&W.

This film discusses black scientists of the present and past. Audio tape accompanies lecture.

Black Muslims Speak From America. Producer/Distributor: TIMELI, 1969. Grade Level: Sr. H.S. through Adult. Running Time: 33 min. Rental: $25. Purchase: $250. B&W.

Who are the Black Muslims? What do they believe in? How do they fit into the social structure of America? These and many more questions are answered as Malcolm Muggeridge interviews a group of seven young Black Muslims.

Black Natchez. Producer/Distributor: LIP. Running Time: 60 min. Rental: $60. Purchase: $350. B&W.

Filmed in Mississippi during the 1964 freedom summer, this film presents a look at elements that social scientists study, such as crowd behavior, social change, the ethnic politician, Negro nationalism, class structure and the generation gap.

Black Politician. Producer/Distributor: PFP, 1970. Grade Level: Intermediate through Adult. Running Time: 15 min. Rental: $15. Purchase: $175. Color.

The contributions made to the democratic process by various black politicians in the past and up to the present day make up the content of this film.

Black Pride: The Emerging American Negro. Producer/Distributor: GSF. Running Time: 22 min. Color.

This film presents the contributions of blacks and their culture.

A Black and White Dictionary. Producer/Distributor: UM, 1968. Grade Level: College, Adult. Running Time: 29 min. Rental: $7. Purchase: $90. B&W.

Professors Robert Vinter of the UM School of Social Work and Albert Wheeler of the UM Medical School, president of the Michigan Conference of NAACP Branches, examine the meaning of "white racism" and other current terms in race relations.

Black and White: Uptight. Producer/Distributor: BFA, 1969. Grade Level: Jr. & Sr. H.S. Running Time: 35 min. Rental: $15. Purchase: $420. Color.

The initial integration of Riverside, California, provides the background for this film. Conflicting positions are expressed in interviews to fully explore the meaning of the 14th Amendment. This film focuses special attention on the area of conflicts between minority and white groups.

Black, White, Gray. Producer/Distributor: BARKTB, 1967. Running Time: 4 min. Color.

Symbols illustrate the history and conflict of the Negro in society. The film expresses the belief that human beings, regardless of race, are the same.

Black World. Producer/Distributor: CBS NEWS-FA, 1968. Rental: $10.50. Purchase: $300.00. Grade Level: H.S. & College. Running Time: 53 min. BW.

Progress of racial equality in the United States as it is viewed by prominent blacks in the country and in Africa. Through use of satellite television, Mr. John Conyers, Democratic congressman of Detroit; Mr. Tom Mboya, Kenyan Minister of Economic Planning and Development in Nairobi; Dr. Alex Dwapong, Chancellor of Ghana University in Accra; and Mr. Floyd McKissick, former National Director of CORE in Harlem are interviewed.

Blind Gary Davis. Producer/Distributor: MGH, 1967. Running Time: 12 min. Code No. 406151. Rental: $12.50. Purchase: $135. B&W.

This film captures the mood of Harlem, leading the viewer through the streets and to the people with the folk music of Gary Davis.

The Blue Dashiki: Jeffrey and His City Neighbors. Producer/Distributor: EBEC/MSU, 1970. Grade Level: Primary and Intermediate. Running Time: 14 min. Rental: Color, $8; B&W, $5.50. Purchase: Color, $167.50; B&W, $86.

Through the eyes of a young boy, we see the resources and opportunities of a city community unfold. The film is designed to stimulate students to observe activities and opportunities in their own neighborhood and to show some of the cultural interests and artifacts of the Afro-American community.

The Blues According to Lightnin' Hopkins. Producer/Distributor: LIP. Running Time: 28 min. Color.

This film presents one of the last of the great country-bluesingers; an educational experience of black Texas and its music.

Blues Maker. Producer/Distributor: EFP. Running Time: 14 min. Rental: $6. Purchase: $85. B&W.

Fred McDowell, one of the last of the old blues musicians and a member of the manual labor pool around Como, Mississippi, performs and talks about his version of the blues, the Mississippi country blues. McDowell's labors are reflected in his songs. The region is reflected in his "bottleneck style" of guitar playing, an old style which originated years ago in the rural backwaters of the Mississippi Delta.

Bobby Seale: Interview in Jail. Producer/Distributor: NET/ADF, 1970. Grade Level: College, Adult. Running Time: 60 min. Rental: $65. Purchase: $225. B&W.

Bobby Seale talks about what's meaningful to him. He gives account of what it's like to be in jail. The politics of the Black Panther Party are all incorporated into Seale's vision, and expressed in their human, personal, day-to-day form.

Body and Soul—Part I. Producer/Distributor: UM, 1968. Grade Level: Jr. H.S. through Adult. Running Time: 25 min. B&W.

An examination of the black Americans' contribution to sports in Amercia is reported by Harry Reasoner. Harry Edwards, leader of the threatened Olympic Games boycott, is interviewed along with leading black athletes Tommie Smith, Lee Evans, Charlie Green, Jim Hines and Ralph Boston. It becomes clear that while a fairly large number of black athletes have succeeded at their specific athletic endeavors, a very small number have ever achieved the status of manager or coach, and a great many of the sports exclude the black man almost entirely. The question is asked, "Is there a difference?" It is answered in the negative.

Body and Soul—Part II—Soul. Producer/Distributor: CBS News. Rental: UM. Purchase: FA, 1968. Grade Level: Jr. H.S. through Adult. Running Time: 25 min. B&W.

Soul music is discussed in detail by singer Ray Charles. Mr. Charles explains that because of isolation and the misery and humiliation suffered by the American black man, he developed many of his own music and dance forms. Only through this outlet of rhythm and sound has the black man been able to release some of his frustration and grief. Singers Mahalia Jackson, Billie Holiday and Aretha Franklin cry out their souls to make a rich contribution to American music.

Booker T. Washington. Producer/Distributor: BFA, 1967. Grade Level: Elementary through Sr. H.S. Running Time: 11 min. Rental: $6.50. Purchase: $130. Color.

This film covers the early years of Booker T. Washington, who was born a slave in 1856, and who later built Tuskegee Institute, which has become a monument to education.

Booker T. Washington. Producer/Distributor: EBF/MSU, 1951. Grade Level: Jr. H.S. through College. Running Time: 20 min. Rental: $7.50. Purchase: $135. B&W.

This film tells the story of Booker T. Washington from childhood to the time when he becomes "probably the greatest Negro in history"; recalls his hardships in obtaining an education, his struggle to free his people from ignorance and poverty, his building Tuskegee Institute, and his tragedies in private life.

The Born Criminal. Producer/Distributor: IU, 1958. Grade Level: Sr. H.S. through Adult. Running Time: 30 min. Rental: $6.75. Purchase: $125. B&W.

This film discusses the relationship of heredity to criminality, and points out common misconceptions concerning physical characteristics as a cause or recognizable symbol of crime. The fallacies in Lombroso's theories of criminality are explained. The presentation stresses the need for education in the area of genetic inheritance as related to criminal tendencies.

Boundary Lines. Producer/Distributor: MGH, 1948. Grade Level: College. Running Time: 10 min. Rental: $5. Purchase: $130. Color.

This film analyzes the symbolism of lines to express ideas of trees, of mountains, and of man. It is a plea to eliminate the arbitrary boundary lines which divide people from each other as individuals and as nations—invisible boundary lines of color, origin, wealth, and religion. Presented in stylized animation by Phillip Stapp and musical score by Gene Forrell.

"Boy": An Experience in the Search for Identity. Producer/Distributor: ADL, 1964. Grade Level: Sr. H.S. through Adult. Running Time: 12 min. Purchase: $55. B&W.

Through imaginative role-playing, a Negro boy indulges in a fantasy which reveals his deep sensitivity to name-calling and stereotyped attitudes toward racial minorities. The hard-hitting dialogue exposes the degradation to which a prejudiced person subjects his fellow human beings. Part of the Study in Color Series.

Boy With a Knife. Producer/Distributor: IFB, 1956. Grade Level: Sr. H.S. through Adult. Running Time: 20 min. Rental: $9. Purchase: $120. B&W.

This film focuses on the attitude of toughness and the security of the gang with which disturbed young people "protect" themselves. It is a case story showing how a group worker attempts to reach this gang of boys who are headed for delinquency. It shows how the worker plans his preventive action and how he attempts to carry out his plan.

Brazil: The Vanishing Negro. Producer/Distributor: AIM/IU, 1965. Grade Level: Sr. H.S. through Adult. Running Time: 30 min. Rental: $6.75. Purchase: $125. B&W.

This film depicts the interracial experiences of the Negro in Brazil and stresses that they differ markedly from the experiences of North American Negroes. Included are visits to the port of Salvador, traditional Afro-Brazilian religious ceremonies, and interviews with Negro Brazilians, who discuss the significance of being Negro in their country. This is one in a series of nine films on the History of the Negro in the United States, South America, and Africa.

Brotherhood of Man. Producer/Distributor: MGH, 1946. Grade Level: Jr. H.S. through College. Running Time: 10 min. Rental: $12.50. Purchase: $135. B&W.

This is an animated film in humorous style which emphasizes the problems of developing one world requiring interracial and intercultural cooperation. Based on the pamphlet "Races of Mankind," by Ruth Benedict and Jean Weltfish.

The Bus. Producer/Distributor: HW, 1962. Grade Level: Sr. H.S. through Adult. Running Time: 62 min. Rental: $25. Purchase: $660. B&W.

In August of 1963 groups from all over the U.S. journeyed to Washington, D.C., for a massive civil rights demonstration. Filmmakers Haskel Wexler and Michael Butler joined the San Francisco delegation and produced this candid document of their trip. The mobile cameras and hidden microphones succeed in presenting an intimate portrait of the participants—their devotion, intensity, and remarkable sincerity.

Business Machine Operators. Producer/Distributor: DEROCH, 1968. Grade Level: Jr. & Sr. H.S. Running Time: 6 min. 25 sec. Purchase: $48.45. Color.

This film portrays the number of jobs and job duties performed by business machine operators. It briefly explains the jobs and gives solid, factual information on career ladders in this field, stressing mobility potential of those with business machine skills. An informative sequence shows data processing machine operator being trained on-the-job to move up into the computer field.

The California Fair Housing Case. Producer/Distributor: EBEC, 1969. Grade Level: Sr. H.S. through Adult. Running Time: 20 min. Rental: Color, $9; B&W, $6.50. Purchase: Color, $232.50; B&W, $119.

This presentation documents the problems of a young Negro couple attempting to purchase a home in a white community. It dramatizes and illuminates the events leading up to the attempt to introduce an anti-open housing amendment into the California constitution.

Can We Immunize Against Prejudice? Producer/Distributor: CMC, 1954. Grade Level: Jr. & Sr. H.S. Running Time: 7 min. Purchase: $50. B&W.

This film demonstrates how three sets of parents try to immunize their children against prejudice by using three different methods. Their methods include the following approaches: setting a good example, knowledge of the facts, and law and order. One day these children return home with evidence of prejudice. Although the film does not solve the problems prejudice presents, it does focus attention and furnish the background for discussion.

The Captive. Producer/Distributor: NCC, 1963. Grade Level: Adult. Running Time: 29 min. Rental: $8. B&W.

This is the story of the hopes, fears, and frustrations of a man struggling to escape the bonds of poverty in the Appalachian region of the United States. The grim way of life and the devastating effects of poverty on Appalachian people in a coal town are portrayed.

The Challenge of Urban Renewal. Producer/Distributor: NBC, 1966. Grade Level: Jr. H.S. through Adult. Running Time: 29 min. Purchase: Color, 327.50; B&W, $167.50.

This film examines the evidence of such problems as urban-suburban deterioration, air and water pollution, and highway jams. Problems created in Detroit and Boston are examined. Illustrates the problems created by mass, unplanned migration from city to suburb. Televised under the title "America, the Beautiful."

A Chance at the Beginning. Producer/Distributor: ADF, 1964. Running Time: 29 min. Rental: $7. Purchase: $85. B&W.

This film shows that pre-school training, especially for children from educationally limited environments, provides a sound foundation for the fullest development of each child's potential. Filmed in a Harlem school.

A Chance for Change. Producer/Distributor: MGH, 1965. Grade Level: College. Running Time: 39 min. Rental: $17.50. Purchase: $225. B&W.

This film reviews the daily schedule of activities—including playground, classrooms, meals, and nature walks—of pre-school children at a Head Start center in a poor Negro community. In this area where no kindergarten or nursery schools previously existed, some useful techniques for this type of operation emerged.

Children of the U.N. Producer/Distributor: IQF, 1954. Grade Level: Primary through Sr. H.S. Running Time: 11 min. Purchase: $75. B&W.

Children of all races and nationalities, whose families work for the U.N., share their experiences with each other.

Children Without. Producer/Distributor: NEA, 1964. Grade Level: Jr. & Sr. H.S. Running Time: 29 min. Rental: $35. Purchase: $110. B&W.

This film comments on the educational problems of the disadvantaged child, based on the Educational Policies Commission Report. The school staff is portrayed as most understanding of the children's problems stemming from inadequate parents and poor environment. The teachers attempt to tailor their educational offering to the needs of these children.

The Chosen People. Producer/Distributor: ADL, 1961. Running Time: 27 min. Rental: $7.50. Purchase: $110. B&W.

This is an effective dramatization of the problems of anti-Semitism in America, originally presented on NBC-TV by the National Council of Catholic Men as part of the "Prejudice, U.S.A." series. In this story, Anne and her friends learn that the Community Club they have selected for their Senior Prom does not admit Jewish people—making it impossible for some of their classmates to attend. In seeking a reason for the club's unwritten "gentlemen's agreement," the teenagers discover irrational prejudice in their own community. A discussion guide is available.

Cities—Crime in the Streets. Producer/Distributor: NET/IU, 1965. Grade Level: Sr. H.S. through Adult. Running Time: 60 min. Rental: $12. Purchase: $200. B&W.

Two important aspects of the crime problem in the United States are police protection and the rehabilitation of juvenile offenders. This film discusses the way in which police protection of citizens from crime is hampered by a shortage of men, poor training, inefficient clerical and communications methods, and problems of community relations. These factors are examined by police experts, criminologists, and others.

Cities of the Future. Producer/Distributor: MGH, 1966. Grade Level: Sr. H.S. through Adult. Running Time: 25 min. Code No. 689313. Rental: $18. Purchase: $325. Color.

This film focuses on the creative planning now in progress to surmount problems in the future. Visiting a dozen cities around the world, the film studies the "clean slate" approach exemplified in new cities like Brasilia, and the "constructive-restoration" approach under way in Philadelphia. Shown are the ideas of such innovators as R. Buckminster Fuller, Japan's Kenzo Tange, Canada's Le Corbusier: cities "weatherproofed" by geodesic domes; megastructures surrounded by greenbelts; multi-level cities; floating cities.

The City and the Poor. Producer/Distributor: NET, 1966. Grade Level: Sr. H.S. through Adult. Running Time: 60 min. Rental: $24. Purchase: $400. B&W.
    In this study of the frustrations, aspirations, and fears of America's poor, sections of Chicago and Los Angeles are examined in an attempt to understand the nature of social welfare work, the lack of motivation among the poor, and the growing impatience prevalent in some poverty areas. Two parts.

Civil Disorder: The Kerner Report. Producer/Distributor: PBL/IU, 1968. Grade Level: Sr. H.S. through Adult. Running Time: 80 min. Rental: $16.50. Purchase: $300. B&W.
    This documentary film was prepared by the National Educational Television Film Service, and is designed to present a statement of the effects of racism, the goals of the Negro revolution, and examples of efforts at relieving Negro unemployment. It also gives an analysis of the Kerner Report by outstanding Negroes. Also included in the film are critical statements by Negro militants in contrast to the more positive views of the late Dr. Martin Luther King. In three parts.

Civil Rights Movement: The Angry Voices of Watts. Producer/Distributor: FI, 1968. Grade Level: Jr. H.S. through Adult. Running Time: 52 min. Rental: $25. Purchase: $250. B&W.
    This film documents the anger of Negroes who witnessed days and nights of riots, the frustration and disappointment of people forced into an unsatisfactory existence not of their own choosing, and the hostilities which are fueling the Black Revolution.

Civil Rights Movement: Historic Roots. Producer/Distributor: FI, 1966. Grade Level: Jr. H.S. through Adult. Running Time: 16 min. Rental: $8.50. Purchase: $102.50. B&W.
    This film presents and reviews the origin of the civil rights movement, starting with the slave trade, slavery, abolitionism, and ending with the Emancipation Proclamation.

Civil Rights Movement: Mississippi Summer Project. Producer/Distributor: FI, 1966. Grade Level: Jr. H.S. through Adult. Running Time: 17 min. Rental: $8.50. Purchase: $102.50. B&W.
    This film discusses the civil rights project that began when hundreds of people gathered in Oxford, Ohio, for non-violent resistance training to prepare for a massive attack on the problems of Negroes in Mississippi.

Civil Rights Movement: The North. Producer/Distributor: FI, 1966. Grade Level: Jr. H.S. through Adult. Running Time: 23 min. Rental: $15.50. Purchase: $151. B&W.
    The tense atmosphere of race relations in many northern cities is de-

picted. The film discusses integration attempts in Chicago, unemployment problems in Elizabeth, New Jersey, and educational problems in Englewood, New Jersey. Inadequate educational facilities, and *de facto* segregation in northern slums are also included.

Civil Rights Movement: The Personal View. Producer/Distributor: FI, 1966. Grade Level: Jr. H.S. through Adult. Running Time: 25 min. Rental: $15.50. Purchase: $151. B&W.

The story of a well-to-do Negro professional family living in a white neighborhood is the point of departure for an exploration of the problem of community race relations. A presentation of Negro stereotypes in fiction and films demonstrates their distortion of the image of the Negro. Also shows the wealthy Negro family in a white Los Angeles neighborhood.

Civil Rights Movement: The South. Producer/Distributor: FI, 1966. Grade Level: Jr. H.S. through Adult. Running Time: 28 min. Rental: $15.50. Purchase: $167.50. B&W.

This film discusses the civil rights movement in the South after the Supreme Court desegregation decision, and recalls Little Rock in 1957, the 1955 Montgomery bus boycott, 1960 Greensboro sit-ins, and 1963 registration day at the University of Alabama. The principle of civil disobedience is traced from Thoreau to Gandhi to Martin Luther King.

The Civil War: A House Divided. Producer/Distributor: MGH, 1969. Running Time: 25 min. Code No. 666005. Rental: $16. Purchase: $275. Color.

This film deals with the significant military operations of the Civil War, the effects of the war on the North and South, the dilemma facing Lincoln as he sought to end the war, and the problems which remained unsolved by the war.

Civil War: Postwar Period. Producer/Distributor: CORF-UM. Grade Level: Jr. & Sr. H.S. Running Time: 16 min. Rental: $3.25. Color.

The problems faced by the nation are clarified through a variety of historical materials combined with live action scenes. The film analyzes the years of crisis, bitterness, and lack of understanding: the conflict between the conservative President Johnson and radical Congress, the "carpetbag" legislation and reconstruction, and the birth of protest groups such as the Ku Klux Klan.

Color Us Black. Producer/Distributor: IU. Running Time: 60 min. Rental: $10.50.

This film shows the black man's struggle in his search for his own identity over and above the white "norm." It is covered from the point of view of Negro students at black Howard University in Washington, D.C. The four-day takeover of the administration building is shown, including the successful ending of the rebellion.

Common Fallacies About Group Differences. Producer/Distributor: MGH, 1957. Grade Level: Sr. H.S. through College. Rental: $8.50. Purchase: $100. B&W.

This film presents, in the field of sociological psychology, popular misconceptions about races, heredity and group differences. This presentation summarizes the fallacies about group differences and makes positive conclusions. It analyzes seven common notions about races, heredity, and group differences in the light of known scientific evidence and shows in what ways they are all fallacies. From the Psychology Series.

Confrontation: Dialogue in Black and White. Producer/Distributor: IU, 1967. Grade Level: Sr. H.S. through Adult. Running Time: 35 min. Rental: $15. B&W.

This film shows militant and moderate Negro and Caucasian citizens exchanging frank views about race after viewing a film of Chicago's West Side produced by a Negro militant. The opportunity for extreme and moderate representatives of both races to confront each other was furnished by WTTW.

Confronted. Producer/Distributor: NET/IU, 1963. Grade Level: Sr. H.S. through Adult. Running Time: 60 min. Rental: $13. Purchase: $250. B&W.

This production explores the issue of Negro integration in schools, jobs, and housing. The film shows demonstrations for Negro employment in construction and in banks. It also probes the depths of prejudice in business and in housing.

The Constitution and Employment Standards. Producer/Distributor: CU/IU, 1958. Grade Level: Sr. H.S. through Adult. Running Time: 29 min. Rental: $6.75. Purchase: $125. B&W.

This film shows the relationship of the Constitution to wage-and-hour legislation by recreating the case of United States v. Darby Lumber Company. It reviews the legal, social, and economic background, and the aftermath of the Fair Labor Standards Act of 1938. The film emphasizes the constitutional standards and their shifting interpretations used by the Supreme Court in judging the constitutionality of federal regulation of labor standards. The role of Supreme Court decision-making in the American governmental system is illustrated.

The Constitution and the Labor Union. Producer/Distributor: CU/IU, 1958. Grade Level: Sr. H.S. through Adult. Running Time: 29 min. Rental: $5.40. Purchase: $125. B&W.

This film shows the relationship of the Constitution to organized labor. Presents the case of Whitaker et al v. North Carolina, in which a group of unions challenged the constitutionality of a state ban on the closed shop, union shop and "union security" provisions. The role of the 14th Amendment in labor struggles is traced. Photographed in Asheville, North Carolina, and other cities.

Cooks, Chefs and Related Occupations. Producer/Distributor: DEROCH, 1968. Grade Level: Jr. & Sr. H.S. Running Time: 7 min. 10 sec. Purchase: $51. Color.

This film shows the multitude of jobs and job duties that exist in this field. It opens with a montage of job sites—trains, planes, ships, restaurants, schools, hospitals—and moves quickly into full dialogue and narration sequences in the kitchen of a large hotel. It shows an M. D. T. A. trained short-order cook on his first move up the ladder, and carefully defines the career and financial potentials of occupations in this field.

The Cool World. Producer/Distributor: OF, 1964. Grade Level: Jr. H.S. through
Adult. Running Time: 104 min. Rental: $100. Purchase: $1,000. B&W.
A group of young black teenagers in Harlem are shown in their attempts
to deal with the reality of their lives in the ghetto. Some of the difficulties they
face are the irrelevance of their education, drugs, crime, their need for money
and the role of a gun in their lives. Although the film is staged, it documents
without passing judgement what pressures these young people sustain and how
they respond.

The Counselor. Producer/Distributor: DEROCH, 1969. Grade Level: Jr. & Sr.
H.S. Running Time: 15⅙ min. Purchase: $80.75.
This film presents a day in the life of a counselor for the Neighborhood
Youth Corps, portraying a number of typical working situations. Meetings with
N.Y.C. enrollees at the counselor's office, at an enrollee's home, on the job site,
and in a group sensitivity session show the counselor building a relationship of
trust and mutual care that helps the enrollees develop self-respect and maturity.

Crime and Delinquency. Producer/Distributor: IU, 1960. Grade Level: College,
Adult. Running Time: 29 min. Rental: $6.75. Purchase: $125. B&W.
In this discussion of the rise in violence and deviant behavior in America,
Dr. Margaret Mead and Dr. Bertram Beck are questioned on the causes of
delinquency and what can be done about the rise in crime. The presentation
includes emphasis on the new problem of suburban delinquency.

Crime in the Streets. Producer/Distributor: NET/IU. Grade Level: Jr. H.S.
through Adult. Running Time: 60 min. Rental: $12. Purchase: $200. B&W.
This film examines the quality of law enforcement and rehabilitation of
offenders in relation to juvenile crime.

Crime Under Twenty-One. Producer/Distributor: KQED/IU, 1958. Grade
Level: Sr. H.S. through Adult. Running Time: 30 min. Rental: $6.75.
Purchase: $125. B&W.
This film concentrates on criminal behavior committed by teenagers. It
points out that juvenile delinquency may be over-exaggerated because of improve-
ments in statistics, reporting, and apprehension influence the total picture of
teen-age crime. A group of young people discuss themselves and their problems.

Crisis in Levittown, Pa. Producer/Distributor: AF, 1963. Grade Level: Jr. H.S.
through Adult. Running Time: 30 min. Rental: $8. Purchase: $150. B&W.
Such issues as the population explosion, the taxpayers' revolt, and the
failure of school bonds and tax legislation are explored in this film, which
examines the causes and effects of various crises in education and expresses a
need for long-range tax reform. This is a true story which made the front page
coast to coast when the first Negro family moved into Levittown, Pennsylvania,
and the camera caught the unrehearsed drama of complex forces released by the
event.

A Crisis in Medicine. Producer/Distributor: NET/IU, 1969. Grade Level: Sr.
H.S. through Adult. Running Time: 15 min. Rental: $5. Purchase: $100.
B&W.
This is a report on the inadequate medical care accorded most blacks

today, a situation aggravated by an increasing decline in the number of blacks entering the medical professions.

Cry, the Beloved Country. Producer/Distributor. AUDIOF, 1952. Grade Level: Sr. H.S through Adult. Running Time: 105 min. Rental: $25. B&W.

The late Canada Lee portrays a simple country priest drawn to the city in search of his son. There, amid the squalor and evil atmosphere, he finds human misery and tragedy in the discovery that his son has been sentenced to death for murder. The setting is South Africa, and the film is based on the best-selling novel and hit play by the same title.

The Cry of Jazz. Producer/Distributor: GROVE. Running Time: 35 min. B&W.

Young Negro intellectuals protest the death of jazz at the hands of the whites, and the plight of blacks in America.

Culture and Crime. Producer/Distributor: KQED/IU, 1958. Grade Level: Sr. H.S. through Adult. Running Time: 30 min. Rental: $6.75. Purchase: $125. B&W.

This film analyzes patterns of culture and how they influence the rise of criminality. The Nazi regime in Germany is used as an example. The presentation points out that accepted behavior in one culture may be a crime in another, and discusses the impact of cultures meeting head-on, thus giving rise to criminal behavior.

Culture for the Millions. Producer/Distributor: WTTWTV/IU, 1961 Grade Level: Sr. H.S. through Adult. Running Time: 29 min. Rental: $6.75. Purchase: $125. B&W.

One common denominator of our culture, according to the narrator, is the peoples' desire for self-improvement. An early manifestation of this desire was an American institution that endured until the late 1920's—"tent Chautauqua." A source of inspiration, education, and entertainment, reaching hundreds of towns throughout the nation, Chautauqua became a major vehicle for lecturers, musicians, and entertainers including such notables as Clarence Darrow, William Jennings Bryan, Samuel Gompers, John Philip Sousa, and the Fisk Jubilee Singers.

Dance: Echoes of Jazz. Producer/Distributor: NET. Grade Level. Sr. H.S. & College. Running Time: 30 min. Rental: $6.75. Purchase: $125. B&W.

Traces the development of the jazz dance in America from the tap dance of the Thirties of the cool, abstract style of the Sixties.

The Dangerous Drugs. Producer/Distributor: NEFA, 1960. Grade Level: Sr. H.S. through College. Running Time: 22 min. Rental: Color, $12.50; B&W, $6. Purchase: Color, $235; B&W, $125.

This film deals with two types of drugs being used illicitly for the purpose of intoxication, stimulation, hypnosis, etc.: the sedative barbiturates, and the stimulative amphetamines, commonly known among the illicit users as "goof balls" and "bennies." Narrated by Ronald Reagan, this film tells an effective story to inform police officers, teachers and others of the uses and the abuses of these drugs.

Daniel Watts. Producer/Distributor: NET/IU, 1967. Grade Level: Sr. H.S. through Adult. Running Time: 30 min. Rental: $7.25. Purchase: $150. B&W.

Daniel H. Watts, editor of the *Liberator* and one of the leading theoreticians of Black Nationalism in America, is interviewed by Donald Fouser and articulates his position on the subjects of the urban riots, the racist revolution to come, anti-Semitism, the origins of leaders for the "Black Power" movement, the meaning of "Black Power," and the role of religion in the Afro-American community.

David Hilliard, On Face The Nation. Producer/Distributor: ADF. Running Time: 27 min. Rental: $50. Purchase: $200. B&W.

In this complete version of CBS "Face The Nation," televised on December 28, 1969, David Hilliard, Black Panther Party Chief of Staff, attempts to establish that the Panther program represents the basic needs and desires of all oppressed people for self-determination and self-defense. He makes clear that "the revolution is still at an educational level because the people are still being deformed politically by the government and the mass media."

A Day in the Life of Jonathan Mole. Producer/Distributor: MGH, 1959. Grade Level: Jr. H.S. through Adult. Running Time: 32 min. Purchase: $135. B&W.

This presentation of a problem of prejudice, and the fallacies on which it thrives, builds a fantasy about courtroom trial testing and a new law intended to restrict employment to people of "pure" racial origin. The Lord Chief Justice, Jonathan Mole, lets his prejudices override just arguments for the defense; he sentences an Indian, a Jew, and an immigrant to a lifetime of "limited opportunity."

Decision at Delano. Producer/Distributor:: CAFM, 1967. Grade Level: Sr. H.S. through Adult. Running Time: 25 min. Rental: $15. Purchase: $325. Color.

In this documentary of the Delano grape-workers' strike in California's San Joaquin Valley, Cesar Chavez, the leader who organized the strike, outlines the problems of the migrant workers. Men and women strikers voice their frustrations with housing, living conditions, wages and education. Growers explain their economic predicament and labor problems.

A Definition of Language. Producer/Distributor: UB/IU, 1958. Grade Level: College, Adult. Running Time: 29 min. Rental: $6.75. Purchase: $125. B&W.

This production reviews and continues the definition of language from the program Language and Writing. It explains the relationship between language and culture, and tells whether one language is older, better, or more difficult to learn than another language. The film also discusses language patterns and how they affect the learning of a language. A film from the Language and Linguistics Series.

Demons in the Streets. Producer/Distributor: WCAUTV, 1966. Running Time: 52 min. Rental: $10.20. Purchase: $200.

This is a story of the efforts of an area youth worker from the Settlement

House to bring about the rehabiliation of one of the worst of the juvenile street gangs, the "Royal Demons." The setting is New York.

The Detached Americans. Producer/Distributor: CAROUF, 1964. Grade Level: Jr. H.S. through Adult. Running Time: 33 min. Rental: $150. Purchase: $145. B&W.

This examination of the problems and reasons for apathy in the United States today depicts typical examples in community life. The theory of the conditioned family relationship is suggested as a cause for not wanting to get involved. The film was produced by WCAU-TV, Philadelphia.

Dialects. Producer/Distributor: UB/IU, 1958. Grade Level: College, Adult. Running Time: 29 min. Rental: $6.75. Purchase: $125. B&W.

Dialect differences in standard English are explained and demonstrated, using guests from five different geographical areas of the United States. A film from the Language and Linguistics Series.

Diary of a Harlem Family. Producer/Distributor: IU. Running Time: 20 min. Rental: $6.50.

This is a poignant view of the plight of one poverty-stricken family living in New York City's black Harlem, seen through the photographs of Gordon Parks, depicting the hostility and violence that can result from such conditions. The impotence of poverty agencies and others leaves the family's difficulties unsolved.

A Different Kind of Neighborhood. Producer/Distributor: UVA. Running Time: 21 min. Color.

The aspects of a big-city neighborhood are presented as seen by a 14-year-old boy, involving questions of urban renewal and/or rehabilitation.

Dr. Leakey and the Dawn of Man. Producer/Distributor: FI, 1967. Grade Level: Sr. H.S. through Adult. Running Time: 51 min. Code No. 083-0004; 083-0008 (edited). Rental: $25; $16 (edited). Purchase: $500; $327.50 (edited). Color.

The original television documentary by National Geographic about Dr. Louis Leakey's discoveries in East Africa, proving his contention that man originated in Africa. Available in an edited version, 26 minutes, in either color or B&W. The edited version highlights Dr. Leakey's dramatic discoveries and their implications for the study of man's earliest past. The film traces the development of the first theories about both the emergence of man and his place of origin and examines the application of modern technology to the study of anthropology.

Do They Really Want Me? Producer/Distributor: AF. Running Time: 28 min. Purchase: Free. Color.

This film attacks some of the traditional myths about jobs for Negroes, white employers, and the fields open to college educated blacks. The presentation is meant to encourage young people to consider careers leading to management–level positions in business, industry, and government. The young people in this documentary film are either students at predominantly Negro colleges or men and women in the business world who are recent graduates of those colleges. Through an informal interviewing technique, the film becomes a lively, unrehearsed dialogue between those two groups. The college students in the film include sophomores and juniors from Grambling College, Grambling, Louisiana; Livingstone College, Salisbury, North Carolina; and Morris Brown College in Atlanta, Georgia.

Do You Think a Job Is the Answer? Producer/Distributor: NET/IU, 1969. Grade Level: Sr. H.S. through Adult. Running Time: 68 min. Rental: $13.50. Purchase: $270. B&W.

This film describes the Jobs Campaign in Detroit; difficulties and progress in hiring and keeping the hardcore unemployed; and the special difficulties of a bus service set up for black workers.

Drafting. Producer/Distributor: DEROCH, 1968. Grade Level: Jr. & Sr. H S. Running Time: 7 min. 23 sec. Purchase: $51. Color.

A panorama of the career horizons open to beginning draftsmen with the ability and interest to advance on the job, this film opens in a construction engineering firm, where young men and women at drafting boards are shown receiving work assignments and employing the tools of their craft. The scene moves to a group discussion and assignment of tasks that will finally result in the design and construction of a suspension bridge. The final outcome of the work done is shown as the film moves to actual construction sites. There is strong emphasis on teamwork and on the fact that apprentice draftsmen are being sought out and helped by employers to obtain the additional education needed to become designers and supervisors.

A Dream to Learn. Producer/Distributor: CMC, 1967. Grade Level: Jr. & Sr. H.S. Running Time: 28 min. Purchase: $150. B&W.

Elementary school children in the Roxbury District of Boston profited from a cultural enrichment program. Learning about Harriet Tubman, W. E. B. DuBois, and Martin Luther King helped them to identify with the Negro race, as well as with America, and to gain confidence in their own status.

The Dropout. Producer/Distributor: IFB, 1961. Grade Level: Sr. H.S. Running Time: 29 min. Rental: $12.50. Purchase: $150. B&W.

The story of one school dropout illustrates the personal problems and the danger to America caused by the high rate of school dropouts. This film considers the reasons which impel students to lose interest in school. It portrays a positive community program of attacking this problem, especially through work experience and remedial reading.

Drug Abuse: The Chemical Tomb. Producer/Distributor: FDI, 1969. Grade Level: Jr. & Sr. H.S. through Adult. Running Time: 19 min. Rental: $15. Purchase: $225. Color.

This film classifies and examines the drugs that are coming into more and more widespread use in American schools and colleges: the anesthetics, the depressants or "downers," "red devils," seconals, the nembutals or "yellow jackets," the tuinals or "rainbows," "hearts," "peaches," airplane glue, gasoline, ether, paint thinner, deodorants, LDS, marijuana and THC ("no-cal alcohol").

The film exposes pitfalls such as dependence, infection, mind alteration, brain damage, accidental doses, and convulsions.

Due Process of Law Denied. Producer/Distributor: TFC, 1952. Grade Level: Sr. H.S. through College. Running Time: 29 min. Rental: $105. B&W.

This presentation dramatizes the dangers of decisions based on emotion and those of denying the constitutional rights of an individual. The film is taken from the 20th Century-Fox feature motion picture *The Ox-bow Incident.* It portrays the lynching of three innocent men by Nevada townspeople in 1885, when an unsubstantiated report of a murder results in the formation of an illegal vigilante group.

Duke Thomas, Mailman. Producer/Distributor: CF. Grade Level: Primary through Elementary. Running Time: 15½ min. Purchase: Color, $180; B&W, $90.

This is a true documentary, taking children into the workday of a real mailman, showing sights and sounds of the post office, contacts with the community along the route, and the "feel" of a day of work. Narrated by a black mailman in his own words.

Encounter at Kwacha House. Producer/Distributor: NFBC, 1969. Grade Level: Sr. H.S. through College. Running Time: 17 min. Rental: $12. Purchase: $100. B&W.

A group of Negro and white youths gather at an interracial club in Halifax, Nova Scotia, to discuss discrimination in employment and housing, the limitations of education for Negroes, the kind of protest action that is taking place in the United States, and what such action might accomplish in Halifax.

The English Language: Patterns of Usage. Producer/Distributor: CORF, 1970. Grade Level: Jr. & Sr. H.S. Running Time: 11 min. Purchase: Color, $130; B&W, $65.

A dialogue between four people of different ages with divergent social, racial and regional backgrounds and professions, demonstrates the many ways words and usage vary. A difference in vocabulary, pronunciation and construction of sentences and phrases, readily apparent in conversation, also reflects a speaker's attitudes in formal and informal situations.

Ephesus. Producer/Distributor: CFS, 1965. Grade Level: Jr. H.S. through Adult. Running Time: 25 min. Rental: $15. Purchase: $150. B&W.

A remarkable example of religious devotion is preserved on film as it happens at a Sunday evening service in a Negro "Holiness" church. The film portrays this religion that believes in the "active" participation of the congregation.

Epitaph for Jim Crow. Producer/Distributor: NET/IU. Running Time: 30 min. Purchase: $85. B&W.

This series of illustrated film-lectures on the dynamics of intergroup relations in the United States focuses on the history and current situation of the Negro American. The historical, political, sociological and psychological forces which shape patterns of prejudice and discrimination are reviewed, and new advances in intergroup relations are discussed. Dr. Thomas Pettigrew of the Harvard University faculty is host narrator.

Fourteenth Generation American This film tells the history of the Negro American, and contributions by Negroes to all aspects of American life are emphasized.

Face to Face Dr. Thomas Pettigrew explores the problems of bringing diverse groups together and the value of various kinds of contact in actually bettering intergroup relations.

A Tale of Two Ladies This film reviews the history of Negro protest against racial discrimination.

The Newest New Negro The meaning and value of the newest forms of direct-action protest against segregation are discussed with Whitney Young, Director of the National Urban League.

Conformity and the Crutch The psychology of bigotry and the difference between pathological bigotry and bigotry arising out of social conformity are discussed in light of recent sociological research.

Employing the Disadvantaged. Producer/Distributor: BNA/UM. Grade Level: Sr. H.S. through Adult. Running Time: 45 min. Rental: $12. Color.

Through a sampling of five individual approaches, this documentary shows how American business and industry are facing up to the challenge of hard-core unemployment. The response of disadvantaged workers to these programs is also shown.

Equal Protection of the Laws. Producer/Distributor: BFI, 1967. Grade Level: Sr. H.S. through Adult. Running Time: 30 min. Rental: $15. Purchase: $330. Color.

This documentary film utilizes the integration of Riverside, California to provide a background for a focus on conflicts between Negroes and Caucasians. Conflicting views concerning the meaning of the 14th Amendment are expressed. The film gives examples of infringement of the principles in the 14th Amendment and furnishes a background for discussions on integration and civil rights.

Equality Under the Law: Lost Generation of Prince Edward County. Producer/Distributor: EBEC/MSU, 1967. Grade Level: Jr. & Sr. H.S. Running Time: 25 min. Rental: $6.50. Purchase: $224. Color.

The schools of Prince Edward County, Virginia, were closed in 1959 by the County Board of Supervisors to avoid integration in accordance with the historic Brown decision of the Supreme Court in 1954. During the period schools were closed, county grants were made to help white children attend private, segregated schools. In 1963 the Supreme Court reaffirmed the Brown decision. Although a Supreme Court injunction opened these schools to Negro and white, many white children continue to attend private schools.

Everybody's Prejudiced. Producer/Distributor: MGH, 1961. Grade Level: Jr. H.S. through Adult. Running Time: 21 min. Rental: $12. Purchase: $155. B&W.

This film presents a comparison between the kind of prejudices we all employ and the unreasoning prejudices of the bigot. The theme of this film is that people are prejudiced against people and things which they do not understand or with which they are unfamiliar. As the film progresses, rational judgment decreases until in the final example, the characteristics of a bigot are evidenced.

Exchanges. Producer/Distributor: ACI, 1969. Grade Level: Sr. H.S. through Adult. Running Time: 10 min. Rental: $15. Purchase: $100. B&W.

An encounter is depicted between a Negro man and a white girl on a train. The film is open-ended, with electronic music and without narration; a mixture of realistic and expressionistic styles.

Eye of the Beholder. Producer/Distributor: REYP, 1955. Grade Level: Sr. H.S. through Adult. Running Time: 25 min. Rental: Color, $40; B&W, $25. Purchase: Color, $300; B&W, $250.

This film dramatizes the story of twelve hours in the life of Michael Gerard, an artist. After a brief introduction of cartoon illustrations which makes the point that we can easily be misled (the old shell game, the top hat illusion, the ambiguous cube figure), we see Michael in his studio, standing amid a disarray of spilled paints and a knife, with an apparently lifeless young woman lying on a couch. From here, the film flashes back to give the impressions Michael has made in the minds of five people with whom he has come in contact: waiter, mother, cabbie, landlord, and cleaning woman.

Family Living and Sex Education. Producer/Distributor: CAROUF, 1968. Grade Level: Primary through Elementary. Running Time: 9½ min. Purchase: $125. Color.

All Kinds Of Babies Provides the child with an understanding of the universality of birth—that all babies come from eggs, either from within or outside the body; and that babies are helpless, must be cared for, and loved.

It Takes a Lot of Growing Reassures the child of his place in the social structure of the family unit. Shows how his father and mother differ physiologically and their role as parents.

Being Boys and Girls How boys and girls become aware of and learn to accept their bodily differences; how they develop, and discover that they will one day become men and women, and parents.

Becoming Men and Women Shows how heredity and environment affect growth and development. Discussed are the boy-girl relationship; the adolescent's social and physical needs; the necessary habits of personal hygiene and tips on nutrition.

Felicia. Producer/Distributor: ADL, 1965. Grade Level: Jr. & Sr. H.S. Running Time: 12½ min. Rental: $7.50. Purchase: $75. B&W.

This film shows the corrosive effects of prejudice. Felicia, a junior in high school, lives with her mother, an older brother and younger sister in Watts. Felicia is black. Many adults in her community are jobless. Most of her classmates see no future for themselves because of their color. But Felicia has a goal—education—and she wants to help make Watts a good place in which to live. Filmed prior to the Watts riot.

The First Hundred Years. Producer/Distributor: HU. Running Time: 28 min. Color.

This film presents the story of Howard University to 1961; its campus and activities; famous graduates and baccalaureates. A prize-winning production.

The First Step. Producer/Distributor: GROVE. Running Time: 6½ min. Rental: $25. Purchase: $95. B&W.

This film documents a handicraft outlet store for the products of black people in Jackson, Mississippi; also shows young people being trained in film techniques.

First World Festival of Negro Arts. Producer/Distributor: CAROUF. Running Time: 20 min. Code No. 407954. Rental: $8.50. Purchase: $180.

What significance can we attribute to Negro art today? How wide is its diffusion and influence within Africa and elsewhere? What has been the scope of its contacts with alien cultures, in particular with European and Western culture? These are some of the main questions which the first World Festival of Negro Arts has helped to answer in this film. Taking place in Africa and attended by the most highly respected experts on African culture, this symposium was arranged to affirm the value and endurance of African art. The film presents impressions of this historic meeting at Dakar, West Africa, focusing on treasures of African art as it explains the influences of Negro culture through the ages and the artistic values it has given to the world. A co-production between UNESCO, the Alexander Sahia Studio (Bucharest) and the Romanian National Commission for UNESCO.

Flatland. Producer/Distributor: MGM.

This is an animated film depicting the tale of a Square who lives in Flatland, and the difficulties he encounters in trying to convince his two-dimensional society of the existence of a third dimension. This is included among films treating prejudice in general.

Follow the Leader. Producer/Distributor: CAROUF, 1968. Grade Level: Elementary through Adult. Running Time: 23 min. Purchase: $135. B&W.

This is an unusual motion picture containing extraordinary camerawork and an original music score. The dialogue is terse and sometimes frightening as improvised by the youthful actors involved in a make-believe children's war-game.

For All My Students. Producer/Distributor: UC, 1966. Grade Level: College, Adult. Running Time: 35 min. Rental: $10. Purchase: $175. B&W.

This film portrays an integrated high school classroom situation; many Negro pupils are failing. The reasons are society, home, the pupils themselves, school curriculum, teachers. Student feelings as well as teacher doubts and frustrations are expressed in order to stimulate meaningful discussion and effective teaching.

Forgotten Man. Producer/Distributor: UM, 1957. Grade Level: College. Running Time: 29 min. Rental: $3.

Milestones in the progress of education in the South are described, including statements by Booker T. Washington; observations by Walter Hines Page; the Supreme Court on desegration.

Frederick Douglass: The House on Cedar Hill. Producer/Distributor: MGH/
    MSU, 1951. Grade Level: Jr. H.S. through Adult. Running Time: 17 min.
    Rental: $12.50. Purchase: $130. B&W.

This is a biography of Frederick Douglass, showing his contributions as a
writer, orator, statesman, and leader of the Negro people. Photographs and
drawings present Douglass alongside such figures as Abraham Lincoln, John
Brown, and Susan B. Anthony. Douglass is presented as part of the vital events
of American history during a major part of the nineteenth century.

Frederick Douglass (Profiles in Courage). Producer/Distributor: SAUDEK/
    MSU. Grade Level: Jr. H.S. through Adult. Running Time: 50 min.
    Rental: $9.

This film shows how Douglass' revelation of his true identity as an
escaped slave in order to work openly for the Abolitionist Movement made him
subject to recapture under the Fugitive Slave Act and forced him to live in exile
until he could raise money to purchase his freedom.

Free At Last. Producer/Distributor: AIM. Grade Level: Sr. H.S. through Adult.
    Running Time: 30 min. Rental: $6.50.

This film uses dramatic readings from the works of Frederick Douglass,
Booker T. Washington, W. E. B. DuBois and Marcus Garvey to trace the history
of the American Negro from emancipation to the end of World War II. The film
also discusses the influence of Washington, DuBois and Garvey on the present
Negro-white position in the United States. Part of the History of the Negro
People Series.

Friendly Game. Producer/Distributor: MMM/MSU, 1968. Grade Level: Sr. H.S.
    through Adult. Running Time: 10 min. Rental: $2.25. Purchase: $135.

A "friendly" game of chess between a white man and a black man
provides an opportunity to examine racist and capitalistic psychology. The film
attempts to establish a new common currency between the races.

From the Inside Out. Producer/Distributor: MGH, 1967. Grade Level: Jr. H.S.
    through Adult. Running Time: 24 min. Rental: $17.50. Purchase: $175.
    B&W.

This film was written and directed by Negro teenagers from North
Richmond, California. It frankly conveys problems of the streets and of discrimination which the Negro teenager faces. Included also are accounts of
projects in communities and the awareness that young people want their world
to be different from the one which black people experienced in the past.

From Runaway to Hippie. Producer/Distributor: FDI. Running Time: 18 min.
    Rental: $14. Purchase: $185. B&W.

This film shows the drop-outs and castaways whose damage to themselves
is only matched by their loss to society. This documentary was filmed where the
kids are, in shabby pads infested with vermin and disease, in doorways and
alleyways where they are often mugged, raped, beaten.

Fury. Producer/Distributor: TFC, 1947. Grade Level: Elementary through Sr.
    H.S. Running Time: 17 min. Rental: $52.50. B&W.

This film is an excerpt from the MGM feature motion picture *Fury.* The

Lynching Sequence shows irresponsible emotional agitators and how they inflame townspeople as they lead a mob in burning the jail when the sheriff refuses to surrender a prisoner being investigated on suspicion of kidnapping. The second segment, the Trial Sequence, portrays the shame and remorse of an entire community proven guilty of mass perjury in a selfish effort to protect twenty-two of its members on trial for lynch murder.

The Future and the Negro. Producer/Distributor: AIM. Grade Level: Sr. H.S. through Adult. Running Time: 75 min. Rental: $15.

This film presents a panel discussion on the subject of the Negro's future. The discussion covers the economic plight of the Negro in the United States and in the Negro nations, and emphasizes racism, which is felt to be deeply ingrained in people of the world. Part of the History of the Negro People Series.

The Future Is Now. Producer/Distributor: AIM, 1963. Grade Level: Intermediate through Adult. Running Time: 24 min. Rental: $5. Purchase: $95.

This film discusses the problem of prejudice towards minority groups in the areas of employment and education. The intensifying need for equality in education and employment is vividly emphasized through documentary interviews with minority group college students—including a Jewish student aware of "executive suite" barriers and a Negro who has broken the barriers and achieved a modicum of success.

The Game. Producer/Distributor: GROVE. Running Time: 17 min. Rental: $35. Purchase: $110. B&W.

This is a film of a New York ghetto, adapted from a play, in cooperation with Mobilization for Youth—an impressionistic presentation acted by Negro and Puerto Rican teenagers.

George Washington Carver. Producer/Distributor: ART. Running Time: 12 min. Purchase: $130. Color.

This documentary film is a sensitive, penetrating study of Dr. George Washington Carver. It presents his philosophy, his work, and his contributions to the field of science.

George Washington Carver. Producer/Distributor: BFA/VIGNET, 1967. Grade Level: Elementary through Sr. H.S. Running Time: 11 min. Rental: $5. Purchase: $70. B&W.

Using historic footage of Dr. Carver at work in his laboratory during the early 1930's, this film provides a documented account of the achievements of this great Negro American who was born a slave in 1864. His many important contributions toward agricultural research in this country are presented.

Getting a Job Is a Job. Producer/Distributor: DIBIE, 1968. Grade Level: Sr. H.S. through Adult. Running Time: 18 min. Purchase: $180. Color.

This informative, sometimes humorous film shows the correct procedure to follow in applying for employment. The film follows two young people as they seek employment, pointing out the right and wrong way of applying for a job.

Ghetto. Producer/Distributor: MYI, 1969. Grade Level: Sr. H.S. through Adult. Running Time: 15 min. Rental: $15. Purchase: $225. Color.

This film follows a day in the life of a young Negro in New York City. It is a frank look at the garbage and pollution of this inner city, told from the point of view of the young participants in a poverty project known as the cultural arts program of MFY-Henry Street. Its director is 20-year-old Richard Mason.

Gone Are the Days (*Purlie Victorious*). Producer/Distributor: AUDIOF, 1963. Grade Level: College, Adult. Running Time: 97 min.

Adapted from the Broadway play *Purlie Victorious*, the film presents a deliberately boisterous parody on segregation, bigotry, and civil rights. All its characters are intentional stereotypes. Ossie Davis is the author, and stars along with his wife, actress Ruby Dee. The film setting is in Georgia and shows the complications that develop when a Negro preacher attempts to build a church. The screenplay is also written by Ossie Davis.

Goodbye and Good Luck. Producer/Distributor: NET/IU, 1967. Grade Level: Sr. H.S. through Adult. Running Time: 30 min. Rental: $7.25. Purchase: $150. B&W.

This is a documentary showing an encounter between Black Power advocates and a Negro veteran from Vietnam. The Black Power arguments as well as viewing a draft protest march tend to confuse this veteran and make him unsure of the value of the role he has just played as a soldier in Vietnam.

Government and the Market. Producer/Distributor: LODGE/IU, 1963. Grade Level: College, Adult. Running Time: 30 min. Rental: $6.75. Purchase: $125. B&W.

This film discusses the roles government plays in the economy and the extent to which government actions have modified the operation of a free market. A film from the American Business System Series.

Grambling College. Producer/Distributor: WABC TV, 1968. Grade Level: Jr. H.S. through College. Running Time: 60 min. Color.

Grambling College, one of the largest predominantly Negro institutions of higher education in the Deep South, has been famous for producing outstanding athletes. This film relates how two men helped combat discrimination against Negroes being accepted on professional football teams.

Grammar. Producer/Distributor: UB/IU, 1958. Grade Level: College, Adult. Running Time: 29 min. Rental: $6.75. Purchase: $125. B&W.

Part I This film examines the structure, patterning, and classification of words, and explains how the linguist defines a word in terms of base, vowels, and stress patterns. It presents examples using nouns, verbs, and pronouns.

Part II This continuation of the discussion of grammar and word classification explains how adjectives, adverbs, and prepositions are indentified by structure rather than meaning. The structure of phrases and sentences are examined. Both films are from the Language and Linguistics Series.

Green Pastures. Producer/Distributor: CFS, 1936. Grade Level: Elementary through Adult. Running Time: 93 min. Rental: $25. B&W.

This film features an all black cast which does a supposedly black folklore version of the Bible. It is a screen adaptation of the famous Broadway play, starring Rex Ingram, George Reed, Eddie Anderson, Oscar Polk, Frank Wilson, and the Hall Johnson Choir. A black minister tells the story of the Bible to his Sunday School children, and the various stories—the creation, Adam and Eve, Noah, etc.—are shown as the children visualize them. Winner of many awards.

Green Power and Black Power. Producer/Distributor: UM, 1968. Grade Level: College, Adult. Running Time: 29 min. Rental: $7. Purchase: $90. B&W.

This program asks if the federal government is exercising its power to use economic sanctions to eliminate the racial discrimination that has produced the drive for Black Power. The no-holds-barred debate among Derrick Bell, deputy director of the Office of Civil Rights for the U.S. Department of Health, Education, and Welfare, Prof. Albert Wheeler of the University of Michigan Medical Center and Prof. Richard Julin of the University of Michigan Law School covers such questions as "Is the government spending enough and spending it wisely?" and "Is the government exercising any of its economic power to induce integration?"

Guilty of Conspiracy. Producer/Distributor: ADF. Running Time: 45 min. Rental: $50. B&W.

This is a series of three films on what happened in Chicago, who conspired, to what purpose, and who were the people involved on both sides. The film features positions set forth by ex-President Lyndon B. Johnson, Chicago's Mayor Dailey, J. Edgar Hoover, and President Richard M. Nixon.

Chicago, the Season's Change This film was made by the American Civil Liberties Union as a defensive answer to the mayor of Chicago. The film is a testimony to the question of who really conspired. Directed by Bill Jersey.

The Streets Belong to the People This film was directed by Ralph Diamond, who spent many days with the demonstrators in Chicago filming their plans, marches, rallies in Grand Park and at the hotel.

Yippie! The third film in the series was partly edited by Jerry Rubin. The film presents more of the action that was evident in the first two.

The Hangman. Producer/Distributor: MGH. Rental: $12.50. Purchase: $150.

Drawings are used in illustrate Maurice Argden's poem about the coward who lets others die to protect himself, and then becomes the hangman's final victim. This animated film conveys, in the simplest terms, the message that we are all responsible humans—and one day liable to answer for it.

Hard Way. Producer/Distributor: NET/IU, 1965. Grade Level: Sr. H.S. through Adult. Running Time: 59 min. Rental: $14.25. Purchase: $250. B&W.

The film focuses on slums, housing projects, public schools, and settlement houses in the St. Louis area. It makes the point that the United States is the richest country in the world and is troubled by the problems of the poor. Today's poor are contrasted with the poor of past generations. An analysis of the problems was done by S. N. Miller, Professor of Sociology at Syracuse University.

Harlem Crusader. Producer/Distributor: EBEC/FI, 1965. Grade Level: Sr. H.S. through Adult. Running Time: 29 min. Rental: $7.50. Purchase: $167.50. B&W.

This film portrays the effectiveness of Mr. Dan Murrow, an American Friends Committee social worker. He and his family lived for 5 years in a ghetto in Spanish Harlem (New York City) ; the film documents his work in a block on 111 Street.

Harlem Wednesday. Producer/Distributor: GROVE, 1969. Running Time: 10 min. Rental: $12.50. Purchase: $135. Color.

Water colors and sketches by Prestopino are combined with original jazz by Benny Carter to suggest the activities of an ordinary midweek day in New York's Harlem. Venice Film Festival award winner.

Harriet Tubman and the Underground Railroad. Producer/Distributor: MGH, 1964. Running Time: 54 min. Code No. 618086. Rental: $29. Purchase: $325. B&W.

This film describes the first nineteen trips Mrs. Tubman, a conductor on the Underground Railroad, made into slave territory between 1850 and 1860. Filmed with a notable cast that includes Ethel Waters, Ruby Dee and Ossie Davis. From the Great Adventure Series. In two parts.

Harvest of Shame. Producer/Distributor: MGH. Running Time: 53 min. Purchase: $275. B&W.

Edward R. Murrow narrates the story of the plight of migratory workers who harvest America's crops in Florida, Georgia, Virginia, New Jersey, New York, Michigan and California. The degradation and exploitation of millions of these workers is pointed out in this film. Arguments for and against the use of these farm workers are given. A CBS Reports documentary.

The Hat. Producer/Distributor: CFS, 1955. Grade Level: Primary through Adult. Running Time: 18 min. Rental: $15. Color.

This is a satirical cartoon about border soldiers and the absurd difficulties that result when one soldier's hat blows over the border line and cannot be retrieved. The film explores the need for world legal authority to establish disarmament and settle international disputes peacefully. With the voice of Dizzy Gillespie.

Head Start in Mississippi. Producer/Distributor: NET/IU, 1966. Grade Level: Sr. H.S. through Adult. Running Time: 60 min. Rental: $12. Purchase: $200. B&W.

This documentary focuses on the controversial Head Start program in Mississippi. The progress which has been made is shown through scenes of the children in their schools and interviews with the Negroes who run the program. Then an administrator from the Office of Economic Opportunity explains on camera why the funds for the Mississippi program are being stopped. The Negroes dispute the charges and claim the white Mississippians refuse to acknowledge that Negroes alone can successfully run a program.

Hear Us O Lord! Producer/Distributor: NET/IU, 1968. Grade Level: Sr. H.S. through Adult. Running Time: 51 min. Rental: Color, $15.50; B&W, $11.25. Purchase: Color, $360; B&W, $210.

School District 151 in Cook County, Illinois, became the first incorporated suburb in the nation ordered to desegregate its schools by means of bussing. To look at the responses of those involved, PBL reporters spent much time with the

Dan Lang family, their two children, and their neighbors in South Holland, Illinois. Many parents petitioned to keep schools closed awaiting an appeal from the district court. Mr. Lang did not want his children going to school with black children because, as he said, "they live differently, they dress differently, and they think differently."

Heavyweight, Inc. Producer/Distributor: TDI. Running Time: 59 min. B&W.

This is the story of Joe Frazier, heavyweight boxing champion of six states; a runaway kid who beat the odds and became a million-dollar corporation. He has lived his life on the premise that, with hard work, anything can be accomplished by blacks.

The Hecklers. Producer/Distributor: ROBECK, 1969. Grade Level: Sr. H.S. through College. Running Time: 35 min. Rental: $30. Purchase: $300. B&W.

This film, in no way a political film, shows actual meetings with leading politicians and very sincere hecklers in action.

Her Name Was Ellie, His Name Was Lyle. Producer/Distributor: DEROCH, 1966. Grade Level: Jr. & Sr. H.S. Running Time: 28½ min. Purchase: $69.70. B&W.

A young man discovers he has syphilis and must reveal the names of all his sexual contacts or expose them and others to the consequences of a deadly epidemic. The film tells how venereal disease is contracted; the insidiousness of the various stages; the importance of early treatment; the serious results if untreated. It underscores the danger of free-and-easy attitudes toward moral standards. The film is helping to combat the spread of venereal disease by bringing the subject out into the open, thus alleviating fear and ignorance.

Heritage of the Negro. Producer/Distributor: AIM. Grade Level: Sr. H.S. through Adult. Running Time: 30 min. Rental: $6.50.

This exploration of the heritage of the Negro examines the civilization and achievements of ancient Africa and their significance to the American Negro today. The film discusses the art, sculpture and present-day pageantry which reflect the old cultures. Part of the History of the Negro People Series.

Heritage of Slavery. Producer/Distributor: FA. Grade Level Sr. H.S. & College Running Time: 53 min. Rental: $10.50. Purchase: $300. B&W.

Examination of slavery and the attitudes established during slavery which still persist today. Descendants of plantation owners and present-day activists are interviewed, demonstrating the parallels between attitudes under slavery and now. Past influences on the present are shown. Graphics and readings from accounts by slave owners and slaves capture the quality of life in the days of slavery. History of slave revolts is reviewed and related to contemporary racial unrest.

Heredity and Environment. Producer/Distributor: KUHT/IU, 1960. Grade Level: Sr. H.S. through Adult. Running Time: 30 min. Rental: $6.75. Purchase: $125. B&W.

This film discusses the heredity-environment relationship in two ways:

environmental effects on the development of an individual, and environmental effects on the parents, which in turn might affect the offspring. The presentation explains the machinery and processes involved in what is actually inherited.

Heritage in Black. Producer/Distributor: EBEC, 1969. Grade Level: Sr. H.S. through Adult. Running Time: 27 min. Rental: $11.50. Purchase: $380. Color.

This film traces the black experience in America from the American Revolution (and the first rebel casualty, a black soldier) forward to the dream of Martin Luther King, Jr., to be "free at last!" Scene after scene documents the black man's intense participation in American life, the vital role he has played in the nation's growth and his contributions in every area of society are depicted.

Heritage of the Negro. Producer/Distributor: NET/IU, 1965. Grade Level: Sr. H.S. through Adult. Running Time: 30 min. Rental: $6.75. Purchase: $125. B&W.

This film explores the heritage of the Negro by examining the civilization and achievements of ancient Africa and their significance to the American Negro today. It explores the art, sculpture and present-day pageantry which reflect the old cultures.

Hey, Mama. Producer/Distributor: CFS, 1969. Grade Level: Sr. H.S. through College. Running Time: 18 min. Rental: $20. Purchase: $135. B&W.

This is an award-winning documentary which follows a typical family through a typical day in the Los Angeles ghetto. There is no narration or commentary; merely the voices and sounds of the people themselves. Among the events shown is an interview with the aging mother of sixteen children now left alone with her "white" TV set; young children marching drill as part of a black power training; a young man visiting a barber shop; a typical party; etc.

There are two versions of this film. In one of them, a particular scene in which profanity is used is abridged so that the profanity is eliminated.

High School. Producer/Distributor: OF, 1968. Grade Level: Jr. H.S. through Adult. Running Time: 74 min. Rental: $100. B&W.

This film deals with the ideology and values of a large urban high school as they emerge through encounters between students, teachers and parents in guidance sessions, college counseling, discipline, faculty meetings, corridor patrol, gym and classroom activity.

The High Wall. Producer/Distributor: MGH, 1952. Running Time: 30 min. Purchase: $135. B&W.

This film analyzes the emotional and mental attitudes behind intolerance and race prejudice, how these are taught to children by various influences in their environment, and how these prejudices qualify conduct.

History of the Negro in America. Distributor: MGHT. Grade Level: Jr. H.S. through College. Running Time: 20 min. each. Rental: $4.25 each. B&W.

Three films, part of the series History of the Negro in America, trace the growth and development of the American Negro in different periods of American history. Individual titles are: Part I, 1619–1860—Out of Slavery; Part II, 1861–1877—Civil War and Reconstruction; Part III, 1877–Today—Freedom Movement.

Hollywood, U.S.A. Producer/Distributor: ATLAP. 1964. Grade Level: Jr. H.S. through College. Running Time: 28 min.

Traces the assimilation of Negroes into the motion picture industry in the year after the 1963 NAACP resolution requesting Hollywood to remove barriers to the employment of Negroes. Pictures Negroes in numerous roles on television and in the motion pictures, including Sidney Poitier's performance in *Lilies of the Field* and his acceptance of the Academy Award for Best Actor in 1963.

Home of the Brave. Producer/Distributor: AUDIOF. Grade Level: College, Adult. Running Time: 86 min. Rental: $20. B&W.

Stanley Kramer's screen adaption of Arthur Laurents' Broadway hit emerges as a drama of exceptional power. A sensitive, educated Negro's wartime problems are shown in a flashback of his life, focusing on his wartime adventures with four white soldiers on a dangerous reconnaissance mission. Frank Edwards plays the Negro soldier.

Hooked. Producer/Distributor: CF, 1966. Grade Level: Jr. & Sr. H.S. Running Time: 20 min. Purchase: $125. B&W.

This is a powerful, sometimes shocking description of the experience of drug addiction told in the words of young (ages 18–25) former addicts who had been "cured" of their addiction for periods of time ranging from three months to two years. They talk with candor and indisputable authenticity about what impelled them to become addicted, how it affected their relationship with others and their perception of themselves, and the aversion and disgust with which they regard the experience in retrospect.

Hospital. Producer/Distributor: OF, 1969. Grade Level: Jr. H.S. through Adult. Running Time: 84 min. Rental: $100. Purchase: $1,000. B&W.

The day-to-day activities in a big city hospital are shown, with particular emphasis on the workings of the emergency ward and out-patient clinic. Relevant scenes include a college student recovering from an overdose of drugs and a young homosexual's session with his psychiatrist. The hospital is shown as an institution dealing with all the social ills of a community, not just strictly medical issues.

House on the Sand. Producer/Distributor: AUDIOF. Grade Level: College, Adult. Running Time: 75 min. Rental: $22.50. B&W.

This adult drama deals with the interracial tensions that result when an Iranian college exchange student falls in love with a Negro girl in the United States. It depicts the disapproval that develops in both the white and Negro communities over their relationship, a disapproval that ends in tragic death for the girl.

How To Live in a City. Producer/Distributor: IU. Grade Level: Sr. H.S. through Adult. Running Time: 30 min. Rental: $5.40. Purchase: $125. B&W.

This film documents the eternal city-bound dilemma—everything so near, but where is there room to stretch? The film examines the open-spaces dream to build a city with more living room, and questions whether the designers are making conformists out of city dwellers with their monotonous architectural designs.

How To Look at a City. Producer/Distributor: IU. Grade Level: Sr. H.S. through Adult. Running Time: 30 min. Rental: $5.40. Purchase: $125. B&W.

New York's ever-changing face is shown as seen by lovers, adventurers, and the star-struck; its buildings, some old and stately, others new and monotonous; the pathos of the old neighborhood; the bustle of the business world. Professor Eugene Raskin, architect and author, points to three fundamental standards used by architects and planners to judge the quality of a city's neighborhoods: human scale, density, and variety.

How To Say What You Mean. Producer/Distributor: KQED/IU, 1958. Grade Level: College, Adult. Running Time: 29 min. Rental: $6.75. Purchase: $125. B&W.

This presentation defines communication as a speaker-illusion relationship. The film explains the difference between a sign and symbol, and discusses the importance in communication of proper translation, which involves finding experiences to match other experiences. The point is made that it is never enough to simply say what you mean, but what you say must mean something to the listener. This involves being able to determine common areas of experience. A film from the Language In Action Series.

Howard E. Mitchell. Producer/Distributor: NET. Running Time: 59 min. Rental: $13. Purchase: $240. B&W.

This film presents scenes illustrative of the problems of the "inner city" and a profile of Howard Mitchell, professor of urbanism and human resources at the University of Pennsylvania, who is working toward solutions for many of these problems. Mitchell encourages his students to become community activists, and they are seen and heard not only in seminars but also at ghetto rallies and community improvement projects. Mitchell discusses the Negro's plight, the needs of the poor, and several rehabilitation projects.

Human Ecology and Drugs. Producer/Distributor: ADF, 1971. Grade Level: Sr. H.S. through Adult. Running Time: 30 min. Color.

The root cause of drug abuse is a feeling of helplessness in a civilization seemingly bent on self-destruction. The cure is a meaningful life. The film unmasks the culture of hypocrisy and emphasizes therapeutic techniques leading to self-determination and the creation of a new life. In production.

Hunger in America. Producer/Distributor: CBS, 1968. Grade Level: Jr. H.S. through Adult. Running Time: 54 min. Purchase: Color, $550; B&W, $275.

Pointing out that the United States is the richest nation in the world, the film pictures a situation of 10,000,000 men, women, and children going hungry daily. These people are the sharecroppers, Indians, and some other minorities. Even with government help, these people suffer from an extremely inadequate diet, as the film relates.

The Hurdler. Producer/Distributor: NYT/ARNO, 1969. Grade Level: Elementary through College. Running Time: 15 min. Purchase: $200. Color.

This film deals with the late Charles Drew, the Negro doctor whose pioneering research in blood plasma led to the modern blood bank system. The film follows Dr. Drew's determined hurdling of racial barriers, from his diligent drive for honors at Amherst through his struggling research in blood plasma to his breakthrough achievement in establishing the first blood banks for the American Red Cross.

I.Q. and Crime. Producer/Distributor: IU, 1958. Grade Level: Sr. H.S. through Adult. Running Time: 30 min. Rental: $6.75. Purchase: $125. B&W.

This film discusses and refutes some often-heard ideas about the relationships between mental ability and crime. Presents interviews with two delinquents—one high, one low in mental ability. Each interview is followed by a discussion of the case.

"I Have a Dream": The Life of Martin Luther King. Producer/Distributor: BFA/MSU. Grade Level: Jr. H.S. through Adult. Running Time: 35 min. Rental: $6.50. Purchase: $210. B&W.

This film tells the story of this dedicated man's life; the forces that brought him to the leadership of his people are explored, with actual news film footage. The film brings a better understanding of the philosophies and ideals that he exemplified. In telling the story of Dr. King, the civil rights movement of the 1950's and '60's plays an integral part. A CBS News documentary.

I See Chicago. Producer/Distributor: AIM, 1964. Grade Level: Jr. & Sr. H.S. Running Time: 28 min. Purchase: $90. B&W.

Interviews with parents and employers are conducted in an effort to determine the conditions that cause high drop-out rates and what is being done to find useful employment for these people. Whitney Young, president of the National Urban League, discusses what should be done to keep these youths in school.

I'm A Man. Producer/Distributor: Yale University, 1970. Grade Level: Sr. H.S. through College. Running Time: 20 min. Rental: $24.00. Purchase: $275.00. B&W & Color.

Appealing to the conscience of white America from the heart of the ghetto, Peter Rosen's film, *I'm A Man*, documents the personal and ideological struggle for freedom and manhood of black militant John Barber. Set in the "model city" of New Haven, Connecticut, the portrait of Barber begins with him, supplemented with the proud and powerful sounds of Muddy Waters singing Bo Didley's "I'm A Man." The film explains why years of immersion in America's cauldron of racial strife and years of non-violent pleas for understanding have converted John Barber and his fellow black intellectuals to radical militancy.

I'm Here Now. Producer/Distributor: BRAN, 1965. Running Time: 30 min. Rental: $15. Purchase: $135. B&W.

This film is comprised of still photographs and film footage taken of many residents in New York's slums. In the summer program of 1965, conducted by the Archdiocese of New York in cooperation with the Office of Economic

Opportunity, a series of recreational activities were conducted in city streets—parades, dances, crafts sessions, carnivals, and variety shows.

I'm Sorry. Producer/Distributor: COMMUN. Grade Level: College, Adult. Running Time: 30 min. Rental: $5.75.

This film presents the story of an older teen-age boy living in the slums of Jersey City. It shows life in a black ghetto; expresses the hundred-year-old feelings of the Negro; and is left open-ended as to the Negro's future.

Immigrant From America. Producer/Distributor: NYT, 1970. Grade Level: Elementary through College. Running Time: 20 min. Purchase: $240. Color.

Beginning with an actual, spontaneous classroom confrontation, the film looks deeply at racism and prejudice in America. It shows how white immigrants gradually scaled the ghetto walls, while millions of blacks became ghetto prisoners.

In the Name of the Law. Producer/Distributor: NBC/UM, 1969. Grade Level: Sr. H.S. through Adult. Running Time: 14 min. Rental: $4.50. Color.

This film discusses how violence characterizes today's society: the endless clash of blacks against white; how each sees what happens differently; how the people of the slums see the police as an army of occupation and the symbol of oppressive power; how arrests are interpreted as racist acts which frequently incite riots; how police are caught between black rage and white fear. The question is raised as to whether the need is for law and order, or for justice.

In Search of a Past. Producer/Distributor: CBS, 1968. Running Time: 53 min. Rental: $9.75. Purchase: $300. B&W.

A six-week visit to Ghana by three black Washington, D.C., high school students was filmed by CBS News. An effort was made to discover how pertinent Africa is to today's black American. Through the eyes of these three young people, African civilization is examined. The students conclude that their heritage is, after all, in the country that their forebears helped to build and defend.

Incident on Wilson Street. Producer/Distributor: MGH, 1964. Running Time: 51 min. Purchase: $250. B&W.

This film demonstrates how a school and teacher trained in guidance react to an in-school "incident" when a child strikes out at her teacher: the child's frustrations, the father's hostility to the child's classmates, the teacher's unwillingness to keep the child in her class, the principal's reactions, and the comprehension of the situation by the child's classmates.

Individual Motivation and Behavior. Producer/Distributor: WGBHTV/IU, 1962. Grade Level: Sr. H.S. through Adult. Running Time: 30 min. Rental: $6.75. Purchase: $125. B&W.

This film deals with individual motivation and behavior within groups. It explores with individuals from the demonstration group the basis for their own actions: one member is anxious to leave; one is disturbed by the arguments; one is looking for the approval of the others; another feels threatened by the "domineering" attitudes of others. A film from the Dynamics of Leadership Series.

The Initiation. Producer/Distributor: PIC, 1969. Grade Level: Sr. H.S. through College. Running Time: 45 min. Rental: $50. Purchase: $350. B&W.

Paul Lammer's visual poem gives the viewer new eyes for seeing the amputee—not just the missing limbs but the bruised and deformed psyche of such a man and his threatened manhood.

Integration: Report I. Producer/Distributor: CMC, 1960. Grade Level: Jr. H.S. through Adult. Running Time: 22 min. Purchase: $135. B&W.

An on-the-spot documentary report of student sit-ins, protest meetings, and rallies in Montgomery, Alabama, Washington, D.C., Greenville, South Carolina, and New York City.

Interview With Bobby Seale. Producer/Distributor: SFN, 1969. Grade Level: Elementary through Sr. H.S. Running Time: 20 min. Rental: $25. Purchase: $150. B&W.

Bobby Seale, sentenced to four years for contempt of court in the Chicago conspiracy trial, was interviewed in San Francisco County Jail by Newsreel in December 1969. He discusses the black nation, women's liberation, and the direction we must take in combatting fascism.

An Interview With Bruce Gordon. Producer/Distributor: MGH, 1964. Running Time: 17 min. Rental: $12.50. Purchase: $150. B&W.

This study provides a good point of departure to a launching of mature discussion of problems of human rights. Bruce Gordon, a 22-year-old organizer of the Student Non-Violent Coordinating Committee, was interviewed in Selma, Alabama, during the drive to register Negro voters. This young man explains his views about life, man, God, human dignity, freedom, and the Civil Rights movement.

Is Justice Color Blind? Producer/Distributor: UM, 1964. Grade Level: Sr. H.S. through Adult. Running Time: 27 min. Rental: $5.50. B&W.

The Honorable Wade H. McCree, U.S. District Court, Eastern Michigan, and Professor R. Julin of the University of Michigan Law School consider whether the American Negro today receives fair treatment in the American scheme of justice. Negro-police relations, legal representation, bail, judge and jury problems are considered. Part of the American Negro Series.

The Island Called Ellis. Producer/Distributor: MGH. Running Time: 53 min. Purchase: $550. Color.

This film presents a history of immigration prior to World War I, showing the problems facing immigrants to this country, the struggle to make a living in a foreign land, and their contributions to the country. The film is narrated by Jose Ferrer. Produced by NBC News-Project 20.

I Wonder Why. Producer/Distributor: CAROUF, 1965. Running Time: 5½ min. Rental: $7.50. Purchase: $75. B&W.

This film tells the story of a young Negro girl as she wonders why some people do not like her. The girl's love for the common elements of life—nature, people, games, and religion—are expressed.

"*J.T.*" Producer/Distributor: CAROUF, 1969. Grade Level: Primary through
Adult. Running Time: 51 min. Purchase: Color, $575; B&W, $275.
"*J.T.*" is the story of J. T. Gamble, a shy, lonely child. Through his devotion to a wounded alley cat, J.T. gets people a little closer to what is real and important in life. And he finds his own pride and dignity as well.

Jackie Robinson. Producer/Distributor: SF, 1965. Grade Level: Jr. & Sr. H.S.
Running Time: 27 min. B&W.
This film presents the life story and deeds of baseball player Jackie Robinson. From Biography Series LC No. FIA66–117.

The Job. Producer/Distributor: ADL, 1964. Grade Level: Sr. H.S. through
Adult. Running Time: 29 min. Purchase: $75. B&W.
This sometimes humorous but biting satire attacks the hypocrisy of using the race angle as a promotion gimmick for "selling" movies, plays, or books. Part of the Study in Color Series.

The Job Corps and You. Producer/Distributor: DEROCH, 1967. Grade Level:
Jr. & Sr. H.S. Running Time: 14½ min. Purchase: $76.50. Color.
This film is designed to show youth how they can gain work experience and occupational training away from home. It shows the Job Corps settings; the types of work experience; the occupational and educational training offered; and other basic information, such as home leave, pay, and recreational activities.

The Job Developer. Producer/Distributor: DEROCH, 1969. Grade Level: Jr. &
Sr. H.S. Running Time: 10¼ min. Purchase: $62.05. Color.
This documentary-style film follows an actual Job Developer from a meeting with a trainee, where he learns the trainee's interests, to meetings with other community agencies and employers, where he seeks out existing job opportunities and develops new openings.

Jobs in the Automotive Trades. Producer/Distributor: DEROCH, 1968. Grade
Level: Jr. & Sr. H.S. Running Time: 10 min. Purchase: $16.20. Color.
This fast-moving film offers a fresh insight into the many interesting and rewarding jobs in automotive trades. It begins with pit mechanics on the track making split-second adjustments on a racing car at the height of the Indianapolis 500, moves into a host of automotive job sites and jobs, and includes an interview scene between a service manager and an applicant seeking an entry job. Actual job duties are described as the work is being performed.

Jobs in the Baking Industry. Producer/Distributor: DEROCH, 1969. Grade
Level: Jr. & Sr. H.S. Running Time: 6½ min. Purchase: $48.45. Color.
The never-ending demand for daily breads and pastries opens many job opportunities for men and women. The baker's art is appetizingly illustrated with scenes showing the making of baked goods from simple breads and pastries to intricately hand-iced cakes.

Jobs in Clerical Work. Producer/Distributor: DEROCH. Grade Level: Jr. & Sr. H.S. Running Time: 10 min. Purchase: $61.50. Color.

This film explores the many opportunities for today's clerical worker and stresses the necessity for every applicant to acquire the basic skill of typing as well as the ability to transcribe rapidly. In the growing adoption of electronic computers throughout the nation, excellent opportunities are becoming available—particularly to those men and women who have acquired skill and experience in clerical work.

Jobs in Cosmetology. Producer/Distributor: DEROCH. Grade Level: Jr. & Sr. H.S. Running Time: 10 min. Purchase: $61.20. Color.

This film explores the wide variety of skills providing gainful employment in the hairdressing and cosmetology profession to thousands of men and women of all ages. It details the procedures and qualifications, as well as the training for a successful career as a licensed beautician.

Jobs in Health. Producer/Distributor: DEROCH, 1967. Grade Level: Jr. & Sr. H.S. Running Time: 10½ min. Purchase: $62.90. Color.

This film portrays many of the jobs and opportunities in health services for youth. Emphasis is put on the duties and responsibilities of nurse aides, orderlies, laboratory and x-ray technicians, therapist assistants, medical secretaries and others.

Jobs in the Sheet Metal Trades. Producer/Distributor: DEROCH, 1969. Grade Level: Jr. & Sr. H.S. Running Time: 9½ min. Purchase: $57.80. Color.

The film opens by showing sheet metal workers assembling sections for helicopter fuselages, then moves on to the fabricating shops where sheet metal working tools and machines are being operated by both men and women. From there the film moves on to a mechanical contractor's shop. A fourth job location is the Metal Sign and Trim Shop.

Jobs in Small & Major Electric Appliance Repair. Producer/Distributor: DEROCH, 1968. Grade Level: Jr. & Sr. H.S. Running Time: 7 min. 10 sec. Purchase: $51. Color.

This film captures the drama and interest of jobs and occupations in a high-demand field. It opens with a full dialogue scene featuring a route repairman and his helper at work during an emergency repair call in a private home; moves into a number of job sites and work situations in repair shops, showing workers repairing both small and major appliances from steam irons to electric stoves. The film includes a scene with an entry worker receiving on-the-job instruction in the repair of a new type of electric knife.

Job Opportunities in Hotels and Motels. Producer/Distributor: DEROCH, 1968. Grade Level: Jr. & Sr. H.S. Running Time: 10½ min. Purchase: $57.80. Color.

A bellhop is interviewed by the hotel's personnel manager to plan his future in the hotel business. Entry-level jobs and promotion possibilities are outlined as the film tours the laundry, housekeeping and engineering departments. Year-round jobs in motels, being similar in scope to those in the larger hotels, are illustrated as the film moves from the front desk, through kitchen and dining room operations, to backstage of the banquet hall and "on stage" in the hotel pub.

Joshua. Producer/Distributor: ADL, 1968. Grade Level: Jr. H.S. through Adult. Running Time: 16 min. Purchase: $100. B&W.

This film presents the conflicts of an 18-year old boy from the black ghetto as he encounters white society; his fears, his pent-up anger, his growing awareness that he can successfully compete in the world outside. The film's plot shows how much can be accomplished when people join together in a common effort.

Just Sign Here. Producer/Distributor: HBBB, 1969. Grade Level: Sr. H.S. through Adult. Running Time: 14½ min. Color.

This film presents a very fair treatment of the credit problem in a low income community, at once revelatory and constructively informative; of general interest, though set in New York's Harlem.

Justice and the Poor. Producer/Distributor: NET/IU, 1967. Grade Level: Sr. H.S. through Adult. Running Time: 60 min. Rental: $13. Purchase: $240. B&W.

The inequities of the poor when faced with legal problems are explored. According to this film, the poor are not well treated by the police, are penalized by the bail system, and have difficulty obtaining a qualified lawyer. A variety of attempts to rectify these problems are presented in this film.

Justice, Liberty and Law. Producer/Distributor: CF, 1968. Grade Level: Sr. H.S. through College. Running Time: 22 min. Purchase: $220. Color.

This film presents an introduction to one of the profound conflicts of a free society: how a government is to enforce order while providing justice and a maximum of freedom to the individual. The film sets the Bill of Rights in historical perspective and provides an introduction to the other films in the series which deal with specific Amendments.

Search and Privacy Discusses the concepts of the 14th Amendment.

Speech and Protest Discusses the concepts of the 1st Amendment.

Interrogation and Counsel Discusses police efficiency and the administration of justice; and the concept of greater protection for the individual against the machinery of law.

Justice Under Law. Producer/Distributor: TFC, 1952. Grade Level: Jr. & Sr. H.S. Running Time: 30 min. Rental: $105. B&W.

This presentation emphasizes the ideal of justice under the laws of the United States. A prosecuting attorney in a murder trial becomes convinced of the innocence of the accused. Instead of seeking the man's conviction, the prosecutor disproves the evidence which appears to implicate the prisoner and obtains his acquittal. (Based on a case in which Homer S. Cummings, 1870–1956, United States Attorney General in President Franklin Roosevelt's administration, was the prosecutor.) Excerpt from a 20th Century-Fox feature motion picture, *Boomerang.*

The Jungle. Producer/Distributor: CF, 1967. Grade Level: Sr. H.S. through Adult. Running Time: 22 min. Rental: $5.10.

This film pictures the life of black ghetto youths. Philadelphia gang members tell their own story as they make this film about their violence, rivalries, and loyalties. The 12th and Oxford Street Gang reacts to success and acceptance of production to become 12th and Oxford Street Film Makers Corporation.

Kindergarten. Producer/Distributor: CAROUF. Running Time: 21 min. Purchase: $120. B&W.
This film emphasizes the value of physical, intellectual, emotional, and social stimulation in kindergarten.

Ku Klux Klan: The Invisible Empire. Producer/Distributor: CAROUF/ADL, 1967. Grade Level: Jr. H.S. through Adult. Running Time: 45 min. Rental: $8. Purchase: $250. B&W.
This CBS Reports film traces the history of the Klan and its resurgence at every point where strides have been made in civil rights. Included are filmed sequences of an actual Klan meeting, footage of a Klan rally and cross-burning held in Ohio, and interviews with Klansmen who reveal the bigoted savagery of this organization whose goal is the total violation of the rights of minority groups.

The Lady in the Lincoln Memorial. Producer/Distributor: NYT/ARNO, 1970. Grade Level: Intermediate through Sr. H.S. Running Time: 28 min. Purchase: $200. Color.
In a dramatic blend of live footage and newsreels, photographs and drawings, this film follows Marian Anderson's career from childhood to her early singing days in churches and small concert halls (and her first taste of Jim Crow trains and "whites only" hotels), through her triumphant concert tours of Europe and America, to her historic concert at the Lincoln Memorial in 1939 after a racist policy denied her the use of Constitution Hall.

Law and Order. Producer/Distributor: OF, 1969. Grade Level: Jr. H.S. through Adult. Running Time: 81 min. Rental: $100. Purchase: $1,000. B&W.
This film is about the routine day-to-day activities of the Kansas City Police Department. The film deals with the role of the police in the toughest district of the city, the nature of their contacts with the community, and the diversity and complexity of the police role in American society. Some of the events in the film include arrests of a car thief and a prostitute, a hold-up of a clothing store, ambulance service, and family fights.

The Law Protects the People. Producer/Distributor: TFC, 1959. Grade Level: Intermediate through Adult. Running Time: 20 min. Rental: $70. B&W.
This film explains the checks and balances of the American judicial system by dramatizing events in the life of a small-town judge who declares unconstitutional a law which was hastily enacted in the closing minutes of a session of the state legislature. Excerpt from an MGM feature motion picture, *A Family Affair.*

Lay My Burden Down. Producer/Distributor: NET, 1966. Grade Level: Sr. H.S. through Adult. Running Time: 60 min. Rental: $120. Purchase: $200. B&W.
This film presents the plight of the southern Negro tenant farmer whose earnings average less than $1,000.00 per year. Economically and educationally,

the future of the tenant farmer's children is not bright; their one hope is the recently obtained right to vote.

Legend of Jimmy Blue Eyes. Producer/Distributor: AUDIOF. Running Time: 22 min. Rental: $15. Color.

An Academy Award nominee and a U.S. entry at the Cannes Film Festival, this modern day version of Negroes in agony and ecstasy is told in a narrative poem style with a jazz score.

Legislative Process. Producer/Distributor: IU, 1954. Grade Level: Jr. H.S. through Adult. Running Time: 28 min. Rental: Color, $10; B&W, $7. Purchase: Color, $250; B&W, 135.

This film uses the General Assembly of Indiana to portray a state legislature in action as it passes a bill through the various steps to become a law. The presentation includes animated sequences to chart the steps in the process and shows the roles played by the House and Senate chambers, the committees, the Legislative Bureau, the Attorney General, the lobbyists, and the Governor in creating the laws of the state.

Lilies of the Field. Producer/Distributor: AUDIOF, 1963. Grade Level: Elementary through Adult. Running Time: 94 min. Rental: $50. B&W.

Sidney Poitier stars in this story of an ex-G.I. who encounters five strangely dressed women attempting to farm some barren Arizona acreage. He accepts a day's work and learns that they are refugee nuns from behind the Iron Curtain to whose order the land has been willed. He also makes the astonishing discovery that Mother Maria intends for him to erect a chapel on the grounds of a collapsed adobe barn. The challenge of the stubborn, demanding, dedicated Mother Superior finds a response in the young man, for he has something to prove to himself as well.

Listen, Whitey. Producer/Distributor: ADF. Running Time: 26 min. Rental: $50. Purchase: $200.

The black community reacts to the assassination of Dr. Martin Luther King.

A Little Fable. Producer/Distributor: CFS, 1960. Grade Level: Primary through Adult. Running Time: 4 min. Rental: $5. Purchase: $60. Color.

A UCLA Animation Workshop film by Bob Pike, this is an award winning stylized cartoon dealing with racial prejudice. It stars Happy Chollie, a little orange blob who has always wanted to be sprayed blue. One day, with his mother's permission, he gets his wish, and rolls happily around town until he meets another blue boy. He invites his new-found friend to supper; and he and his friend are instructed to first wash off their blue paint. They do, whereupon his mother decides there isn't enough supper for the boy friend, and he is asked to go home. The boy friend, who is green underneath his blue paint, reluctantly obeys; and after he is gone Happy Chollie's mother informs her son that "I don't mind you bringing home blue boy friends . . . but from now on make sure they're orange underneath."

Lonnie's Day. Producer/Distributor: CORF, 1969. Grade Level: Elementary through Sr. H.S. Running Time: 13½ min. Purchase: Color, $162.50; B&W, $81.25.

Filmed by cameramen who virtually lived with a Negro family for two months, *Lonnie's Day* is an honest, sympathetic portrayal of life in a big-city public housing project, giving a keener awareness of the basic concerns of a ghetto child.

Losing Just the Same. Producer/Distributor: NET/IU. 1966. Grade Level: Sr. H.S. through Adult. Running Time: 60 min. Rental: $12. Purchase: $200. B&W.
The despair of many Negroes living in urban centers in the United States is highlighted by a mother with ten children. In spite of being on welfare and being surrounded by poverty, this mother dreams of success for her children. Her son drops out of high school to earn money to realize his dream of owning a fine car. When the boy is accused of arson and sent to jail, the dreams of both the mother and son are shattered.

M. D. T. A. (Manpower Development Training Act). Producer/Distributor: DEROCH, 1967. Grade Level: Jr. & Sr. H.S. Running Time: 5 min. Purchase: $42.50. Color.
This film shows how the M. D. T. A., through experienced instructors, provides counseling and assistance in developing employable skills in job areas with established labor shortages.

Making It. Producer/Distributor: MTP, 1970. Grade Level: Elementary through Adult. Running Time: 27 min. Rental: Free. Color.
This film demonstrates how young Negro men have achieved job success. Black youth can now follow in their footsteps. It focuses on average young people, and it stresses the need for better employment, education, housing and control of their own destiny.

Malcolm X, Struggle for Freedom. Producer/Distributor: ADF. Running Time: 25 min. Rental: $22.50.
This film shows Malcolm X in Europe and Africa—three months before his last speech.

Man Alive—The World Health Organization. Producer/Distributor: MGH.
Narrated by Sir Alec Guinness, the film traces the history of the World Health Organization.

Management, Motivation & The New Minority Worker. Producer/Distributor: RTBL. Running Time: 43 min. Rental: Color, $60; B&W, $40. Purchase: Color, $450; B&W, $275.
This film deals frankly and openly with the problems encountered by leadmen, foremen or supervisors in handling hard-core employees. For those who teach supervisors in this difficult area, this film provides a vehicle which carries the discussion to the heart of the problem.

Marijuana. Producer/Distributor: CAROUF, 1969. Grade Level: Intermediate through Adult. Running Time: 52 min. Purchase: $275. B&W.
This film documentary is about the "turned-on" generation and the widespread use of marijuana by youth today. Judges, lawyers, congressmen, policemen, and the young people involved express their views.

Marian Anderson. Producer/Director: LES-MSU. Grade Level: Sr. H.S. & College. Running Time: 30 min. B&W. Rental: $4.75.

Vignettes of the great singer's life, from her early years through her Town Hall recital, where she presents a program of favorites, including such traditional spirituals as "O, What a Beautiful City," "He's Got the Whole World in His Hand," "Crucifixion," and "Deep River."

Marked For Failure. Producer/Distributor: MSU, 1965. Grade Level: Jr. H.S. through Adult. Running Time: 59 min. Rental: $12. Purchase: $200. B&W.

This film examines the educational handicaps of children from depressed areas. In describing proposed solutions, particular attention is focused on a pre-nursery pilot project in the New York City schools. Documentary film footage is included to illustrate important points.

Martin Luther King. Producer/Distributor: ROBECK, 1968. Grade Level: Sr. H.S. through College. Running Time: 30 min. Rental: $25. Purchase: $250. B&W.

This is an unusual filmed interview with the Rev. Dr. Martin Luther King, Jr., winner of the Nobel Peace Prize.

Martin Luther King, Jr.: From Montgomery to Memphis. Producer/Distributor: BFA, 1969. Grade Level: Jr. H.S. through Adult. Running Time: 26½ min. Rental: $15. Purchase: $170. B&W.

Dr. Martin Luther King, Jr. first rose to national prominence as a result of his courageous leadership in a struggle against bus segregation in Montgomery, Alabama. Influenced by his example, and often under his active guidance, a mass movement developed to oppose the pervasive system of segregation in the South. Civil rights campaigns in Albany, Georgia, and Birmingham, Alabama, and the massive march in Washington, helped bring about meaningful civil rights legislation. Dr. King was awarded the Nobel Peace Prize in 1964. In Memphis, on April 4, 1968, Martin Luther King, Jr. was assassinated.

Martin Luther King: The Man and the March. Producer/Distributor: NET/IU, 1967. Grade Level: Sr. H.S. through Adult. Running Time: 83 min. Rental: $17. Purchase: $325. B&W.

This documentary records the preparations for the "Poor People's March" and Dr. Martin Luther King's role in it. Dr. King is shown soliciting support at rallies, schools, and from people he met during his travels. The picture also shows his aides working for support from other ethnic groups. This film ended prematurely because of the tragic death of Dr. King.

Martin Luther King: A Man of Peace. Producer/Distributor: JOU, 1964. Grade Level: Elementary through Adult. Running Time: 30 min. Rental: $15. Purchase: $200.

This film shows portions of sermons, speeches and interviews with Martin Luther King, giving an insight on his ethic of love and its power against injustice. He describes his philosophy of non-violence and its pacifist roots in both the Old and New Testaments of the Bible and in Gandhi and his methods. This film also shows him accepting the Nobel Peace Prize.

Men In Cages. Producer/Distributor: CAROUF, 1966. Grade Level: Sr. H.S.
through Adult. Running Time: 52 min. Purchase: $275. B&W.

This CBS Reports film investigates the criminal—from first offender to
the hardened repeater—and his life behind bars. CBS News Correspondent
Roger Mudd and Reporter Warren Wallace take the viewer into some of the
worst penal institutions in the country. Among the matters touched upon are the
overcrowding of jail systems, the confinement of young first offenders with
hardened repeaters, and the difficulties in finding work for men who have been
removed from the world for a number of years. This film is about the sort of
people who go to prison, what happens to them there, and what is being done
and can be done to keep them from returning after they have served their
terms.

The Messenger From Violet Drive. Producer/Distributor: NET/IU, 1964. Grade
Level: Sr. H.S. through Adult. Running Time: 30 min. Rental: $6.75.
Purchase: $125. B&W.

Elijah Muhammad, leader of the controversial Black Muslin movement,
discusses Muslim views, including their desire for total separation of blacks from
white in America.

Mingus. Producer/Distributor: ADF. Running Time: 60 min. Rental: $125.

This film presents a psychological and social portrait of the great jazz
artist, Charlie Mingus.

A Minority Problem. Producer/Distributor: ADL. Grade Level: Jr. H.S. through
Adult. Running Time: 28 min. B&W.

This film analyzes the problems and possibilities of adopting minority
children.

Mixed Marriages. Producer/Distributor: ROBECK, 1969. Grade Level: Sr. H.S.
through College. Running Time: 30 min. Rental: $30. Purchase: $300.
B&W.

This film depicts problems and troubles that may face a mixed marriage—a marriage between a man and a woman of different races.

Moonlight Witness: Abe Lincoln, Lawyer. Producer/Distributor: TFC, 1967.
Grade Level: Elementary through Sr. H.S. Running Time: 20 min.
Rental: $70. B&W.

In the midst of his preparations for his debates with Stephen A. Douglas,
Abraham Lincoln defends William Armstrong, the son of a friend and bene-
factor, who is charged with murder. Lincoln's skillful defense, highlighted by
his famous use of "The Farmer's Almanac" to refute testimony of the prosecu-
tion witness, wins his client's acquittal.

A Morning for Jimmy. Producer/Distributor: AIM, 1964. Grade Level: Sr. H.S.
Running Time: 28 min. Rental: $5. Purchase: $90.

The story of a young Negro boy who encounters racial discrimination
while seeking employment, but who learns a lesson for the future. Jimmy
becomes aware that with proper education and training he can obtain employment in a field of his choice and can attain a place in society.

My Childhood: Hubert Humphrey and James Baldwin. Producer/Distributor: BFI, 1966. Grade Level: Jr. H.S. through Adult. Running Time: 49 min. Rental: $30. Purchase: $300. B&W.

The two-part film is an absorbing study of contrasts in the childhoods of two famous Americans—one white, from a small town, and loved; the other black, from an urban ghetto, and rejected. The film underscores the effects that parental influence and environment have on the forming of a man. Part I: Hubert Humphrey's South Dakota. Part II: James Baldwin's Harlem.

My City. Producer/Distributor: MLA, 1969. Grade Level: Elementary. Running Time: 20 min. Rental: $10. Purchase: $300. Color.

Experiences of three children show positive approaches to the opportunities in their respective big-city hometowns. The film is designed to develop an appreciation of one's environment on the part of children growing up.

My Own Yard To Play In. Producer/Distributor: MGH, 1959. Running Time: 7 min. Purchase: $110. B&W.

This social documentary of children at play was photographed on the streets of New York. Included are the songs, thoughts, and fantasies of these children. This film offers insight into children's behavior, creativity, and adaptation to environment.

The Name of the Game Is . . . Basketball. Producer/Distributor: MTP, 1969. Grade Level: Sr. H.S. Running Time: 28 min. Rental: Free. Color.

In thrilling action and instructive slow motion, Oscar Robertson, John Havlicek, Wes Unseld, Elvin Hayes, and 11 more great stars of the NBA demonstrate the techniques that brought them stardom. Includes fitness tips.

Negro American. Producer/Distributor: BFA, 1966. Grade Level: Jr. H.S. through Adult. Running Time: 15 min. Rental: $70. Purchase: $165. Color.

This film portrays briefly the history of the Negro from the time he was transported from Africa into slavery in this country to the present. Included are the accomplishments of many Negro Americans, such as Frederick Douglass, George Washington Carver, and Booker T. Washington. Negroes doing their part in wars, territorial expansion, government, and in the struggle for equality are also presented. This film focuses on the values of education to Negro people and furnishes a background for discussion of the American Negro.

The Negro and the American Promise. Producer/Distributor: NET/IU, 1963. Grade Level: College, Adult. Running Time: 60 min. Rental: $73. Purchase: $250. B&W.

The late Dr. Martin Luther King, the late Malcolm X, Dr. Kenneth Clark, and James Baldwin discuss their motivations, doctrines, methods, goals, and place in the American Negro's movement for social and racial equality.

Negro Heroes From American History. Producer/Distributor: BFA/MSU. Grade Level: Intermediate through Jr. H.S. Running Time: 11 min. Rental: $4. Purchase: $125. Color.

This film is an introduction to the history of the Negro in America, through the biographies of several heroes from the Revolutionary War to the present day. The film demonstrates the richness of the Negro contribution and its deep roots in our history. An Atlantis-Simons Film.

Negro in Pennsylvania History. Producer/Distributor: DIS, 1968. Running Time: 24 min. Rental: $5.10.
This film traces the Negro movement from the South to Pennsylvania, from colonial times through Civil War to the present, and shows the effects of abolition efforts and stations in the underground railway system. Advances and problems in education, employment and civil rights are described. Uses still photos and film clips.

Negro Slavery. Producer/Distributor: MGH, 1969. Running Time: 25 min. Code No. 666006. Rental: $16. Purchase: $275. Color.
This film shows the development of slavery as an institution in the United States and depicts the life of the American slave. It explores the history of slavery in the United States and its development into an important part of the economy of the country. It depicts the life of the American slave and describes the gradual division of American society over the slavery issue, which culminated in the Civil War.

The Negro and the South. Producer/Distributor: AIM. Grade Level: Sr. H.S. through Adult. Running Time: 30 min. Rental: $6.50.
This film interviews both Negroes and whites of Mississippi to depict "the Southern way of life." White persons interviewed include a mayor, a sheriff, and a judge. Negroes interviewed include a teacher, a mechanic, and a minister. Part of the History of the Negro People Series.

Neighborhood Youth Corps. Producer/Distributor: DEROCH, 1967. Grade Level: Jr. & Sr. H.S. Running Time: 7½ min. Purchase: $51. Color.
This film demonstrates how young people can stay in school and continue their education while earning needed money and gaining work experience at jobs that need to be done, or, if they have dropped out, how they can gain work experience, earn money and be helped to employment opportunity.

New Mood. Producer/Distributor: AIM. Grade Level: Sr. H.S. through Adult. Running Time: 30 min. Rental: $6.50.
This film reviews the civil rights struggle of the past decade and traces the impact of the new Negro militancy on both white and Negro Americans. It also reviews the implications of the 1956 Supreme Court decision repudiating the doctrine of "separate but equal" facilities in public schools and elsewhere. Part of the History of the Negro People Series.

New Thing. Producer/Distributor: NTAAC, 1969. Running Time: 17 min. Color.
This film deals with the program of young black cultural organizations located in Washington, D.C. The film seeks to make young blacks proud of themselves and of their heritage by giving definition to the culture of the black community and by developing appreciation for it. The film creates an atmosphere in which creative exchange inspired by experienced artists can occur.

The Newcomers. Producer/Distributor: UMC, 1963. Grade Level: Adult. Running Time: 29 min. Rental: $8. Purchase: $140. B&W.

The migration of families from Appalachia into Cincinnati in search of work is pictured with all of the frustrations that face a displaced people. To meet a problem of such dimensions the need for agencies to pool their resources is also emphasized.

The Newest New Negro. Producer/Distributor: NET. Running Time: 30 min. Purchase: $85. B&W.

The meaning and value of the newest forms of direct-action protest against segregation are discussed with Whitney Young, Director of the National Urban League.

A Nice Kid Like You. Producer/Distributor: UC/EMC, 1969. Grade Level: Sr. H.S. through Adult. Running Time: 38 min. Rental: $15. Purchase: $250. B&W.

Drugs, sex, parents, and the failures of modern America as seen through the eyes of college students are discussed forthrightly and on-camera in this documentary film.

No Handouts for Mrs. Hedgepeth. Producer/Distributor: NCF/UM. Grade Level: Jr. H.S. through Adult. Running Time: 27 min. Rental: $8.50. Color.

Poverty is shown through the eyes of a Durham, North Carolina, domestic as she moves back and forth between the shack she lives in and the plush home of her employer. The film offers insight into lives of the working poor, and questions United States' commitment to its disadvantaged.

No Hiding Place. Producer/Distributor: EFLA. Grade Level: Sr. H.S. through Adult. Running Time: 50 min. Rental: $8. Purchase: $250. B&W.

The film exposes the evils of "block-busting" perpetrated by unscrupulous real estate dealers upon suburban home owners. It dramatically traces the events in a neighborhood into which a Negro family has just moved, and it reveals how block-busting tactics create panic and tension, frequently causing the collapse of an entire community.

No Hiding Place: Minority Life in the Suburbs. Producer/Distributor: ADL, 1969. Grade Level: Sr. H.S. through Adult. Running Time: 58 min. Purchase: $240. B&W.

This documentary probes the racial tensions in a suburban town. Through interviews, residents reveal that the problems of the black community have no effect on the majority of whites. But a minority of black and white residents who "dare to trust each other" seek to establish meaningful communication.

No Jail Can Change Me. Producer/Distributor: UC/EMCC, 1968. Grade Level: College, Adult. Running Time: 30 min. Rental: $10. Purchase: $180. B&W.

This film presents an interview between Warren Wells, a 21-year-old black man who since the age of ten has spent all but a few scattered months of his life in correctional institutions, and a counselor from the Northern California Service League. The interview, following six months of regular interviews, was videotaped in a county jail, preparatory to Wells' release, and is a study of an inmate's attempt to deal with the authorities who control his freedom and his life.

No Man Is an Island. Producer/Distributor: CAROUF, 1961. Grade Level: Jr. H.S. through Adult. Running Time: 29 min. Purchase: $135. B&W.

This film presents the story of a young Causcasian man and a Negro whose friendship matured during army service. Attempting to continue their friendship in civilian life, both are confronted with the prejudices of families and friends. This picture makes a strong appeal to the conscience of anyone who professes a religious faith.

No Other Choice. Producer/Distributor: MGH. Rental: $6. Purchase: $75.

This film stresses cooperation as an essential part of human activity.

No Tears for Kelsey. Producer/Distributor: AF, 1969. Grade Level: Sr. H.S. Running Time: 27 min. Rental: Color, $16.75; B&W, $10.75. Purchase: Color, $270; B&W, $135.

Kelsey escaped the slums because he learned to squelch his emotions. Now his teenage daughter has run away from home, lost her virginity, used pot, totally rejected her parents' values and been taken to juvenile hall for truancy. But Kelsey is controlled. He asks "Why?" She answers that they never listened to her, but the "Beautiful People" did. Then she breaks and reveals that all was not so beautiful.

No Vietnamese Ever Called Me Nigger. Producer/Distributor: ADF. Running Time: 65 min.

Black Vietnam veterans and Harlem residents speak out against Vietnam, link it to domestic racial crisis.

Not Left To Chance. Producer/Distributor: IU, 1954. Grade Level: Sr. H.S. through Adult. Running Time: 20 min. Rental: $5. Purchase: $100. B&W.

This film presents a group discussion about common community problems. Illustrates good discussion techniques as a PTA president, a dean, a minister, a restaurant owner, a health officer, and a county sheriff deal with problems of venereal disease and juvenile delinquency.

Not in My Block. Producer/Distributor: AF/AIM, 1963. Grade Level: Sr. H.S. Running Time: 48 min. Rental: $7.50. Purchase: $125.

This film presents an analysis of the housing situation as it affects the Negro minority in the urban community. Interviews with executives, banks, real estate agencies and builders reveal the problem as they see it. Interviews with Negroes of low income, middle-class and upper middle-class families reveal their experiences in obtaining housing.

Nothing But a Man. Producer/Distributor: BFI, 1963. Grade Level: Sr. H.S. through Adult. Running Time: 92 min. Rental: $50. B&W.

This film highlights the predicament of all people whose basic situation is that of Duff and Josie: the difficulty of being a man, of preserving dignity and integrity, and living in peace and hope, under oppressive economic, social, and political conditions. This film was awarded the 1965 National Council of Churches of Christ Prize for a picture which portrays human society and its cultural environment in such a way as to enhance general understanding of the family of man in its richness and variety.

The Novel: Ralph Ellison on Work in Progress. Producer/Distributor: NET/IU, 1966. Grade Level: Jr. H.S. through Adult. Running Time: 30 min. Rental: $6.75. Purchase: $125. B&W.

This film presents an interview with Mr. Ralph Ellison, during which he discusses his philosophy as to writers, American novels, the unity of the American spirit, and the genesis of his first novel, *The Invisible Man.* Further insight into the personality of Mr. Ellison is provided by a brief synopsis of his life and views of the interior of his apartment. He discusses his work in progress and reads from it; then he goes on to comment on how the Negro church has contributed to the eloquence of most Negro writers as well as to the American literary heritage in general. Mr. Ellison discusses his role as a teacher and how teaching keeps him in touch with the younger generation.

Now. Producer/Distributor: ICAIC-SFN, 1964. Grade Level: H.S. through College. Running Time: 5 min. B&W.

Presents a montage which captures the spirit and tempo of the civil rights movement, assembled from news footage and skills. Lena Horne sings the song "Now."

Now Is the Time. Producer/Distributor: CAROUF, 1968. Grade Level: Jr. H.S. through Adult. Running Time: 36 min. Purchase: $200. B&W.

This film serves warning that the black man is no longer satisfied with being a second-class citizen. The script—which includes the history of the Negro from the slave trade to the present—is drawn from the works of Langston Hughes, Countee Cullen, Malcolm X, Stokely Carmichael, and James Baldwin. The actors are Ruby Dee and Ossie Davis. This picture focuses on the feeling that all black patience has been exhausted. This documentary was produced by WCAU-TV Philadelphia.

Nutrition and Dental Care in Pregnancy. Producer/Distributor: IU, 1959. Grade Level: Sr. H.S. through Adult. Running Time: 29 min. Rental: $6.75. Purchase: $125. B&W.

This film discusses the dietary needs of the expectant mother and stresses the importance of proper diet for maintaining the mother's dental health and for developing the baby's teeth. A specialist in nutrition and a dentist serve as consultants.

Of Black America: Portrait in Black and White. Producer/Distributor: CBS, 1968. Grade Level: Elementary through Adult. Running Time: 54 min. Rental: $25. Purchase: $300. B&W.

This series of 8 films produced by CBS News examines various facets of historical and contemporary history of the black man in America. It includes filming in America and Africa and makes use of such personalities as John Conyers, and Bill Cosby.

This examination of black attitudes toward the white community and white attitudes toward the black community was produced with the use of a nationwide poll. CBS News prepared a 45-minute questionnaire and interviewed some 1,500 people. The results of these interviews show people's attitudes and feelings on the race question to be both subtle and complex.

Of Black America: Black History: Lost, Stolen, or Strayed. Producer/Distributor: CBS, 1968. Grade Level: Elementary through Adult. Running Time: 54 min. Rental: $35. Purchase: Color, $575; B&W, $300.

This film is a Bill Cosby guided tour through a history of attitudes—black and white—and their effects on the black American. It is a portrayal of some of the things that happen to an American if he is black. Cosby reviews black American achievements omitted from American history texts, the absence of recognition of Africa's contributions to Western culture, and the changing Hollywood stereotype of the black American.

Of Black America: The Black Soldier. Producer/Distributor: CBS, 1968. Grade Level: Elementary through Adult. Running Time: 26 min. Rental: $15. Purchase: $170. B&W.

This film narrated by Bill Cosby, illustrates the history of black American participation in America's armed forces. Paintings, drawings, cartoons and etchings of famous battles, as well as rare silent news footage of World War I, World War II, the Korean War and the war in Vietnam are shown.

Of Black America: Black World. Producer/Distributor: CBS, 1968. Grade Level: Elementary through Adult. Running Time: 53 min. Rental: $35. Purchase: Color, $575; B&W, $300.

In an international round-robin conversation, moderated by Mike Wallace, the black man's position in the world today is examined. Panelists Rep. John Conyers, Jr., in Washington, D.C., the Hon. Thomas Mboya of Kenya in Nairobi, Floyd McKissick of the Congress of Racial Equality in New York, and Dr. Alex Kwapong, Vice Chancellor of the University of Ghana, discuss the civil rights movement in America and how it looks to Africans.

Of Black America: Body and Soul—Body, Part I. Producer/Distributor: CBS, 1968. Grade Level: Elementary through Adult. Running Time: 24 min. Rental: $20. Purchase: Color, $300; B&W, $170.

An examination of the black American's contribution to sports in America is reported on by Harry Reasoner. Harry Edwards, leader of the Olympic Games boycott, is interviewed along with leading black athletes Tommie Smith, Lee Evans, Charlie Green, Jim Hines and Ralph Boston.

Of Black America: Body and Soul—Soul, Part II. Producer/Distributor: CBS, 1968. Grade Level: Elementary through Adult. Running Time: 28 min. Rental: $20. Purchase: Color, $300; B&W, $170.

Soul music is discussed in detail by singer Ray Charles. Mr. Charles explains that because of isolation and the misery and humiliation suffered by the American black man, he developed many of his own music and dance forms. Only through this outlet of rhythm and sound has the black man been able to release some of his frustration and grief. Singers Mahalia Jackson, Billie Holiday, and Aretha Franklin are presented.

Of Black America: The Heritage of Slavery. Producer/Distributor: CBS, 1968. Grade Level: Elementary through Adult. Running Time: 53 min. Rental: $35. Purchase: Color, $575; B&W, $300.

This film is an examination of slavery and the attitudes established during slavery which still persist today. CBS News reporter George Foster interviews descendants of plantation owners and present-day black activisits, demonstrating the parallels between attitudes under slavery and now. Graphics and readings from accounts by slave owners and slaves capture the quality of life in the days of slavery.

Of Black America: In Search of a Past. Producer/Distributor: CBS, 1968. Grade
 Level: Elementary through Adult. Running Time: 53 min. Rental: $35.
 Purchase: Color, $575; B&W, $300.
    A six-week visit to Ghana by three black Washington, D.C., high school students was filmed by CBS News. An effort was made to discover how pertinent Africa is to today's black American.

Omowale—The Child Returns Home. Producer/Distributor: AIM. Grade Level:
 Sr. H.S. through Adult. Running Time: 30 min. Rental: $6.50.
    This film pictures John Williams, Mississippi-born Negro, on an odyssey to Africa to explore his ancestral roots. Williams explores the relationship of the American Negro to Africa and the Africans. The film emphasizes that the Negro in the United States is several generations removed from the African Negro, both culturally and economically. Part of the History of the Negro People Series.

111th Street. Producer/Distributor: BRAN, 1962. Grade Level: Sr. H.S. through
 Adult. Running Time: 32 min. Rental: $6.60.
    This film presents a dramatic sequence of the difficult initial contact of a street club worker with a delinquent gang in New York. There is the testing out, the jeering, the suspicion, and the "freeze," which give the worker cause to question his ability and to seek support from his supervisors. Finally the worker accomplishes his first real breakthrough, but feels that his ultimate victory, should he achieve it, is infinitesimal compared with the magnitude of the problem.

One People. Producer/Distributor: ADL, 1946. Grade Level: Primary through
 Adult. Running Time: 10½ min. Purchase: $60. Color.
    This film shows how the United States was settled by groups of every nationality, and points out the various contributions of each group. An animated film, narrated by Vincent Price.

Operation Airco: A Story of Opportunity. Producer/Distributor: AIRCO, 1969.
 Grade Level: Elementary through Adult. Running Time: 13 min. Rental:
 Free. Color.
    This informational film describes Airco's integrated program with Cleveland's "AIM" project to train inner-city dropouts and high school men for careers in welding.

Operation Bootstrap. Producer/Distributor: EBEC, 1969. Grade Level: Sr. H.S.
 through College. Running Time: 58 min. Rental: $50. Purchase: $300.
 B&W.
    This film presents the story of the volunteer program that grew out of the ruins of Watts (Los Angeles)—how this program grew, expanded, and became a source of African cultural pride. A woman volunteer—on relief herself—made the first start with a welfare recipient's union where people could talk out their

problems. Profanity and the venting of pent-up feelings suggest teacher previewing before classroom use. Open discussions to help both blacks and whites discover more about each other reflect the language of the streets.

Operation Breadbasket. Producer/Distributor: FI, 1969. Grade Level: Jr. H.S. through College. Running Time: 65 min. Rental: $28.50. Purchase: $600. Color.

This film, written, directed, and narrated by Robert Culp, reports on the Operation Breadbasket arm of the Southern Christian Leadership Conference. Using methods of peaceful picketing, abstaining from buying certain products, and "buy-ins" of Negro produced or distributed products, Operation Breadbasket has obtained many jobs for blacks and supported small business men in its community. The film traces the history of Breadbasket since its inception in 1966 by Reverend Martin Luther King.

Opportunities in the Machine Trades. Producer/Distributor: DEROCH, 1968. Grade Level: Jr. & Sr. H.S. Running Time: 7 min. 10 sec. Purchase: $51. Color.

This film is a graphic presentation of the many job opportunities for beginners in this field. The film stresses good pay for entry workers and points out avenues for career advancement, including shop ownership for those who have mastered their trade. The picture opens with a testimonial. An actual shop owner drives home the opportunity theme with a case in point: M. D. T. A. graduates in his own shop who are on the way to advancement. Film moves to floor of machine shop depicting entry workers employed alongside experienced craftsmen and learning from them. We see workers at various machines and learn something about their operation and the work they perform. The film concludes showing a number of machinists' jobs in tool and die-making with operators manning complicated tool- and die-making machinery.

Opportunities in Sales and Merchandising. Producer/Distributor: DEROCH, 1967. Grade Level: Jr. & Sr. H.S. Running Time: 11¼ min. Purchase: $66.30. Color.

This film portrays the career opportunities in sales and merchandising occupations; how entry jobs fit into the career ladder; work settings; levels of occupations and information about preparatory work experience available through part-time work or a summer job in the retailing industry. Actual work settings and the occupational skills to be found in sales and merchandising are shown.

Opportunities in Welding. Producer/Distributor: DEROCH, 1968. Grade Level: Jr. & Sr. H.S. Running Time: 7 min. 11 sec. Purchase: $51. Color.

The film opens with a close-up of spot-welding in shop; cuts to manual welding, horizontal and vertical, and to instructional scene. It moves to job sites in shipyard where again we see the interest and challenge in welding jobs with workers performing automatic trackrod welding, flexcore and short-arc welding. Other job sites and jobs follow—from shop scenes showing the many kinds of welds and welding jobs that go into making boilers and fork-lift trucks, to aircraft maintenance showing workers using Heliarc equipment. It climaxes on construction site twenty stories up with plate and girder welding.

Or Die. Producer/Distributor: PSU-TAD, 1968. Grade Level: Sr. H.S. through
    Adult. Running Time: 18 min. Rental: $3.80.

    The film shows representative activities of Synanon, a social movement
run by former drug addicts. Includes a sequence on the Game, a form of group
therapy. The members of the Game group strip away any lies and excuses used
by any participant to rationalize his behavior. A sense of community life and
social action are shown to redirect self-destructive energies toward positive goals.

Organizing for Power—The Alinsky Approach. Producer/Distributor: FI/
    NFBC. B&W.

    A series of 5 films examining a method of organizing communities into
effective action units based on participatory democracy.

    People and Power Alinsky talks about his philosophy and the dynamics
of organization. 17 min. Purchase: $100. Rental: $8.50.

    Deciding to Organize A group of concerned citizens from Dayton, Ohio,
consult Alinsky on the means of creating an effective organization. 34 min.
Purchase: $170. Rental: $15.50.

    Building an Organization The obstacles encountered by a new community
action organization in Buffalo, N.Y., as it begins to work for recognition. 38 min.
Purchase: $190. Rental: $18.50.

    Through Conflict to Negotiation A community action group in Rochester,
New York, confronts the community's largest employer on the issue of corporate
responsibility and the employment of minority groups. 45 min. Purchase: $225.
Rental: $21.50.

    A Continuing Responsibility As demonstrated in the Woodlawn Organi-
zation in Chicago, Alinsky's techinque creates ongoing organizations firmly
rooted in the community. 43 min. Purchase: $225. Rental: $21.50.

The Other Face of Dixie. Producer/Distributor: CAROUF, 1962. Grade Level:
    Jr. H.S. through Adult. Running Time: 54 min. Purchase: $250. B&W.

    Although violence and conflict connected with racial segregation in some
southern cities received much publicity, this film depicts examples in other
communities in which the South demonstrated peacefully integrated schools,
wholesome Negro-white social and business relations, and mutual respect for
civil rights. The film was designed to present an inspirational impact.

Our Country Too. Producer/Distributor: AIM. Grade Level: Sr. H.S. through
    Adult. Running Time: 30 min. Rental: $6.50.

    This film explores the inner world of the American Negro—his values,
attitudes and impressions of life. Interviews at various places, including an
African rite in Harlem, a Negro debutante ball, the office of a Negro newspaper
and a Negro-owned radio station, help to depict the Negro's view of his world.
Part of the History of the Negro People Series.

Our Immigrant Heritage. Producer/Distributor: MGH. Running Time: 32 min.
    Purchase: $330. Color.

    This film traces the history of immigration in the United States, describ-
ing its social impact from the Revolutionary period to the present, and shows
how few groups have escaped discrimination at some time.

Our Race Problem. Producer/Distributor: NET/IU, 1959. Grade Level: Sr. H.S. through Adult. Running Time: 29 min. Rental: $6.75. Purchase: $25. B&W.

Part I: This film presents two points of view regarding the race problem in America. Harry Ashmore, editor of the *Arkansas Gazette* of Little Rock, represents the Liberal point of view. William Simmons, editor of the *Citizens Council* of Jackson, Mississippi, takes the conservative position. The interviewer is Dr. Houston Smith, Professor of Philosophy at Massachusetts Institute of Technology.

Part II: This film continues the discussion of the race problem in America. Dr. Benjamin Mays, President of Morehouse College in Atlanta, Georgia, and Mr. Charles Burton, Assistant County Agent in Greenville, Mississippi, present the Negro point of view. Both are interviewed by Dr. Houston Smith.

Palmour Street (Study in Family). Producer/Distributor: SEFPS, 1953. Grade Level: College, Adult. Running Time: 27 min. Rental: $5. Purchase: $162. B&W.

This film illustrates basic mental health concepts by showing ways parents can influence their children's mental and emotional growth, using the example of a Georgian Negro family and the mother's responsibility as stabilizing influence when the father is injured at work.

Panther Lawyer Speaks. Producer/Distributor: ADF. Grade Level: Sr. H.S. through Adult. Running Time: 36 min. Rental: $40.

This discussion between Panther attorney Charles Garry and Dr. Carlton Goodlett includes such topics as the history and persecution of the Black Panther Party, Bobby Seale's treatment at the Chicago Conspiracy Trial, the future of the Party, and the relation between U.S. imperialism abroad and fascism in the ghettos.

Paul Lawrence Dunbar: American Poet. Producer/Distributor: VIGNET. Grade Level: Intermediate through Sr. H.S. Running Time: 14 min. Purchase: $165. Color.

This film portrays the life of the American poet Paul Lawrence Dunbar, a Negro whose poems reflect pride in his race and heritage. It relates his struggles from age 13 when his father, an escaped slave who fought in the Civil War, died to his time of world wide fame. When he died at 33 years of age, he had already fashioned out of his rich heritage a wealth of poems, songs, plays, and novels.

People Are Different and Alike. Producer/Distributor: CORF, 1967. Grade Level: Primary through Intermediate. Running Time: 11 min. Purchase: Color, $130; B&W, $65.

This film shows that differences among people are easily seen by how they look, where they live, what they own. But it also emphasizes the likenesses of people—they all need friendship and love, food and a place to live; they want an education, fun and happiness. The film shows vividly that people are more alike than different.

The People Left Behind. Producer/Distributor: NET/IU, 1967. Grade Level: Sr. H.S. through Adult. Running Time: 31 min. Rental: $7.25. Purchase: $150. B&W.

This film shows the plight of unskilled labor in Mississippi. The people have no work because of the cotton picking machine, automatic machinery, the minimum wage laws, and removing land from cultivation. Both constructive and non-comprehending views of the plight of the unskilled laborers are presented.

Picture In Your Mind. Producer/Distributor: MGH, 1949. Running Time: 17 min. Purchase: $175. Color.
Phillip Stapps' animation presents the early roots of prejudice and the reasons why any group, tribe or nation, thinks its way of life is superior to the other man's mode of living. A plea is made to every individual viewer to reexamine his own thinking.

A Piece of the Action. Producer/Distributor: NBC/UM, 1967. Grade Level: Sr. H.S. through Adult. Running Time: 17 min. Rental: $6.50. Color.
This case history of the Detroit riots of 1967, where forty-three Americans were killed and thirty-eight injured, shows the response from industry and government, which resulted in programs for training workers, creating jobs and providing business opportunities. The presentation suggests that we can and must find ways to solve the problem of poverty in the black ghettos.

A Piece of the Cake. Producer/Distributor: NET/IU, 1969. Grade Level: Sr. H.S. through Adult. Running Time: 58 min. Rental: $13. Purchase: $240. B&W.
This film documents the efforts of Westinghouse Electric Corporation to recruit and train the hard-core unemployed and notes the problems relating to black and white attitudes.

Police and the Community. Producer/Distributor: DIBIE, 1969. Grade Level: Elementary through Adult. Running Time: 24 min. Rental: $8. Purchase: $260. Color.
This film examines the problems that have contributed to the tensions existing between the police and the community. Emphasis is placed on police relations with minority citizens. It presents a direct approach to the problem and offers suggestions as to what the police and the citizen might do to improve police and community relations.

Police Power. Producer/Distributor: NET/IU. Running Time: 60 min. Rental: $12. Purchase: $200. B&W.
This film presents a debate on the role of police power in a modern democratic society, including related issues such as conflicts between civil liberties and police methods, attitudes of the police and the public toward one another, and the effect of Supreme Court decisions on police authority.

Police Unit 2A26. Producer/Distributor: AEF, 1969. Grade Level: Jr. H.S. through Adult. Running Time: 18 min. Rental: $20. Purchase: $200. Color.
This documentary tells the vivid story of two policemen, one Negro and one white, as they go through a typical day. We see Officers Al Harvey and Denny Tipps with their families, learn of their hopes, see them at their station, and follow them in their patrol car at night. The film attempts to provide an insight on the problems of the police: from the student to the worker in the

ghetto, from a potential police officer to a teacher, from veteran policemen themselves to the general public.

Porgy and Bess. Producer/Distributor: Samuel Goldwyn, 1959. Grade Level: Sr. H.S. through Adult. Running Time: 116 min. Rental: rates by application. Color.

This film adaptation now available in 16mm features the well-known black entertainers Sydney Poitier, Dorothy Dandridge, Sammy Davis and Pearl Baily. Directed by Otto Preminger, the 1959 epic was written for screen by N. Richard Nash from the musical by George Gershwin.

The Poor Pay More. Producer/Distributor: NET/IU, 1967. Grade Level: Sr. H.S. through Adult. Running Time: 60 min. Rental: $12. Purchase: $200. B&W.

This film shows the various ways the poor pay more for food, furniture, appliances, etc. It portrays how they are bilked by finance companies, and it shows how government and private individuals are attempting to correct these evils.

Portrait in Black and White. Producer/Distributor: CBS NEWS-FA, 1968. Grade Level: Jr. H.S. through Adult. Running Time: 54 min. Rental: $9.75. Purchase: $300.00.

This examination of black attitudes toward the white community and white attitudes toward the black was produced with the use of a nation-wide poll. CBS News prepared a 45-minute questionnaire and interviewed some 1,500 people. The results of these interviews show attitudes and feelings on the race questions to be both subtle and complex.

Portrait of a Disadvantaged Child: Tommy Knight. Producer/Distributor: MGH, 1965. Grade Level: College, Adult. Running Time: 16 min. Rental: $3.80. Purchase: $125. B&W.

This is a documentary highlighting a day in the life of a slum child. The viewer is introduced to special problems, needs, and strengths of the inner city child, and is shown factors hindering Tommy's ability to learn. The film presents the contrast in home life and parental attitudes of disadvantaged children, showing that some homes are supportive and others neglectful. The viewer comes to understand that these children are not a nameless, faceless mass, but individuals with problems that must be treated as such, if they are to become effective citizens.

Portrait of the Inner City. Producer/Distributor: MGH, 1965. Grade Level: College, Adult. Running Time: 17 min. Rental: $3.80. Purchase: $125. B&W.

This camera-eye view of the streets, schools, and living quarters in the inner city of a large, urban community gives the viewer some idea of what life is like in the inner city, reflecting its uplifting as well as its degrading aspects. A shoeshine man, porter, carwash man, junkman, and an older brother serve as models for young Tommy Knight. Techniques for communication between school and inner city are shown.

Portrait of the Inner City School: A Place To Learn. Producer/Distributor:
     MGH, 1965. Grade Level: College, Adult. Running Time: 19 min. Rental:
     $4.60. Purchase: $125. B&W.
     This film shows a variety of teaching techniques, some good, some
ineffective, some harmful, and shows unconscious discrimination against the
culturally disadvantaged pupil. The film discusses how textbooks can discrim-
inate through illustrations and written materials which are unfamiliar to the
inner city child. Teachers discuss methods which have proved successful or
harmful. The viewer comes to see that school can be a place for the inner city
child to learn and grow toward maturity, or a place of confinement where the
child is forced into failure and frustration.

Portraits in Ebony. Producer/Distributor: ROBRTS. Grade Level: Jr. H.S.
     through College. Running Time: 30 min. Color.
     Depicts outstanding American Negro athletes in action in baseball, basket-
ball, football and track. Narration is in sports jargon.

Preparing for the Trial. Producer/Distributor: KETCTV/IU, 1958. Grade
     Level: Sr. H.S. through Adult. Running Time: 30 min. Rental: $6.75.
     Purchase: $125. B&W.
     This film continues the documentary-drama of a civil lawsuit based on an
automobile injury case, and dramatizes how both sides prepare for the trial.
This portion includes final checks on witnesses, conferences between the lawyers
and their clients, and research into the decisions of the courts in related cases. A
film from the Action at Law Series.

President Kennedy Speaks on the Bill of Rights. Producer/Distributor: TFC,
     1967. Grade Level: Elementary through Sr. H.S. Running Time: 4 min.
     Rental: $17.50. B&W.
     Photographed shortly before his tragic death on November 23, 1963, for
theater presentation to the nation on Bill of Rights Day, December 15, 1963, this
film presents President John F. Kennedy addressing American citizens on the
history and significance of the sacred privileges of the American way of life
guaranteed by the first ten Amendments to the United States Constitution.

The Price of a Life. Producer/Distributor: AFIC, 1968. Grade Level: Sr. H.S.
     through Adult. Running Time: 29 min. Rental: $6.10. Purchase: $100.
     B&W.
     This film traces the entire probation process, from the present investiga-
tion of a 25-year-old offender on his way to becoming a habitual criminal to the
means and methods by which probation can be strengthened with the more than
400,000 probationers now in the community.

Property Values and Race. Producer/Distributor: CCUSF. Running Time: 24
     min. Rental: $2. B&W.
     This film deals with what happens to property values when non-whites
move into a neighborhood. It is based upon an exhaustive study made by Dr.
Luigi Laurenti—over 10,000 home sales analyzed in San Francisco, Oakland and
Philadelphia. It gives the facts, supported by: (1) experiences in other cities;
(2) testimony of experts; and (3) statements of neighborhood residents.

Prudence Crandall. Producer/Distributor: IQF, 1964. Grade Level: Intermediate through College. Running Time: 50 min. Purchase: $300. B&W.

This portrait of one of the first attempts at school integration is about a Quaker school teacher in Connecticut in the nineteenth century who tries against violent opposition to maintain a school for Negro girls. Part of the Profiles in Courage Series.

Pull the House Down. Producer/Distributor: CAROUF, 1969. Grade Level: Jr. H.S. through Adult. Running Time: 38 min. Purchase: Color, $375; B&W, $225.

This film is a reflective, profound dialogue between two men of conviction: Harry Reasoner, and his son Stuart. Here they talk about the antagonism the "Establishment" feels toward its young, and the hostility with which the young rebels react. They range over such diverse topics as drugs, sexual promiscuity in suburbia, racism, greed, campus revolt, and the war in Vietnam.

Purchase and Use of the Car. Producer/Distributor: NET/IU. Running Time: 30 min. Rental: $5.40. Purchase: $125. B&W.

This film discusses how to buy a new car, how to buy a used car, the variable and fixed costs of car operations, economies in operating your car, and advertised gadgets. A film from the Driver Education Series.

The Quiet One. Producer/Distributor: AUDIOF/MSU, 1948. Grade Level: College, Adult. Running Time: 67 min. Rental: $25.

This film tells the story of a Negro boy, scarred with the rejection and indifference of his parents. Withdrawn into a state of shame and loneliness, he is sent to the famed Wilwyck School for treatment. There, under the guidance of a psychiatrist and counselor, he is slowly brought into the realization of his attitude and the actualities of a more normal life.

The Rafer Johnson Story. Producer/Distributor: ETM. Running Time: 53 min. B&W.

This film presents the story of a great athlete, decathlon champion and the first member of the Peace Corps.

A Raisin in the Sun. Producer/Distributor: AUDIOF. Running Time: 127 min. Rental: $25.

Lorraine Hansberry wrote the screenplay for this drama adapted from her own Drama Critics Circle Award winning Broadway production. The principal players are from the original cast. The story is one of humor, turmoil and pathos revolving around a Negro family, the Youngers, living in three crowded, sunless rooms on Chicago's South side. The squalid routine of their lives is suddenly disrupted when Lena Younger receives a $10,000 check from the company that insured her husband. The resulting dissension over disposition of the money results in a sinewy character study that comes closer than any previous film to define the Negro point of view.

Referred for Underachievement. Producer/Distributor: CMC, 1966. Grade Level: College, Adult. Running Time: 35 min. Purchase: $210. B&W.

This film presents an actual family intake interview between a psychiatrist; Leo, a 12-year-old referred for underachievement in school; his mother; father; older brother John; and three younger sisters. The session is lively, complex, sometimes hectic. As it progresses, the family's responses to the interviewer's questions reveal interrelationships and attitudes which have caused Leo to be identified as the patient. It is a good example of how family interviewing can help the mental health worker diagnose a situation and decide on the best course of therapy. It was produced specifically to give trainees a concrete illustration of an actual session and to stimulate discussion. Filmed by Dr. Edward A. Mason, Laboratory of Community Psychiatry, Dept. of Psychiatry, Harvard University. Ten study guides are included with each print.

Remedy for Riot. Producer/Distributor: MSU, 1968. Grade Level: Jr. H.S. through Adult. Running Time: 37 min. Rental: $7.25. Purchase: $200. B&W.
This film is based on findings by the President's Advisory Commission on Civil Disorders and presents the ghetto as a tinder box which can easily flare into disorder, murder, and looting. This is a CBS News Special Report.

The Report of the National Advisory Commission on Civil Disorders. Producer/ Distributor: ADL, 1968. Grade Level: Sr. H.S. through Adult. Running Time: 29 min. Purchase: $75. B&W.
This documentary is an interview by Dore Schary, producer, director and playwright, as he talks with Father Theodore Hesburgh, President of Notre Dame University and member of the U.S. Commission on Civil Rights. They discuss the Advisory Commission findings and call for individual commitment to purge prejudice from the American society.

The Revolution in the Colonial World. Producer/Distributor: IU, 1959. Grade Level: Sr. H.S. through Adult. Running Time: 29 min. Rental: $6.75. Purchase: $125. B&W.
This film discusses the revolution that has taken place in the colonial world and the present conflict between the remaining colonial powers of the West and the newly independent countries of Asia and Africa. Points out the major issues involved in this conflict by providing a condensed re-enactment of the U.N. committee debate on Algeria in 1955.

The Revolving Door. Producer/Distributor: AFIC, 1968. Grade Level: Sr. H.S. through Adult. Running Time: 30 min. Rental: $6.10. Purchase: $100. B&W.
This film follows the minor offender in a cycle of arrest-detention-trial-jail-release. Scenes include lower court and jail, trials in groups, visiting, eating, and recreational conditions. The film emphasizes the need to reform jail, probation, and rehabilitation, and shows pilot programs to ease the court's burdens and to provide presentencing information.

Richard Hunt: Sculptor. Producer/Distributor: EBEC, 1969. Grade Level: Jr. H.S. through Adult. Running Time: 12 min. Rental: Color, $6.50; B&W, $5.50. Purchase: Color, $167; B&W, $86.
This film studies the work and philosophy of the young black artist who has become one of America's foremost sculptors.

The Road Ahead. Producer/Distributor: AF/AIM, 1964. Grade Level: Sr. H.S. Running Time: 28 min. Rental: $5. Purchase: $90.

This film presents the dramatic and sensitively told story of a Negro and a white youth suddenly faced with jobless futures. Tim, who never completed high school, learns that job opportunities are scarce with his limited education. William, on the other hand, finds that his high school diploma opens the door to a promising future in a large electronics plant where he can receive on-the-job training for a skilled position.

Roosevelt City, Inc. Producer/Distributor: NET/IU, 1969. Grade Level: Sr. H.S. through Adult. Running Time: 9 min. Rental: $3.35. Purchase: $75. B&W.

This study of the newly incorporated Alabama city designed as a haven of self-determination for indigenous black citizens examines the program of self-determination. Because the city has very little money, all government officials and those providing community services, such as the police, are unpaid. It is stressed that there is an attempt to make all people desire to be involved in the operations of city government. This is one of a group of NET productions produced by black film makers to acquaint all people with black America.

The Run From Race. Producer/Distributor: IU, 1964. Grade Level: Sr. H.S. through Adult. Running Time: 29 min. Rental: $6.10. Purchase: $125. B&W.

This film depicts life and problems in a Negro community in Philadelphia. Negroes—a minister, a university professor, a real estate salesman, and a housewife—discuss the race and status story. The shambles of the colored center is set against the new town houses. The program asks the critical question—why do some stay when a neighborhood begins to integrate? Why do some run?

Sam. Producer/Distributor: AF, 1969. Grade Level: Jr. & Sr. H.S. Running Time: 27 min. Rental: Color, $16.75; B&W, $10.75. Purchase: Color, $270; B&W, $135.

Sam, an old vaudevillian, is the only human being left after the computers take over the world. They have kept him alive because of his unique talent. They create an experimental model programmed to be an actor and thus take his place. He is tortured as they seek to learn his routines. But he escapes and hides, determined to die with the secret of his talent. Then a little boy rouses him, and in time wins his heart.

Sanctuary and Spear: The Church in Revolution. Producer/Distributor: UM 1964. Grade Level: Sr. H.S. through Adult. Running Time: 30 min. Rental: $7. Purchase: $90. B&W.

The Reverend Louis Johnson, Pastor of Friendship Baptist Church in Detroit, describes, with the aid of pictures, the story of the Negro Church, a refuge in the nineteenth and early twentieth centuries, which has become in our time the church militant. The Reverend Gordon Jones of St. Andrew's Episcopal Church in Ann Arbor describes the role of white churches in the civil rights movement. Both men discuss the ecumenical side effects of the Negro revolution. Part of the American Negro Series.

Saul Alinsky Went to War. Producer/Distributor: MGH/UM, 1968. Grade Level: Sr. H.S. through Adult. Running Time: 57 min. Rental: $10. B&W.

This film is a portrait of Saul Alinsky, a white man in the middle of the Black Power revolution. He hires himself out to the poor and oppressed, instructs them in the art of protest, and sends them to do battle against the establishment through marches, sit-ins and riots. The film explores his thinking and working philosophy and his tactics in action; the "war" on Eastman Kodak by black people in 1964 serves as a case study of Alinsky's special brand of protest.

The Savages. Producer/Distributor: UC/EMC, 1967. Grade Level: College, Adult. Running Time: 25 min. Rental: $10. Purchase: $160. B&W.

This is a controversial film about black ghetto youth which the filmmaker calls "an introduction to contemporary inhumanity." The question posed for viewers is carried in the title: Is it the people or their surroundings which are savage?

The School's Environment. Producer/Distributor: EALING. Grade Level: Elementary. Running Time: 28 min. Color.

An inner-city fifth grade class learns to identify, categorize and map their immediate city environment.

A Second Chance. Producer/Distributor: NET/IU, 1966. Grade Level: Jr. H.S. through Adult. Running Time: 60 min. Rental: $12. Purchase: $200. B&W.

This film tells the story of a group of boys who are school dropouts, beginning with their departure from New York City and ending after their first 300 days at Fort Rodman, a Job Corps camp near New Bedford, Massachusetts. The problems, defeats, and triumphs of the teachers and trainees during this period are candidly shown as the boys progress from lonely individuals to a cohesive group.

The Seekers. Producer/Distributor: BFI, 1968. Grade Level: Sr. H.S. through Adult. Running Time: 31 min. Rental: $40. Purchase: $390. Color.

This is an honest film, unscripted, about young ex-drug abusers who tell about the physical and psychological damage they suffered, and how they learned to face reality instead of escaping from it through drugs.

Segregation: Northern Style. Producer/Distributor: CBS. Grade Level: Jr. H.S. through Adult. Running Time: 33 min. Purchase: $145. B&W.

This CBS Reports documentary film delves deeply into the social problems encountered by a Negro couple trying to buy a home in the suburban community of Bergen County, New Jersey. The evasions of less-than-ethical real estate brokers are seen and heard by the use of cameras with telephoto equipment and hidden tape recorders. The fact that most white home owners refuse to sell to Negroes is repeatedly stressed. Shown as a contrast, however, is the heartening demonstration of the successful integration of the Glenwood Lake Section of New Rochelle, New York.

Segregation in the Schools. Producer/Distributor: MGH/MSU, 1954. Grade Level: Sr. H.S. through Adult. Running Time: 28 min. Rental: $5.50.

This film presents the reactions of the citizens of two southern cities to the Supreme Court ruling against segregation in the schools. Those interviewed included both Negro and white civic leaders, teachers, parents, and students. From the See It Now Series.

Selected Negro Spirituals. Producer/Distributor: EBEC, 1952. Running Time: 10 min. Rental: $2.25. B&W.
 This film presents the contributions of the Negro spiritual song to American culture. A group of Negro singers present "Nobody Knows De Trouble I Seen," "Joshua Fit De Battle Of Jericho," and "Deep River."

Selma-Montgomery March—1965. Producer/Distributor: ADF. Running Time: 17 min. Rental: $20. Purchase: $100.
 The film depicts the historic march, protest and demand for voting rights.

Semester of Discontent. Producer/Distributor: NET/IU, 1965. Grade Level: Sr. H.S. through Adult. Running Time: 60 min. Rental: $12. Purchase: $200. B&W.
 Faculty, students, administration, and educational experts from major universities examine conditions at the University of California (Berkeley), Princeton, and Cornell. Discussed are the changing demands and attitudes of the teaching profession and the strain placed upon universities by the demand to make higher education available to everyone.

A Sense of the Future. Producer/Distributor: UM, 1964. Grade Level: Sr. H.S. through Adult. Running Time: 30 min. Rental: $5.50. Purchase: $90. B&W.
 Featuring Dr. Charles Stewart, Assistant Director of the Human Relations Commission of the Detroit Public Schools, the program takes us into the classrooms where we learn why Negro drop-out rates are disproportionately high and what school and community can do about it. Part of the American Negro Series.

Sexuality and Crime. Producer/Distributor: KQED/IU, 1958. Grade Level: Sr. H.S. through Adult. Running Time: 30 min. Rental: $6.75. Purchase: $125. B&W.
 This film discusses the delicate but serious problem of sex and crime. It explains three categories; offense motivated by sexual desire, profit from sex, and sex deviation. American and British attitudes toward this problem are contrasted.

Sit-In. Producer/Distributor: MGH. Running Time: 54 min. Code No. 672006. Purchase: $250. B&W.
 This film tells the story of sit-ins from their inception, as Negro customers walked up to the lunch counters in six downtown Nashville stores and sat down to a historic mid-afternoon snack, at 3:15 on Tuesday, May 10, 1960. This film focuses on the event, the consequences that flowed from it, and the little known story of how this explosive issue was settled peacefully. Negro students are shown attending workshops in which they rehearse for the ordeal they will have to undergo when they sit at white lunch counters. White sympathizers are also shown being abused by their aroused neighbors and revealing how, for the first

time, they're able to understand "this tremendous humiliation." The film contains actual newsreel footage and interviews with people who were involved in the Nashville sit-in demonstrations. Narrated by Chet Huntley. An NBC White Paper production.

1619–1860: Out of Slavery. Producer/Distributor: MGH, 1965. Grade Level: Jr. H.S. through Adult. Running Time: 20 min. Rental: $4.25. Purchase: $115. B&W.

This film traces the history of the promise of freedom and equality for all. The presentation shows the steps which led to the Civil War; slavery practiced in Ancient Greece and Rome; civilization as it existed in West Africa on the eve of slave trade; the uprooting of Negroes from Africa and their passage into bondage in the New World; the life of the Negro in the North and South as a free man and as a slave, as a patriot during the American Revolution, and as a participant in the abolitionist movement. Part of the History of the Negro in America Series.

1861–1877: Civil War and Reconstruction. Producer/Distributor: MGH, 1964. Grade Level: Jr. H.S. through Adult. Running Time: 20 min. Rental: $4.25. Purchase: $140. B&W.

This film shows the political conflict over slavery and the Civil War, what Negroes did to win their freedom in that war, why Lincoln issued the Emancipation Proclamation, and the problem of reconstructing the nation when the war was over. The film pictures the brief but exciting period of reform—the reconstruction that followed the war. It sets forth information on the Emancipation Proclamation, the 13th, 14th and 15th Amendments and their efforts toward the Negro's newly won freedom. Part of the History of the Negro in America Series.

1877–Today: Freedom Movement. Producer/Distributor: MGH, 1960. Grade Level: Jr. H.S. through Adult. Running Time: 20 min. Rental: $4.25. Purchase: $140. B&W.

This film shows the Negro: abandoned by the North, shut out of political life in the South, suffering under Jim-Crowism, forced into share cropper-tenant farm life, or penned up in black ghettos of the big cities. The film discusses the cultural renaissance of the Negro of the 1920's; the battle for survival in the depression years; the effect of the New Deal; and the civil rights movement. Part of the History of the Negro in America Series.

Skipper Learns a Lesson. Producer/Distributor: ADL, 1951. Grade Level: Primary. Running Time: 9½ min. Purchase: Color, $135; B&W, $70.

This film tells the story of a little girl and her dog, Skipper, who move into a new neighborhood. Skipper refuses to play with other dogs but learns his lesson, and the children demonstrate that they can get along well together regardless of race, color, or national origin.

Slavery. Producer/Distributor: AIM. Grade Level: Sr. H.S. through Adult. Running Time: 30 min. Rental: $6.50.

Based on the actual testimony of former slaves, this film tells of the tragic and sometimes humorous experiences of life in the old South. It relates small incidents in the lives of many slaves and depicts the liberation of slaves by the Yankee troops. Negro spirituals are used to help tell the story of slavery. Part of the History of the Negro People Series.

Slavery and Slave Resistance. Producer/Distributor: NYT, 1969. Grade Level: Elementary through College. Running Time: 26 min. Purchase: $325. Color.
The achievements of William Wells Brown, Phyllis Wheatley, Frederick Douglass, and other ex-slaves are documented in this film.

So That Men Are Free. Producer/Distributor: MGH. Grade Level: College, Adult. Running Time: 25 min. Rental: $5.60.
This film depicts the story of Peruvian Indians on the Vicos hacienda who are raised from poverty, ignorance, despair, and an overwhelming sense of inequality to a position of dignity, enlightenment, and responsibility.

So You Want To Be on the Team. Producer/Distributor: NEW, 1968. Grade Level: Elementary through Sr. H.S. Running Time: 11 min. Rental: $12. Purchase: $120. Color.
Sound advice to young people with athletic ability, from prominent athletes, to stay in school; also shows white and black youth teaming up together.

Social Security. Producer/Distributor: TFC, 1952. Grade Level: Jr. & Sr. H.S. Running Time: 10 min. Rental: $35. B&W.
This is a documentary film study of the Social Security Act at the time of its passage into law. The various aspects of the Act are interpreted and the procedures of enrollment, salary deductions and compensation are shown.

Social Worker. Producer/Distributor: UEVA, 1968. Grade Level: College, Adult. Running Time: 17 min. Rental: $6.10. Purchase: $209. Color.
This film depicts how the concern of the social worker is reflected in service to people, as individuals, as families, in groups and communities. By use of professional knowledge and skills, and empathy with people strengthened by self-knowledge and professional values, the social worker is able to deal effectively with the social problems and adjustments necessary in a complex world.

Some of My Best Friends Are White. Producer/Distributor: ROBECK, 1968. Grade Level: Sr. H.S. through College. Running Time: 30 min. Rental: $25. Purchase: $250. B&W.
This provocative film examines America's complex racial problem from an unusual angle: it looks at the middle-class Negro and his approach to the problem of racial equality. This film asks direct questions and gets frank answers from successful, middle-class Negroes—among them: Gordon Parks, *Life* magazine's celebrated photographer-poet-author-composer.

Some Won't Go. Producer/Distributor: ADF. Rental: $65. Purchase: $375.
This documentary film examines each draft-resister's reasons for not wanting to be in the military. Each man speaks for himself, in his own language, with his own gestures, from his own experience. The film shows the young man

in the army who has gone AWOL; the young man doing alternative service; and the young men who have fled to Canada to seek refuge there.

Something of Value. Producer/Distributor: TFC, 1959. Grade Level: Sr. H.S. through Adult. Running Time: 10 min. Rental: $35. B&W.
    This film is an excerpt from the feature film of the same title, and shows how adult prejudices and conventions imposed upon the relationship of an African native and a white settler destroy the friendship and homelife they had shared from boyhood. The story reveals the problems they face in a society of race prejudices as they try to rebuild their friendship. Contains an introduction by Winston Churchill.

Something That's Real. Producer/Distributor: NET/IU, 1969. Running Time: 28 min. Color.
    Tape-recorded comments of four Negroes of the New England Telephone & Telegraph Co. provide a representative idea of what it feels like to be black in a white society. The film presents fresh viewpoints.

The South: Health and Hunger. Producer/Distributor: NET/IU, 1969. Running Time: 23 min. Rental: $6. Purchase: $150. B&W.
    This film examines the health needs of black residents in the deep South, covering a range of problems from sanitation to a high rate of childbirth mortality among mothers. Inadequate nutrition, the lack of water, and the too few medical facilities which are encountered by many black residents of the deep Sough are probed in this film. These problems affect both the physical and mental development of southern blacks. Also seen are interviews with the only black obstetrician in Mississippi and a midwife. This film is one of a group of NET productions produced by black film makers to acquaint all people with black America.

The South: Roots of the Urban Crisis. Producer/Distributor: EBEC, 1969. Grade Level: Jr. H.S. through College. Running Time: 27 min. Rental: Color, $10; B&W, $7.50. Purchase: Color, $327.50; B&W, $167.50.
    This film takes a candid look at some paradoxical aspects of our society and the evils arising therefrom. Case studies of southern workers and interviews with representatives of the urban poor illustrate how the cyclical pattern which links poverty to violence has many of its roots in the South. Startling visuals show the contrast between rich and poor. Southern affluence does not reach unskilled blacks and whites. They carry their poverty with them to northern cities where the vicious cycle continues. Poor education leads to low-paying jobs—lack of money leads to frustration—and frustration may even lead to violence.

Southern Accents, Northern Ghettos. Producer/Distributor: BFI, 1968. Grade Level: Jr. H.S. through Adult. Running Time: 50 min. Rental: $30. Purchase: $300. B&W.
    Here is the poignant case history of a black family dramatizing one of the great dilemmas facing our nation today: black families who flee southern rural poverty for northern cities only to become trapped on welfare and in black inner city ghettos. The film explains the existence of the northern ghettos by

profiling the people who live in them and describing how and why they are there.

Southern Consumers' Cooperative. Producer/Distributor: NET/IU, 1969. Grade
    Level: Sr. H.S. through Adult. Running Time: 9 min. Rental: $3.35. Pur-
    chase: $75. B&W.
A cooperative operated entirely by blacks has been started in Louisiana.
Organized originally as a farming enterprise by a black parish priest, the
cooperative includes a shrimp boat, a loan company, a gas station and has now
expanded into a manufacturing role of producing candy for large chains. The
cooperative charges an entry fee of $5.00 and further entails signing a contract
to invest at least $300 more. This film is one of a group of NET productions
produced by black film makers to acquaint all people with black America.

The Southerner. Producer/Distributor: IU, 1960. Grade Level: Sr. H.S. through
    Adult. Running Time: 29 min. Rental: $6.75. Purchase: $125. B&W.
This film visits the town of York, South Carolina, to seek the values
dominant in the southern way of life. It discusses the characteristics of southern
living and tells why the ways of the South are not always compatible with other
sections of the country. The film shows historic landmarks of York including
plantations, churches, houses, and industry. Two parts.

Spud's Summer: Interracial Understanding. Producer/Distributor: MGH. Run-
    ning Time: 26 min. Purchase: $300. Color.
This film depicts the feelings and experiences of Spud, a 6-year-old boy
from the slums of Harlem, on the occasion of his first visit to the country. In
moving from the unwholesome life of a New York ghetto to an improved rural
environment, Spud reveals the broadening of his experiences and changes in his
ideals. This film won the San Francisco Film Festival's International Award.

Standing Room Only. Producer/Distributor: MGH. Running Time: 25 min.
    Code No. 689301. Purchase: $300. Color.
Examining the proposition that the world can support an ever-rising
population, the film depicts ideas for distributing food surpluses, exploiting the
oceans, and increasing agricultural productivity. Surveying the alternate approach, it discusses advance methods of birth control and shows two family-
planning programs in action. Such questions are asked as: Will today's population explosion reach crisis proportions by the next century, and is there an
underutilization of the world's resources?

Still a Brother: Inside the Negro Middle Class. Producer/Distributor: MGH,
    1968. Running Time: 90 min. Rental: $40. Purchase: $400. B&W.
This is a picture of the progress of the middle class Negro. This group,
which parallels the white middle class but is virtually separate, comprises
around 5,000,000 people. These people are shown at work, play, and home. The
huge Negro market is contrasted with the limited Negro ownership. Such
concepts as black nationalism, Afro-American culture, religion, and "soul" are
included.
This presentation comes in three sections: the social and business life of
the Negro middle class; its reaction and involvement on the civil rights struggle;
and the newer mental revolution which may be signalling a separatist movement

of withdrawal from the mainstream of American society. This is a National Educational Television documentary.

Storefront. Producer/Distributor: MTP. Running Time: 47 min. Rental: Free. B&W.

A kind of mental health first-aid station for people seeking help with personal and family troubles, the three centers in New York's South Bronx are staffed with nonprofessionals indigenous to the neighborhood. This documentary records the recruitment and training of one group of selectees: white, Puerto Rican, Negro.

Story of Dr. Carver. Producer/Distributor: EBEC, 1956. Grade Level: Jr. H.S. through Adult. Running Time: 10 min. Rental: $2.25. B&W.

Relates how as a Negro slave boy George Washington Carver received an education, became a scientist, and worked to the benefit of the southern farmer.

Street Corner Research. Producer/Distributor: CMC, 1967. Grade Level: College, Adult. Running Time: 30 min. Purchase: $180. B&W.

This film records the initial contact and first interview in an experimental program to prevent juvenile delinquency, in which the psychologist or social worker actively seeks out his client. In the film, Dr. Ralph Schwitzgebel, a psychologist, approaches two boys in Harvard Square and offers to pay them if they agree to take part in his project. The mobile camera then focuses on the first interview, where the boys are surprisingly frank and reveal significant material. The film was produced to induce discussion; a detailed study guide including background material, the spoken dialogue in the film, questions for discussion and a bibliography accompanies the film. Filmed by Dr. Edward A. Mason, Laboratory of Community Psychiatry, Department of Psychiatry, Harvard University.

The Struggle At Hand. Producer/Distributor: UM, 1964. Grade Level: Sr. H.S. through Adult. Running Time: 29 min. Rental: $5.50. B&W.

Bayard Rustin, Deputy Director of the 1963 March on Washington, discusses with University of Michigan Professor Albert Wheeler why the Negro must choose non-violence rather than violence in the current revolution. Part of the American Negro Series.

Study in Color. Producer/Distributor: ADL, 1964. Grade Level: Sr. H.S. through Adult. Running Time: 28 min. Purchase: $75. B&W.

A trilogy of films consisting of *Boy, The Job,* and *Study in Color,* films which represent a strong indictment of racial prejudice. They appeal to moral considerations and impel audiences to analyze their inner feelings about color and race.

Each film is an entity and can be used either alone or as a series. They are most suitable for adult audiences who are concerned with the cultural, philosophical, psychological and ethical aspects of race prejudice. Senior high school and college students will also find these films interesting and provocative.

Two players discuss "color" in separate soliloquies; one is a white man who wears a Negro mask, the other a Negro wearing a white mask. Through the use of these threatrical devices the members of the audience are given an opportunity to place themselves in the role of the Negro and to try to empathize with his deepest feelings.

A Study in Paper. Producer/Distributor: IFB, 1966. Grade Level: Sr. H.S. through College. Running Time: 4½ min. Rental: $5. Purchase: $50. B&W.

Utilizing animated newspaper tear-outs representing War and Peace and without using words, a struggle is depicted between these two personified ideas. War always destroys anything constructive that Peace does, until at last Peace destroys War itself; then all weapons disappear. This film is excellent to stimulate discussion in the area of human relations. Produced at Syracuse University.

Suburban Living—Six Solutions. Producer/Distributor: NFBC, 1954. Running Time: 59 min. Purchase: $250. B&W.

This film shows six suburban neighborhoods, five abroad and one in North America, and discusses important factors of this way of living. It points out that as the population of the world grows, problems of living in large cities multiply also. It is a presentation of how planning in some of the world's largest cities can make living much more pleasant through proper housing, and rental costing about one-sixth of people's incomes.

The Summer Children. Producer/Distributor: UCLA, 1966. Running Time: 44 min. Purchase: $210. B&W.

The project of an experimental summer session for eighty-five disadvantaged children was conceived by Dr. John I. Goodlad. These children were bussed to the elementary laboratory school of the University of California, Los Angeles. This documentary film is a record of the actual experiences of children and teachers in their adventure in learning. The film won a prize at the International Film Festival in Salerno, Italy, 1967.

Superfluous People. Producer/Distributor: MGH, 1952. Running Time: 54 min. Rental: $25. Purchase: $275. B&W.

This film argues that welfare aid is both a material and moral problem. It employs interviews with occupants of slum areas and city administrators and leaders to make its point. Originally a CBS TV Production. Available in two parts.

Talking Ourselves Into Trouble. Producer/Distributor: KQED/IU, 1958. Grade Level: College, Adult. Running Time: 29 min. Rental: $5.40. Purchase: $125. B&W.

This film discusses the area of general semantics and develops the idea that one's language determines the limits of one's world. It illustrates the way in which undifferentiated reactions to words lead to a communications deadlock. A film from the Language In Action Series.

Take a Giant Step. Producer/Distributor: RTBL. Running Time: 25 min. Rental: $27.50. Purchase: Color, $300; B&W, $185.

Filmed on location in the riot-torn Watts area of Los Angeles, this film follows the progress of a former Negro rioter, Lester Johnson, through his development period until he becomes a productive and valuable employee. This film sheds light on hiring practices, developing the potential of unskilled workers, changing attitudes and solving knotty supervisory problems.

Take an Option on Tomorrow. Producer/Distributor: DEROCH, 1964. Grade Level: Jr. & Sr. H.S. Running Time: 28½ min. Purchase: $106.25. B&W.
A dramatic report on the many "youth-help" programs either directed or aided by the New York State Division for Youth, this film demonstrates how the philosophy, methods and resources of these experimental programs are brought to bear in rehabilitating juvenile offenders, and how the dynamics of group counseling are applied to the problems of troubled and under-privileged youth.

Teach Me! Producer/Distributor: TFC, 1968. Grade Level: Sr. H.S. through College. Running Time: 20½ min. Rental: $150. Color.
A beginning teacher discovers during her first year's experience in a large inner city high school that satisfactions and rewards of motivating disadvantaged students outweigh environmental problems and handicaps.

Teamwork. Producer/Distributor: FIP. Running Time: 20 min. B&W.
This film depicts the story of "Redball Highway," a Negro unit which fought during World War II.

The Tenement. Producer/Distributor: CAROUF, 1967. Grade Level: Jr. H.S. through Adult. Running Time: 40 min. Purchase: $240. B&W.
This film depicts five Negro families living in a Chicago tenement; the property is owned by a realty company which does not keep the building in good repair. In these families the attitudes range from grim determination to provide the children with the necessary education to escape the slums to one of hopeless withdrawn indolence. The tenement was razed for urban renewal; this caused the tenants to move from one slum to another. The film shows these people as being rejected not by a building but by life.

Testing Intelligence With the Stanford-Binet. Producer/Distributor: IU. Grade Level: College, Adult. Running Time: 18 min. Rental: $3.90. Purchase: $75. B&W.
This film pictures the administering of various test items from the Stanford-Binet Intelligence Test to four children. It also explains the meaning of mental age and the calculation of the intelligence quotient.

That's Me. Producer/Distributor: CAROUF, 1969. Running Time: 15 min. Purchase: $150. B&W.
This is a film of a Puerto Rican boy who finds adjustment to the demands of life in New York City difficult. A conscientious social worker is trying to help him. This film contains both wit and realism, as the struggle for adjustment proceeds.

There Must Be a Catch. Producer/Distributor: CMC, 1968. Grade Level: Jr. H.S. through Adult. Running Time: 12 min. Purchase: $144. Color.
This significant film portrays a young man, newly motivated by a state employment counselor, being "screened out" by the narrow, unrealistic hiring

policy of a personnel office. The silent anguish of the job-seeker who deserves a better reception, juxtaposed with the frustration of an employer who can't find "competent" help, produces a dramatic impact.

They Beat the Odds. Producer/Distributor: DIBIE, 1966. Grade Level: Sr. H.S. through Adult. Running Time: 22 min. Purchase: $220. Color.

This review of the lives of several successful Negroes in various occupations points out that although at birth the odds were heavily against any of them achieving such heights in his field, through diligent effort and persistent study they did succeed.

Thinking Seventeen. Producer/Distributor: UC/EMC, 1969. Grade Level: College, Adult. Running Time: 16 min. Rental: $6. Purchase: $96. B&W.

This film is a study of what is on the mind of one black teenager of Oakland, California. Seventeen-year-old Dennis Johnson rambles through a surprising commentary, giving his views on life, including black militants, racism, college, jobs, and his own suspicions and hopes.

The Third Chance. Producer/Distributor: UM, 1964. Grade Level: Jr. H.S. through Adult. Running Time: 28 min. Rental: $7. Purchase: $90. B&W.

Professor Dwight L. Dumond, noted prize-winning University of Michigan historian, considers the Negro American's African heritage and attempts to explain why the Negro failed to achieve freedom after the American Revolution and the Civil War. Part of the American Negro Series.

Thursday's Child. Producer/Distributor: CEF. Running Time: 18 min. Rental $10. Purchase: $100. Color.

Photographed and recorded on the spot with actual participants, this film delves into the human problem-solving world of the community counselors. These women, white and black, create a direct link between the school and the home. They cross the invisible line that separates teachers from many parents. They teach money-saving methods of preparing meals and purchasing needs, sewing, housekeeping, all the practical arts of family living. Produced for C. S. Mott Foundation.

A Ticket to Freedom. Producer/Distributor: AIM, 1968. Grade Level: Jr. & Sr. H.S. Running Time: 23 min. Rental: $13.50. Purchase: $299. Color.

A ticket to freedom is the symbol of what happened to Homer Plessy when he took a seat in a railroad car reserved for whites. In 1892, such a step resulted in jail and years of legislative wrangling. As Josh White sings the ballad of Plessy, one sees history spring to life in the forms of Nat Turner, Ralph Bunche, Martin Luther King, Jr., Jessie Owens and Jackie Robinson. It ends with the hope that the black man and the white man will, together, work against bigotry, hostility and discrimination.

A Time for Building. Producer/Distributor: CON/MSU. Running Time: 60 min. Rental: $15. Purchase: $250. B&W.

This film shows the reactions of various groups after seeing *A Time of Burning*, its parallel film. The scenes present the provocative discussion by four panelists who were actively involved in the production of that film. Highly charged discussions in communities from Maine to Mississippi reveal differing attitudes on the part of both white and black viewers. A CBS News documentary.

A Time for Burning. Producer/Distributor: MGH, 1966. Running Time: 58 min.
Rental: $25. Purchase: $275. B&W.

This documentary probes the American conscience. Although painful, it bares the smoldering tensions between Negroes and whites. This is an emotion-packed presentation. Rev. William Youngdahl is attempting to bring integration in spirit and deed to his white congregation. Ernest Chambers, a Negro barber, feels the church is the place where there should be evidence of enlightenment, not ignorance.

To Find a Home. Producer/Distributor: ADL. Grade Level: Sr. H.S. through
Adult. Running Time: 28 min. Purchase: $100. B&W.

This film shows the experiences of a Negro family trying to rent an apartment in a middle-sized northern city. They are refused. Another Negro family has a similar experience, but eventually find an apartment manager who has a policy of equal opportunity. Based on actual experience, this film helps the audience examine their own attitudes.

To Live Together. Producer/Distributor: ADL, 1950. Running Time: 34 min.
Purchase: $85. B&W.

By presenting the difficulties encountered and experiences shared by children at an interracial summer camp, the film shows that to learn democracy, children must have a chance to live it.

To Touch a Child. Producer/Distributor: MF, 1968. Grade Level: College, Adult.
Running Time: 29 min. Rental: $10.30.

Flint, Michigan school and civic leaders organize a diversified program to use school buildings and facilities during evenings and vacation periods, when school is not open. This film shows how educational, recreation, health, and enrichment programs can benefit both school system and families in the community.

To Work in a White World. Producer/Distributor: UMTVC, 1968. Grade Level:
Sr. H.S. through Adult. Running Time: 29 min. Rental: $7. Purchase:
$90. B&W.

Five Detroit high school seniors and two executives from Michigan Bell Telephone Co. get together to show how it feels to leave the ghetto for the first time. George Higgins, of the U-M Bureau of Industrial Relations, serves as host on this University of Michigan Television Center program, and welcomes Edward Hodges III, General Employment Manager of Michigan Bell, and Fred Gaulzetti, Manager of Michigan Bell's Non-Management Employment Activities.

The students confront Gaulzetti with, "Why do we have to adjust to your culture; why don't you come to ours?" "Because I've got what you want," responds Gaulzetti. "Money."

Tomorrow's World: Feeding the Billions. Producer/Distributor: MGH. Rental:
$35. Purchase: $600.

The various ways man has devised to increase the amount of food available are the subject of this important film.

Town Planning. Producer/Distributor: IFB, 1959. Grade Level: Sr. H.S. through
    Adult. Running Time: 15 min. Rental: $8. Purchase: $95. B&W.
    This film shows some of today's urban problems as they stem from the
fact that in the past cities generally grew without any planning. This picture
portrays how past mistakes can be corrected by re-planning.

The Toymaker. Producer/Distributor: MGH, 1964. Running Time: 15 min.
    Purchase: $150. Color.
    This is a film of two hand puppets who discover they are not identical:
one is spotted and the other is striped. This is the cause of trouble between
them. After an exhausting battle, they go to the Toymaker and find that he
created both and loves them equally. Although one has spots and the other has
stripes, they realize they are basically the same.

The Trial: The Case for the Defendant. Producer/Distributor: KETC/IU, 1958.
    Grade Level: Sr. H.S. through Adult. Running Time: 30 min. Rental:
    $6.75. Purchase: $125. B&W.
    This film concludes the documentary-drama of a civil lawsuit based on an
automobile injury case, dramatizing the defendant's day in court. Scenes include
direct and cross examinations of all witnesses in the case for the defendant, show
the jury being instructed on the law by the court and the final arguments by the
lawyers, and concludes with the deliberation of the jury and its verdict. A film
from the Action at Law Series.

The Trial: The Case for the Plaintiff. Producer/Distributor: KETC/IU, 1958.
    Grade Level: Sr. H.S. through Adult. Running Time: 30 min. Rental:
    $6.75. Purchase: $125. B&W.
    This film continues the documentary-drama of a civil lawsuit based on an
automobile injury case, dramatizing the beginning of the trial. This portion
shows how prospective jurors are chosen and questioned to determine possible
bias, explains how the jury is finally selected and sworn in, presents both
lawyers making opening statements to the jury, and concludes with the direct
and cross examinations of all witnesses in the case for the plaintiff. A film from
the Action at Law Series.

A Tribute to Malcolm X. Producer/Distributor: NET/IU, 1969. Grade Level:
    Sr. H.S. through Adult. Running Time: 15 min. Rental: $5. Purchase: $100.
    B&W.
    The influence of Malcolm X upon the present black liberation movement
is reported upon in this film. His life is recollected through an interview with
his widow, Betty Shabazz. Malcolm X, whose father was killed and whose
mother was committed to a mental institution when he was a child, became a
minister of Islam and a leader of the black struggle until his assassination. This
film is one of a group of NET productions produced by black film makers to
acquaint all people with black America.

Troubled Cities. Producer/Distributor: NET/IU, 1966. Grade Level: Sr. H.S.
    through Adult. Running Time: 60 min. Rental: $12. Purchase: $200.
    B&W.
    This documentary examines the attempt being made to solve problems
brought about by the urban population explosion, such as slums, racial im-

balance in schools, and needs of untrained or illiterate rural immigrants. Such attempted solutions as urban rehabilitation, bussing children, and antipoverty programs are discussed by mayors of some major U.S. cities.

The Troublemakers. Producer/Distributor: SFN, 1965. Grade Level: Adult. Running Time: 54 min. Rental: $50. B&W.
This film precedes the Newark riots by one year, yet carries a danger warning for the future because of the complete lack of hope among the ghetto people. Community efforts to improve living conditions are met with failure.

A Trumpet for the Combo. Producer/Distributor: SF. Grade Level: Jr. & Sr. H.S. Running Time: 8 min. Rental: $2.25.
An open-ended film designed to encourage discussion of ethical and moral questions among high school students, this production presents the case of a school combo in need of a new trumpet player. Two boys try out, and while there is no doubt that Randy is the better player, the teacher-director of the music department puts pressure on the group to choose Bruce, a Negro boy who needs the chance to develop. The issue is what should come first, the excellence of the band or the opportunity it will give?

24th and Tomorrow. Producer/Distributor: ACI, 1967. Grade Level: Sr. H.S. through Adult. Running Time: 22 min. Rental: $15. Purchase: $160. B&W.
This film tells the story of one New Yorker who sets a good example and involves his neighbors' interest in cleaning up his street and moving on to attack many important local problems. This documentary shows Davis Platt picking up litter, amazing his neighbors, and interesting them in the project. They fight housing conditions, rat and pest infestations, and improve disposal conditions.

The Union Man. Producer/Distributor: NET/IU, 1965. Grade Level: Sr. H.S. through Adult. Running Time: 60 min. Rental: $12. B&W.
Examining the trade unionism in Australia, England, and the United States, this film centers on a comparative study in the evolution of trade unions in Australia and the meaning of trade unionism to Australians. Filmed in Sydney, Australia; England; and Detroit, Michigan, top union officials, representative of organized labor, consider the different facets of unionism.

Uptown: A Portrait of the South Bronx. Producer/Distributor: CAROUF, 1965. Running Time: 27 min. Rental: $12.50. Purchase: $175. B&W.
This portrait of a New York City slum provides a documentary study of a Puerto Rican and Negro ghetto community. Focuses on the street life, activities, mores, tempo, and daily existence.

Urban Renewal or Negro Removal? Producer/Distributor: NET/IU. Running Time: 13 min. Rental: $4.60. Purchase: $75. B&W.
This film examines the urban university's role concerning expansion in low-income neighborhoods.

Vandalism: Crime or Prank? Producer/Distributor: IFB, 1964. Grade Level: Sr. H.S. through Adult. Running Time: 5 min. Rental: $6. Purchase: $75. Color.

This film scrutinizes such questions as: Is vandalism a crime or a prank? Does an adult who witnesses vandalism have an obligation to report it, especially if it is done by someone he knows? Both points of view about a citizen's obligations are explored here. Through this open-ended film this controversial subject is pursued.

Verdict for Tomorrow. Producer/Distributor: ADL, 1961. Grade Level: Sr. H.S. through Adult. Running Time: 28 min. Purchase: $100. B&W.

A documented account of the Eichmann trial, narrated by Lowell Thomas, this film is based on actual footage gathered during the trial in Jerusalem, but is a reminder of Nazism and Jewish persecution rather than a "dated" legal presentation. Produced by Capitol Cities Broadcasting Company.

Veronica. Producer/Distributor: JAS, 1969. Grade Level: Sr. H.S. through College. Running Time: 27 min. Purchase: $300. Color.

A cinema verité portrait of a black teenager who is president of a predominately white high school in New Haven, Connecticut, this film concerns Veronica's attempt to maintain her own identity in an increasingly polarized society.

Voting Procedures. Producer/Distributor: IU, 1955. Grade Level: Sr. H.S. through Adult. Running Time: 14 min. Rental: $4.60. Purchase: $75. B&W.

This film describes the qualifications and procedures of registration and voting. It explains voting by paper ballot and by machine with both the "split ticket" and "straight ticket" methods. The presentation demonstrates the step-by-step process at the polls and emphasizes the care that is taken to insure the secrecy of the ballot. Both a closed primary and a general election are shown.

W. C. Handy. Producer/Distributor: BFA, 1967. Grade Level: Jr. H.S. through Adult. Running Time: 14 min. Rental: $6.50. Purchase: $165. Color.

The film reflects the political, economic, and sociological conditions in America during the period 1890–1950. It depicts the cultural contribution of an outstanding Negro composer, William Christopher Handy, the "Father of the Blues." The influences which demanded Handy's simple philosophies and uncomplaining acceptance of the blows of fate show that work, determination, and talent can help in achieving one's goals.

Walk in My Shoes. Producer/Distributor: MGH, 1963. Running Time: 54 min. Purchase: $250. B&W.

This film explores the world of the Negro-American, showing Negroes from all walks of life, such as a taxi driver and a comedian, Dick Gregory, and presents their views on race relations.

Wanted: A Place To Live. Producer/Distributor: ADL/MSU, 1959. Grade Level: Sr. H.S. through Adult. Running Time: 15 min. Rental: $3.25.

This presentation of situations involving acceptance of a roommate is designed to provoke discussion of the problem of racial discrimination. One situation deals with a Negro as an applicant; another with a Jew.

Water. Producer/Distributor: CMC, 1961. Grade Level: Primary through Adult. Running Time: 14½ min. Purchase: $174. Color.

The central theme of this film is simple but urgent: there is as much water now as there ever was, but increasing demands and increasing pollution have brought us to the verge of a world-wide water crisis. Designer Philip Stapp has used animation, live action and collage to underscore the fact that advanced countries such as the United States face problems as serious as those usually associated with underdeveloped, arid lands. The film shows how the alternative to future dust bowls, famine and human misery is cooperative planning reaching across state and national boundaries to put the waters of the earth to the service of all mankind.

Watts: Riot or Revolt? Producer/Distributor: ADL, 1965. Grade Level: Sr. H.S. through Adult. Running Time: 45 min. Purchase: $250. B&W.

This CBS Reports documentary on the Watts, Los Angeles, riot during the summer of 1965 examines the situation in terms of the nationwide civil rights struggle. From a completely unbiased point of view, the program presents opinions representing both the Negro and white community as it attempts to answer whether the violence in Watts was an irrational riot or a planned revolt stemming from social and economic injustice. Newsreel footage of the clash and interviews with community leaders give enlightened testimony to the problems which created the situation.

Watts Towers Theatre Workshop. Producer/Distributor: KCETTV/IU, 1968. Grade Level: Sr. H.S. through Adult. Running Time: 28 min. Rental: $10. Purchase: $240. B&W.

This film documents an experiment in adapting conventional drama, improvisation, and pantomime to an unconventional situation, the Watts area of Los Angeles.

The Way It Is. Producer/Distributor: NET/IU, 1967. Grade Level: Sr. H.S. through Adult. Running Time: 60 min. Rental: $12. Purchase: $200. B&W.

This film shows the chaos of the ghetto school, including what is being done in Junior High School 57 of the Bedford-Stuyvesant section of Brooklyn. Workers with a NYU special learning project are shown in classroom. Scenes include teacher's meetings, and visits with children. The presentation shows that moderate success in reaching children was achieved with the adoption of many different approaches.

The Way Out. Producer/Distributor: HDI/UM, 1968. Grade Level: Sr. H.S. through Adult. Running Time: 44 min. Rental: $11.25. Color.

This film presents a general orientation to minority group workers, a discussion between two successful white supervisors, the reaction of two racist white workers to working with blacks and a dialogue between a white supervisor and a black employee.

We Shall Overcome. Producer/Distributor: UM, 1964. Grade Level: Sr. H.S. through Adult. Running Time: 30 min. Rental: $7. Purchase: $90. B&W.

For a look into the future of the Negro revolution by civil rights leaders, Professor Albert Wheeler of the University of Michigan moderates a panel which includes Mr. Damon J. Keith, Co-Chairman of the Michigan Civil Rights Commission; Mrs. Gloria Brown, head of Detroit CORE; Professor Beulah Whitby, long time civil rights leader and chairman of the Department of

Sociology at Mercy College in Detroit; and Mr. Charles Wells, psychiatric social worker and former NAACP official. Part of the American Negro Series.

The Weapons of Gordon Parks. Producer/Distributor: MGH/CON, 1966. Grade Level: Sr. H.S. through Adult. Running Time: 28 min. Rental: $25. Purchase: $275. Color.

This story of Gordon Parks, *Life* photographer, shows a constructive way of dealing with the race problem. He voices the hope that his children and grandchildren in their struggle for success will take the path of love, not hatred. In recounting his own struggle, he noted that his mother did not allow him to take refuge in the excuse that he had been born black.

The Welfare. Producer/Distributor: UC/EMCC, 1966. Grade Level: College, Adult. Running Time: 17 min. Rental: $6. Purchase: $100. B&W.

This documentary film, prepared by the Welfare Department of a city, reflects the frustrations and problems of a case worker and a young Negro woman receiving welfare aid. The social worker was dismayed by the mass of paper work and red tape, but the recipient's problem was more fundamental. When her husband failed to find employment, he was forced to move out of the household so the recipient and her four children could qualify for aid to needy children. This film raises important questions about the nature of this system of assistance.

The Welfare Revolt. Producer/Distributor: NET, 1968. Grade Level: Sr. H.S. through Adult. Running Time: 60 min. Rental: $13. Purchase: $240. B&W.

This film is a report documenting the complaints of welfare recipients and their attempts to change the system by organizing local unions. Complaints range from the need for additional money to the impossibility of establishing a normal courtship with a man. In separate interviews, union leaders discuss the unions' goal as one of forcing a change by means of group pressure. The federal government's emphasis on training programs is described. Organized demonstrations are shown in Cleveland and in Washington, D.C.

We'll Never Turn Back. Producer/Distributor: BFA. Grade Level: Sr. H.S. through Adult. Running Time: 30 min.

Using interviews and film clips of Negroes in the South trying to make democracy live, this film is a study in the struggle for achievement of social justice in our country.

What About Prejudice? Producer/Distributor: MGH. Grade Level: Elementary. Running Time: 12 min. Purchase: Color, $140; B&W, 70.

Bruce Jones's schoolmates dislike him, but the reasons for their dislike are never revealed. The film portrays the damage done to Bruce by his schoolmates and the individual's emotional reaction when the truth is finally learned that they are prejudiced regarding Bruce's parental origin.

What Color Are You? Producer/Distributor: EBEC, 1968. Grade Level: Elementary. Running Time: 15 min. Rental: $9. Purchase: $200. Color.

This film examines and answers questions for primary-elementary level pupils on the biological, anthropological, sociological aspects of race.

What Harvest for the Reaper? Producer/Distributor: NET/IU, 1968. Grade
    Level: Sr. H.S. through Adult. Running Time: 59 min. Rental: $13. Pur-
    chase: $240. B&W.

This documentary describes how a group of farm workers get caught in a
system that keeps them perpetually in debt. Workers are recruited in Arkansas
and transported to Long Island on credit. They work on the farms there but save
nothing because of the economic system which keeps them in debt. The labor
camps and the type of work are shown. Growers and processors present their
side and are refuted by the Migrant Chairman, Suffolk County Human Relations
Commission.

What Will You Tear Down Next? Producer/Distributor: NET/IU, 1964. Grade
    Level: Sr. H.S. through Adult. Running Time: 29 min. Rental: $6.75.
    Purchase: $125. B&W.

This film examines the old versus the new, a conflict in reshaping a
metropolitan complex: the physical problems encountered, and the reaction of
people when they learn that generations-old traditions surrounding the old
neighborhood are about to be destroyed in the name of 20th Century progress.
The film probes the rationale behind the change, namely what should be torn
down when a city rebuilds.

Whatever Happened to Law? Producer/Distributor: TDI. Running Time: 60
    min. Color.

Narrated by E. G. Marshall for WFIL/TV, this film includes comments
by Roy Wilkins of NAACP; a sociologist; two famous lawyers and a penologist.
The discussion deals with the failure of our systems of social and criminal
justice and its victims. The first half deals specifically with the Negro.

What's In It for Me? Producer/Distributor: DEROCH, 1966. Grade Level: Jr. &
    Sr. H.S. Running Time: 28½ min. Purchase: $69.70. B&W.

An unemployed youth with a wife and child faces a life of frustration and
poverty unless he can obtain the necessary training for a skilled job. He is
encouraged by a Youth Opportunity Center counselor to enroll in an M.D.T.A.
program. Gradually, he gains the knowledge, confidence and self-respect needed
to get a secure job with a future. This is a dramatic story of disadvantaged
youth, filmed entirely on location, with a cast consisting of young people from
the neighborhood portraying themselves.

When I'm Old Enough . . . Goodbye! Producer/Distributor: DEROCH, 1962.
    Grade Level: Jr. & Sr. H.S. Running Time: 28½ min. Purchase: $69.70.
    B&W.

This film presents the story of a bright, ambitious, likable youth who
makes the serious mistake of dropping out of high school before graduation to
get a job—and learns, too late, that without education he faces a dim future. His
motives for dropping out and the problems he encounters on the outside are
vividly presented.

Where Is Jim Crow? Producer/Distributor: UC/EMC, 1967. Grade Level: Jr.
    H.S. through Adult. Running Time: 30 min. each. Rental: $10 each. Pur-
    chase. $180 each. B&W.

A Conversation With Brock Peters This actor emphasizes that roles for Negroes are now more numerous, less stereotyped than formerly, and more interesting. He feels that Hollywood must become accustomed to having more than one Negro star at a time.

A Conversation With Godfrey Cambridge Comedian Godfrey Cambridge calls attention to little-known facts about Negro contributions to the growth of America. He explains also the challenges, frustrations, and limitations facing Negro entertainers. Most important, he emphasizes the necessity of both white and Negro races learning more about each other.

A Conversation With Lena Horne Miss Horne discusses herself as a Negro pin-up symbol, the role of the Negro woman as dominating and strong, and the importance to a healthy Negro society of having Negro female strength assume proper proportions.

A Conversation With Stokely Carmichael Stokely Carmichael, spokesman for the "Black Power" concept of the Negro revolution, describes his feelings about violence, destruction, brutality and racial strife associated with the Freedom Movement. He considers civil rights legislation ineffective because legislators wrote these laws only to stop Negro agitation and because great apathy grips this country inasmuch as the people do not really participate in decision making.

Where Shall We Live? Producer/Distributor: UM, 1964. Grade Level: Sr. H.S. through Adult. Running Time: 30 min. Rental: $7. Purchase: $90. B&W.

Detroit Common Councilman and Professor of Sociology at Wayne States University, Melvin Ravitz, with the aid of pictures and drawings, analyzes the most emotional of the race questions: housing. Part of the American Negro Series.

Where the Action Is. Producer/Distributor: USNAC, 1967. Grade Level: Elementary through Sr. H.S. Running Time: 28 min. Rental: $10.30. Color.

This film depicts work in today's complex technological world and shows how vocational and technical education can prepare young people through proper training, particularly at the post-secondary level. The presentation also focuses on the problem of 80% of the young people who do not complete college in terms of jobs, training for these jobs, and their future.

Where Is Prejudice? Producer/Distributor: NET/IU, 1967. Grade Level: Sr. H.S. through Adult. Running Time: 60 min. Rental: $13. Purchase: $240. B&W.

The film depicts a workshop of college students representing many religions and various racial groups as they bared the prejudice and bigotry that is within many people who think they are free of it. The week-long confrontation took place under the guidance of Dr. Max Birnbaum, director of the Human Relations Laboratory at Boston University.

Where Were You During the Battle of the Bulge, Kid? Producer/Distributor: AF/AIM, 1968. Grade Level: Sr. H.S. Running Time: 27 min. Rental: Color, $16.75; B&W, $10.75. Purchase: Color, $270; B&W, $135.

A father and teenage son clash when the son refuses to attend school because a friend, who has written a challenging article for the school paper suggesting that congressmen who voted for the Viet Nam War should serve in the army as buck privates, is expelled on the excuse that his clothing is improper. The father tells the boys they must conform to school rules whether they like them or not, but then his boss "asks" him to do an expensive advertising campaign for a fraudulent product. He recognizes the parallel, and each one is left to his own decision.

White Guilt: Black Shame. Producer/Distributor: UM, 1964. Grade Level: Sr. H.S. through Adult. Running Time: 30 min. Rental: $7. Purchase: $90. B&W.

Dr. James Comer describes, with the aid of pictures, two profound psychological barriers to brotherhood and what he feels can be done about them. Part of the American Negro Series.

Who Am I? Producer/Distributor: UM, 1964. Running Time: 30 min. Rental: $7.50. Purchase: $90. B&W.

Featuring Dr. James Comer of the U.S. Public Health Service, a specialist in preventive mental health, the program considers the Negro child's search for identity and what a lack of identity means to any child. Part of the American Negro Series.

Who Do You Kill? Producer/Distributor: CAROUF, 1964. Grade Level: Sr. H.S. through Adult. Running Time: 51 min. Rental: $8. Purchase: $250. B&W.

From the "East Side—West Side" television series, this story of a young Negro couple living in a rat-infested slum is an indictment against poverty and prejudice.

William Faulkner's Mississippi. Producer/Distributor: BFI/UM, 1967. Grade Level: Sr. H.S. through Adult. Running Time: 49 min. Rental: $30. Purchase: $300. B&W.

This film, narrated by Zachary Scott and Montgomery Clift, deals with Faulkner's novels, which show universal problems of evil as represented by family disintegration. The film includes readings from the following books written by Faulkner: *Absalom, Absalom; Intruder in the Dust; Requiem for a Nun; The Mansion; The Town;* and *The Unvanquished.* In two parts.

Willie Catches On. Producer/Distributor: MGH. Rental: $14. Purchase: $180.

This film discusses the development of prejudice in one man, showing him as a child becoming aware of the diverse racial and religious groups as "different," and as an adult with a sure sense of discrimination.

Winter Comes to the City. Producer/Distributor: CORF, 1970. Grade Level: Primary through Elementary. Running Time: 11 min. Purchase: Color, $140; B&W, $70.

This film shows many sights, sounds and activities of an urban winter and gives youngsters a basis for a variety of language arts and science projects.

Witness to the Accident. Producer/Distributor: KETC/IU, 1958. Grade Level: Sr. H.S. through Adult. Running Time: 30 min. Rental: $6.75. Purchase: $125. B&W.

This film continues the documentary-drama of a civil lawsuit based on an automobile injury case. This portion dramatizes the defendant's first meeting with his lawyer and the filing of an answer to the plaintiff's petition. The film demonstrates how the lawyers for the plaintiff and the defendant take depositions of the principal parties to the dispute, and shows how the witnesses to the accident are questioned and their statements recorded. A film from the Action at Law Series.

The Work Supervisor. Producer/Distributor: DEROCH, 1969. Grade Level: Jr. & Sr. H.S. Running Time: 8 min. Purchase: $53.55. Color.

This film about a Neighborhood Youth Corps work supervisor depicts a variety of actual work and training situations wherein the Supervisor teaches his trainees not only the fundamentals of machine and tool operations, but also the basic prerequisites of getting along with other people.

The World of Julian Bond. Producer/Distributor: NET/IU, 1969. Grade Level: Sr. H.S. through Adult. Running Time: 11 MIN. Rental: $3.35. Purchase: $75. B&W.

This film is a candid study of the young Georgia legislator in which he explains why, as an integrationist, he would still adopt some black separatist policies. The recent career of Julian Bond, member of the Georgia State Legislature, is reviewed following his protest candidacy as the first black man to be nominated for the Vice Presidency at a Democratic National Convention. Bond believes that segregation in the South is causing black capitalism and community control. Scenes show him campaigning in New York for Paul O'Dwyer, a white liberal, and then returning to his own political duties in Atlanta. This film is one of a group of NET productions produced by black film makers to acquaint all people with black America.

The World of Piri Thomas. Producer/Distributor: NET/IU, 1968. Grade Level: Sr. H.S. through Adult. Running Time: 60 min. Rental: Color, $18; B&W, $13. Purchase: Color, $420; B&W, $240.

Piri Thomas is a painter, ex-con, poet, and ex-junkie. He is also the author of the book, *Down these Mean Streets.* In this film, Thomas takes the viewer on a tour of Spanish Harlem, where two-thirds of the 900,000 Puerto Ricans in the United States live. This is home for a "forgotten people" and a place where children tire of living because they see no hope for escaping ghetto life. Piri Thomas pleads for understanding of this life plagued by filth, narcotics, and crime—a life which no people should have to endure.

World War I—Negro Soldier. Producer/Distributor: VDEF, 1969. Grade Level: Elementary through College. Running Time: 1 min. 24 Sec. Rental: $10.50. Purchase: $25.50. B&W.

Film clips show the Negro soldier in World War I, including scenes of cannon firing and receiving medals for bravery. A fact sheet includes number of Negroes enlisted, Negro officers, regiments and fighting in the trenches.

World War II—Negro Pilot. Producer/Distributor: VDEF, 1969. Grade Level: Elementary through College. Running Time: 2 min. 20 sec. Rental: $18.67. Purchase: $45.33. B&W.

Short filmed sequences picture the Negro pilot in World War II. Included are Negro pilots preparing for raid on Casino, the 99th fighter squadron checking bomb racks and maintenance of planes. A fact sheet presents extensive data on the air corps at Tuskegee Institute in Alabama.

World War II—Negro Soldier. Producer/Distributor: VDEF, 1969. Grade
   Level: Elementary through College. Running Time: 1 min. 50 sec.
   Rental: $12.83. Purchase: $31.17. B&W.
   This film shows the contributions and life of Negro soldiers in World War
II, showing various shots of pilots receiving medals for bravery, taking off and in
flight, European battlefronts, Negro WACs and soldiers marching in review. A
fact sheet gives extensive data on Negroes' contributions to World War II.

Worlds Apart. Producer/Distributor: ADL, 1966. Grade Level: Sr. H.S. through
   Adult. Running Time: 16 min. Rental: $5. Purchase: $50. B&W.
   In this teacher-training film, techniques for developing a sense of self-
esteem, teaching concept information and language efficiency are demonstrated
in a pre-kindergarten class supervised by the Institute for Developmental
Studies. These techniques have been devised to bridge the gap between the
world of the ghetto and the "all white suburban world" of textbooks. In a
sequence filmed at a parents-teachers meeting, a vital aspect of the Institute's
program, mothers relate how they reinforce their children's school experiences.

Yea Kids—Views on a Volunteer Project. Producer/Distributor: UMTVC, 1968.
   Grade Level: College, Adult. Running Time: 29 min. Rental: $7. Purchase:
   $90. B&W.
   The University of Michigan's tutorial project is one of the oldest, largest
and most successful in the United States. This film examines the process of
evolution that keeps the project in touch with the rapidly changing school
system and the Negro community which the project primarily serves.

The Years of Reconstruction: 1865–1877. Producer/Distributor: MGH, 1969.
   Running Time: 25 min. Code No. 666008. Rental: $16. Purchase: $275.
   Color.
   The period of Reconstruction was a time of tremendous resentment and
bitterness. This film shows the conflict between advocates of a "hard" peace and
advocates of a "soft" peace and the economic, social, and political problems
facing the freed Negro.

You Can Be a Doctor. Producer/Distributor: MGH, 1969. Running Time: 15
   min. Code No. 666019. Rental: $12.50. Purchase: $200. Color.
   This film is an informative presentation of medicine as a career opportunity for black youth.

You Can't Run Away. Producer/Distributor: TFC, 1952. Grade Level: Sr. H.S.
   through Adult. Running Time: 32 min. Purchase: $105. B&W.
   When a Negro is arrested for the murder of a white man, a white boy
whose mind is "too young to be cluttered" believes the Negro's claim of
innocence. He convinces his uncle, the town prosecutor, that a careful investigation should be made. The boy, the prosecutor, and a fearless sheriff bring the
real murderer to justice and thwart a lynch mob. Excerpt from an MGM feature
motion picture, *Intruder in the Dust.* Three reels.

The Young Greats. Producer/Distributor: WFILTV, 1968. Grade Level: Jr. H.S.
   through Adult. Running Time: 52 min. Purchase: $550. Color.
   This film tells the story of the Young Great Society, a self-directed, self-

financed organization in the ghetto communities of Philadelphia, and explores the efforts of its organizer, Herman Wrice, one-time gang leader.

You're No Good. Producer/Distributor: MGH. Grade Level: Sr. H.S. through Adult. Running Time: 28 min. Rental: $6.10.

This film dramatizes the feelings of a high school dropout: his frustrations, drives, and fantasies.

Youth and the Law. Producer/Distributor: IFB, 1963. Grade Level: College, Adult. Running Time: 36 min. Rental: $15. Purchase: $225. B&W.

This film presents the role of the police in community organizations as they attempt to guide youthful energies into constructive channels. This film is helpful in aiding youth's understanding of juvenile behavior and the responsibility of policemen for the general welfare. This mental health film was sponsored by the Pennsylvania Department of Public Welfare.

Films (8mm)

Afro-American Music, Its Heritage. Producer/Distributor: CGW, 1969. Grade Level: Elementary through Sr. H.S. Running Time: 16 min. Code No. CGE 100/2. Purchase: $185.

This film begins with the primitive drums of West Africa leading into a similar rhythmic beat of a contemporary jazz quartet. From a Yoruba tribe work chant and the Talking Drum to the plantation life in America, the evolution of the spiritual, the blues, ragtime, and Dixieland jazz is explored. Then up the Mississippi River to other parts of the country and on to New York for the Big Band or Swing Era of the thirties and forties.

Black History—Lost, Stolen, or Strayed. Producer/Distributor: BFA, 1968. Grade Level: Jr. H.S. through Adult. Running Time: 54 min. B&W & Color.

This film studies black people's contributions to the development and wealth of the United States, and points out that these contributions have not usually been part of the history taught in this country. Narrated by Bill Cosby. From the Of Black America Series.

The Black Soldier. Producer/Distributor: BFA, 1968. Grade Level: Jr. H.S. through Adult. Running Time: 25 min. B&W.

This film surveys the history of the black American's participation in the armed forces of the United States from the Revolutionary War to the war in Vietnam. From the Of Black America Series.

Black World. Producer/Distributor: BFA, 1968. Grade Level: Jr. H.S. through Adult. Running Time: 53 min. B&W & Color.

The progress of racial equality in the United States is viewed by prominent blacks in this country and in Africa. The film describes varied feelings towards Africa and discusses restlessness among college students, interracial marriage, religion, the black African's view of Vietnam and problems of racism. Democracy is contrasted with other forms of government. Narrated by Mike Wallace. From the Of Black America Series.

Black Theatre: Then and Now. Producer/Distributor: CGW. Grade Level: Elementary through Sr. H.S. Running Time: 22 min. Code No. CGE 200/1.

This film traces the development of theatre in America and the black man's involvement with it, beginning with the career of Ira Aldridge, the first great black actor. Today's black involvement in theatre is shown, with great strides made in all phases of theatre.

Harlem Wednesday. Producer/Distributor: CON/MGH. Running Time: 10 min. Code No. 409018. Purchase: $90.

This film shows a group of Harlem scenes by the painter Gregorio Prestopino and is presented against a big band jazz background played by Bennie Carter's jazz orchestra. Painting and sketches are arranged so as to suggest activities of an ordinary mid-week Harlem day.

The Hurdler. Producer/Distributor: NYT/ARNO, 1969. Grade Level: Elementary through College. Running Time: 16 min. Purchase: $160. Color.

This film deals with the late Charles Drew, the Negro doctor whose pioneering research in blood plasma led to the modern blood bank system. The film follows Dr. Drew's determined hurdling of racial barriers, from his diligent drive for honors at Amherst through his struggling research in blood plasma to his breakthrough achievement in establishing the first blood banks for the American Red Cross.

My City: Atlanta, Pittsburgh, New York. Producer/Distributor: MLA. Grade Level: Elementary. Running Time: 20 min. Purchase: $200. Color.

This film provides insights into the world of urban children. Using real-life situations, it shows how they interpret and react to their environment.

Negro American. Producer/Distributor: BFA, 1966. Grade Level: Jr. H.S. through Adult. Running Time: 15 min. Color.

This animated film relates the history of the Negro in the United States, showing his struggle for freedom and the contributions of his race. Education is suggested as one solution to his problems.

Negro Heroes From American History. Producer/Distributor: ATLAP/ICF, 1969. Grade Level: Elementary through Sr. H.S. Running Time: 11 min. Color.

This film presents the history of the three major African heroes of American history and demonstrates the richness of the Negro's contribution to the United States.

Audiotapes

Adam Clayton Powell in Berkeley. Producer/Distributor: PTL, 1968. Code No. A-2376. Running Time: 28 min. 3¾ IPS. Purchase: $7.50.

The colorful and controversial congressman from Harlem talks to an audience of 4,000 students in the lower plaza of the Student Union on the University of California campus.

African Heritage of the American Negro. Producer/Distributor: ALESCO, 1968. Grade Level: Sr. H.S. Running Time: 18 min. 3¾ IPS. Purchase: $10.72 each.

An African Ambassador to the United States explores the relationship of black America to Africa, recalls the glory of great past African civilizations, calls for black unity, and suggests that black Americans gain greater economic control over their lives. From the Political Science Series.

Ashley Montagu on Racism. Producer/Distributor: PTL, 1967. Code No. A-2360. Running Time: 80 min. 3¾ IPS. Purchase: $13.50.

The noted writer and anthropologist talks about "Race, Racism, and Possible Solutions." Recorded at the First Unitarian Church in San Francisco.

As the Negro Sees It. Producer/Distributor: WT, 1968. Running Time: 25 min. 3¾ IPS. Purchase only.

A discussion by Whitney Young of the Urban League and Rep. John Conyers, Jr.

A Black Ghetto Community Center. Producer/Distributor: PTL. Code No. 524. Running Time: 120 min. 3¾ IPS. Purchase: $16.50.

Leonard Moore, director of the West Oakland Community Center in the heart of Oakland's black community, talks with Elsa Knight Thompson about their projects, classes, employment office, sports, recreation, and a regular newsletter for communication purposes.

Black Heritage. Producer/Distributor: VIMC, 1970. Grade Level: Elementary & Jr. H.S. Code No. VRT-562. 3¾ IPS. Purchase: tapes, $7.75 each, $203 set; cassettes, $8.75 each, $231 set.

A series of twenty-eight tape biographies of black Americans who have made important contributions to American life and culture. Thirty-five booklets accompany each tape. Subjects covered in series include: Abolitionists; Actors and Entertainers; Armed Forces; Business and Industry; Civil Rights; Education; Explorers; Government and Public Service; Investors; Literature; Medicine; Science; Sports.

The Black Man's Role During the Civil War and Reconstruction Days. Producer/Distributor: PTL. Code No. 006.2. Running Time: 120 min. 3¾ IPS. Purchase: $16.50.

Includes a history of the Ku Klux Klan, the life of Frederick Douglass, and a profile of black poet Paul Lawrence Dunbar.

Black Power and White Power. Producer/Distributor: PTL, 1967. Code No. A-2383. Running Time: 58 min. 3¾ IPS. Purchase: $10.50.

Lou Hartman interviews Anna Braden of the Southern Conference Educational Fund on the effect of black power organizing on the poor white communities in the southern mountains.

The Black Man's Struggle. Producer/Distributor: WILSNH, 1969. Grade Level: Elementary through Sr. H.S. Code No. S7-T. Running Time: 18 min. 3¾ IPS. Purchase: $63.20, set of 16 tapes.

The recordings pose such questions as: "Why do blacks protest?" "What has been white reaction, and why?" "What have been the consequences for American society?" These episodes present a balanced sampling of black efforts to win equal rights. Titles are: Before the Mayflower; The Middle Passage; Life On a Plantation; Before Emancipation; Nat Turner; Underground Railroad; Frederick Douglass; Civil War; Black Power in the 1870's; Klu Klux Klan; After Reconstruction; World War I; Black Protest Begins; Towards Civil Rights; The Military; Black Power.

Black Self-Help. Producer/Distributor: WSU. Running Time: 30 min. 3¾ IPS. Purchase only.

Part of the Seeds of Discontent Series.

A Choice of Two Roads. Producer/Distributor: PTL, 1960. Code No. ALW 512. Running Time: 60 min. 3¾ IPS. Purchase: $10.50.

Malcolm X, Bayard Rustin, and moderator Jon Donald discuss the direction of the civil rights movement and its choices. A program recorded from the perspective of mid-1960.

Contemporary Black Nationalism. Producer/Distributor: PTL. Code No. 006.5. Running Time: 120 min. 3¾ IPS. Purchase: $16.50.

This tape covers the evolution of SNCC from Bob Moses through H. Rap Brown; black nationalist movements from Noble Drew Ali in 1913 through Malcolm X; Nina Simone's banned song "Mississippi Goddam"; Martin Luther King's critique of the 1968 President's National Advisory Commission on Civil Disorders.

Dr. Martin Luther King at Berkeley. Producer/Distributor: PTL, 1957. Code No. AL-457. Running Time: 45 min. 3¾ IPS. Purchase: $9.

A speech given in Wheeler Auditorium on the University of California campus. A brief interview follows.

Early Civil Rights Movements. Producer/Distributor: PTL, 1964. Code No. AL-1419. Running Time: 78 min. 3¾ IPS. Purchase: $12.

A scholarly talk by John Hope Franklin, Professor of History at the University of Chicago, and author of several books on integration and its problems.

El Pueblo Follow-Up: The Social Workers Teach-In. Producer/Distributor: PTL. Code No. 115.2. Running Time: 180 min. 3¾ IPS. Purchase: $18.

The teach-in discussed was sponsored by the Social Workers Union Local 535 and held on the Diablo Valley College campus June 22, 1968. Its purpose was to discuss grievances of several social workers who lost their jobs in the El Pueblo area near Pittsburg, Calif. The grievances arose directly from decisions made by the social workers following the violent events occurring in the El Pueblo ghetto.

The Emotional Roots of Racism. Producer/Distributor: PTL, 1969. Code No. 100. Running Time: 65 min. 3¾ IPS. Purchase: $12.

Dr. Price M. Cobbs, black psychiatrist and co-author of the best selling book *Black Rage,* talks about the emotions underlying racism.

Father James Groppi of Milwaukee Speaks. Producer/Distributor: PTL, 1969. Code No. 099. Running Time: 75 min. 3¾ IPS. Purchase: $12.

Recorded at Sacramento State College during the symposium entitled "Racism in America: Past, Present and Future." Father Groppi, Roman Catholic priest from Milwaukee who gained nationwide attention through his militant actions for black justice, addresses the symposium.

From the First Reconstruction to the Second. Producer/Distributor: MGH, 1968. Code No. 75590. Running Time: 25 min. 3¾ IPS. Purchase: $10.

Focuses on crucial myths and realities in Southern history during the century since the Civil War.

Great Men and Great Issues in United States History: Reconstruction and Negro Civil Rights, 1865–1900. Producer/Distributor: WILSNH. Code No. S5-T. 4 tapes. Purchase: $15.80.

Available on LPs and cassettes, the four tapes in this series are Thaddeus Stevens and Negro Civil Rights; The Impeachment of President Andrew Johnson; Frederick Douglass Fights for Negro Civil Rights; and Booker T. Washington Educates His People.

"A Groovy Rebellion." Producer/Distributor: PTL, 1966. Code No. A-2080. Running Time: 62 min. 3¾ IPS. Purchase: $10.50.

A conversation with members of the Mission Rebels, Inc., a neighborhood club formed in the Mission District of San Francisco. The Rebels have declared their own war on poverty. Participants include the Rev. Jesse James, Ray Towbis, Olga Weir and Luis Marcial.

Growth of the Black Muslim Movement in the U.S. Producer/Distributor: PTL, 1962. Code No. AL-976. Running Time: 41 min. 3¾ IPS. Purchase: $9.

A talk on the growth of the movement by C. Eric Lincoln, a black sociologist. Recorded at the Conference on Law Enforcement and Racial and Cultural Tensions held in Berkeley.

Have Slums, Will Travel. Producer/Distributor: CSDI. Running Time: 60 min. 3¾ IPS.
Recorded by Lois Lomax.

Higher Horizons in Speech Communication. Producer/Distributor: GEL, 1967. Grade Level: Sr. H.S. through Adult. 3¾ IPS. Purchase: $249.
"Higher Horizons" provides thirty tapes and two lesson books which are synchronized for audio-visual use. The emphasis of the program is on the student throughout—on his needs and abilities. Tape and Lesson Sequence: Orientation; Pronunciation; Speech Sounds; Speech Music; Word Usage; Vocabulary Development; and Communication Techniques.

"I Have a Dream." Producer/Distributor: PTL, 1963. Code No. AS-1166. Running Time: 17 min. 3¾ IPS. Purchase: $6.
The Rev. Martin Luther King, Jr., delivers his best-known speech before the participants in the March for Freedom and Jobs in Washington.

Integration Is Impossible. Producer/Distributor: PTL, 1969. Code No. 098. Running Time: 45 min. 3¾ IPS. Purchase: $9.
Kenneth Goode, Assistant to the Executive Vice-Chancellor at the Univ. of California in Berkeley, speaks at the Symposium on Racism held at Sacramento State College.

Interview With James Baldwin. Producer/Distributor: PTL, 1963. Code No. AS-1141. Running Time: 33 min. 3¾ IPS. Purchase: $7.50.
Some perceptive comments and observations about literature and civil rights by the well-known author.

James Baldwin in Harlem. Producer/Distributor: PTL, 1963. Code No. ALW 566. Running Time: 58 min. 3¾ IPS. Purchase: $10.50.
The famed author returns to his neighborhood for a talk delivered at the Church of the Master.

James Baldwin in Oakland. Producer/Distributor: PTL, 1963. Code No. AS-1167. Running Time: 30 min. 3¾ IPS. Purchase: $7.50.
Baldwin speaks about "growing and living in a white world" before the students of Caslemont High School, a school with a majority of black students.

James Baldwin in San Francisco. Producer/Distributor: PTL, 1963. Code No. AS-1150. Running Time: 17 min. 3¾ IPS. Purchase: $6.
Baldwin delivers a brief talk at the Masonic Memorial Temple on Nob Hill.

James Bevel on Black Power. Producer/Distributor: PTL, 1966. Code No. A-2148. Running Time: 42 min. 3¾ IPS. Purchase: $9.
Rev. James Bevel of the Southern Christian Leadership Conference, speaking at a Conference on Black Power sponsored by the SDS Berkeley chapter.

The Last Citizen. Producer/Distributor: NTR. Running Time: 30 min. Purchase. A series.

The Negro in America This recording is concerned with problems of the Negro in America and discusses various opinions gathered from across the United States on these problems.

The Negro, Organized Religion, and the Church What is the meaning and background of the segregated church and what is the changing role of the Negro church? Opinions from across the United States on the Negro in America are discussed.

The Negro Worker in the City Dr. Rayford Logan, Professor of History at Howard University, discusses the significant incidents of the Negroes' labor situation since the end of the Civil War.

Laurens Van Der Post on the Psychological Origins of Racial Prejudice. Producer/Distributor: PTL, 1961. Code No. AL-803; AL-804. Running Time: 85 min. 3¾ IPS. Purchase: $13.50.

The noted South African author speaking in San Francisco under the sponsorship of the Analytical Psychology Club and the Society of Jungian Analysts. The talk is followed by a lively question and answer session.

"Let's All Join the Fight for Freedom." Producer/Distributor: PTL, 1962. Code No. AL-690. Running Time: 40 min. 3¾ IPS. Purchase: $9.

One of the landmark speeches made by the Rev. Ralph Abernathy, Martin Luther King's successor in the non-violent civil rights struggle. The talk was delivered to 400 high school students at the American Friends Service Committee conference on goals for young Americans.

The Life of W. E. B. DuBois: "Back to Africa" and Harlem in the 20's. Producer/Distributor: PTL. Code No. 006.3. Running Time: 120 min. 3¾ IPS. Purchase: $16.50.

A one-hour sequence on the life of DuBois, including his speeches, personal anecdotes by DuBois and his friends and relatives. Also included are thoughts on the racial attitudes of presidents Theodore Roosevelt and Woodrow Wilson.

Lives of Black Entertainers. Producer/Distributor: PTL. Code No. 006.4. Running Time: 120 min. 3¾ IPS. Purchase: $16.50.

Discusses black people in the show business world—biography of Paul Robeson with his songs and speeches; Stepin Fetchit; Marian Anderson and others.

Lives and Times of Some Famous and Not-So-Famous Black Personalities. Producer/Distributor: PTL. Code No. 0061. Running Time: 120 min. 3¾ IPS. Purchase: $16.50.

Episodes from the lives of Crispus Attucks, Nat Turner, Harriet Tubman, Phyllis Wheatley, Dred Scott and others.

Malcolm X—A Discussion. Producer/Distributor: PTL, 1965. Code No. ALW 612. Running Time: 52 min. 3¾ IPS. Purchase: $10.50.

Participants in this informal discussion on the late Black Muslim leader include James Shabazz, John Charles, and Joanne Grant.

Malcolm X—A Retrospective. Producer/Distributor: PTL, 1966. Code No. ALW
611. Running Time: 59 min. 3¾ IPS. Purchase: $10.50.
A documentary on the life of Malcolm X from his first impact on black
power and the Black Muslim movement in 1960, to his death in 1965. Recorded
over a span of 5 years.

Martin Luther King. Producer/Distributor: PTL, 1963. Code No. AL-1064. Running Time: 48 min. 3¾ IPS. Purchase: $9.
Recording of King's famous letter from a jail in Birmingham, Alabama.

Martin Luther King at Berkeley. Producer/Distributor: PTL, 1967. Code No. A-
2005. Running Time: 73 min. 3¾ IPS. Purchase: $12.
A talk sponsored by the Inter-Fraternity Council, given from the steps of
Sproud Hall on the University of California campus.

Martin Luther King at Hunter College. Producer/Distributor: PTL, 1968. Code
No. 007. Running Time: 40 min. 3¾ IPS. Purchase: $9.
Recorded March 10, 1968, one month before King's murder. He received
the annual Brotherhood Fund Contribution from Local 1199 Drug and Hospital
Employees Union in New York City. Dr. King talks about his plans for the
immediate future.

A Martin Luther King Memorial in Central Park. Producer/Distributor: PTL,
1968. Code No. ALW 725. Running Time: 78 min. 3¾ IPS. Purchase: $12.
Excerpts from a rally held in New York City on April 5, 1968, the day
following Dr. King's murder. The speakers include Ossie Davis, Dr. Benjamin
Spock, James Forman, and others.

Martin Luther King at Santa Rita. Producer/Distributor: PTL. Code No. A-2354.
Running Time: 23 min. 3¾ IPS. Purchase $7.50.
Dr. King speaking at a rally outside the gates of Alameda County's
rehabilitation detention center. The occasion was a demonstration in support of
the anti-Vietnam War people inside the gates.

Martin Luther King at Stanford University. Producer/Distributor: PTL, 1967.
Code No. A-2043. Running Time: 52 min. 3¾ IPS. Purchase: $10.50.
The topic of this talk is "The Civil Rights Movement and its Direction,
Leadership and Goals for the Future."

Martin Luther King at Yale. Producer/Distributor: PTL, 1962. Code No. ASW
1011. Running Time: 33 min. 3¾ IPS. Purchase: $7.50.
A sermon entitled "Dimensions of Complete Life," delivered in Battrel
Chapel on the Yale University campus.

Martin Luther King on "The Future of Integration." Producer/Distributor:
PTL, 1961. Code No. ASW 1005. Running Time: 34 min. 3¾ IPS. Pur-
chase: $7.50.
A talk delivered at the Ford Hall Forum by the late civil rights leader.
His outlook for integration as seen from his vantage point in 1961.

Memorial for Malcolm X. Producer/Distributor: PTL, 1965. Code No. ALW 588.
Running Time: 62 min. 3¾ IPS. Purchase: $10.50.
A special memorial program held in New York for the late leader of the
Black Muslims. Many prominent American Negro leaders delivered brief remarks.

Metropolitan Development—A Racial Frontier. Producer/Distributor: PTL,
1961. Code No. AL-817. Running Time: 38 min. 3¾ IPS. Purchase: $9.
Dr. Joseph D. Lohman, dean of the School of Criminology at the University of California at Berkeley, discusses the fact that we are rebuilding our old
cities in the light of a new ethic, while our new cities are building under the old
ethic. Recorded at the Council for Civic Unity in San Francisco.

National Unitarian Black Caucus. Producer/Distributor: PTL, 1968. Code No.
109. Running Time: 70 min. 3¾ IPS. Purchase: $12.
Three members of the newly formed Black Caucus within the Unitarian-
Universalist Church, talk with Elsa Knight Thompson about their aims and
programs. Participants are Hayward Henry, chairman of the caucus from
Boston; Larry Williams of the Berkeley Unitarian Fellowship; and George T.
Johnson, director of the Unitarian-Universalist Project of the East Bay.

The Negro American Citizen. Producer/Distributor: VIMC, 1969. Grade Level:
Elementary through Sr. H.S. 2 IPS. Purchase: $198 set; $33 each.
An audio pictorialization of the American Negro, his heritage, the
development of his ethnic group, and his role as an American citizen. Editorial
content and development of this series was produced under the personal
direction of Mrs. Elizabeth Koontz, who is a past president of the Department of
Classroom Teachers, NEA. Forty-two reel to reel tapes or cassettes. **VRT-564-A
The Negro from 450 B.C. to 1865:** Prehistoric Africa (450 B.C. to 1400); From
Nativeland to American Shores (1400–1619); Into Bondage and Slavery (1619–
1776); The Negro in the North Under Slavery (1776–1860); The Negro in the
South Under Slavery (1776–1860); The Abolitionist Movement (1860–1865).
VRT-564-B Reconstruction to Disfranchisement: Out of the Depths of Slavery;
Freedom and Citizenship; The Negro and the Law; The Negro and Industrial
Expansion; The Negro and Educational Advancement; The Negro and Dis-
franchisement. **VRT-564-C The Twentieth Century—Genesis of a New Life
(1900–1928):** The Negro and Politics; The Negro and the Economy; the Negro
and the Rise of Organizations; The Negro and the Armed Forces; New
Dimensions on Education for Negroes; Negro Migration from the South. **VRT-
564-D The Great Depression—World War II (1929–1945):** The Negro and
the New Deal Era; Back to Africa Movement; New Religious Influences; New
Horizons in Cultural Attainment; The Negro and Public Education; The Negro—
Competitor in Sports. **VRT-564-E The Negro and the New Order (1946–
1954):** The Search for Justice; The Quest for Equal Educational Opportunity;
Equality and Access; Employment Opportunities and Job-Training; Negro
Breakthrough in Sports; Supreme Court Decision and Rights Theory. **VRT-
564-F The Forward Thrust Toward First-Class Citizenship (1954–1966):**
Arousing the National Conscience; The Rise of a New Leadership Class; Agencies
and Organizations Involved in Civil-Rights Movement; Influence of Legislation
on Status of Negroes; Emergence of Negroes Into Mainstream of American Life;
"To Fulfill These Rights." **VRT-564-G Negroes—American Too:** In the Political World; In Educational and Religion; In the American Economy; In the Living
Arts; In Organizations; In Athletics.

The Negro and the Public Schools. Producer/Distributor: NTR. Grade Level: Jr. H.S. through College. Running Time: 29 min.

Doorway to the Future. The struggle for integration in the public schools. Jackson Beck narrates.

The Negro As an American. Producer/Distributor: CSDI. Running Time: 30 min. 3¾ IPS.

Robert C. Weaver speaks on the Negro as an American citizen.

Negro History and Culture Series. Producer/Distributor: AVDC. Grade Level: Sr. H.S. through Adult. Running Time: 30 min. Purchase.

The purpose of this series of programs is to acquaint students with the historical, social, and cultural factors contributing to the oppression of the Negro in America, the variety of responses to his plight, and his attempts to liberate himself. **TP-132 Introduction** Seymour Leventman, of the Univ. of Pennsylvania, introduces this series with an explanation on who the American Negro is and why he should be studied; the unwritten history of the Negro and the Negro in a white man's society. **TP-133 African Origins** Dr. Leo Hansberry of Hansberry College, in Nigeria, discusses cultural background of the first slaves in America, slavery in Africa, and African cultural heritages affecting modern Negroes. **TP-134 Africa and Slavery** A continuation of TP-133. **TP-135 Slavery in America** Dr. Martin Duberman, of the Univ. of Pennsylvania, covers the trip from Africa, the nature and status of American slavery, and how slavery in this country differed from slavery elsewhere. **TP-136 Life Under Slavery** Continuation of TP-135. **TP-137 Slave Revolts** Lerone Bennett discusses Negro revolts, their leaders, and results and effects on slaves and the slavery system. **TP-138 The Free Negroes** Dr. Benjamin Quarles, Prof. of History and Chairman of the History Dept. at Morgan State College, Baltimore, Maryland, covers who free Negroes were, their number, where they were from, occupations, way of life and regional locations. Also discussed is the status and role of the Negro before and after emancipation. **TP-139 Emancipation, Reconstruction and the Restoration of Supremacy** Dr. Quarles discusses the responses of slaves to freedom, conflicts, and divided loyalties between "loving masters" and "liberating" northerners and conditions leading to "black codes" and Jim Crow laws. **TP-140 The Dawn of Freedom** Dr. Seymour Leventman covers the heritage of slavery, the social meaning of freedom and the emergence of the "new bondage." **TP-141 Negro Population and Its Distribution** Dr. St. Clair Drake, Prof. of Sociology at Roosevelt College, Chicago, Illinois, discusses size, growth, and regional distribution of the Negro population. Also covered are contrasts between life in the rural South and urban North, migration, its origins and effects. **TP-142 Social and Economic Stratification of the Negro Community** Dr. St. Clair Drake discusses the historical background, occupational, educational, and economic differences of upper, middle and lower classes of the Negro community. **TP-143 Color Consciousness Among Negroes** Mrs. Carrie Bash, sociologist, gives historical background of when color became socially important, extent to which Negroes accept white man's higher evaluation of light skin, and relationship between color and status in the Negro community. **TP-144 Religion and the Church** Dr. C. Eric Lincoln, well-known black sociologist, examines the history of the church as earliest means of communal expression, the changing role of the minister, and the church as a vehicle for class and political values. **TP-145 The Family** Dr. Joseph Hymes, Prof. of Sociology and Chairman of the Dept. at North Carolina College, discusses the historical background of the family under slavery, the roles of the husband, wife, children, and reasons for instability of the lower class family. **TP-146 The Family and Socialization** Dr. Hymes discusses child rearing, teaching, and techniques of the Negro family, class differences, and the effect on children of the mother-centered family. **TP-147 Leaders and Folk Heroes.** Lerone Bennett covers the historical leaders, eminent persons, and spokesmen; how they got to be outstanding; and the values, ideals and aspirations of these folk heroes. **TP-148 Social Movements and Race Consciousness** Dr. Wilson Record, sociologist, reviews the early protest movements, ideologies and causes, the Washington and Tuskegee vs. DuBois and Niagara movement, and the effects of Booker T. Washington's leadership. **TP-149 Folk Literature** Dr. Tristram Coffin, Prof. of History and Folklore at Univ. of Pennsylvania, and Dr. Willis James, of Spellman College, Atlanta, Georgia, trace the origins, forms, styles, ideals and adoption of white values. **TP-150 Modern Literature** Dr. Nick A. Ford, of the Univ. of Pennsylvania, deals with the early Negro writers and their books, romantic and protest style. Dr. Ford covers the angry young writers and expressions of protest. **TP-151 Negro Press** Lerone Bennett discusses the history and growth of the Negro press, where it is located and who controls it, the focus, orientation, content and audience. **TP-152 Negro Music—Folk and Spiritual** Dr. Willis James, head of the Music Department, Spellman College, talks about the origins, forms, and styles of Negro folk music, its functions in Negro culture, expression of values, ideals, protests, and resignation. **TP-153 Negro Music—Jazz** Dr. James covers Negro jazz, sacred and secular origins, and functions in Negro life. **TP-154 The Negro in the Theater** Dr. Walter Turpins, Prof. of English at Morgan State College, discusses the historical origins, actors, playwrights and their audiences, the classics and emergence of "race" plays. **TP-155 The Negro Intellectual** Dr. Ulysses Lee, Prof. of English and specialist in Cultural History at Morgan State College, gives background, occupations, values, and the roles in Negro life of the intellectual. Also discussed is intellectualism among Negroes. **TP-156 Negro School System** Dr. Virgil Clift, Prof. of Education at New York University, talks about the origins, northern missionaries and their influence on the Negro school system, its structure and approach to education. **TP-157 The Negro at the Crossroads** Dr. Seymour Leventman discusses the effect of life in the rural agricultural South on Negro values and effects of segregation and exclusion. Dr. Leventman also covers the Negro's preparation for life in urban, industrial society. **TP-158 Prejudice and Discrimination** Dr. Leventman discusses the nature of and distinction between prejudice and discrimination. Typical reactions of Negroes and attitudes of Negroes toward other minorities, particularly Jews. **TP-159 Stereotypes and the Negro Image in Society** Dr. Leventman traces the nature of stereotypes and function in intergroup relations and speaks of the extent to which Negroes accept or reject stereotypes of themselves. **TP-160 Crime and Delinquency** Dr. Marvin Wolfgang, sociologist and criminology specialist, discusses the Negro crime rate and types of crimes which predominate; cites reasons for difference from whites. **TP-161 Mental Health** Dr. Robert Kleiner, Temple Univ. sociologist, talks about unwillingness among Negroes, differences by class, occupation, education and religion. **TP-162 Negro Personality** Dr. Kleiner traces "typical" traits resulting from oppression, male-female differences, defensive and offensive traits. **TP-163 The Negro in the American Economy** Dr. Andrew Brimmer, member of the Federal Reserve Board, discusses income and occupation distribution, male-female representation in work, poverty, and unemployment. **TP-164 Professionals, Businessmen and Consumers.** Dr. Brimmer discusses the role of physicians, lawyers, and newer professionals; Negro business and businessmen; Negro consumer patterns. **TP-165 The Negro Community in Transition** Dr. Seymour Leventman discusses the Negro community and its influence in American society, political and international forces, and the decline of colonialism. **TP-166 Generational Changes and Conflicts** Dr. Martin Oppenheimer, Assistant Prof. of Sociology, Harford College, covers the following: differing responses to being Negro among various age groups; breakdown of ghetto mentality; sit-ins and open demonstrations of protest. **TP-167 Negroes and Education** Dr. Virgil Clift gives the background of illiteracy and low achievement among Negroes, the problems of aspirations, motivations and low evaluation of intellectual attainment, segregation and desegregation in Negro education. **TP-168 Reawakening of Race Conscious** Dr. C. Eric Lincoln says that race now has a new social and political meaning for Negroes. Dr. Lincoln discusses the development of racial pride among lower class Negroes and the relation to African nationalism. **TP-169 The New Protest** Dr. Wilson Record discusses social origins of recent protest movements, direction, targets and goals, and the organization of protest. **TP-170 Negro Organizations and Their Ideologies** Dr. Record deals with changing strategies and tactics of the Negro organization, the failure of the Communist Party to appeal to the Negro, Americanism, Christianity, and non-violence as ideologies. **TP-171 The New Negro in a Mass Society** Dr. Seymour Leventman is host for his series of lectures on the extension of social services and public welfare programs and the effect of bureaucratization on Negro status. He also touches on the increasing migration to Northern cities.

The Negro in America. Producer/Distributor: PTL. Code No. AL-1475; AL-1476. 3¾ IPS. Purchase: $18.

A conference sponsored by the University of California in Berkeley. Leon Litwack, author of *North of Slavery*, discusses the emerging patterns of discrimination in 19th Century America; followed by Peter I. Rose, author of *They and We: Racial and Ethnic Relation in the United States.*

Negro Journalism and Negro Art. Producer/Distributor: NTR. Running Time: 30 min.

This program raised the question, "In what way does segregation affect Negro journalism and art?" Commentaries are from across the United States. Part of The Last Citizen Series.

Negro Looks at the Fourteenth Amendment. Producer/Distributor: CSDI/ NAACP. Running Time: 60 min. 3¾ IPS.

An attorney answers questions about Supreme Court cases.

Negro Rights in Africa and America. Producer/Distributor: PTL, 1960. Code No. ALW 506. Running Time: 46 min. 3¾ IPS. Purchase: $9.

Bayard Rustin, civil rights leader in America, and Kenneth Kaunda, President of the United National Independence Party in Northern Rhodesia, compare notes on a strikingly similar problem.

A Negro Votes. Producer/Distributor: PTL, 1959. Code No. A-2420. Running Time: 30 min. 3¾ IPS. Purchase: $7.50.

A study of black voting philosophy, concentrating on the Los Angeles area. Produced by Gene Marine and Loren Miller.

New Deal of Expectations. Producer/Distributor: PTL, 1967. Code No. A-2387. Running Time: 42 min. 3¾ IPS. Purchase: $9.

Ted Vincent, producer of the "Black Power Origins," provides an historical analysis of how the New Deal failed the Negroes, and therefore laid the foundations for today's black power movement.

The Poetry of the Blues. Producer/Distributor: NTR. Running Time: 30 min. Purchase.

Langston Hughes, distinguished poet, playwright and world traveler is the guest of Florence Baker Lennon as they discuss the poetry of the blues. Part of the Enjoyment of Poetry Series.

The People's Alternative to Urban Renewal. Producer/Distributor: PTL, 1968. Code No. 116. Running Time: 58 min. 3¾ IPS. Purchase: $10.50.

Robert Goodman, assistant Professor of Architecture at MIT and President of Urban Planning Aid, talks with Duncan Ray. He points out how ghetto community groups can initiate their own urban planning.

Police in the Ghetto. Producer/Distributor: PTL, 1968. Code No. 011.1 Running Time: 49 min. 3¾ IPS. Purchase: $9.

Four youths from the Hunter's Point area of San Francisco discuss police problems and make some suggestions for change. The moderator is Herb Kutchins of the San Francisco Bail Project.

Profiles in Black History. Producer/Distributor: PTL. Code No. 111. Running Time: 25 min. 3¾ IPS. Purchase: $7.50.

The lives of Martin Luther King, Jr., and George A. P. Bridgewater are briefly outlined by Charles M. Smith.

The Quest for Freedom (Afro-American History Series). Producer/Distributor: TU, 1969. Jr. & Sr. H.S. Running Time: 15 min. 3¾ IPS. Purchase: $6.50, each.

This series of tapes constitutes an introduction to major Negro personalities and Negro participation in American history from 1500 to the present. The series includes: **4401 Men of Adventure:** Estevanico; Jim Beckworth; Ben York; Jacob Dodson; Negro cowboys; Matthew Henson. **4402 Men of Sports:** Tom Molineaux; Jesse Owens; Joe Louis; Willie Mays; Wilt Chamberlain; Jim Brown. **4403 Abolitionists:** Sojourner Truth; Harriet Tubman; Frederick Douglass; Henry Highland Garnet; Martin Delany. **4404 Patriot Soldiers:** Revolutionary War; Civil War; The Buffalo Soldiers; World War I; World War II; B. O. Davis, Jr. and Sr. **4405 Scientist and Inventors:** Benjamin Banneker; Charles Drew; Percy Julian; Elijah McCoy; Garret Morgan; Norbert Rillieux; George Washington Carver; Jan Matzeliger; Granville Woods. **4406 Makers of Music:** W. C. Handy; William Grant Still; Duke Ellington; Marian Anderson; Leontyne Price; Fisk Jubilee Singers; Roland Hayes; Harry Belafonte. **4407 Performers of the Stage and Screen:** Ira Aldridge; Bert Williams; Charles Gilpin; Richard Harrison; Canada Lee; Katherine Dunham; Diana Sands; Sidney Poitier; Sammy Davis, Jr. **4408 Distinguished Educators:** John Chavis; Booker T. Washington; William E. B. DuBois; Mary McLeod Bethune; Samuel Shepherd. **4409 Modern Abolitionists:** Walter White; Martin Luther King; James Farmer; Roy Wilkins; Whitney Young; A. Phillip Randolph. **4410 Men** of Government: Robert Smalls; Blanche K. Bruce; Hiram Revels; Robert Weaver; Edward Brooke; Thurgood Marshall; Ralph Bunche; John Conyers; Carl Stokes; Richard Hatcher. **4411 Literary Figures:** William Wells Brown; Phyllis Wheatley; Langston Hughes; Gwendolyn Brooks; Lorraine Hansberry; Richard Wright; Ralph Ellison; James Baldwin. **4412 Men of Business:** Robert Abbott; Robert Vann; S. B. Fuller; Madame C. J. Walker; C. C. Spaulding; John H. Johnson.

Race: An Abused Classification. Producer/Distributor: PTL, 1964. Code No. AL-1423. Running Time: 67 min. 3¾ IPS. Purchase: $12.
A good summation of the anti-racist arguments as delineated by William McCord.

Race Rebuilding and the Renewal of Life. Producer/Distributor: PTL, 1962. Code No. AL-765. Running Time: 64 min. 3¾ IPS. Purchase: $10.50.
Architect and author Allen Temko talks about cities and the ghetto before the Council for Civic Unity in San Francisco.

Racism in Perspective. Producer/Distributor: PTL, 1969. Code No. 102. Running Time: 65 min. 3¾ IPS. Purchase: $12.
Ronald V. Dellums, black City Councilman from Berkeley, provides an illuminating talk on racism at the Sacramento State College Symposium.

Racism: Nazi and American. Producer/Distributor: PTL, 1964. Code No. AL-1566. Running Time: 117 min. 3¾ IPS. Purchase: $16.50.
John Howard Griffin, author of *Black Like Me,* speaks at the Santa Clara Writers Institute. He discusses some of the problems involved in writing his best selling book.

Reconstruction and Negro Civil Rights. Producer/Distributor: WILSNH, 1968. Grade Level: Elementary through Sr. H.S. Code No. S5-T(6). Running Time: 18 min. 3¾ IPS. Purchase: $15.80.
Covers the years from 1865 to 1900. Titles are: Thaddeus Stevens Argues for Radical Reconstruction; The Impeachment of President Johnson; Frederick Douglass Fights for Negro Rights; Booker T. Washington Educates His People. Four tapes.

Roots of Jazz Series. Producer/Distributor: NTR. Grade Level: Jr. H.S. through Adult. Running Time: 30 min.
Duke Ellington This program covers twenty years, from 1923–1943, with Duke Ellington and his orchestra. Features quotes from jazz experts, personal interviews with jazz musicians, and some of Duke Ellington's music. **Negro Spirituals** This tape discusses the years of slavery and Negro religious and spiritual music in the South. **Negro Work Songs and Blues** This tape discusses the origin of Negro work songs and the blues.

The Role of the Black Woman in America. Producer/Distributor: PTL. Code No. ALW 750. Running Time: 50 min. 3¾ IPS. Purchase: $10.50.
A discussion by four black women on their role in the American social, political, and economic scheme. The participants are Peachie Brooks, Verta Smart Grosvenor, Flo Kennedy, and Elinor Norton.

A Salute to Ella Baker. Producer/Distributor: PTL. Code No. ALW 691. Running Time: 60 min. 3¾ IPS. Purchase: $10.50.

A program in honor of the woman who was instrumental in building the civil rights movement, recorded at a dinner in her honor at the Hotel Roosevelt in New York, April 24, 1968, and sponsored by the Southern Christian Education Fund. Among the speakers are Stokeley Carmichael, H. Rap Brown, Floyd McKissick, Anne Braden, Karen Zinn, and Miss Baker.

Social Stress and Urban Violence. Producer/Distributor: MGH 1968. Code No. 75586. Running Time: 22 min. Purchase: $10.

An analysis of riot-related psychosocial stresses felt by black ghetto residents and also discusses riot-prevention measures.

A Special Program Commemorating Negro History Week, 1962. Producer/Distributor: PTL, 1962. Code No. AL-732; AL-733. Running Time: 68 min. 3¾ IPS. Purchase: $12.

Produced by Elsa Knight Thompson and Mike Tigar. The second part contains an interview with Jomo Kenyetta.

The Teaching of Negro History. Producer/Distributor: MGH, 1968. Code No. 75603. Running Time: 25 min. Purchase: $10.

A discussion of the right and wrong reasons for teaching Negro history and the necessity of raising the hardcore issues.

A Tribute to Paul Robeson. Producer/Distributor: PTL. Code No. ALW 1583-C. Running Time: 150 min. 3¾ IPS. Purchase: $18.

Produced on the occasion of his seventieth birthday, this is a tribute to the athlete, actor, singer and extraordinary man—his songs and his thoughts.

The Urban Plantation. Producer/Distributor: PTL, 1968. Code No. A-2367. Running Time: 50 min. 3¾ IPS. Purchase: $10.50.

An interview with Neil Eddington who did his field work for a doctorate in anthropology in the black ghetto area of Hunter's Point in San Francisco. He discusses black attitudes and the relevance of the social scientist.

Violence in A Black Community Producer/Distributor: PTL, 1968. Code No. 115.1 Running Time: 150 min. 3¾ IPS. Purchase: $18.

In April of 1968, violence broke out in the all-black El Pueblo suburb of Pittsburg, California, forty miles east of San Francisco. During the incident, gunfire was exchanged and a state of emergency was declared. This is an interview with participants and others closely connected with the events.

The White Man's Stake in Black Liberation. Producer/Distributor: PTL, 1969. Code No. 107. Running Time: 30 min. 3¾ IPS. Purchase: $7.50.

Carl Braden of the Southern Conference Educational Fund speaking on this important subject. He is the editor of the *Southern Patriot.*

Whitney Young, Jr. on Civil Rights Issues. Producer/Distributor: PTL, 1968. Code No. 167. Running Time: 60 min. 3¾ IPS. Purchase: $10.50.

The executive director of the National Urban League speaks at the national convention of the League of Women Voters held in Chicago, April 1968.

X-Ray Procedures and Black People. Producer/Distributor: PTL, 1968. Code No. 103. Running Time: 62 min. 3¾ IPS. Purchase: $10.50.
Chester Aaron, chief technologist in the x-ray Department at Alta Bates Hospital in Berkeley, Calif., discusses the practice of many x-ray technicians in routinely giving heavier x-ray exposures to black people.

Filmstrips (silent)

Advanced Reading Skills. #136. Producer/Distributor: EGH, 1961. Grade Level: Intermediate through Jr. H.S. Purchase: $5.25, each. Color.
A special set of filmstrips intended for readers with a wide range of ability and achievement. Speed has not been stressed; the aim is to have pupils read better. Detailed objectives and explanations are contained in the teaching manual. **136A** Reading Activities; 35 frames. **136B** Related Reading Activities; 34 frames. **136C** Literature and Famous Places; 34 frames. **136D** Origin and Meaning of Words; 43 frames. **136E** Knowing and Selecting Words; 40 frames. **136F** Associating Facts and Ideas; 36 frames. **136G** Creative Talent; 49 frames. **136H** Introduction to Shakespeare; 49 frames. **136I** Oral and Written Composition; 43 frames. **136J** Three Great Writers: Washington Irving, Edgar Allan Poe, Mark Twain; 36 frames.

Air Pollution and You. Producer/Distributor: CAF, 1967. Grade Level: Jr. H.S. through College. 47 frames. Purchase: $7.50. Color.
This filmstrip outlines the basic problem of air pollution, its principal effects on health and property, some approaches to its control, and briefly describes the Federal Program. Additionally, the importance of the citizen's role in control efforts is discussed.

American Negroes. Producer/Distributor: TA, 1969. Grade Level: Elementary. 43 frames. 8 in series. Purchase: $48, set.
This series of American Negroes in history includes a selection of personalities such as Harriet Tubman, Frederick Douglass, Sojourner Truth, Booker T. Washington, George Washington Carver, Mary McLeod Bethune, Martin Luther King, Jr., and Jackie Robinson. Each filmstrip devotes itself to the life of one of these personalities.

American Negro Pathfinders. Producer/Distributor: BFA, 1969. Grade Level: Elementary to Adult. 6 in series. Purchase: $7.25, each; $42, set.
This captioned filmstrip series depicts the outstanding contributions to

American society of six prominent Negro leaders. These leaders are Martin Luther King, Jr., A Philip Randolph, Gen. Benjamin O. Davis, Jr., Dr. Mary McLeod Bethune, Justice Thurgood Marshall, and Dr. Ralph Bunche. Using constructive action instead of violence, each person furthered the cause of human dignity, individual freedom, and social justice. They succeeded in spite of the prejudice that can exist among people. The lives and accomplishments of these Negroes serve as an inspiration to young people of any race or background.

Before and After the Civil War. Producer/Distributor: AVMC. 7 in series. Purchase: $6.50, each; $42, set.

The filmstrips cover the period prior to and immediately following the Civil War. They deal with emerging sectionalism, Nat Turner, Compromise of 1850, Dred Scott Decision, secession, reconstruction, Fort Sumter, and Civil War generals.

City and State. Producer/Distributor: NYT, 1965. Grade Level: Jr. H.S. through College. 52 frames. Purchase: $6. B&W.

A filmstrip showing growing problems faced by state and local governments in coping with increasing need and demand for services.

Civil War. Producer/Distributor: EBEC, 1958. Grade Level: Elementary through Sr. H.S. 50 frames. Purchase: $48, set. Color.

Eight filmstrips presenting hundreds of accurate and realistic paintings which will help the student acquire a deep and lasting appreciation of a tragic era in our nation's past. Questions for review and discussion are included at the end of each filmstrip. 1. Causes of the Civil War. 2. From Bull Run to Antietam. 3. From Shiloh to Vicksburg. 4. The Civil War at Sea. 5. Gettysburg. 6. Sherman's March to the Sea. 7. Road to Appomattox. 8. Reconstruction Period.

Current Problems in the U.S. Producer/Distributor: CAF. Grade Level: Jr. H.S. through College. 5 in series. Purchase: $4, each. B&W.

These filmstrips focus on many of the issues of our times.

The American Negro: The Quest for Equality 1965; 43 frames. Analyzes the problems and progress of the American Negro today; highlights advances made from the 1963 March on Washington to the 1964 Civil Rights Act.

The Nation's Health: Problems and Progress 1963; 43 frames. Discusses community health problems, and the cost of maintaining good health. Describes non-compulsory forms of hospitalization, medical protection, and the Medicare plan for older citizens.

City and Suburb: Crisis and Opportunity 1964; 45 frames. Discusses the urban crisis and the problems associated with rapid and haphazard suburban growth.

Youth: The Search for Identity 1968; 46 frames. Shows some of the underlying causes for youth's search for a new identity, and how these causes are reflected in behavior and youth's overall concept of life.

Crisis in Urban Development 1968; 46 frames. Explains how the economic growth and well-being of the United States is dependent on cities, and discusses the role of the Department of Housing and Urban Development.

Frederick Douglass. Producer/Distributor: ALESCO. Purchase: $39.75, set.

The life of an American slave who became one of the leading Negro-

Americans of the 19th century—a presidential adviser, a brilliant editor, and an outstanding orator.

The Fundamentals of Thinking. Producer/Distributor: EGH, 1962. Grade Level: Intermediate through Jr. H.S. 9 in series. Purchase: $5.25, each. Color.

A filmstrip series on thinking; a unique topic developed from the original research and theory of Dr. Louis E. Raths, distinguished service Professor of Education, Newark State College, Union, N.J. This potential learning concept is outlined in nine filmstrips devoted to nine basic thinking skills. **151A** Comparisons; 26 frames. **151B** Assumptions; 26 frames. **151C** Classifying; 24 frames: **151D** Critical Thinking; 26 frames. **151E** Problem Solving; 26 frames. **151F** Interpreting; 32 frames. **151G** Summarizing; 26 frames. **151H** Observing; 27 frames. **151I** Analyzing; 28 frames.

Fundamentals of Vocabulary Building. Producer/Distributor: EGH, 1961. Grade Level: Jr. H.S. 35 frames. Purchase: $5.25, each; $42.50, set. Color.

These filmstrips are designed to help increase sight vocabulary and reading vocabulary. The set includes a study in configuration, an exercise in visualization, reasoning and judgment. **147A** Name the Right Word; 35 frames. **147B** Words that Rhyme; 39 frames. **147C** Synonyms; 37 frames. **147D** Homonyms; 42 frames. **147E** Find Another Word; 34 frames. **147F** Prefixes and Suffixes; 30 frames. **147G** Singular and Plural; 38 frames. **147H** Seeing Words Clearly; 37 frames. **147I** The Dictionary and Other Reference Books; 36 frames.

George W. Carver. Producer/Distributor: ALESCO. Purchase: $39.75, set.

The life and achievements of a great Negro scientist whose inventiveness and dedicated work in agriculture brought a better life to thousands of farmers.

George Washington Carver. Producer/Distributor: ART. 72 frames. Purchase: $6.

This is the story of the great scientist whose selfless devotion converted the unwanted peanut into scores of useful new products.

George Washington Carver, the Plant Doctor. Producer/Distributor: EGH. Grade Level: Intermediate through Jr. H.S. 24 frames. Purchase: $5.25.
This filmstrip deals with Dr. Carver's contributions to science.

Harriet Tubman. Producer/Distributor: SVE. Grade Level: Elementary through Jr. H.S. Single Strip. Color.

Highlights the life of the remarkable woman respectfully called "Black Moses"; the "Conductor" of the underground railroad to freedom.

The Heritage of Afro-American History. Producer/Distributor: TA, 1970. Grade Level: Elementary through College. 40 frames. 9 in series. Purchase: $7.50, each; $67.50, set.

This library of nine full-color filmstrips traces the history and heritage of Afro-Americans, and demonstrates how Negro history is deeply entwined with American history. From African origins to the current struggle for equality, Afro-American history is filled with noble leaders, important events, and the great challenge of freedom and justice for all citizens living in America. The series includes: From Africa to the New World, 1000–1713; Life in the New American Colonies, 1713–1792; The Plantation System, 1790–1850; From Abolition Movements to Civil War, 1850–1865; From Reconstruction to Jim Crow, 1865–1898; The Long Hard Struggle, 1898–1942; Changing Currents of Civil Rights, 1942–1960; Years of Challenge, 1960–Present; Leaders Who Left Their Mark.

History of the American Negro. Producer/Distributor: MGH, 1965. Code No. 405360. 37 frames. 8 in series. Purchase: $8.50, each; $60, set. Color.

This series of filmstrips is designed to provide accurate information about the history of the American Negro from the beginning of slavery to the present.

From Africa to America This filmstrip examines the different forms of slavery that existed before 1500, and contrasts them with Negro slavery as it was practiced in America during the colonial period. It then describes the economic conditions that existed during that time which caused slavery to flourish: the need for cheap labor, the ease with which Negroes could be transported from Africa to America to satisfy this need, and the lack of any other forms of profitable servitude such as Indians or white indentured servants.

Slavery in the Young American Republic This filmstrip covers the advances the Negro made in securing his freedom and equality during and immediately after the Revolutionary War, and discusses the anti-slavery attitudes of Washington, Jefferson, and other leading patriots of the time. It explains why slavery was losing ground in both the North and the South until four factors caused its rebirth in the South toward the end of the 18th century: the Industrial Revolution in England; the invention of the cotton gin; the westward spread of cotton growing; and the continuance of the slave trade.

Slavery in a House Divided In the period before the Civil War, most Negroes worked as slaves in Southern cotton fields. This filmstrip describes the life of these slaves and the life of the free Negro, North and South, from 1830 to 1860. It shows how Frederick Douglass, Harriet Tubman, and many others joined with white sympathizers to work for the abolition of slavery. It describes the brutal treatment of the Negroes that finally shocked the Northerners into siding with the abolitionists, and examines various other issues.

The Negro in the Civil War and Reconstruction This filmstrip examines the part the Negro played in the Civil War, and how he distinguished himself on the battlefield by his bravery and valor. It explains the true significance of the Emancipation Proclamation, and describes the Reconstruction period that followed the war when Lincoln tried to get the South back on its feet economically. This filmstrip also examines the formation of the Freedman's Bureau and the part the Bureau played in revitalizing the South by helping the Negro in education, in securing jobs, and in assuring his voting rights. It also explores the revival of anti-Negro feelings by Southern extremists and the drastic measures they used against the Negroes who were now beginning to stand up for their rights.

Negro in the Gilded Age Describes the setbacks the Negro faced after the Reconstruction period, including his right to vote, his political influence, and the loss of much of his former freedom. It shows how ex-rebels regained control of the Southern legislatures and undid the work of Reconstruction days by declaring the Civil Rights Act of 1875 unconstitutional. This filmstrip illustrates the educational disadvantages of separate but rarely equal schools, and describes the sharecropper system that kept Negroes on the farms under conditions reminiscent of the old slave days.

The Negro Faces the Twentieth Century This informative filmstrip shows the impact of segregation on the Negro between 1900 and 1933. It describes the migration of Negroes to northern cities and their entry into the labor market and the armed forces during World War I. It examines the beginnings of organizations to improve the lot of the Negro, such as the NAACP. This filmstrip also describes the rise of a new Negro leadership and the Harlem Renaissance of the 1920's.

Negro Fights for the Four Freedoms This filmstrip covers the administration of President Franklin D. Roosevelt and shows the measures he took to insure Negro equality in employment and education. The Great Depression is studied as well as the effect World War II and the Korean War had on integrating the armed forces. Great emphasis is placed upon the increasing opportunities for the Negro brought about in part by his growing political influence and by his participation in the defense industry and the armed forces. This filmstrip illustrates why this was a period of progress for the nation in general.

The Threshold of Equality This final filmstrip in the series briefly reviews the history of the Negro in America, showing how a Negro society arose within the overall white world. It then details the dramatic gains made by Negroes in the last decade, including the increase in their appointments to political posts and the passage of the Civil Rights Bill. It explains the significance to all Americans of the Nobel Peace Prizes awarded to Ralph Bunche and Dr. Martin Luther King, and studies the emergence of the new African nations and their effect on the world.

Law and Order in a Troubled America. Producer/Distributor: CAF, 1968. Grade Level: Jr. H.S. through College. 44 frames. Purchase: $7.50. Color.

This filmstrip points out the main causes of crime and lawlessness. It also shows that the system of law and order in America is in urgent need of repair and explores law enforcement problems.

John Henry and His Mighty Hammer. Producer/Distributor: TA, 1970. Grade Level: Elementary. 40 frames. Purchase: $6.

This filmstrip tells the exciting story of John Henry, a Negro who drives steel railroad spikes faster than any man alive. This folk tale hero lays the tracks for the Chesapeake and Ohio Railroad in Virginia, hammers through mountains of solid rock, and wins a contest against a drilling machine.

Leaders of America. Producer/Distributor: EGH. Grade Level: Elementary & Jr. H.S. Purchase: $5.25.

A filmstrip series devoted to outstanding leaders who play an important part in the American heritage. **65H** George Washington Carver, the Plant Doctor; 24 frames. **65I** George W. Goethals; 25 frames.

Let's Have Fun. Producer/Distributor: SE. Purchase: $5.25, each.

A delightfully informative filmstrip series to help stimulate students in special education classes. A variety of scientific facts about nature are presented, along with the guidance principle of encouraging them to seek advice from older persons when confronted with a burdensome problem. **204A** Peter's Garden. **204B** Bill's Robin. **204C** Jim's Doghouse. **204D** Betty's Wild Flowers.

Little Citizen. Producer/Distributor: OED. Purchase: $35.10.

This filmstrip will help to provide word-picture relationships and help to build a larger more meaningful vocabulary for use in oral communication.

A Picture History of the Civil War. Producer/Distributor: EBEC, 1962. Grade Level: Jr. & Sr. H.S. 50 frames. 8 in series. Purchase: $48, set. Color.

Eight filmstrips showing illustrations, photographs, paintings, drawings and eyewitness battle scenes of the Civil War. A reading script provides rich and meaningful commentary to the captionless filmstrips. 1. The South Declares Its Independence. 2. Federal Armies Invade the South. 3. Armies and Navies of the Civil War. 4. South Fights Back. 5. Gettysburg and Vicksburg. 6. Civil War on Home Fronts. 7. Grant Takes Command. 8. The Confederate Armies Surrender.

Population Explosion. Producer/Distributor: NYT, 1967. Grade Level: Jr. H.S. through College. 51 frames. Purchase: $6, each. B&W.

A filmstrip showing the effect of poverty, hunger, illiteracy, and political instability, especially in less developed areas of Asia, Africa, and Latin America.

The Reverend Dr. Martin Luther King, Jr. Producer/Distributor: ALESCO. Purchase: $8.50, each.

The life and objectives, accomplishments, and death of the great Negro-American leader. Stresses his advocacy and use of non-violent direct action, and his impact upon America and the world.

Robert Smalls. Producer/Distributor: ALESCO. Purchase: $39.75.

The life and daring exploits of a slave who became a national naval hero during the Civil War and was later elected to represent South Carolina in the U.S. House of Representatives.

The Roots of War (1830–1860). Producer/Distributor: SSSS, 1969. Grade Level: Sr. H.S. 4 in series. Purchase: $6, each.

Four filmstrips showing the Negro revolt against slavery. 1. Emerging Sectionalism, 24 frames. 2. Nat Turner, 24 frames. 3. Slavery, 24 frames. 4. Social Reformers, 24 frames.

Slavery in America. Producer/Distributor: AHF. 6 in series. Purchase: $36, set.

This set of six full-color, silent filmstrips describes the conditions of being an indentured servant in the 1660s; relates the experiences of a young African Negro as he is carried across the Atlantic in the hold of a slave ship; a southern plantation owner discusses his views and a northern abolitionist points out the immorality of slavery; describes Gerrit Smith's relationship with John Brown and observes John Brown as he wonders whether or not to attack Harpers Ferry; explains the events leading up to the Emancipation Proclamation and follows the dilemma of a freed Negro and his problem of survival; describes the problems faced by a northern schoolteacher who comes south to teach Negroes and relates George Peabody's efforts to provide freed Negroes with an education.

The Story of America's People. Producer/Distributor: EGH, 1966. Grade Level: Elementary & Jr. H.S. Purchase: $5.25, each.

A filmstrip documentary illustrating the arrival, growth, and achievement patterns of the leading ethnic groups, and their unique contributions to our culture. Tracing ancestry back to many foreign lands, every American can be proud of the renewed strengths, vigorous resolutions, and monumental attainments that made America great.

The Teacher and Integration. Producer/Distributor: NEA, 1967. 50 frames. Purchase: $8.

Presents a positive viewpoint and includes information for working in racially integrated schools.

Understanding Citizenship. Producer/Distributor: BFA, 1958. Grade Level: Elementary & Jr. H.S. 29 frames. 3 in series. Purchase: $7.25, each; $21, set. Color.

The Bill of Rights and the Pledge of Allegiance are bases on which to build an understanding of how citizenship functions. Three strips show what the documents do for us, and how they protect the individual citizen as he goes about his way. They also stress the need to preserve our heritage of both individual and collective freedom. The series can be made a part of both group and individual study about our country and its form of government.

"Unfree" Laborers (1765–1790). Producer/Distributor: SSSS, 1969. Grade Level: Sr. H.S. 24 frames. Purchase: $6, each. Color.

This filmstrip shows an African aboard a slaving ship who must choose either slavery or death.

Filmstrips (sound)

About Venereal Diseases. Producer/Distributor: BFA. Grade Level: Jr. & Sr. H.S. 45 frames. 33⅓ RPM. Purchase: $12.

Concentration is placed on the causes, effects, and treatment of the two most prevalent venereal diseases, syphilis and gonorrhea. Emphasis is placed on the early detection of the diseases, the fact that they are curable, the need to report them to responsible health authorities, and the avoidance of "quack-type" cures.

African Background and Early Days of the American Experience. Producer/Distributor: ALESCO. Grade Level: Jr. & Sr. H.S. 44 frames. Purchase: $17.49.

After recalling and illustrating the African heritage of black Americans, this filmstrip depicts the inhumanity of the slave trade and the slave's life on the New World plantations. Includes teacher's manuals. One 12″ LP.

Afro-American Art. Producer/Distributor: ALESCO, 1968. Grade Level: Sr. H.S.
Single Strip. 82 frames. 33⅓ RPM. Purchase: $15.95.

A panorama of Afro-American Art from the 19th Century to the present.
Touches upon a variety of styles, themes, and materials, and gives biographical
information about some of the artists. One 12″ LP.

The Afro-Americans' Life From 1770–1861. Producer/Distributor: ALESCO.
Grade Level: Jr. & Sr. H.S. 50 frames. Automatic Changer. Purchase:
$17.49.

This filmstrip emphasizes the economic importance of slavery to the
colonies; the role of Negroes in the American Revolution; outstanding black
leaders of this period; slave rebellions and abolitionism; and the ever-increasing
divisions between North and South. Includes teacher's manuals.

American Negroes. Producer/Distributor: LLI. Purchase: $50.

Eight filmstrips reveal the life and time of such Negro leaders as Harriet
Tubman, Frederick Douglass, Booker T. Washington, Jackie Robinson, So-
journer Truth, Martin Luther King, George Washington Carver, and Mary Mc-
Leod Bethune.

Artists At Work: Joe Overstreet—Soul Painter. Producer/Distributor: HANDY,
1969. Grade Level: Jr. H.S. through College. Single Strip. 58 frmaes. 33⅓
RPM. Automatic Changer. Purchase: $12.45. Color.

Helpful in art classes, and also of value in counseling students on careers
in art, giving a first hand look at the craftsman at work. It serves to provide an
insight into the creative processes.

Artists at Work. Producer/Distributor: HANDY, 1969. Grade Level: Jr. H.S.
through College. 5 in series. 33⅓ RPM. Automatic Changer. Purchase:
$57.25. Color.

Candid photography provides an exciting insight into four techniques of
modern art-painting, sculpturing, printmaking and the use of the lost-wax
process. The artist expresses his thoughts on the philosophies which are involved in and influence the creation of a particular piece.

Black Folk Music in America. Producer/Distributor: SVE, 1970. Grade Level:
Elementary through Sr. H.S. 55 frames. 4 in series. 33⅓ RPM. Purchase:
$32.50, with records; $36.50, with cassettes.

This series of filmstrips chronicles the history of black music in America
from early Jamestown to today. Artwork, compelling narration and songs performed by Brother John Sellers combine to create a powerful portrayal of
black musical heritage. The filmstrips include the titles: Songs of Slavery; Black
Songs of the Civil War; Black Songs After the Civil War; Black Songs of Modern
Times.

Black History. Producer/Distributor: LIBFSC, 1969. Grade Level: Jr. H.S.
through College. 55 frames. 4 in series. 33⅓ RPM. Purchase: $20. Color.

The filmstrips in this series relate the history and circumstances which
have marked the black man's journey from bondsman to responsible citizen.
Part I Africa–Past; Part II 1492–1865; Part III 1865–1915; Part IV 1915 to
Present. Record also available.

Black History Program. Producer/Distributor: MMPI. 15 in series. Purchase: $375.

This series of sound filmstrips is designed to give a cultural and historic background of black Americans from their beginnings in Africa through the present time.

Black Leaders of the Twentieth Century. Producer/Distributor: IBC. Grade Level: Elementary through Jr. H.S. 10 in series. Purchase: $90.

The biographies of ten black leaders in 20th Century America are presented in terms of their personal achievements and their contributions to American life. This particular selection of personalities was based on the diversity of their contributions, backgrounds, and schools of thought. Included are leaders in politics, the arts, science, labor, and education. Because they were drawn from several generations, even within the 20th Century, a study of all ten suggests in capsulated form where Black America has been, how far it has gone, and where it is heading. Included are Martin Luther King, Mary McLeod Bethune, Charles Drew, Langston Huges, Malcolm X, Percy Julian, Carl Stokes, and Lorraine Hansberry. Five records.

Black Men in Blue. Producer/Distributor: RMI, 1969. Grade Level: Elementary.

A discussion of the bravery and encurance, problems and accomplishments of the Ninth and Tenth Negro Cavalry Regiments after the Civil War. Stresses the success of their work despite racial prejudice encountered from white settlers and army men. These "Buffalo Soliders" were a major force in maintaining peace and furthering civilization in the Southwest.

The Black Odyssey: Migration to the Cities. Producer/Distributor: GA. 2 in series. Purchase: $35, with records; $39, with cassettes. Color.

This program relates historically defined questions to current national developments. **Part I** reviews the Underground Railroad, post-Civil War terrorism, migration to Homestead Act lands. Students learn how World War I industrial needs and cotton crop failures spurred mass Negro movement to the North and examine the impact of the Depression, World War II and the post-war years of continued black migration to the cities. **Part II** contrasts migrants' hopes with realities they faced: limited economic gains, Jim Crow employers and unions, segregated and inferior housing, odds against black-owned businesses. Students trace the Negroes' changing relationship to the labor movement. Finally, the program examines contemporary issues, including: the rise of militant leadership struggles against job discrimination and restricted educational opportunities for blacks.

Black Political Power. Producer/Distributor: AVMC. 6 in series. Purchase: $15, each; $90, set.

This filmstrip is a behind-the-scenes look at what it takes for a black citizen to achieve political success in this country. Lives of important black people include Julian Bond, State Representative of Georgia; Yvonne Brathwaite, California State Representative; Shirley Chisholm, U.S. Representative, New York; John Conyers, Jr. U.S. Representative, Michigan, Carl Stokes, mayor, Cleveland, Ohio. The series puts political insight into campaigning in human terms.

Black Rabbits and White Rabbits: An Allegory. Producer/Distributor: SCHLAT. Grade Level: Elementary through Sr. H.S. Single Strip. 45 frames. 33⅓ RPM. Automatic Changer. Purchase: $21, with record; $24, with cassette. Color.

Tells the story of two communities, each developing its own customs and way of life in its own territory. One day, the white rabbits capture and enslave some of the black rabbits. After many generations, the black rabbits revolt and enslave the white rabbits. The allegory ends when a little white rabbit questions the superiority of his masters. Accompanied by a teacher's guide.

A Boat Named George. Producer/Distributor: OED.

The theme is working with others. George is working hard on a big "construction" project. Bob wants to help, but he's afraid to ask. George needs the help, but he's afraid his request will be rebuffed. A few words from their kind teacher bridges the gap.

Chains of Slavery (1800–1865). Producer/Distributor: EBEC, 1969. Grade Level: Jr. & Sr. H.S. 6 in series. 33⅓ RPM. Automatic Changer. Purchase: $36. Color.

Six filmstrips explaining social injustices in the North and the formation of a closed society in the South. Black participation in the Civil War and the "military necessity" for the Emancipation Proclamation are illustrated.

11701 Harriet Tubman 49 frames. A fast-paced study of one of the most fascinating women of the pre-Civil War period—in the view of many abolitionists, "the greatest heroine of the age."

11702 Frederick Douglass 53 frames. The life of the outstanding black intellectual, Frederick Douglass: his early and brutal slave-labor confinement, his escape to the North, his life as an inspired voice of the abolition movement, his days as an exile in England, as adviser to John Brown, sympathizer to Abraham Lincoln, eloquent recruiter for the Union Army, champion of the poor and homeless freed men in the South, "Father of the Negro Protest Movement."

11703 Black People in the Free North, 1850 52 frames. New England and particularly the city of Boston are observed. Viewers see early groups, such as the New England Anti-Slavery Society founded in 1832 by white abolitionists; see the effect of mass Irish immigration on jobs once held by Afro-Americans; watch the injustice of fugitive slave arrests; see the demonstrations of an aroused public; note the work of many factions opposed to abolition.

11704 Black People in the Slave South, 1850 55 frames. Mississippi is the focal point used to explore the overwhelming social and economic changes worked by the invention of the cotton gin. This "Wild Frontier" of the Cotton Kingdom shows the "slave industry" of the 1830's; the social difference between the "big house" Afro-American, the field hand, and the craftsman; the dramatic changes in southern attitudes fostered by pro-slavery propaganda; the growing frustration of the southern black and the techniques he employed to divert his master while plotting escape.

11705 Nat Turner's Rebellion 46 frames. What immediate effects did Nat Turner's rebellion have on the conditions and treatment of slaves? What were its long-range effects? What other black uprisings occurred in American history? Nat Turner's name was a shock-word to white people in the South before and after the Civil War. It pictures tensions that turned a "good slave" into a brutal killer, propelled a fearful white society into hysteria, and caused unspeakable atrocities.

11706 Black People in the Civil War 51 frames. Shows the dilemma of a president's struggle to save the union, and it presents highlights of famous battles—Port Hudson, Miliken's Bend, Fort Wagner, Fort Pillow.

Cities U.S.A. Producer/Distributor: GA, 1966. Grade Level: Jr. & Sr. H.S. 113 frames. 33⅓ RPM. Automatic Changer. Purchase: $18. B&W & Color.
Part of the Improving American Ways of Life Series.

Civil War and Reconstruction. Producer/Distributor: ALESCO, 1968. Grade Level: Jr. & Sr. H.S. Single Strip. 44 frames. 3 in series. 33¾ RPM. Purchase: $17.59 each. Color.
These films show how the black man helped the Union forces during the Civil War; his achievements during the reconstruction period; and the subsequent rise of discrimination, black codes, and the Ku Klux Klan. One 12″ LP.

Cultural and Social Aspects of Struggle for Civil Rights. Producer/Distributor: ALESCO, 1968. Grade Level: Jr. & Sr. H.S. Single Strip. 42 frames. 6 in series. Purchase: $17.49 each. Color.
Traces the history of the Negro church as an organization, and stresses its role as a source of spiritual strength, political power, and training for leadership. Touches upon various Civil Rights Acts of the 1960's. One 12″ LP.

Children of the Inner City. Producer/Distributor: SVE. Grade Level: Elementary. 55 frames. 6 in series. 33⅓ RPM. Purchase: $7, each; $49.50, with record; $55.50, with cassettes.
Presents the warm, true-to-life stories of six families—their origins, language and customs, their difficulties in adapting to urban society. Each family represents a different racial, religious or national minority group; all of them are U.S. citizens. The titles are: Jose, Puerto Rican Boy; Ernesto, Mexican-American Boy; Gail Ann, Kentucky Mountain Girl; Eddie, American Indian Boy; Fred, Black American Boy; Cynthia, Japanese American Girl. Three records.

Dropping Out: Road to Nowhere. Producer/Distributor: GA, 1964. Grade Level: Jr. & Sr. H.S. 85 & 79 frames. 33⅓ RPM. Automatic Changer. Purchase: $35. Color.
A two-part filmstrip from the series Improving American Ways of Life.

Exploding the Myths of Prejudice. Producer/Distributor: SCHLAT, 1967. Grade Level: Elementary through Jr. H.S. 106 frames. 2 in series. 33⅓ RPM. Automatic Changer. Purchase: $36, with records; $42, with cassettes. Color.
This set attempts to answer such questions as: What is prejudice? Are there pure stocks of people? What causes dark and light skin? Is the white race smarter than others? Accompanied by a teacher's guide and one LP record or two cassette tapes.

Fred, Black American Boy. Producer/Distributor: SVE. Grade Level: Elementary. 54 frames. Purchase: $11, with records; $13, with cassettes. Color.

This color filmstrip presents dreams and realities of Fred, an urban black boy. Photographed on-site in a changing neighborhood, it portrays both the joys and the hostilities Fred and his family encounter.

Frederick Douglass: The Fight for Equal Rights. Producer/Distributor: MGH, 1969. Code No. 40518. Series. Purchase: $11.50.

This sound-filmstrip emphasizes the role of an individual in the development of our nation. Part of the Biography Series.

George Washington Carver: A Study in Genius. Producer/Distributor: RMIF, 1967. Grade Level: Elementary through Sr. H.S. 65 frames. 33⅓ RPM. Purchase: $15. Color.

The inspiring story of a slave boy whose ambition and love of God and nature brought him a college professorship, two doctorates, and national fame for his great contributions to mankind. Shows Tuskegee Institute and the laboratory where Dr. Carver started his long day's work at 4:00 A.M., and the national shrine in his honor.

People Are Like Rainbows. Producer/Distributor: OED. Series.

The theme is the importance of being yourself. Susan and Maria are friends. They share many things; the same games and songs, the same nice teacher. But they are very different. Maria draws and paints, while Susan prefers to play outdoors. That is the way the world is—many different people, similar in some ways and very different in others. Part of the Getting to Know Me Series.

Ghettos of America. Producer/Distributor: SCHLAT/BOW, 1967. Grade Level: Elementary through Jr. H.S. 60–75 frames. 4 in series. 33⅓ RPM. Automatic Changer. Purchase: $60, with records; $72, with cassettes. Color.

This correlated set of sound filmstrips presents everyday life in Harlem and Watts through the eyes of the people who live there. In each presentation, the camera and narrator follow a teenage boy and share in his experiences and in those of his family and the people of his neighborhood. The program dramatizes the way ghettos are created and preserved. Accompanied by a teacher's guide and two LP records or four cassette tapes.

Growing Up Black. Producer/Distributor: SCHLAT, 1968. Grade Level: Elementary through College. 49–75 frames. 4 in series. 33⅓ RPM. Automatic Changer. Purchase: $60, with records; $72, with cassettes. Color.

This sound filmstrip set attempts to create an understanding of what it feels like to grow up black in America, based on in-depth interviews with five Negroes of various backgrounds. Presents childhood experiences to depict the realities of being black in a white society. Accompanied by a teacher's guide and four LP records or cassette tapes.

Harlem People and Places. Producer/Distributor: ALESCO, 1966. Grade Level: Primary. Single Strip. 38 frames. Series. 33⅓ RPM. Purchase: $15.95. Color.

This film explores a Harlem community and discusses the lives, problems, and occupations of the people. One 10″ LP.

The Harlem Renaissance and Beyond. Producer/Distributor: GA. 96 & 111
frames. 2 in series. Purchase: $37.50, with records; $41.50, with cassettes.
Color.

Black poetry and prose offer students valuable insights into the historic
Negro experience in America, as photos and art reflect the social conditions of
Harlem. **Part I** portrays Harlem as post-World War I "race capital," new center
of white literary interest. Langston Hughes' Jesse B. Simple personifies new
concern for ordinary black people as opposed to the "talented tenth." Gripping
poetry by Hughes, Countee Cullen and Claude McKay capture Harlem's early
hopes and her cruel disillusionment during the twenties. **Part II** begins with
Richard Wright's *Native Son* and its vivid portrait of Negro life in the thirites.
Gwendolyn Brooks' poetry describes and condemns World War II discrimination. Students hear major black writers debate the role of race involvement in
their work and the program concludes with examination of socially relevant
poems by today's militant and moderate black poets.

Health Careers. Poducer/Distributor: ELAC. 61 & 46 frames. Purchase: $7.

Students and graduate members of the occupations and professions are
shown at their work, revealing modern facilities, colorful working areas, and the
human relationships that exist between the patients and members of the health
team.

Herbie's Dream. Producer/Distributor: BIF, 1959. Grade Level: Elementary. 88
frames. 33⅓ RPM .Purchase: $9. B&W & Color.

Shows children why they need to eat the right kind of food, why they
must brush their teeth often, and why they should visit the dentist regularly.

A History of Black America. Producer/Distributor: UEVA, 1969. Grade Level:
Jr. & Sr. H.S. 8 in series. 33⅓ RPM. Automatic Changer. Purchase: $6,
each; $68, set. Color.

The African Past 42 frames. An eclectic view of the ancient Africa,
including the findings of recent archaeological studies by Dr. Louis Leakey and
writings from the histories of Greece, Rome, Egypt, and Israel to outline the
black Sudanese empires such as Ghana and Songhay. Ends with the 15th Century
beginnings of the slave trade.

Firebrands and Freedom Fighters 41 frames. Presents the politics and
personalities involved in the abolitionist movement, the underground railroad,
the Fugitive Slave Law, John Brown's raid at Harper's Ferry, and the election of
Abraham Lincoln.

From Freedom to Disappointment 41 frames. Traces the events and
activities which followed the Civil War, including the establishment of the
Freedman's Bureau, the battle against black illiteracy, the political successes of
Robert Brown Elliott and R. B. S. Pinchback, the entrenchment of the "separate
but equal" doctrine, Booker T. Washington's advocacy of vocational education
for blacks, and the resultant opposition from white labor unions at the turn of
the century.

Hope, Disillusionment and Sacrifice 46 frames. Chronicles the advances
made against segregation during the 1940's and 1950's, the accomplishments of
Negroes in the Korean conflict, the beginnings of nonviolent protest and boycotts, the achievements under the Kennedy administration, the rise of militant
groups, and the assassination of Martin Luther King, Jr.

New Leadership and the Turning Tide 41 frames. Contrasts the opposing philosophies of Booker T. Washington and W.E.B. DuBois and discusses the establishment of the NAACP, the national recognition of Negro musicians, the black role in World War I, the beginnings of progress in the civil rights struggle, and Marcus Garvey's failure to provide the leadership so sorely needed for blacks during this crucial period.

The Plantation South 45 frames. Examines the plantation system from 1800 to 1830, pointing out its effects on the slave families. The revolts resulting from the slavery system are described, including those led by Gabriel Prosser, Denmark Vesey, and Nat Turner.

Progress, Depression and Global War 38 frames. Points out the accomplishments of Negroes such as Louis Armstrong in jazz, Langston Hughes in drama, James Weldon Johnson in poetry, and Oscar DePriest, Thurgood Marshall, and Asa Philip Randolph in politics and civil rights movements. Gives reasons for the resurgence of the Ku Klux Klan, segregation and discrimination in World War II, and some favorable Supreme Court rulings.

Slavery and Freedom in the English Colonies 40 frames. Attributes the colonial acceptance of outright Negro slavery to the establishment of indentured immigrants. Conflicting opinions about slavery and its importance to the economy of the colonies are presented, culminating in the large-scale liberation of slaves after the American Revolution and the reasons for the resurgence of slavery and the emergence of the plantation system.

The History of the Black Man in the United States. Producer/Distributor: EAV, 1970. Grade Level: Jr. H.S. through College. 8 in series. 33⅓ RP. Purchase: $72.50.

This sound filmstrip set traces the history of the black man in the United States from Colonial times to the present. The visuals are presented in paintings, cartoons, photographs, and other forms of illustration contemporary to the times discussed. The correlated narration incorporates quotations from people involved in the events described, excerpts from literature and music. A teacher's manual includes a full text of the narration.

Part I: The Colonial Period: The Unwilling Immigrants Early Africa; the origins of the slave trade and the conditions of slavery North and South; the paradox of slavery in the context of the spirit of independence; the Revolutionary War and black participation; post-Revolutionary diminution of slavery.

Part II: The Abolitionists Mounting opposition to slavery from 1800 to Fort Sumter; motives of the white abolitionists such as Garrison, and the influence of the blacks themselves; slave rebellions and the Underground Railroad; Nat Turner and Harriet Tubman; the economic and political factors; the Dred Scott case.

Part III: The Civil War Blacks view the Civil War as "the war to abolish slavery," while Lincoln seeks to preserve the Union; the Emancipation Proclamation; black men under arms and initial resistance to them by Union forces; Robert Smalls; Frederick Douglass; David Walker.

Part IV: Reconstruction The political and social problems of the postbellum period; Andrew Johnson; the freed blacks attempt to adjust to their new status while northern direction of Reconstruction heightens tensions in the South; the failure of Reconstruction and the rise of racism.

Part V: Black Renaissance The revival of a distinct black culture in the post-World War I period; Harlem in the 1920s; the art and artistry of Toomer,

Cullen, Cuney, Dunbar, Ellington, Johnson, Hughes, Holiday, Bessie Smith; the dual existence of the black intellectual in a white world.

Part VI: The Black Man in the Depression The adversity of the black experience is intensified by the Crash of 1929; sharecroppers move to northern ghettos; the significance of religion and the power of black religious leaders; Jessie Owens, Joe Louis, others; World War II and discrimination in industry and armed forces.

Part VII: Racism and the Kerner Commission Report The Kerner Commission examines the foundations and subtleties of racism in the U.S.; examples of how children's literature, movies, journalism, and other media foster racism; the violence of the 1960s and the Commission's warning that U.S. society threatens to split into white and black entities.

Part VIII: Black Protest Movements The blacks' unabating quest for equal rights throughout U.S. history; the continuing conflict between exponents of gradual and immediate implementation of rights; B. T. Washington, W. E. B. DuBois; Montgomery bus boycott; integration of public schools; Dr. King; Malcolm X; Black Power; ghetto uprisings.

Image Makers. Producer/Distributor: EGH, 1969. Grade Level: Jr. & Sr. H.S. 10 in series. 33¾ RPM. Purchase: $77.

This series of ten sound filmstrips presentations traces the rise to prominence of ten outstanding contemporary Negroes in ten varying fields of endeavor. **216A** Matthew Henson; 43 frames. **216B** Jackie Robinson; 46 frames. **216C** Marian Anderson; 53 frames. **216D** Dr. Ralph Bunche; 56 frames. **216E** Thurgood Marshall; 51 frames. **216F** Mary McLeod Bethune; 52 frames. **216G** Dr. Charles Drew; 55 frames. **216H** Gwendolyn Brooks; 52 frames. **216I** Edward W. Brooke; 53 frames. **216J** Martin Luther King, Jr.; 58 frames.

I Never Looked at It That Way Before. Producer/Distributor: GA, 1966. Grade Level: Jr. & Sr. H.S. 68 & 76 frames. 33⅓ RPM. Automatic Changer. Purchase: $35. Color.

A two-part selection from the series Improving American Ways of Life.

John Brown. Producer/Distributor: IFB. Purchase: $13.

This sound filmstrip tells the story of John Brown and his time, using Benet's description of Harper's Ferry and Brown's trial. Presents excerpts from an autobiographical letter of Brown's; his last speech to the court, and a speech by Frederick Douglass examining Brown's place in history. One LP.

John Brown: Martyr or Madman. Producer/Distributor: LEPI. Code No. 102. Purchase: $34.

As the storm-clouds of hatred and rampant emotion gathered prior to the Civil War, certain human actions seemed likely to ignite the opposing guns at any moment. Driven by a consuming passion to abolish the hated institution of slavery, Brown contributed dramatically to the schism which finally drove the Union and Confederacy tragically apart. Songs include "Clear The Track"; "Racing With The Sun"; "Abolitionists Hymn"; and "John Brown's Body."

The KKK: Our Anti-Social Klub. Producer/Distributor: LEPI. Code No. 103. Purchase: $34.

This study traces the history of the Klan, its leaders, its activities, its goals and hopefully its death. In two parts.

Language Art Series. Producer/Distributor: ALESCO, 1968. Grade Level: Sr. H.S. 84 & 86 frames. 33⅓ RPM. Single Strip. 303 in series. Purchase: $15.95, each. Color.

Afro-American Literature (Part I). The story of the creation and development of Afro-American literature from the 1700's through the 1920's. Ranges from work songs and folk tales to slave narratives, novels, and poems by major writers of this time. One 12" disc.

Afro-American Literature (Part II). With the 1930's, Afro-American literature turned from imitation of white writing to a concern for social protest and polemics. Major writers of modern times are high-lighted, and the future of the black writer as an artist is discussed. One 12" disc.

Leading American Negroes. Producer/Distributor: SVE, 1965. Grade Level: Elementary through Adult. 6 in series. 33⅓ RPM. Purchase: $6.50, each; $45, with record; $51, with cassettes.

This set of sound filmstrips depicts the contributions of Negroes to American culture. Included are Mary McLeod Bethune, George Washington Carver, Benjamin Banneker, Robert Smalls, Frederick Douglass, and Harriet Tubman.

Learning About Sex and Love. Producer/Distributor: CAFM, 1967. Grade Level: Jr. & Sr. H.S. 56 frames. 33⅓ RPM. Automatic Changer. Purchase: $46. Color.

This filmstrip begins with babyhood; continues through early child-parent relationships and pre-teens into the teen years. It covers the weaning from parental controls to youth's more mature role, and relations to the opposite sex. Sex functioning is described, the value of wholesome communication between youth and parents, youth and friends; the importance of knowledge, attitudes, values and skills in sex understanding.

Learning to Measure. Producer/Distributor: RMIF. Grade Level: Kindergarten. Single Strip. Purchase: $15.

Informal treatment is given the yardstick and tape measure in comparing the height of children, weighing children and things with different types of scales; measuring with spoons and cups; observing seconds, minutes and hours on clock; noting dates on the calendar, such as birthdays, weeks, and months, and various uses of the thermometer. Negro actors are used.

The Legacy of the Civil War. Producer/Distributor: EGH. 4 in series. Purchase: $34.

A filmstrip documentary relating how the economic, social, and political forces of the Civil War affect today's critical issue of civil rights with haunting, bitter strife and turbulant upheaval. Adaptable to courses in American History, Political Science, Economics, Problems in American Democracy, Civics, and Sociology. This series challenges the student to think, become involved in the problems discusses, and understand the broad concepts of this traumatic era. Subjects are: The Rise of Southern Nationalism Before the Civil War; The Civil War Considered as a Revolution; Presidential vs. Congressional Reconstruction; and Civil Rights and The Legacy of the Civil War.

The Letter. Producer/Distributor: RMIF. Grade Level: Kindergarten. Single
   Strip. Purchase: $12.50.
   Carefully chosen pictures using Negro actors follow the progress of a letter
from a little boy's house to his grandparents' house. Included are the correct
addressing of the letter, the mailing, how the mailmen handle the letter in the
post office, and how it reaches grandpa's mail box.

Listen! Jimmy! Producer/Distributor: QED.
   Jimmy has an overpowering need for recognition—and a very loud voice.
After each classmate's contribution during sharing time, Jimmy has to top it
with a better one. Soon the other children just stop listening to him. Finally,
Jimmy finds the right way to succeed—by doing instead of talking and wins the
respect of his classmates.

Martin Luther King, Jr. Producer/Distributor: EEM. Grade Level: Primary. 40
   frames. 33⅓ RPM. Automatic Changer. Purchase: $8. B&W.
   This filmstrip tells the story of the son of a minister who grew up realiz-
ing there was something different about his family because they were Negro.
The story includes this Negro leader's winning of the Nobel Prize and his tragic
death in 1968.

Minorities Have Made America Great. Producer/Distributor: SCHLAT, 1967.
   Grade Level: Elementary through Jr. H.S. 37–63 frames. 6 in series. 33⅓
   RPM. Automatic Changer. Purchase: $84, with records; $102, with cas-
   settes. Color.
   Each filmstrip traces the story of a different ethnic group from early in
American history to the present time, relating their accomplishments, struggles
and obstacles faced. Accompanied by teacher's guide and six records or cassette
tapes. Included are: Negroes: Slavery; Negroes: Reconstruction to Present;
Jews; Italians; Germans; and Irish.

The Negro in American History: Legacy of Honor. Producer/Distributor: NEA,
   1967. Grade Level: College, Adult. 110 & 37 frames. 2 in series. 33⅓ RPM.
   Purchase: $7, each. Color.
   Part I. Presents the role of the Negro in the discovery, exploration, and
settlement of the New World Territories; Negro participation in the American
Revolution and in the development of a young nation; Negro contributions to
science, the arts and Americn society.
   Part II—Suggestions for Teaching. Provides suggestions and sources of
help and materials for teaching about the Negro in American history. For
teachers only. Accompanied by one 12″ LP, a printed script and program guide.

Negro Cowboys. Producer/Distributor: RMIF. Grade Level: Elementary
   through Sr. H.W. Single Strip. 57 frames. 33⅓ RPM. Purchase: $20. Color.
   Relates the story of the long and largely ignored role of the Negro
Cowboy in the development of the West. Good Guys and bad guys, mountain
men and cattle drivers, gold prospectors and rodeo riders are identified and
portrayed.

Neighborhoods Change. Producer/Distributor: CORF, 1967. Grade Level: Primary. 51 frames. 6 in series. 33⅓ RPM. Automatic Changer. Purchase:
   $47.50. Color.

The camera, observing a wide variety of neighborhoods, opens children's eyes to evidences of change. In the city, pupils see expressways being built, old buildings being torn down and replaced. They see nationality sections being absorbed, evidences of decay and new sections. The necessity for cooperation among people to create better neighborhoods is emphasized.

Neighborhoods in the City With the aid of the camera, the many faces of a big city come up for inspection. Two children travel a paper route, visit the zoo, and go to school. Along the way, they meet three basic types of city neighborhoods: industrial, business and residential. They see that every neighborhood depends upon people and services for its needs. The filmstrip provides a close look at life in one of the residential sections.

Neighborhoods in the Country 50 frames. Farm neighborhoods differ greatly from other neighborhoods, youngsters will quickly discover from this filmstrip. Pupils also learn that there are many kinds of farms—wheat, vegetable and dairy farms, cattle ranches and diversified farms.

Neighborhoods in Small Towns 48 frames. This filmstrip takes children to the suburb to find out its special characteristics. They look at its shopping center, homes with plenty of space, a sprawling modern school, the park with the swimming pool, the village hall and the commuter train station.

Neighborhoods of Many Kinds 50 frames. This introductory filmstrip provides a sweeping over-view of many different kinds of neighborhoods, focusing briefly on dwellings, people, businesses and industries in small towns, big cities, suburbs and country sides.

The Period of 1877 to 1930. Producer/Distributor: ALESCO. Grade Level: Jr. & Sr. H.S. Single Strip. 50 frames. 4 in series. 33⅓ RPM. Purchase: $17.49, each. Color.

Jim Crow laws, unique Negro achievements in various fields, the role of black Americans in World War I, and the Harlem Renaissance are included in this survey of the period. One 12″ LP.

Portrait in Black—America. Producer/Distributor: LEPI. Code No. 101. Purchase: $34.

Depicts the black man's march to full equality, a march which began before the American Revolution as black men and women made their mark in history as scientists, soldiers, poets and men-of-letters. This is an intimate and colorful look at this special slice of history. Songs include "No More Auction Block"; "Michael Rowed the Boat Ashore"; "Marching Song of the First Arkansas"; and "Kingdom Coming." In two parts.

The Rev. Dr. Martin Luther King, Jr. Producer/Distributor: SVE, 1968. Grade Level: Elementary through Sr. H.S. Single Strip. 43 frames. 33⅓ RPM. Purchase: $8.50.

This sound filmstrip on the life of Dr. Martin Luther King, Jr., objectively presents his crusade for the rights and dignity of all men, revealing the events that shaped the life of Dr. King.

Robert and His Family. Producer/Distributor: SVE. Grade Level: Elementary. Purchase: $31, with records; $35, with cassettes.

This 1967 Freedoms Foundation Award Winner is on-site photography with story-type narration portraying the life of Robert Anderson, a primary-grade black boy living in an urban area. Story is told with humor and simplicity. The set of four color filmstrips and two records or two cassettes have the following titles: (1) Robert's Family at Home; (2) Robert's Family & Their Neighbors; (3) Robert Goes Shopping; (4) Robert and Father Visit the Zoo.

The Search for Black Identity. Producer/Distributor: GA. 3 in series. Purchase: $35, with records; $39, with cassettes.

Proud Heritage from West Africa Part I begins by defining the West African Savannah and rain forest regions to which most black Americans trace their ancestry. Part I concludes by examining the influence of Islam on West African literature and education. Part II begins with the Yoruba tribal myth of creation and explores the political and cultural life of Oyo, Benin and Ashanti Forest Kingdoms. Program reviews social fragmentation caused by the slave trade, European colonization and current resurgence of interest in West African culture by Africans and black Americans.

Malcolm X Part I describes Malcolm's deprived childhood, his adolescence in the ghetto, prison years and self-education, his association with the Black Muslims and rise to national prominence. Part II explores Malcolm's changing philosophy during the last months of his life; his African tour and espousal Afro-American unity in a world brotherhood of non-whites, his increasingly less dogmatic view of white people, his partial estrangement from an American black community unsure of his new direction. Throughout the program, comments by today's black leaders indicate Malcolm's continuing development and his influence as the "first black militant."

Martin Luther King Part I traces black leadership from Frederick Douglass on, and introduces Dr. King as a part of this tradition. Excerpts from actual speeches infuse each event with Dr. King's eloquence, conviction and personal impact. Part II follows his contribution through the Greensboro sit-ins, the freedom rides, Birmingham, the March on Washington and Selma, Alabama. Program invites discussion of the goals and non-violent methods Dr. King advocated.

Rush Toward Freedom. Producer/Distributor: SCHLAT, 1970. Grade Level: Jr. H.S. through College. 93–152 frames. 8 in series. 33⅓ RPM. Automatic Changer. Purchase: $108, with records; $132, with cassettes. Color.

This series puts the Civil Rights movement into a meaningful perspective and gives the student an insight into the history and present course of this dynamic social change. Discusses most of the significant events and people of 15 years, including: Little Rock, "Ole Miss," Rosa Parks and the bus boycott, lunch counter sit-ins, police dogs, southern filibusters, voter drives, freedom rides, assassination of Malcolm X, Black Muslims, Stokely Carmichael, Resurrection City, and Mayor Stokes and Hatcher. The narration has highlights from individuals who have taken part in this crucial drama, including: Dr. Martin Luther King, Jr., George Wallace, Medgar Evers, John F. Kennedy, Orville Faubus, and James Meredith. Accompanied by a teacher's guide and eight records or cassette tapes.

Separate and Unequal (1865–1910). Producer/Distributor: EBEC, 1969. Grade Level: Elementary through Sr. H.S. 53 frames. 6 in series. 33⅓ RPM. Automatic Changer. Purchase: $36. Color.

Organized in terms of key men, events and places, this series examines such major events as the passage of the Black Codes which subordinated black people in Southern society and the Supreme Court's decision (Plessy vs. Ferguson) which upheld the validity of separate-but-equal laws.

Booker T. Washington: National Leader. This filmstrip shows the beginning of Booker T. Washington's work, and his unswerving dedication to freedom through education. His famous Atlanta Exposition Speech is discussed.

Bishop Turner: Black Nationalist. From an historic scene in the Georgia State Legislature in 1868, this filmstrip moves to Dr. Ralph Abernathy's statement that "for all civil rights leaders, Bishop Turner remains the symbol of the black man's struggle for equality and self-respect."

Black People in the North, 1900. Depicts the black ghetto in Philadelphia in 1900, exploring the question of the prejudice of white Philadelphians, and traces the development of social, economic and political changes.

Black People in the South, 1877–1900. This chronology of the aftermath of the Radical Reconstruction period develops the influence of "carpetbaggers," the problem of Grant's administration, the contribution of Northern whites who came to help rebuild the South, the dispute surrounding the Hayes-Tilden election, "Rednecks" vs. "Federals," the plight and confusion of blacks freed by law yet steadily losing their rights as citizens.

Separate but Equal. Moving from Louisiana in 1896, when Homer Plessey was arrested for refusing to leave a railroad coach reserved for white passengers, to Alabama in 1955, when Mrs. Rosa Parks was arrested for refusing to yield her seat in the "white" section of a city bus, this filmstrip traces the important socio-political and legal patterns which affected the intervening years. Supreme Court decisions are highlighted by using the court's own words, and prominent court figures are shown stating their opinions.

Slavery: America's Peculiar Institution. Producer/Distributor: ZP. 2 in series. Purchase: $25.

This filmstrip has been designed to offer insight into present-day problems by helping students gain a better understanding of the period in U.S. history when slavery was a legal and political institution in many parts of the country. Included is a detailed teacher's guide and bibliography.

Part I—Background of Slavery. Traces the origins of slavery from beginnings in ancient Greece and Rome. Shows the beginning of the slave trade by Portugal, Spain, and later by the English. Portrays the capturing of slaves and life aboard the slave ships. Shows the seasoning process in the West Indies and aboard the slave ships. Shows the seasoning process in the New World.

Part II—Slavery in America. Traces the beginning of slavery in the United States, the problems the institution created, and the reasons for the enslavement of Negroes. Contrasts slavery as it developed in the North and South and shows how slavery created problems for those who drafted the Declaration of Independence and the founding fathers at the Constitutional Convention.

Strike Three! You're In. Producer/Distributor: OD.

Tim is great at arithmetic, but who likes mathematicians? He'd rather play his favorite game, baseball, only he can't play as well as his classmates. As a matter of fact, they can't add very well and badly need a scorekeeper. Of course

212　　　　　　　　　　　Multimedia Materials for Afro-American Studies it's Tim. Using his special abilities, Tim is accepted as a needed member of the team.

Struggle for Civil and Human Rights. Producer/Distributor: ALESCO, 1968. Grade Level: Jr. & Sr. H.S. Single Strip. 48 frames. 5 in series. 33⅓ RPM. Purchase: $17.49. Color.

This filmstrip reviews the black man's role in America life since 1930, and focuses on his struggle for freedom, first class citizenship, and civil rights. Ends with the 1963 march on Washington, D.C. One 12″ LP.

Studies in the History of Black Americans. Producer/Distributor: SILBUR. 10 in series. 33⅓ RPM. Automatic Changer. Purchase: $99.

African Ancestry. After surveying the diverse geography and distinct cultural groups of Africa, this filmstrip gives strong emphasis to African history from its settlements of 5,000 years ago, through the emergence of Ghana and Mali as powerful empires, to the spread of the Islamic faith and the development of the great educational and cultural centers. Depicted here are the African's abliity to govern, his drive for knowledge, and his skill in opening routes of trade. This filmstrip shows the rise of the trans-Sahara slave trade, followed by the export slave trade and the eventual subjugation of Africa.

Black Participation in the Civil War. Supplying materials missing from classroom texts, this account reveals how black volunteers were at first refused by Union forces; how objections were raised against the formation by blacks of home-guard units; and how Bull Run resulted in a number of important policy changes. Examines the factors behind the Emancipation Proclamation. Shows the raising of all-black regiments, and black troops in every major Union campaign except one.

Black Revolution 1966–. This filmstrip shows why black people came to feel that the gains made by nonviolent direct action in regard to voting, southern universities, interstate buses, public accommodations of all kinds, and employment in defense plants depended on protection. Students hear the voice of Malcolm X calling for black unity in the march toward freedom. Resentment is seen exploding the ghettos of Watts and Newark. The Rev. Jesse Jackson explains why he thinks economics is the answer. The mayor of Gary Indiana, whose successful campaign is described, explains why he thinks political power is the solution.

Black Viewpoints on the American Revolution. Opening with the death of Crispus Attucks in the Boston Massacre and the courage of Peter Salem at Bunker Hill, this filmstrip reveals the changing attitude of the colonists to black military volunteers. It depicts the rale of black men in the American Revolution, crossing the Delaware with Washington, fighting along with the Green Mountain Boys, and using their navigational skills. Shown also is the post-Revolutionary period, with some blacks, as in Massachusetts, being granted the right to vote; some being set free and even receiving state pensions, as in Virginia; and others being returned to the auction block.

Broadening Perspectives. This filmstrip brings out the recognized valor of segregated black troops in World War I, their acceptance in Europe, and their return to lynchings and exclusion. Students learn the causes of the northward migration from 1915 onward. They see the conditions which greeted new arrivals in northern cities and led to the formation of the Urban League. The views of Booker T. Washington are contrasted with those of W. E. B. DuBois and

William Monroe Trotter, as are those of Marcus Garvey with DuBois and A. Phillip Randolph. This filmstrip takes in the effects of the Depression and later the withholding of defense jobs from black people. Students see how Randolph and others forced an end to military segregation after World War II, and how housing segregation continued.

The Civil Rights Movement 1954–1966. Opening with an account of a school girl telling how she was met with bayonets when she attempted to enter her high school in Little Rock, this film puts into perspective the march of recent history—Rosa Parks, Dr. Martin Luther King, and the Montgomery Bus Boycott, the sit-ins, protest, marches—and the reaction, such as the bombing of eight black churches in 1962. Classes see how all this relates to Dr. King's campaign in Birmingham and a public reaction that impelled Congress to pass the Civil Rights Act of 1964. Students learn how the Student Nonviolent Coordinating Committee tested this law with a voter registration drive.

Frederick Douglass. The period between the Revolution and the Civil War is here revealed through the life of a vigorous leader whose activities spanned this whole important era. Drawing largely upon Douglass's own works, the filmstrip recounts how this remarkable man escaped from slavery, joined Garrison's wing of the Abolition Movement, and later broke with it. It explains why he wrote his autobiography, went abroad, had his freedom purchased, and began publishing the North Star. Students learn what reaction met Douglass when he tried to work in a New Bedford shipyard or send his children to Rochester public schools which he later saw integrated.

Jim Crow and the "Progressive." The gradual loss of adequate schooling and the right to vote and the collapse of the Freedmen's Bank are here contrasted with the amount of racial mingling surprised travelers observed in the South. Students see the results of "separate but equal" and the Jim Crow laws of the 1880's and 1890's. Students also learn how prisoners were leased to private individuals for chain-gang work and how lynchings were advertised like picnics. Documented here are the decimation of black registration by the "correct interpretation" device used by registrars; the helplessness of the well-disposed whites against the ruthless; and the temporary unity of poor whites and blacks achieved by Tom Watson and the populists, who, although defeated, bequeathed the nation a number of reforms.

Reconstruction? This filmstrip reveals how Presidential handling of Reconstruction resulted in all-white local governments, courts, and schools. Students see how Congress proposed handling readmission of the southern states, how the Freedmen's Bureau oversaw the division of former plantations, how education under black leadership was begun, and how the plan of Thaddeus Stevens for "40 acres and a mule" was defeated. Also brought home to students are the small, personal realities of the post-war period, such as the seeking of legal marriage denied during slavery. Seen as well is the fearful white reaction to talented black political leadership, a reaction which built up to the Humburg Massacre and the rise of the Ku Klux Klan.

Slavery in America. This filmstrip contrasts Spanish and English slavery to show why the latter resulted in greater hopelessness, weakening of family structure, and general demoralization. It reveals how expediency drove slaves to pretenses of simplemindedness and how the slaveholder's concept of black people shackled many people of both races until very recent times. Studied here is the revolt in Haiti led by Toussaint L'Ouverture and the effects it had on American slaves and slaveholders. Students encounter the plans of Denmark

Vesey and Nat Turner, the operations of the underground railroad, of Harriet Tubman, and of unknown people who tell in their own words how they escaped or led others to freedom successfully.

The Trap. Producer/Distributor: BR/UC. Purchase: $15.

A sound filmstrip on the look, the causes and the despair of poverty. It presents a dramatic picture of one of the most dangerous problems facing the United States today—the immediate and long effects of poverty in an affluent society. Accompanied by a discussion guide. One LP.

They Have Overcome. Producer/Distributor: SCHLAT, 1967. Grade Level: Elementary through Sr. H.S. 82–101 frames. 5 in series. 33⅓ RPM. Automatic Changer. Purchase: $72. Color.

Five prominent Negroes tell how they achieved their present distinguished status in spite of almost insurmountable odds. In their own words, they recall the important experiences and events that shaped their lives. Included are Dr. James Commer, Claude Brown, Dr. Dorothy Brown, Gordon Parks, and Charles Lloyd. Accompanied by a teacher's guide and five LP records or cassette tapes.

Tobacco and Alcohol: The $50,000 Habit. Producer/Distributor: GA, 1967. Grade Level: Jr. & Sr. H.S. 76 & 78 frames. 33⅓ RPM. Automatic Changer. Purchase: $35. Color.

A two-part selection from the series, Improving American Ways of Life.

Understanding Your Love Feelings. Producer/Distributor: CAFM, 1967. Grade Level: Jr. & Sr. H.S. 56 frames. 33⅓ RPM. Automatic Changer. Purchase: $46. Color.

Love is presented in the filmstrip as a growth process that can come many times into the life of a person and take many different forms. Presents the importance of knowing when you are in love and how you can appraise mature love.

Who Am I? The Search for Self. Producer/Distributor: CAFM, 1967. Grade Level: Jr. & Sr. H.S. 61 frames. 33⅓ RPM. Automatic Changer. Purchase: $46. Color.

This filmstrip is addressed to teenagers on their role and position in the home, school and community; how you see yourself and how others see you; how your self-image begins to form in early years and the importance of self-understanding to a healthy mature life. The different treatment given to boys and girls from childhood up tends to shape their emotional and psychological characteristics, and these masculine or feminine characteristics sometimes becomes confused. What we can do to overcome such problems is graphically explained.

You and Your Pet. Producer/Distributor: LYCEUM, 1967. Grade Level: Primary. Single Strip. 43 frames. Purchase: $15. Color.

This is a quietly integrated filmstrip to aid the teacher in presenting elementary aspects of health, hygiene and nutrition—along with love and gentleness for animals.

Multimedia kits

Afro-American History Fact-Pack. Producer/Distributor: EDLACT. Grade
Level: Jr. & Sr. H.S. Media Kit Contents: 1 12″ LP record. Filmstrips. 141
frames. Book. Purchase: Complete kit, $85.90; Slide set (60 slides), $20;
Flashcard set (50 cards, 11⅜″ × 15″), $15; Book, *Afro-American History
Highlights*, $4.95.

This unique kit provides a way to dramatize Afro-American history. The
filmstrip reveals and traces the Black Man's dramatic role in history from the
origin of man in East Africa to his recent realization of black pride. It includes
information about the development of agriculture, surgery and education in
ancient Africa, Black Pharaohs, ancient black cultures in Africa, the enslavement of African peoples, slave experience in the U.S., and black leaders and
heroes from ancient times to the present.

Black Americans in Government. Producer/Distributor: BLC, 1970. Grade
Level: Elementary & Jr. H.S. Media Kit Contents: 5 Records. 5 Filmstrips. Pictures. 1 Teacher's Filmstrip Guide.

The first release in a new and comprehensive Afro-American History and
Culture Series. These unique materials are designed to provide information on
black histroy and culture for existing curricula in such areas as urban problems,
civil rights, and the legislative and judicial processes; to provide materials for
black studies curricula; and to provide materials to promote understanding and
recognition of black Americans' contributions to the United States. The five
people featured are: Thurgood Marshall; Robert Weaver; Edward Brooke;
Shirley Chisholm; Patricia Harris.

The Black Man's Struggle. Producer/Distributor: PPC. Media Kit Contents: 8
Records. Purchase: $47.60.

Beginning with the Jamestown Colony and ending with today's Black
Power Movement, these 16 dramatized episodes portray the black man's efforts
to win equal rights and opportunities throughout American history.

Black Political Power. Producer/Distributor: DOUBLE, 1969. Grade Level: Jr.
& Sr. H.S. Media Kit Contents: Records. Filmstrips. Purchase: $90.

In this series of five sound filmstrips, the viewer takes a behind-the-scenes
look at what is involved in a black citizen's achievement of political success in
this country. Here is a cross-section of blacks already holding important offices
on the city, state and national level. Julian Bond, Shirley Chisholm, John
Conyers, Jr., Carl Stokes, and Yvonne Brathwaite.

Ghetto. Producer/Distributor: SSSS, 1970. Media Kit Contents: Simulations. Purchase: $20.

A game of mobility which simulates the pressures the urban poor live under and the choices that face them as they seek to improve their life situation. Students have the experience of planning the life strategies for a poor person and of meeting with discouragement, frustrations and occasional good luck. Teaches that moving ahead demands wise and strategic use of time and illustrates that an early investment in education pays off throughout life. Also makes clear that there are great barriers to completing one's education in ghetto schools. As the player becomes involved in trying to improve the life situation of a person living in the ghetto, he realizes how poor work, school and living conditions can perpetuate themselves, breed anger and frustration and sometimes inspire heroic community action. (7 to 10 players.)

Growing Up Black. Producer/Distributor: SCHLAT. Media Kit Contents: 4 Records. 4 Filmstrips. Teacher's Guide. Purchase: $58.45.

These recordings deal with the different forms of racism met by black youth in America. It enables students to role-play skits of their own making.

Historical Highlights in the Education of Black Americans. Producer/Distributor: NEA, 1969. Media Kit Contents: Filmstrip. 1 12" LP. History booklet. Purchase: $10.

Throughout our nation's history, there have been Americans who struggled against prejudice and hatred to obtain good education for black children. The struggle is being carried on today.

Negro History. Producer/Distributor: SVE. Code No. MM-43K. Media Kit Contents: Filmstrips. Pictures. Displays. Book. Purchase: $91.

The kit is packaged in a sturdy, easy-to-use-and-store carton with contents listed inside the cover. The items listed below are included in the kit: Filmstrips: **742-SAR** Leading American Negores (set of 6 full-color filmstrips with 3 back-to-back records). **244-3R** The Rev. Dr. Martin Luther King, Jr. (black & white filmstrip, record, and guide). Book: **43-A** Great Negroes, Past and Present (150 biographies, fully illustrated). Picture-Display Portfolios: Each contains 24 plastic-coated, 2-color prints—11" x 14"; brief biographical sketches. **43-B** Negroes in Our History **43-C** Modern Negro Contributors **43-D** Negroes of Achievement (1865–1915). Overhead Transparencies: **OT-10S** Great American Negroes (set of 6 transparencies with guide).

Silhouettes in Courage. Producer/Distributor: EA. Purchase: $45 set.

A new motivating, fully documented history of black America. Over 500 actors and musicians have joined forces to bring 2,500 years of authentic black American history. **Volume 1** Narrated by Ossie Davis; **Volume 2** Narrated by Brock Peters; **Volume 3** Narrated by Frederick O'Neal; **Volume 4** Hear words of black leaders Martin Luther King, James Meredith, Malcolm X.

Soul Brothers: Men of Thought, Men of Action. Producer/Distributor: DOUBLE, 1969. Grade Level: Jr. H.S. through College. Media Kit Contents: Records. Filmstrips. Pictures. Purchase: $130.

Through the eyes of these men more than two hundred years of the American experience—from 1730 to the present—are vividly recreated in a new multimedia sound filmstrip series.

Sunshine. Producer/Distributor: SSSS. Media Kit Contents: Simulations. Purchase: $10 each.

A simulation of current racial problems in a typical city. Students are "born" by pulling race identity tags from a hat at the beginning of the simulation. During the remainder of the game, students wear their identities. The class is divided into a mythical city with six neighborhoods with varying degrees of segregation and integration in housing and schooling. While studying the history of the Negro from slavery to the present, students also research ways of solving current racial problems. Pre- and post-attitude tests on racial toleration show the teacher and the class the results of the experience.

Recordings (discs)

Adventures in Negro History (Vol. I & II). Producer/Distributor: PEPI 1966. 33⅓ RPM. Purchase.

A recorded series of adventures in the history and development of Negroes in American life.

American History in Ballad and Song. Producer/Distributor: FRSC, 1960. Grade Level: Jr. H.S. Code No. FH 5801. LP. 6 sides. 33⅓ RPM. Purchase: $13.39.

A chronological history of America told in ballads and songs.

American Negro Folk and Work Song Rhythms. Producer/Distributor: FRSC, 1960. Grade Level: Elementary. Code No. FC 7654. 12″ LP. 2 sides. 33⅓ RPM. Monaural. Purchase: $4.45.

Ella Jenkins and the Goodwill Spiritual Choir of Chicago celebrate the musical heritage of the black American. Simple work songs, rhythmic chants, and inspiring spirituals voice his suffering, his warm humor, his aspirations for freedom and equality. A special section on the spiritual features "This is the Way I Pray," others. Percussive instruments and hand-clapping accompany the songs.

American Negro History. Producer/Distributor: EAV. Code No. 350-22. LP. 2 sides. 33⅓ RPM. Purchase: $6.50.

The history of American Negro in song and prose. Read by Langston Hughes.

Amos Fortune, Free Man. Producer/Distributor: NARI. Grade Level: Elementary through College. Code No. 3008. LP. 33⅓ RPM Purchase: $5.95.

A documentary that tells how Prince At-Mun was captured, sold into slavery, and finally freed. Based on a book by Elizabeth Yates.

Anthology of Negro Poets. Producer/Distributor: FRSC, 1955. Grade Level: Jr. & Sr. H.S. Code No. FL 9791. 12″ LP. 2 sides. 33⅓ RPM. Monaural. Purchase: $5.95.
  Langston Hughes, Sterling Brown, Claude McKay, Margaret Walker, Countee Cullen, and Gwendolyn Brooks read from their works. Biographies of the poets are included in the album.

Anthology of Negro Poets in the U.S.A. Producer/Distributor: FRSC, 1955. Grade Level: Jr. & Sr. H.S. Code No. FL 9792. 12″ LP. 2 sides. 33⅓ RPM. Monaural. Purchase: $5.95.
  Arna Bontemps reads the poetry of James Weldon Johnson to a musical background of "God's Trombones."

An Anthology of Negro Poetry for Young People. Producer/Distributor: FRSC, 1958. Grade Level: Elementary & Jr. H.S. Code No. FC 7114. 10″ LP. 2 sides. 33⅓ RPM. Monaural. Purchase: $4.15.
  Arna Bontemps reads poems by Langston Hughes, Countee Cullen, Paul Laurence Dunbar, Claude McKay, and others.

The Autobiography of Frederick Douglass, Part I. Producer/Distributor: FRSC/ALESCO, 1966. Grade Level: Jr. & Sr. H.S. 12″ LP. 2 sides. 33⅓ RPM. Purchase: $6.67.
  Read by Ossie Davis, this record is based on three autobiographies that Douglass wrote, this record covers the first 30 years of his life from his birth as a slave to his work as a newspaper editor. Includes descriptive notes. A second record covers the last 48 years of Douglass' life, and also includes descriptive notes.

The Autobiography of Frederick Douglass, Part II. Producer/Distributor: FRSC, 1966. Grade Level: Elementary through Sr. H.S. Code No. FH 5522. 12″ LP. 2 sides. 33⅓ RPM. Monaural. Purchase: $5.95.
  An inspiring LP for American history classes, taken from books, speeches, and journals of the former slave who rose to become a brilliant speaker and editor. The contents also include Douglass's impression of his childhood; his eyewitness accounts of slave life and his escape from it; and his story of the publication of the *North Star,* the newspaper he established in 1847. His words are read by actor Ossie Davis.

Ballads of Black America. Producer/Distributor: HBMP. 8″ LP. 33⅓ RPM. Purchase: $1.95, each.
  Dramatizes original ballads about the black heroes. The record is accompanied by six page booklet with an illustrated transcript of the narration and a three-color poster showing a portrait of the leader and, on the reverse side, the music and words to the ballads. The following names are featured: Harriet Tubman, Frederick Douglass, The Deacons for Defense and Justice, Leroy "Satchel" Paige.

Been Here and Gone. Producer/Distributor: FRSC. Code No. FA 2659. 12″ LP. 33⅓ RPM. Purchase: $5.79.
    An album which documents Negro music from the South.

Been in the Storm So Long. Producer/Distributor: RSC, 1967. Grade Level: Jr. & Sr. H.S. Code No. FS 3842. 12″ LP. 2 sides. 33⅓ RPM. Monaural. Purchase: $5.79.
    This recording attempts to show that isolated pockets of rich regional culture still exist. Recorded on location on Johns Island one of the Sea Islands off South Carolina, it reflects the life of the Sea Island Negroes. Because of their isolation from the mainstream of modern life they were able to preserve their unique folkways, which express themselves in hymns, spirituals, fables concerning Bible. The album is also recommended to students of American speech, social studies, and folk music.

Belafonte at Carnegie Hall. Producer/Distributor: RCA. Grade Level: Jr. & Sr. H.S. Code No. LSO-6006. 12″ LP. 4 sides. 33⅓ RPM. Stereo. Purchase: $7.45.
    These songs are sung by Harry Belafonte, accompanied by an orchestra conducted by Robert Corman.

The Believers. Producer/Distributor: RCA, 1969. Grade Level: Jr. & Sr. H.S. Code No. LSO-1151. 12″ LP. 2 sides. 33⅓ RPM. Purchase: $3.72.
    The Black Experience in Song. An original cast recording of the current Off-Broadway musical hit. Selections trace the blacks' passage from Africa to the southern slave plantations, from the country-side to the city and the current resurgence of nationalist militancy.

Bessie Smith: The World's Greatest Blues Singer. Producer/Distributor: CR. Purchase: $5.98.
    This collector's item is a reissue of Miss Smith's entire recorded output— 160 selections—on ten LPs, which are offered in two-disk sets. The selections have been arranged in chronological order and organized so that the complete set will be in sequences. The first set is now available. Bessie Smith: The World's Greatest Blues Singer consists of her first and last sixteen recordings.

Beyond the Blues. Producer/Distributor: LLI. Code No. PM 81. 12″ LP. 33⅓ RPM. Purchase: $5.95.
    American Negro poetry read by Brock Peters, Gordon Heath, Vinette Carroll, and Cleo Laine.

Black America: The Sounds of History. Producer/Distributor: NBC. Grade Level: Jr. & Sr. H.S. Purchase: $80.
    An audio history of black people in America from their African roots to the conflicting currents of black thought in the present day. There are 30 divisions in the series. **African Heritage (Pre-History–1500)**: Kingdoms & Heroes; West African Homeland. **Black Cargoes (1450–1800)**: Pillage of West Africa; The Middle Passage. **Slavery Takes Hold (1619–1860)**: Colonial Slavery; The Cotton Kingdom. **Toward Freedom (1619–1860)**: Slave Resistance; Abolitionist Crusade. **Black Achievements (1490–1860)**: Explorers and Patriots; Builders of a New Nation. **Civil War (1860–13865)**: White Man's War; Black Man's Struggle. **Reconstruction (1865–1900)**: A Taste of Freedom; Restoration of

White Rule. **Separate and Unequal (1876–1900)**: Jim Crow in the North; Jim Crow in the South. **Black Leadership (1860–1918)**: Era of Booker T. Washington; Challenge of W. E. B. DuBois. **Harlem Renaissance (1918–1929)**: Black Politics; Black Culture. **Blacks in the Depression (1929–1939)**: Last Hired, First Fired; Roosevelt & Black Politics. **World War II and Beyond (1939–1954)**: The War Effort; The Struggle Resumed. **Civil Rights Movement (1954–1969)**: Toward Integration; Rise of Black Power. **Black Achievements (1986–1969)**: Builders of Industrial America; Spread of Black Culture. **Black Spokesmen (1800–1969)**: Voices of the 19th Century; Voices of the 20th Century.

Black Contributors to American Culture. Producer/Distributor: SVE. Grade Level: Elementary through Sr. H.S. 33⅓ RPM. Purchase: $40.

Four albums; eight records. Encompasses the contributions of 32 prominent Afro-Americans in the areas of Science, Government, Human Rights, Music, Arts, Literature, and Theatre.

The Black Heritage in Song. Producer/Distributor: VSC, 1970. Purchase: $5.98.

This recording is a beginning in the attempt to collate and preserve the contributions of black composers and arrangers of choral music. Contents of "The William Dawson Song Book": "Oh What a Beautiful City," "Soon Ah Will Be Done," "Ain'-a That Good News," "There is Balm in Gilead," "Ezekiel Saw De Wheel," "Behold The Sar," "Every Time I Feel The Spirit," "Mary Had A Baby," "Lit'l Boy Child," "Jesus Walked This Lonesome Valley," "King Jesus Is A-Listening," "Hail Mary."

Black Image Makers. Producer/Distributor: EGH, 1969. Grade Level: Jr. & Sr. H.S. Code No. S 1508. 12″ LP. 2 sides. 33⅓ RPM. Purchase: $22.50.

Narrated by Rosko, a well-known disk jockey and written by Wendy Rydell. Narrations present the biography and the spirit of these persons: **Record 1** Matthew Alexander Henson, Jackie Robinson; **Record 2** Marian Anderson, Dr. Ralph Bunche; **Record 3** Thurgood Marshall, Mary McLeod Bethune; **Record 4** Dr. Charles Drew, Gwendolyn Brooks; **Record 5** Edward Brooke, Martin Luther King.

The Black Man in America. Producer/Distributor: LLI. Code No. H.G. 120. 12″ LP. 33⅓ RPM. Purchase: $5.95.

Studs Terkel interviews James Baldwin.

Black Pioneers in American History (19th Century). Producer/Distributor: CRI. Code No. TC-1252. Purchase: $7.50.

Narrated by Eartha Kitt and Moses Gunn, this record portrays the lives and contributions of such black heroes as Frederick Douglass and Nat Love. It carries background sound effects in an effort to portray reality.

Black Protest. Producer/Distributor: LLI/EAV, 1970. Grade Level: Sr. H.S. & College. Code No. 6RR862. 6 sides. 33⅓ RP. Monaural. Purchase: $18.95.

The protests of American Negroes against slavery, oppression, and discrimination are presented in selections of the words, and some actual voices, of the black people. Speeches by Martin Luther King, Jr., Malcolm X, Stokely Carmichael, and others.

Blues Roots. Producer/Distributor: PRSI, 1964. Grade Level: Sr. H.S. & College. 12" LP. 33⅓ RPPM. Purchase: $5.95, each.

RF16 Chicago—The 1930's. Includes performances by Big Bill, Memphis Minnie, and Johnny Temple. **RF14 Mississippi.** Includes performances by Tommy Johnson, the Mississippi Jug Band, Joe Williams, and Robert Johnson. Both discs compiled and annotated by Samuel B. Charters.

Booker T. Washington. Producer/Distributor: CMSR, 1968. Code No. CMS 540. LP. 2 sides. 33⅓ RPM. Monaural. Purchase: $5.95.

Excerpts from *Up From Slavery* read by Chuck Daniel.

Call of Freedom. Producer/Distributor: FRSC, 1962. Grade Level: Elementary. Code No. FC 7566. 12" LP. 2 sides. 33⅓ RPM. Monaural. $5.79.

A playlet on slavery and emancipation in the U.S., performed by a class of elementary school children. Side 2, starting with "We Shall Overcome," presents freedom songs recorded throughout the world.

The Country Blues (Vol. 1). Producer/Distributor: PRSI, 1964. Grade Level: Jr. H.S. through College. Code No. RF 1. 12" LP. 2 sides. 33⅓ RPM. Monaural. Purchase: $5.95.

Early rural Recordings of folk artists. Edited by Samuel B. Charters. Includes songs sung by Blind Lemon Jefferson, Lonnie Johnson, Cannon's Jug Stompers, and Peg Leg Howell.

The Dream Keeper: Producer/Distributor: FRSC 1955. Grade Level: Jr. & Sr. H.S. Code No. FC 7102. 10" LP. 2 sides. 33⅓ RPM. Monaural. Purchase: $4.15.

Written and narrated by Langston Hughes, who shows how his poetry developed from specific experiences and ideas. A trip to the "Waterfront Streets;" an idea that people should treasure their dreams becomes another famous poem. As Hughes says, "All the progress that human beings have made on this earth of ours grew out of dreams."

Dred Scott Decision; John Brown's Last Speech. Producer/Distributor: ALESCO/EEM, 1968. Grade Level: Sr. H.S. 12" LP. 2 sides. 33⅓ RPM. Purchase: $7.22.

This recording on Side 1 presents the history, meaning, and import of the famous Supreme Court decision regarding slavery. Side 2 offers a dramatic presentation of the abolitionist's life and principles. Good background material is included in the readings.

Duke Ellington's Concert of Sacred Music. Producer/Distributor: RCA. Grade Level: Jr. H.S. Code No. LPS-3582. 12" LP. 2 sides. 33⅓ RPM. Stereo. Purchase: $3.10.

Ellington's vital and contemporary affirmation of faith in a musical language.

Ethel R. Dennis. Producer/Distributor: LLI. Purchase: $5.95.

This black author, lecturer, and educator presents a panorama of noted black personalities and leaders during ancient times who helped shape world civilization. Based on talks she has given on her popular radio program in New Haven, Connecticut.

Everybody's Got a Right to Live. Producer/Distributor: PRSI. Grade Level: Jr. H.S. through College. Code No. BRS 308. 12" LP. 2 sides. 33⅓ RPM. Stereo. Purchase: $5.95.

Eleven songs are presented on this disc.

The Fisk Jubilee Singers. Producer/Distributor: FRSC, 1955. Grade Level: Jr. & Sr. H.S. Code No. FA 2372. 12" LP. 2 sides. 33⅓ RPM. Monaural. Purchase: $5.95.

This group from Fisk University introduced Negro spirituals to the music world in 1871. From then on, similar groups—also selected from the student body of Fisk University—have made concert tours under the same name.

Frederick Douglass. Producer/Distributor: CMSR, 1969. Grade Level: Jr. H.S. through College. Code No. CS 570. LP. 2 sides. 33⅓ RPM. Monaural. Purchase: $5.95.

Read by Brock Peters. The story and thoughts of the great Afro-American leader, from his autobiography.

Free At Last. Producer/Distributor: GORDY. 12" LP. 33⅓ RPM. Purchase: $4.95.

Presents excerpts from Dr. Martin Luther King's most important speeches and sermons: "I've Been to the Mountain," "I Have a Dream" "Free at Last," and "Drum Major Instinct Sermon".

George Washington Carver. Producer/Distributor: ETM. 12" LP. 33⅓ RPM. Purchase.

Carver's career is highlighted under the headings: A Young Negro's Thirst for Learning; Call to Tuskegee; Sweet Potatoes and Peanuts; Professor Carver Impresses Congress.

The Glory of Negro History. Producer/Distributor: FRSC, 1966. Grade Level: Elementary through Sr. H.S. Code No. FC 7752. 12" LP. 2 sides. 33⅓ RPM. Monaural. Purchase: $5.95.

Written by poet Langston Hughes, this record discusses how Negroes first came to the Americas as sailors; the triumphs and tragedies of the Negro people; the story of George Washington Carver, the chemist-botanist who discovered that the prosaic peanut had undreamt of uses. The voices of Mary McLeod Bethune, pioneer educator, and Ralph Bunche, Nobel Prize winner and U.N. official are heard. It is recommended for American history classes. Told through the use of African chants and American Negro folk songs.

Great Moments in Negro History. Producer/Distributor: SSSS, 1966. Grade Level: Elementary through Sr. H.S. 12" LP. 2 sides. 33⅓ RPM. Monaural. Purchase: $3.75.

This record unveils the saga of the American Negro, a people whose labor, sweat and tears have helped make America great. Covered are Crispus Attucks, the first man to die in the War for Independence; Harriet Tubman, creator of the Underground Railroad; Hiram Rhodes, first Negro U.S. Senator; and Martin Luther King, Nobel Peace Prize winner, among others.

Great Negro Americans, Vol. I. Producer/Distributor: ALESCO. Grade Level: Jr. & Sr. H.S. 12" LP. 2 sides. 33⅓ RPM. Purchase: $6.62.

Short biographical sketches of ten famous Negro Americans who achieved success in such fields as business, music, publishing, medicine, and athletics. Includes teacher's guide.

A Hand Is on the Gate. Producer/Distributor: VER. Code No. H191. 12″ LP. Purchase.

An all Negro revue which won acclaim during the 1966 Broadway theater season.

The History of the American Negro. Producer/Distributor: LLI. LP. Purchase: $64.

Eight color filmstrips, along with recordings, help develop a basic understanding of the evolution of the Negro race in America and an appreciation of the problems faced and the contributions made by an emerging ethnic group in a large society. From Africa to America; Slavery in the Young American Republic; Slavery In "A House Divided"; The Negro In Civil War and Reconstruction; The Negro In The Gilded Age; The Negro Faces The 20th Century; The Negro Fights For The Four Freedoms; The Threshold Of Equality.

History of Jazz. Producer/Distributor: FRSC, 1968. Grade Level: Elementary through Sr. H.S. Code No. FJ 2811. LP 2 sides. 33⅓ RPM. Monaural. Purchase: $4.45 each.

FJ2801 The South; **FJ2802** The Blues; **FJ2803** New Orleans; **FJ2804** Jazz Singers; **FJ2805** Chicago No. 1; **FJ2806** Chicago No. 2; **FJ2807** New York: (1922–34); **FJ2808** Big Bands (1924–34); **FJ2809** Piano; **FJ2810** Boogie Woogie; **FJ2811** Addenda.

History of Jazz: The New York Scene. Producer/Distributor: PRSI, 1965. Grade Level: Sr. H.S. & College. Code No. RF 3. 12″ LP. 2 sides. 33⅓ RPM. Monaural. Purchase: $5.95.

Documentary recordings by Mamie Smith (accompanied by Perry Bradford's Jazz Hounds, 1920—Crazy Blues); Fletcher Henderson and his Orchestra, 1925 (Sugar Foot Stomp); Clarence Williams' Washboard Five, 1928 (Log Cabin Blues), and others. Edited by Samuel B. Charters.

An Introduction to Gospel Song. Producer/Distributor: PRSI, 1965. Grade Level: Sr. H.S. & College. Code No. RF 5. 12″ LP. 2 Sides. 33⅓ RPM. Monaural. Purchase: $5.95.

Compiled and edited by Samuel B. Charters, this recording includes performances by the Fisk University Jubilee Quartet, Tuskegee Institute Singers and the Pace Jubilee Singers with Hattie Parker.

The Invincible Louisa. Producer/Distributor: NARI. Grade Level: Elementary through H.S. Code No. 3009. LP. 33⅓ RPM. Purchase: $5.95.

Based on a book by Cornelia Meigs, this recording portrays the part the Alcotts played in the Underground Railroad; it also covers Louisa's feelings about slavery and her participation in the events leading to the Emancipation Proclamation.

In White America. Producer/Distributor: LLI. Code No. HG 135. 12″ LP. 33⅓ RPM. Purchase: $6.95.

This critically acclaimed off-Broadway production dramatizes the history of the Negroes' struggle or equality in America from the days of slavery to the present in narrative and song. Also available on Columbia Records.

James Baldwin Reads James Baldwin. Producer/Distributor: CMSR, 1967. Grade Level: Sr. H.S. & College. Code No. CMS 517. LP. 2 sides. 33⅓ RPM. Monaural. Purchase: $5.95.

The celebrated writer reads excerpts from his novels *Giovanni's Room* and *Another Country.*

Jerico-Jim Crow. Producer/Distributor: FRSC, 1966. Grade Level: Jr. & Sr. H.S. Code No. FL 9671. 12″ LP. 2 sides. 33⅓ RPM. Monaural. Purchase: $11.90.

Performed by the original cast. It is a documentary musical about music. It contains freedom songs, spirituals, and traditional songs, along with narration depicting the Negroes' struggle for freedom and equality. Good for drama and music classes.

John Brown's Last Speech/The Dred Scott Decision. Producer/Distributor: ETM. Code No. EAD-15. Purchase: $5.95.

This record is a narration of events which carry the listener back to the time of John Brown and the Dred Scott Era. The audio presentations are designed for introducing the black experience.

Langston Hughes. Producer/Distributor: CRI/ALESCO. Grade Level: Jr. & Sr. H.S. 12″ LP. 33⅓ RPM. Purchase: $7.22.

Side 1: 27 poems; Side 2: 23 poems. When the "poet laureate of Harlem" depicts the despair and frustration, hopes, and aspirations of the New York ghetto, he also expresses the feelings of other black Americans throughout the nation. Read by Ruby Dee and Ossie Davis. A collection of sharp, witty, and thought-provoking dialogues on various aspects of black and white American life (from Hughes' *Simple*) read by Ossie Davis is available on a second record at the same price.

Leadbelly's Last Sessions. Producer/Distributor: FRSC, 1954. Grade Level: Jr. & Sr. H.S. Code No. FO 2941. 12″ LP. 4 sides. 33⅓ RPM. Monaural. Purchase: $8.92.

Recordings by Leadbelly, who was a forerunner of Contemporary folk music.

Music Down Home. Producer/Distributor: FRSC/ALESCO, 1965. Grade Level: Sr. H.S. Code No. FA 2691. 12″ LP. 4 sides. 33⅓ RPM. Purchase: $12.72.

The 33 pieces included here form a representative collection of authentic Negro country folk music covering a variety of song types, instruments, and moods. Includes descriptive notes.

Negro Folk Music of Alabama. Producer/Distributor: FRSC. 12″ LP. Purchase: $6.79, each.

FE4417 Vol. 1 Includes field calls, lullabies, ring games, work songs, folktales, and chain-gang songs. **FE4418 Vol. 2** Includes religious songs, with notes by Harold Courlander.

Negro Folk Music of Africa and America. Producer/Distributor: EAV Code No. 5RR862. LP. 33⅓ RPM. Stereo. Purchase: $15.90.

Recordings made in Africa, South America, Haiti, Puerto Rico, Mississippi, Alabama and provide a cross section of musical styles and instruments.

Negro Folk Songs for Young People. Producer/Distributor: FRSC/ALESCO, 1960. Grade Level: Jr. & Sr. H.S. Code No. FC7533. 12″ LP. 2 sides. 33⅓ RPM. Purchase: $5.79.

Authentic Negro worksongs, blues, and spirituals reflecting the life and history of black Americans. Includes descriptive notes with texts of songs, and selections sung and written by Leadbelly.

Negro Poets. Producer/Distributor: LLI. Code No. PM 79. 12″ LP. 33⅓ RPM.

Langston Hughes, Sterling Brown, Claude McKay, Countee Cullen, etc., read from their works.

Negro Prison Camp Folk Songs. Producer/Distributor: FRSC. Code No. FE4475. 12″ LP. Purchase: $6.79.

Includes notes by Pete Seeger.

The Negro Woman. Producer/Distributor: FRSC, 1966. Grade Level: Jr. & Sr. H.S. Code No. FH 5523. 12″ LP. 2 sides. 33⅓ RPM. Monaural. Purchase: $5.79.

The personal, intimate reminiscences of courageous Negro heroines, including Sojourner Truth, Harriet Tubman, Frances Harper, and Mary McLeod Bethune. With great skill and dignity, all of these women fought prejudice against Negroes and prejudice against their sex. Recommended for classes in American history (Civil War suffragette movement) and social studies.

Negro Poets in the U.S.A. Producer/Distributor: LLI. Code No. PM 80. 12″ LP.

Arna Bontemps reads from works covering 200 years.

Negroes in America. Producer/Distributor: LLI. Purchase: $10.95.

From slavery to freedom to civil rights. Black Americans and their goals. Splits in the civil rights movement. Progress in education and jobs. White backlash. The new Negro militancy.

New Jazz Poets. Producer/Distributor: PRSI, 1961. Grade Level: Sr. H.S. & College. Code No. BR 461. 12″ LP. 2 sides. 33⅓ RPM. Monaural. Purchase: $5.95.

Compiled and edited by Walter Lowenfels. On the record: "Jitterbugging in the Streets" (Calvin C. Hernton); "The Second Coming" (John Morgan); "Autumn, 1964" (Peter La Forge); "March on the Delta" (Art Berger).

On the Road to Selma. Producer/Distributor: LLI. Code No. HG 139. 12″ LP. 33⅓ RPM. Purchase: $5.95.

The story of the march to Selma, Alabama.

The Original Confession of Nat Turner. Producer/Distributor: CMSR/ALESCO, 1968. Grade Level: Sr. H.S. 12″ LP. 2 sides. 33⅓ RPM. Purchase: $5.70.

Read by Brock Peters. Dramatic reading of the legal confession made by the leader of a famous nineteenth-century American slave revolt—followed by a discussion of Nat Turner and his rebellion by Brock Peter and two scholars.

Our Voices, Our Faces. Producer/Distributor: LLI. Code No. HG-140. 12" LP. 33⅓ RPM. Purchase: $6.50.
Collection of monologues on Civil Rights, written and performed by Lillian Smith.

Reconstruction and Negro Civil Rights. Producer/Distributor: PPC. 4 sides.
Set of two records—Dramatizations of events from 1865 to 1900: Thaddeus Stevens argues for Radical Reconstruction; President Johnson is impeached; Frederick Douglass fights for Negro rights; Booker T. Washington educated his people.

Richard Wright. Producer/Distributor: LLI. Purchase: $12.95.
Brock Peters reads a condensation of *Black Boy*, the autobiography by a man who grew up in the pre-Civil Rights Act era in the South.

Roots, an Anthology of Negro Music in America. Producer/Distributor: CR. 33⅓ RPM. Purchase: $4.98.

The Sit-In Story. Producer/Distributor: FRSC, 1960. Grade Level: Jr. & Sr. H.S. Code No. 5502. 12" LP. 2 sides. 33⅓ RPM. Monaural. Purchase: $5.79.

Songs of the American Negro. Producer/Distributor: LLI. Purchase: $5.95.
Sung by Michael Larue. Notes by John Franklin and Ralph Knight.

Sound of Harlem. Producer/Distributor: EAV. Grade Level: Sr. H.S. & College. Code No. 8RR360. LP. 6 sides. 33⅓ RPM. Stereo. Purchase: $14.95.
An anthology of jazz played by some of the most important figures of music: Louis Armstrong, Bessie Smith, Cab Calloway, Fats Waller, Ethel Waters, Benny Carter and others.

The Story of Jazz. Producer/Distributor: FRSC, 1955. Grade Level: Jr. & Sr. H.S. Code No. FC7312. 10" LP. 2 sides. 33⅓ RPM. Monaural. Purchase: $4.15.
Written and narrated by Langston Hughes. He explains the rise of jazz illustrated with excellent samples of the blues, ragtime, and bebop.

To Live and Die in Dixie. Producer/Distributor: PRSI, 1967. Grade Level: Sr. H.S. & College. Code No. BR 470. 12" LP. 2 sides. 33⅓ RPM. Monaural. Purchase: $5.95.
John Beecher, rebel and poet, cuts at racial injustice with knifesharp precision. Bigotry and the indifference of man to the suffering of others is dramatized in a selection of his poetry. Complete text and introduction.

Vinie Burrows. Producer/Distributor: LLI. Purchase: $6.50.
The black scene in prose, poetry and song. A one-woman show with guitar accompaniment which includes works from Stephen Vincent Benet, Sojourner Truth, Robert Hayden, Langston Hughes, and others.

Walk Together Children: The Black Scene in Prose, Poetry, and Song. Producer/Distributor: SAC. Code No. 1030. Purchase: $5.95.

Vinie Burrows brings her dramatic ability to a presentation of song and verse.

We Shall Overcome. Producer/Distributor: PRSI, 1963. Grade Level: Jr. H.S. through College. Code No. BR 592. 12″ LP. 2 sides. 33⅓ RPM. Monaural. Purchase: $5.95.

This documentary of the March on Washington August 28, 1963, contains excerpts of all the participants, their songs and speeches. Also includes the complete speech of Dr. Martin Luther King, "I Have A Dream."

We Shall Overcome. Producer/Distributor: FRSC, 1964. Grade Level: Jr. & Sr. H.S. Code No. FD 5591. 12″ LP. 2 sides. 33⅓ RPM. Monaural. Purchase: $5.95.

These songs are often included in the selections sung by Civil Rights workers. The types ranged from spirituals to gospel songs, such as, "There's a Meeting Here Tonight," "Rock My Soul," "Hold On," "We Shall Overcome." Contributions were made by the Montgomery Gospel Trio, the Nashville Quartet, and Guy Carawan.

What Is Jazz? Producer/Distributor: MFL. 12″ LP. 33⅓ RPM. Purchase: $3.62.

Leonard Bernstein looks at jazz with Birch Clayton, Bessie Smith, Louis Armstrong, and others.

William Melvin Kelley Reads William Melvin Kelley. Producer/Distributor: CMSR, 1967. Grade Level: Sr. H.S. & College. Code No. CMS 525. LP. 2 sides. 33⅓ RPM. Monaural. Purchase: $5.95.

Mr. Kelley reads excerpt from his novel "A Different Drummer" and his complete short story "The Only Man On Liberty Street."

WNEW's Story of Selma. Producer/Distributor: FRSC. Code No. FH5595. 12″ LP. Purchase: $5.79.

Pete Seeger, Len Chandler, and others sing and discuss the impact of civil rights events on song-making and how freedom songs are composed.

You'll Sing a Song and I'll Sing a Song. Producer/Distributor: FRSC, 1966. Grade Level: Elementary. Code No. FC 7664. 12″ LP. 2 sides. 33⅓ RPM. Monaural. Purchase: $5.79.

Ella Jenkins provides for children's participation. There are places for them to clap, hum, come in on the chorus, and play finger cymbals. Her songs are international in scope; some are based on Negro folk music. The interracial Urban Gateways Children's Chorus is featured in this play-a-long recording which Miss Jenkins developed through methods tested in classroams and workshops. LP for nursery school and the elementary grades.

Slides

Afro-American Artists: 1800–1968. Producer/Distributor: ALESCO, 1968. Grade
   Level: Jr. & Sr. H.S. 40 in set.
   A set of slides surveying the serious work of Negro artists in America
since 1800. Vividly depicts the life, feelings, and experiences of the black man in
America during that time.

The Art of Black America. Producer/Distributor: AVMC, 1969. 20 in set. Purchase: $1, each. Color.
   These full-color reproductions of paintings by black artists are published
with accompanying biographies of the artists and commentary on each painting.
Paintings reveal life in America as seen through the eyes of the artist over the
last 150 years. The reproductions are supplied lacquered and mounted on 90
point board. Artists include Charles Alston, Jacob Lawrence, Hughie Lee-Smith,
Hale Woodruff, and Robert Duncanson.

Contemporary Black Artists. Producer/Distributor: SAND. 47 in set. Purchase:
   $58.75. Color.
   An exhibition of 30 contemporary black artists was shown at the Minneapolis Institute of Arts in October, 1968. The exhibition is currently touring
major museums throughout the country. During its tour the exhibition was
expanded and its title changed to "Contemporary Black Artists." This Sandak
slide set documents the revised exhibition.

Study prints/pictures/ posters/graphics

Black America—Yesterday and Today. Producer/Distributor: DCC, 1969. Grade
   Level: Elementary. Code No. A1865. 20 in set. 11″ x 14″. Media Descrip-
   tion: Teaching Pictures. Purchase: $3.95.
   Presents an overview of Negro American history and the contributions of
Negroes to America. Pictures in full color, teacher's manual with background

information, stories, quotations, discussion guidelines, poetry by Negro writers. The set includes: 1 Before Slavery, 2 Ships brought Slaves, 3 Three Great People, 4 Fredrick Douglass—Abolitionist, 5 Harriet Tubman—Moses of Her People, 6 Black Men Fought for Their Own Freedom, 7 Pickney Behton Steward Pinchback—Reconstruction Politician, 8 Jim Crow Laws, 9 Black Man Helped Build America, 10 Mary McLeod Bethune—Teacher, 11 Dr. Charles Richard Drew—Surgeon, 12 Garrett A. Morgan—Inventor, 13 Black Explorers, 14 Integrated Armed Forces, 15 Integrated Schools, 16 Dr. Ralph Johnson Bunche—Peacemaker, 17 Dr. Martin Luther King, Jr.—Drum Major for Justice, 18 Black Writers—Poems by Black Writers, 19 Art by Black People, 20 Black Is Beautiful.

Business and Professions. Producer/Distributor: AAPC, 1969. Grade Level: Elementary through Jr. H.S. Code No. P-5. 24 in set. 11" x 14". Media Description: Study Prints. Purchase: $4.95.

Successful black capitalist date as far back as the 1700s and black professionals have ranged far beyond the "preacher-teacher" limits to serve not only their community but the larger society as well. Personalities discussed include: W. Q. Atwood, James Forten, Richard T. Greener, John Merrick, William Whipper, Claude Barnett, Kenneth Clark, Judge Parker, C. C. Spaulding, Paul Williams, and others.

Champions of Human Rights. Producer/Distributor: AAPC, 1969. Grade Level: Elementary through Jr. H.S. Code No. P-8. 24 in set. 11" x 14". Media Description: Study Prints. Purchase: $4.95.

After the Emancipation the Negro's struggle moved to the areas of the civil rights guaranteed by the Constitution, and in the mid-60s broadened to include the area of those human rights difficult to insure through legislation. Each print contains a brief biography and source references.

Civil War (Slavery to 1863) Series 3. Producer/Distributor: DPA. 10 in set. 11" x 14". Purchase: $5.

Kit contains: Photograph of John Brown; Advertisement for Uncle Tom's Cabin; Slaves working on a plantation, circa 1862; Slaves before their cabin, circa 1861; Harriet Tubman and a Slaves-for-Sale poster; Confederate dead, Antietam, 1862; Union artillerymen preparing for battle of Fair Oaks; Pauline Cushman, actress and Northern spy; Charleston, S. C. Mercury announces Secession; Fort Sumpter, before and after its bombardment.

Crisis in Pictures. Producer/Distributor: DPA. 21 in set. Purchase: $13.50.

The pictures in this series make controversial problems very visible. Teaching guide and information are printed on the reverse side. Included among the pictures are: Riot; and Goodbye Dr. King.

Education and Religion. Producer/Distributor: AAPC, 1969. Grade Level: Elementary through Jr. H.S. Code No. P-6. 24 in set. 11" x 14". Media Description: Study Prints. Purchase: $4.95.

These two areas are grouped together because so many of the early educators were ministers, and vice versa. Latter-day religious figures have made significant contributions to the social and civic welfare of black people. John Hope, Charles S. Johnson, Alain Locke, Robert Moton, William Scarborough, Arthur Schomberg, Richard Allen, James A. Healy, Daniel Payne, Mordecai

Johnson, Benjamin Mays, Inman Page, Charles Wesley, Father Divine, Elijah Muhammad, Adam C. Powell, Sr. ,Howard Thurman, among others are discussed. Each print contains a brief biography and source reference.

Famous Black Americans. Producer/Distributor: AVMC, 1970. Grade Level: Elementary through Jr. H.S. Code No. 20600. 12 in set. 15" x 11½". Media Description: Color Study Prints. Purchase: $15.

Outstanding men and women have emerged in the black American's historic struggle for equality and individuality. The 12 main portraits included in this series of prints are: Frederick Douglass, Booker T. Washington, George Washington Carver, Benjamin Oliver Davis, Jr., Thurgood Marshall, Charles Drew, M.D., Martin Luther King, Jr., Willie Mays, Marian Anderson, S. B. Fuller, W. C. Handy, and Sidney Poitier. In addition to the main biography on the reverse of each print are drawings and information on two other personalities in the same field for a total of 36 famous black Americans.

Famous Contemporary Negroes. Producer/Distributor: ALESCO. Grade Level: Jr. & Sr. H.S. 15 in set. 8" x 10". Media Description: B&W posters. Purchase: $1.56, each.

A set of handsomely produced photographs on heavy poster stock. Each contains a brief biographical note about the famous person represented.

Famous Negroes of the Past. Producer/Distributor: ALESCO. Grade Level: Jr. & Sr. H.S. 12 in set. 8" x 10". Media Description: B&W posters. Purchase: $1.56, each.

A set of handsomely produced photographs on heavy poster stock. Each contains a brief biographical note about the famous person represented.

Fighters for Freedom. Producer/Distributor: AAPC, 1969. Grade Level: Elementary through Jr. H.S. Code No. P-7. 24 in set. 11" x 14". Media Description: Study Prints. Purchase: $4.95.

In the early years of our country, the Negro fought freedom's battle on two fronts. He fought as a patriot for independence and union, and he fought as a black man for his personal freedom. Anthony Burns, Joseph Cinque, Alexander Crummell, Henry Garnet, Josiah Henson, Lermain W. Loguen, Robert Purvis, Joseph Roberts, "Pap" Singleton, William Still, etc. Each print contains a brief biography and source references.

A Gallery of Great Afro-Americans. Producer/Distributor: VIMC, 1969. Grade Level: Elementary through Jr. H.S. Code No. VSP-2. 50 in set. 11" x 14". Media Description: Study Print Posters. Purchase: $20.

Fifty posters highlight the contribution of Afro-Americans, from the Revolutionary War to the present. Includes a brief paragraph about each person or event. Features: James Aristead; Arthur Ashe; Crispus Attucks; Benjamin Banneker; James Beckworth; Mary McLeod Bethune; Jane Bolin; Edward E. Brooke; William E. Dubois; Charles Evers; Patricia R. Harris; Matthew A. Henson; Henry Johnson; James Weldon Johnson; Martin L. King; Lewis Howard Latimer; Dred Scott; and others. Civil War Soldiers; Soldiers in the West; William Still; Sojourner Truth; Harriet Tubman; Nat Turner; Ralph H. Bunche; Richard Cain; William H. Carney; George W. Carver; Afro-American Congressmen; Frederic E. Davison; Martin R. Delany; Fredrick Douglass; Charles R. Drew; Henry Lewis; Nat Love; March on Washington; Thurgood

Marshall; Jan Matzeliger; Garrett A. Morgan; Constance Motley; Gordon Parks; A. Philip Randolph; Booker T. Washington; Robert C. Weaver; Ida B. Wells; Phillis Wheatley; George H. White; Walter White; Daniel Hale Williams.

Ghetto School Teaching. Producer/Distributor: DPA. 8 in set. Purchase: $4.80.
    A young white teacher working without supplies in a predominately black school developed receptive attitudes for learning while using simple and available materials like leaves, wood scraps, nails, rocks, old newspapers, and the children's needs and talents. The experiences of the children and the teacher are described on the back of color prints made while class was in progress.

Government and Judicial. Producer/Distributor: AAPC, 1969. Grade Level: Elementary through Jr. H.S. Code No. P-9. 24 in set. 11″ x 14″. Media Description: Study Prints. Purchase: $4.95.
    From the time he acquired citizenship, the Afro-American became involved in politics and served on many levels of government. Most of the individuals in this portfolio were elected or appointed to federal offices. Ebenezer D. Bassett, Henry P. Cheatham, Robert B. Elliott, Jefferson F. Long, James M. Trotter, Jonathan J. Wright, Shirley Chisholm, William L. Dawson, Patricia H. Harris, Hobart Taylor, etc. Each print contains a brief biography and source references.

Important Dates in the History of the Negro People in Our Country. Producer/ Distributor: ART. 17″ x 24″. Purchase: $2.
    A panoramic view of American Negro history—including major cultural, economic, and political events. This illustrated three-color scroll calendar is a pictorial record, with brief comments, of achievements of great Negro leaders and their notable contributions to the American heritage. Accompanied by a factsheet containing well-written, condensed, historical material, and a helpful list of book references. Excellent for classroom bulletin boards.

Important Negro Inventors. Producer/Distributor: CURTAV. 6 in set. 8″ x 10″. Media Description: B&W glassy prints. Purchase: $3.

Large Pictures. Producer/Distributor: ASSOC, 1929–1970. Grade Level: Elementary through Sr. H.S. 6 in set. 19″ x 24″. Purchase: $1, each; 6 for $5.
    Frederick Douglass, Booker T. Washington, Abraham Lincoln, Paul Laurence Dunbar, Phillis Wheatley, Toussaint L'Ouverture, George Washington Carver, Gen. Benjamin O. Davis and Mary McLeod Bethune for assembly halls and offices. Large enough to be seen and easily recognized at a distance.

Lithographs of Fifteen Distinguished Negroes. Producer/Distributor: ASSOC, 1929–1970. Grade Level: Elementary through Sr. H.S. 6 in set. 11″ x 14″. Purchase: .50, each; 6 for $2.
    Lithographs, finished in black tone of a size to allow a suitable margin for framing. The following are available: Frederick Douglass, Booker T. Washington, Paul Laurence Dunbar, Samuel Coleridge-Taylor, James Weldon Johnson, George W. Carver, Phillis Wheatley, Colonel Charles Young, W. E. B. DuBois, Roland Hayes, Henry O. Tanner, Carter G. Woodson, Dean Kelly Miller, Marian Anderson, Gen. Benjamin O. Davis, and Ralph Bunche.

Modern Negro Contributors. Producer/Distributor: AAC, 1966. Grade Level: Elementary through Jr. H.S. Code No. P-2. 24 in set. 11″ x 14″. Media Description: Study Prints. Purchase: $4.95.

Pictures included in this collection represent individuals who have attained a position of importance in their professions. Richmond Barthe, Edward W. Brooke, Ralph Bunche, Dean Dixon, Katherine Dunham, Duke Ellington, John H. Johnson, Thurgood Marshall, James B. Parsons, Sidney Poitier, Leontyne Price, William Grant Still, Charles White, and others. Each print contains a brief biography and source references.

The Negro Experience in America. Producer/Distributor: DPA. 48 in set. Purchase: $22.

This set of black history prints gives an unparalleled visual history of the Negro in America. These pictures encompass salient Negro-American events that took place during more than three hundred years of history. These pictures provoke intense interest and discussion.

Negro Family. Producer/Distributor: IC. Code No. 132. 40 in set. Purchase: $2.50.

Pictures for flannel board.

Negro Heroes and Heroines of the Revolutionary War. Producer/Distributor: CURTAV. 8″ x 10″. Media Description: B&W glossy prints. Purchase: set of 15, $7.50; set of 12, $6; set of 6, $3.

Negroes of Achievement 1865–1915. Producer/Distributor: AAPC, 1968. Grade Level: Elementary through Jr. H.S. Code No. P-3. 24 in set. 11″ x 14″. Media Description: Study Prints. Purchase: $4.95.

Each print features a Negro who overcame the handicaps of the post-Civil War period (1865–1915) to achieve social stature. Though many are not famous, they are important because they represent the thousands of Negroes who disprove the historical stereotype of the period. Included are: Martin R. Delaney; Mifflin Wister Gibbs; John Mercer Langston; John R. Lynch; Samuel A. McElwee; James C. Matthews; Hiram Revels; John H. Smythe; James J. Spelman; Rev. Henry McNeal Turner; George W. Williams; Granville T. Woods; Miss Maria Louise Baldwin; Mrs. Cora L. Burgan; Mrs. Mary Ann Shadd Cary; Mrs. Katie Chapman Davis; Mrs. Frances Ellen Watkins Harper; Mrs. C. A. Johnson; Madam Elizabeth Keckley; Miss Mary E. P. Mahoney; Mrs. W. E. Matthews; Mrs. Josephine St. Pierre Ruffin; Miss Gertrude J. Washington; Miss Ida B. Wells. Each print contains a brief biography and source references.

The Negro History Program Package. Producer/Distributor: AAPC, 1964–1968. Grade Level: Elementary through Jr. H.S. 24 in set. 11″ x 14″. Media Description: Study Prints. Purchase: $14.85.

Three portfolios with 24 two-color plastic coated prints in each; 72 pictures of noteworthy Negroes from Crispus Attucks to Senator Brooke. Each print contains a brief biography and source references. From this collection of 72 pictures may be assembled groups of individuals who contributed to science, business, government and law, the arts, etc.

Negroes in Our History. Producer/Distributor: AAPC, 1964. Grade Level: Elementary through Jr. H.S. Code No. P-1. 24 in set. 11″ x 14″. Media Description: Study Prints. Purchase: $4.95.

This portfolio includes important contributors to America's progress, Benjamin Banneker, Blanche K. Bruce, Frederick A. Douglass, Jan Ernest from Crispus Attucks to the late Mary McLeod Bethune. Robert S. Abbott, Garrett A. Morgan, Mary Church Terrell, Maggie Walker, Robert Smalls, Carter G. Woodson, Jan Ernest Matzelinger, Frederick A. Douglass, Blanche K. Bruce, Benjamin Banneker, and others. Each print contains a biographical sketch and source references.

Pictures of Distinguished Negroes. Producer/Distributor: ASSOC, 1929–1970. Grade Level: Elementary through Sr. H.S. 100 in set. 5½"–17½". Purchase: $7.50.
This history of the Negro race is told with the pictures of its great men and women. All pictures are suitable for framing.

Portraits of Twentieth-Century Americans of Negro Lineage. Producer/Distributor: AAPC. 24 in set.

The Posters. Producer/Distributor: PPC. 15 in set. Purchase: $29.50.
Fifteen vivid multi-picture posters, with colorful backgrounds in three different colors, illustrate the contributions of Afro-American people to America's history.

Reprints Concerned with Black America. Producer/Distributor: LIFERP, 1969. Grade Level: Jr. & Sr. H.S. 8 in set. 10" x 13". Media Description: Magazine reprints.
Taken as a unit, these reprints examine the complex subject of growing tensions between black and white men from as many vantage points as *Life* writers and photographers have presented it to readers over a period of 30 years. These materials have been specially organized and updated for use in the schoolroom. Each reprint is available in large quantities and at low enough prices to make it practical to provide each student with his own copy to refer to during classroom discussion.
Bitter Years Of Slavery Profiles Negro rebels, heroes and martyrs of the slave period, from colonial days to Emancipation.
The Cycle Of Despair Features Gordon Parks' searing photos of ghetto life and an analysis of the riot Commission Report.
Hard Reality Of Freedom Shows why Reconstruction was in fact a false dawn of freedom for many.
The Mobilization Of Black Strength Discusses roots of Black Power, from the founding of the NAACP in 1910 to the present.
The Negro Leadership. Defines the basic attitudes of moderate and extreme Negro civil rights leaders.
The Origins Of Segregation Traces Negro history from sophisticated African civilizations through the years of slave trade.
A Separate Path Of Equality Examines self-expression of the Negro in politics, in poetry and in prose throughout history.

Scenes From the Life of the Negro. Producer/Distributor: ASSOC, 1929–1970. 6 in set. 11" x 14". Purchase: $.50, each; 6 for $2.
The Cripus Attucks Monument, Paul Cuffe's Tomb, Nat Turner in Action, the John Brown Monument, the Home of Frederick Douglass, the

Lincoln Memorial, the Booker T. Washington Monument, and the Home of Paul Laurence Dunbar.

Science and Invention. Producer/Distributor: AAPC, 1969. Grade Level: Elementary through Jr. H.S. Code No. P-4. 24 in set. 11″ x 14″. Media Description: Study Prints. Purchase: $4.95.
Purchase: $2.50.
This portfolio includes contributors to the fields of medicine, biology, mathematics, and other sciences, as well as inventors of farming, industrial, transportation, and communications devices. Only authenticated pictures and achievements are included. Andrew Beard, Lewis Latimer, Elijah McCoy, Norbert Rillieux, H. C. Webb, Otis Boykin, Charles Buggs, Meredith Gourdine, F. M. Jones, Rufus Stokes, etc. Each print contains a brief biography and source references.

The Slave Trade and Its Abolition. Producer/Distributor: JACK. Code No. JD6. Purchase: $2.50.
Consists of packaged documents pertinent to some major historical event. An authentic reproduction showing contemporary documents, maps, charts, engravings, prints, costumes, paintings, diaries, etc.

Smaller Pictures for School Work. Producer/Distributor: ASSOC. Grade Level. Elementary through Sr. H.S. 24 in set. 1¾″ x 2″. Media Description: Small pictures for school work. Purchase: $.50, set.
Twenty-four very small pictures of the following: John B. Russwurm; Robert R. Moton; Granville T. Woods; Edward W. Blyden; Joseph C. Price; Ira Aldridge; Toussaint L'Ouverture; Alexandre Dumas; Alexander Pushkin; Robert Brown Elliott; Hiram Revels; B. K. Bruce; Phillis Wheatley; Benjamin Bannaker; Frederick Douglass; Booker T. Washington; Paul Laurence Dunbar; Samuel Coleridge-Taylor; James Weldon Johnson; William E. B. DuBois; Roland Hayes; Henry Ossawa Tanner; Carter Godwin Woodson; Colonel Charles Young.

Transparencies

Afro-American History. Producer/Distributor: AEVAC, 1968. Grade Level: Sr. H.S. Code No. AF-41. Purchase: $115. Series. Color.
This series of 18 transparencies offers a flexible program for studying Black History from pre-Colonial explorers through Martin Luther King. Through the use of sequential overlays, the transparencies trace Afro-American influence and contributions to American art, industry and culture. The printed Teacher's Guide explains and analyzes subject matter, outlines suggested lesson procedure, and offers specific ideas for stimulating classroom discussions. The

complete set includes 18 transparencies with 49 overlays. Individual titles of the transparencies are: Before the Mayflower; The Nation Begins; Chronology of Negro History; Reluctant Slaves; Abolition; Evils of Slavery; The New Amendments of Freedom; The Failure of Reconstruction; Civil Rights—Supreme Court; The Western Frontier; The Negro Organizes; Black Education; Black Churches; The Negro and the Arts—"Harlem Renaissance"; Inner City Life; Military Tradition; Non-Violence—"I Had a Dream"; The Emergence of Black Power.

Adventures of Huckleberry Finn. Producer/Distributor: TECED, 1970. Grade Level: Jr. & Sr. H.S. Code No. 72026. Series. Purchase: $58. Color.

Nineteen transparencies with eleven overlays, this series was edited by William Sullivan, English Dept., Trumbull High School, Trumbull, Conn. It was designed to facilitate and enrich the teaching of Huckleberry Finn as a vital and meaningful work. The titles include Mark Twain, Journey down the Mississippi, Huck and Jim, Satire and Point of View, etc.

Biographies of Outstanding Negro Americans. Producer/Distributor: DESED, 1967. Grade Level: Elementary through Sr. H.S. Purchase: $48.95, per vol. Series.

Five volumes consisting of 12 transparencies each showing portraits of outstanding figures and events in Negro History. Contents of each volume follow: **RJ-106:** Crispus Attucks—Paul Revere; Peter Salem; War of 1812 Battle of New Orleans; Crew Members of the Confederate Steamer Planter; Four Officers; Major Martin Delancy; Sergeant W. H. Carney; Phalanx Regiment; Charge of Duncan's Brigade; Phalanx soldiers; Charge on Fort Wagner. Alexander Dumas; R. H. Terrell; Mrs. M. C. Terrell; Madam C. J. Walker; Charles W. Chesnutt.

RJ-110 Paul Dunbar; Ida B. Wells; Hon. J. M. Langston; George W. Carver; W. E. Dubois; Pushkin; Judson Lyons; Dr. W. F. Penn; Percy Julian; Prof. Scarborough; Rev. H. H. Proctor; John Chavis.

RJ-111 Sojourner Truth; Langston Hughes; Daniel Hale Williams; Mary McLeod Bethune; A. Philip Randolph; E. Franklin Frazier; Alain Locke; Granville T. Woods; Archibald Grimke; Clarence C. White; Carter G. Woodson; Norbert Rillieux.

RJ-112 Jan Matzelinger; Dr. Ernest Just; Mrs. G. E. Johnson McDouglad; Countee Cullen; William Grant Still; John Patterson Green; Dr. Charles Drew; S. R. Ward; Ira Aldridge; Henry H. Garnet; Benjamin Banneker; James Weldon Johnson.

Biographies of Outstanding Negro Americans. Producer/Distributor: LA, 1969. Grade Level: Jr. H.S. Code No. 920.AO-SR. Purchase: $109. Series. Brown Print.

Complete series of 53 transparencies with storage box and teacher's manual.

The Black American: Past and Present. Producer/Distributor: HSPC. Code No. H100. Purchase: $5. Series.

Traces the struggles and achievements of the black American from his African heritage to the present generation. Included with the set are six transparencies, 18 spirit master duplicating pages, and teacher's text. Topics covered are ancient African civilizations, the slave trade, Civil War, Reconstruction, outstanding personalities, and achievements in science, arts, medicine, government, entertainment, etc.

Compromise of 1850. Producer/Distributor: 3M, 1964. Grade Level: Jr. H.S. through Adult. Single. 8″ x 10″. Color.
From the U.S. Area Maps—Topographic and Geopolitical Features Series. One overlay.

Early Negro History. Producer/Distributor: CES, 1969. Grade Level: Elementary through Sr. H.S. Code No. Neg. 1. Purchase: $32.50. Series. Color.
A series of 13 transparencies relating to early Negro history, including Africans in New World; Slave Traders; Jamestown Arrivals; Slavery Routes; African Continent showing map outlines; Skills and Occupations; Timbuktu; Negroes in North; Negroes in South; Phillis Wheatley; Revolution Heroes; Benjamin Banneker; Aboltion Movement. Series is accompanied by printed teacher's guide with information on content of each transparency, suggested use in the classroom, and suggested project on subject.

Fifteenth Amendment, the Right to Vote Without Regard to Race. Producer/ Distributor: AEVAC, 1967. Grade Level: Jr. through Sr. H.S. Code No. GT33. Purchase: $41.10, set. Single. 10″ x 10″. Color.
Color transparency from the series, Constitutional Amendments, Eleventh Through Seventeenth.

Free and Slave States. Producer/Distributor: HAMMND, 1968. Grade Level: Jr. & Sr. H.S. Code No. 8415. Purchase: $6.50. Single. 10″ x 10″. Color.
From the American History I-A Series.

Freedom Rider Bus in Flames at Anniston, Alabama. Producer/Distributor: COLBRN. Grade Level: Jr. H.S. through College. Single. 10″ x 10″. B&W.
This is a single transparency from the series, World History—From World War I.

Great American Negroes. Producer/Distributor: SVE, 1965. Grade Level: Intermediate through Adult. Code No. OT-10S. Purchase: $9.95. Series. Color.
A set of six two-color transparencies, with printed teacher's guide. Two-color artwork presents portraits of great American Negroes. Transparencies include portraits of Mary McLeod Bethune, George Washington Carver, Benjamin Banneker, Robert Smalls, Frederick A. Douglass, and Harriet Tubman.

A History of Afro-Americans. Producer/Distributor: SCOTT, 1970. Grade Level: Jr. & Sr. H.S. Code No. 71012. Purchase: $55. Series. Color.
Book I: The African Heritage A set of transparencies tracing Africa's people from the origin of man in Kenya through the development of agriculture, animal husbandry, and the use of metals in prehistoric times. The West African Berber, Ghana, Hausa, Mali, and Songhay civilizations are presented in their political, economic, social, and cultural ramifications. The transparencies on everyday life during the late 15th Century prepare for the next set which opens with the slave trade at the time of Columbus.
Book II: Jamestown to Emancipation The history of the Afro-American in the Western Hemisphere from the Fifteenth to the Twentieth Century is traced in this second series. Black explorers and settlers, indentured servitude and the

transition to slavery are presented. The slave cycle, the burgeoning slave trade are analyzed. Comparisons are drawn between North and South American slavery, house and field slavery, blacks captured and blacks born into slavery. Topics include the slaves' quest to go North, slave revolts, and the effects of dehumanization on blacks and whites.

Book III: The Road to Freedom: 1865 to the Present This part of the series continues Afro-American history and culture from the reconstruction to the present. Segregation, the fight for equality, the current status of the black community and the quest for jobs, education, and political power are presented in a comprehensive series of transparencies designed for use in U.S. history, Afro-American History, and Problems of Democracy.

A History of the Negro Contribution to Civilization. Producer/Distributor: DESED, 1967. Grade Level: Elementary through Jr. H.S. Purchase: $48.95. Series.

A History of Negro Soldiers of the United States. Producer/Distributor: DESED, 1967. Grade Level: Elementary through Jr. H.S. Purchase: $48.95. Series.
Portraits of prominent Negro Americans. A set of 14 transparencies.

How Safe Are Our Drugs? Producer/Distributor: EGH. Code No. 052. Purchase: $54.75. Series.
This series of 22 transparencies with 20 overlays shows how the Food and Drug Administration (FDA) protects the health of the nation. The transparencies tell what a drug is and how it can help or harm. The guide accompanying the series gives detailed information pertaining to the paragraphs in FDA publication No. 44 with which the series is correlated.

Key Supreme Court Decisions. Producer/Distributor: AEVAC, 1967. Grade Level: Jr. & Sr. H.S. Code No. GT30. Purchase: $43.75. Series. 10" x 10". Color.
Part I: 1803–1905 This set of seven color transparencies shows the far-reaching effects of major Supreme Court decisions on American government, business, and private life. Among the historic decisions included in the series are John Marshall and National Supremacy, Dred Scott Decision, Munn vs. Illinois, Swift and Company vs. the U.S. The series includes projectural-overlays, carrying case, and teaching notes.
Part II: 1911–1966 Emphasizes the social revolution begun in the 1930's and the recent cases involving the concept of individual rights. Examines the changing interrelationships between the functions of the government and the nature of the American social structure. 1. The Apportionment Cases; 2. Civil Rights; 3. Criminal Due Process Cases; 4. New Deal Cases; 5. Released Time Cases; 6. Rule of Reason (Standard Oil).

Legislation Affecting Slavery Prior to Civil War. Producer/Distributor: EGH. Grade Level: Jr. & Sr. H.S. Code No. 020-7. Purchase: $8.20. 12⅛" x 9¾". Color.
This transparency from the series Territorial Growth and History of the U.S. is from the larger series United States History.

Legislation Affecting Slavery Prior to Civil War. Producer/Distributor: DCAEP, 1964. Grade Level: Jr. & Sr. H.S. Purchase: $8.20. Single. 10″ x 10″. Color.
Color transparency with three overlays from the series United States History.

Missouri Compromise. Producer/Distributor: 3M, 1964. Grade Level: Jr. H.S. through Adult. 8″ x 10″. Color.
Two color transparencies with one overlay each from the series. U.S. Area Maps—Topographic and Geopolitical Features.

Negro History: 1800–1865. Producer/Distributor: CES, 1969. Grade Level: Elementary through Sr. H.S. Code No. NEG-2. Purchase: $37.50. Series.
A series of 15 transparencies relating to Negro history from 1800–1865, including Paul Cuffe of Massachusetts; Ira Aldridge, who won international fame on the stage as Othello; plantation conditions; Negro population; Nat Turner; Frederick Douglass; Henry "Box" Brown; Negro literary abolitionists; William Lloyd Garrison; the Amistad Case; James Beckwourth; Prudence Crandall; Sojourner Truth and Harriet Tubman. Series is accompanied by printed teacher's guide with information on content of each transparency, suggested use in the classroom, and suggested project on subject.

Negro History: 1865–1919. Producer/Distributor: CES, 1969. Grade Level: Jr. & Sr. H.S. Code No. NEG-3. Purchase: $65. Series. Color.
This first section of this series of 26 transparencies is entitled "Reconstruction Woes" and includes the transparencies: Adjustment to Freedom; New Status: Education; Black Potential Leaders; National Recognition; Migration; Jim Crow; Low Pay. The second section of the series, "Some Steps Forward," includes the transparencies: Ida B. Wells; Philanthropic Help; Booker T. Washington; Tuskegee Institute; W. E. B. DuBois; NAACP. The third section, "Science and Invention," outlines with transparencies the substantial contributions made by blacks in the field of science. Jan Matzeliger and Granville Woods; McCoy and Latimer; George Washington Carver; Matt Henson. Fourth section, "Black Frontier," includes Nat Love; Negro Cavalry. Fifth section, "War Activities," includes San Juan; Discrimination in WW I; and Negro War Contributions. The last three transparencies include Negro History; Musicals; Writers.

Negro History: 1920–1945. Producer/Distributor: CES, 1969. Grade Level: Jr. & Sr. H.S. Code No. NEG-4. Purchase: $50. Series. Color.
Divided into three sections, this series of 20 transparencies begins with the "twenties" covering Race Riots; Migration (showing large migration from the South to large industrial centers in the North); Marcus Garvey; Theater (showing rise of serious Negro actors); Music; Science and Education; Harlem; Poets and Writers.
The second section on Depression and New Deal includes the transparencies: Jobless Negroes; Father Divine; New Deal Projects; "Black Cabinet"; A. Philip Randolph; Louis and Owens; Marian Anderson.
The section on World War II includes transparencies to show Military Discrimination; Racial Diffiiculties; Davis and Miller; Ground Divisions; In Summing Up.

Negro History since 1945. Producer/Distributor: CES, 1969. Grade Level: Jr. &
   Sr. H.S. Code No. NEG-5. Purchase: $70. Series. Color.
   This series of 28 transparencies begins with a section entitled "March for
Equality" which includes Violence Erupts; Voting Rights; The Desegregation
Decision; Autherine Lucy; Bus Boycott; Little Rock; James Meredith; Freedom
Riders; Selma and D.C. Marches. The second section "Some Famous Negroes"
covers famous men and women in sports, opera, higher education, and political
campaigns, including Jackie Robinson and Althea Gibson; Ralph Bunche;
Ralph Ellison; Richard Wright and James Baldwin, Leontyne Price and Sidney
Poitier; John Hope Franklin, Robert Weaver, Edward Brooke, Julian Bond,
and Carl Stokes; Third section on "Organizations and Leaders" includes
NAACP, Martin Luther King; Malcolm X; Black Power. The last section, entitled "Where Do We Stand?," includes transparencies on education, jobs, housing, and family structure.

Negro Heritage. Producer/Distributor: TA, 1968. Grade Level: Elementary
   through Jr. H.S. Code No. 003N. Purchase: $74.95; $2.50, each. Series.
   Color.
   A collection of 31 transparencies which reveals the lives of Negro artists,
educators, explorers, statesmen, heroes, scientists, and leaders. This unit,
through its portrayal of people of history and notables of today, reveals the
man, his times, and his contributions. Included with each transparency is a free
supplementary biographical data fact sheet in narrative form. Transparency
titles are: Jim Beckwourth; Robert Smalls; Frederick Douglass; Sojourner
Truth; Mary McLeod Bethune Crispus Attucks; Peter Salem; Henry O. Tanner;
Ira Aldrich; Estevanico; Charles Drew; Harriet Tubman; Benjamin Banneker;
James Weldon Johnson; Richard Allen; Dred Scott; Matthew Henson; Jan
Matzeliger; A. Philip Randolph; Marian Anderson; Martin Luther King, Jr.;
Jackie Robinson; Ralph Bunche; Langston Hughes; Rafer Johnson; Duke
Ellington; Louis Armstrong; Benjamin Davis, Jr., Thurgood Marshall; Gwen-
dolyn Brooks; Constance Baker Motley.

Negro in America. Producer/Distributor: LPC. Code No. T-40. Purchase:
   $49.95. Series.
   A series of 10 transparencies with charts showing differences in education,
employment, income, birth rate, etc., of the Negroes and whites in America.
Each chart is based on authoritative statistics and information. Titles of the
transparencies are: Population of the United States—By Race; Distribution of
Family Incomes for Negroes and Whites; Years of School Completed for Negroes
and Whites; Percentage of Negro and White Young Adults in School; Live Birth
Rates for Negroes and Whites; Type of Family for Negroes and Whites; Unemployment rates for Negroes and Whites; Expected Responsiveness by Negroes
and Whites to Government Officials; Political Participation of Negroes and Whites
in Southern States.

Reconstruction. Producer/Distributor: HAMMND, 1969. Grade Level: Jr. & Sr.
   H.S. Code No. 8419. Purchase: $6.50. Single. 10″ x 10″. Color.
   This transparency is from the American History Series.

Reconstruction in the South, 1865–1877. Producer/Distributor: NYSTRO, 1968.
   Grade Level: Elementary through Sr. H.S. Code No. TQJ. Purchase.
   Single. 8″ x 10″. Color.

This transparency is from the American History Series. The series depicts key events in United States history from the age of discovery and exploration to the present.

Reconstruction of the South after the Civil War. Producer/Distributor: DCAEP. Grade Level: Jr. & Sr. H.S. Single. 10″ x 10″. Color.
This transparency is from the series U.S. History. Contains one overlay.

Territory Opened to Slavery by Kansas-Nebraska Act. Producer/Distributor: 3M, 1964. Grade Level: Jr. H.S. through Adult. Single. 8″ x 10″. Color.
Color transparency from the Series, U.S. Area Maps—Topographic and Geopolitical Features.

The Thirteenth Amendment: The Abolition of Slavery. Producer/Distributor: AEVAC, 1967. Grade Level: Jr. &Sr. H.S. Code No. GT33. Purchase: $41.10, set. Single. 10″ x 10″. Color.
Color transparency from the series, Constitutional Amendments, Eleventh Through Seventeenth.

The Use and Misuse of Drugs. Producer/Distributor: EGH. Grade Level: Jr. & Sr. H.S. Code No. 051. Purchase: $59.75. Series. 12⅛″ x 9¾″.
This series of 20 transparencies shows why information on drug labels should be followed exactly; it also covers the points of when to use self-medication and the dangers of misusing stimulants, depressants and narcotics. It describes the hallucinogens and their abuse are included. Narcotics are mentioned only briefly since they do not fall under FDA's jurisdiction. FDA Publication, Life Protection Series No. 46, accompanies this series.

White Man Kicks a Negro Reporter in Little Rock. Producer/Distributor: COLBRN. Grade Level: Jr. H.S. through College. Single. 10″ x 10″. B&W.
From the series, World History—From World War I.

Video tapes/telecourses/kinescopes

The American City: Millstone or Milestone? Producer/Distributor: WMSBTV, 1969. Grade Level: Adult. Running Time: 90 min. B&W. Rental.
In a 90-minute dialogue, the American City is discussed by social activist Saul Alinsky, architect Peter Blake, newspaper columnist Sydney Harris, Theologian Richard Rubenstein, and civil rights leader Floyd McKissick. One of the questions considered is: Would the urban crisis be solved if the racial crisis were

solved? Among the subjects covered are urban education, industrialization, automation, segregation, integration, social morality, black power, and black nationalism.

Beautiful Dreamer. Producer/Distributor: WUCMTV, 1969. Grade Level: Elementary through Adult. Running Time: 44 min. Rental.
    A WUCM production of a controversial play written by Scott Cunningham and performed by the Poor Peoples Theater of New York City as a tribute to the late Martin Luther King, Jr., and the continuing struggle for human rights. The play is both "message theater"—a drama with a theme—harmonious race relations, and entertainment.

Because We Believe Things Can Be Better. Producer/Distributor: WVIATV, 1969. Grade Level: Jr. & Sr. H.S. Running Time: 30 min. B&W. Rental.
    This is a series of half-hour human relations programs of skits and songs written by participants in a summer project at the Progressive Center in Scranton, Pennsylvania's central city. The program was performed by young people at the Center's Festival in which they perform monologues, sketches, and songs to develop the theme of race relations. Songs emphasize the idea of brotherhood, and the solos are accompanied by guitar.

Black Horizons. Producer/Distributor: WQEDTV, 1969. Grade Level: Adult. Running Time: 30 min. Color. Rental.
    A weekly half-hour series produced for and by members of the black community. With host-producer, Ralph Proctor, Black Horizons, is designed to reveal the cultural heritage of the black and to place in historical perspective the significant contributions made by these Americans. In addition to studio interviews and discussions, the series offers filmed highlights of programs which may be of interest to blacks, i.e., Black Arts Festival held at the University of Pittsburgh.

Black on Black. Producer/Distributor: WCNYTV, 1969. Rental.
    This Afro-American program in magazine format provides a platform for blacks to speak to other blacks, and to the community at large, about matters of concern to black citizens. In addition to using black artists, journalists, craftsmen, and entertainers, Black on Black invites representatives from community organizations representing a broad cross-section of black opinion. Examples of features: discussion of the Black Revolution by college students; African dance program; local Negroes today and slaves of the past in the state; soul music and entertainment sections.

Black Peoplehood. Producer/Distributor: WVIZTV, 1969. Running Time: 30 min. Color. Rental.
    A series of nine programs, Black Peoplehood, was written, produced, and edited by members of Cleveland's black community. Black consultants from various occupations advise on the programs which are filmed in and around the community. Art and music are original, done by new talent in order to give members of the community a sense of participation. Examples of programs: The Black Man and Politics; The Black Man and Religion; The Black Man and Literature; The Black Man and Community Power; The Black Man and Business.

Black Perspective. Producer/Distributor: KCETTV, 1969. Rental.

Black Perspective, a national organization of black newsmen and communicators, sponsors a program similar to "Meet the Press." The panel interviews a guest, ranging from candidates for mayor, the President of Operation Bootstrap, the president of San Francisco State College, and others.

Black Thing. Producer/Distributor: WMVSTV, 1969. Rental.

A local television series produced by Black News. Examples of presentations: poet Rocky Taylor reads "My Black Woman", while the poem is interpreted by dancer Fern Caulker; cameras follow a black model through a day in her life; the artist, William Christian, is interviewed; the Ko-Thi Dancers present a historical review of religion.

Black Voices. Producer/Distributor: KTCATV, 1969. Grade Level: Sr. H.S.
 Running Time: 60 min. Rental.

A black production dealing with social and economic problems confronting the black population of the Twin Cities, Black Voices serves as a showcase for black art, theater, and history. The programs vary from panel discussions, audience participation, live entertainment, and a "Black Calendar" once a month which reviews contributions and landmarks of black people. Examples of program topics: Black Man in Business; White Racism; Black Patrol; Stillwater Prison Treatment of Black Inmates; Center for Advanced African Understanding; Civil and Human Rights. Fifty-two programs.

Brother Man. Producer/Distributor: WVIZTV, 1969. Grade Level: Adult. Running Time: 60 min. Color. Rental.

A series of ten programs concerned with issues, activities, and talent in Cleveland's black community. Topics and talent for each show are suggested by a group of consultants representing a cross-section of the black community. Examples of programs: an interview with Willa Wright who talks about the origin of the spiritual and sings; an editorial on the significance of the mayoralty election and policemen in booths on election day in the black wards; a film of "Carl's Corner", a boutique run by Women for Carl Stokes for Mayor; and many other locally centered problems.

Dick Gregory: The Black Man in Rural America. Producer/Distributor: WUCMTV, 1969. Grade Level: College, Adult. Running Time: 29 min. B&W. Rental.

Dick Gregory was asked to talk about the problems of the rural black man in America. With an all-black panel including a local television newsman, a Baptist minister, a city councilman, an instructor of black culture at a local high school, and the editor of the Saginaw Afro-Herald, he explores the problems of the rural black man both in the North and in the South.

Jambo! Producer/Distributor: WNYETV, 1968. Grade Level: Intermediate through Sr. H.S. Running Time: 18:30. B&W. Rental.

Job Line. Producer/Distributor: WILLTV, 1969. Rental.

A weekly program listing specific employment opportunities for the underemployed and underskilled in the Urbana area. Each week a guest is interviewed to offer detailed information about training programs and career opportunities, often a specialist who gives tips about how to respond in a personal interview and the importance of a job seeker's attitude. Job Line's black host emphasizes that all jobs listed are from equal opportunity employers.

Martin Luther King, Jr.—The Man and the Dream. Producer/Distributor: WNYETV, 1968. Grade Level: All ages. Running Time: 28 min. 30 sec. B&W. Rental.

This program was awarded an EMMY by the New York Chapter of the National Academy of Television Arts and Sciences.

Negro Contributions to American Music. Producer/Distributor: WNYETV, 1969. Grade Level: Elementary. Running Time: 28 min. 30 sec. B&W. Rental. Originally used as a program during Negro History Week.

New Mood/New Breed. Producer/Distributor: WHYYTV, 1969. Grade Level: All ages. Running Time: 29 min. Rental.

A weekly series exploring the new mood of black awareness, unity, independence, and self-determination as expressed by today's black Americans—produced by the Delaware Valley black community. Examples: The dissemination of African culture and history from two "new breed" viewpoints—that of the director of an Afro-American dance company and that of the proprietors of an Afro-American business enterprise, a shop dealing in Afro-American merchandise. Members of the organization "IN" (Interested Negroes) which places junior high school males with successful white collar, blue collar, business and professional Negroes for a day in their work life, explain how they motivate students to stay in school and prepare for a career.

On Being Black. Producer/Distributor: WGBHTV, 1969. Rental.

A series of original television dramas about what it is like to be black in white America. Producer Luther James trys to find plays about blacks which illustrate the tensions, the conflicts, and the humor of life in a black community. The idea for using dramas is that the playwright can often illuminate human experience in ways that cannot be realized through the documentary. Examples: Danger Zone (black priest dealing with drug addiction problem of his people); Face in the Mirror (alcoholism problem); Black Girl (story of a girl who wants to become a dancer).

Once a Ghetto. Producer/Distributor: WILLTV. Rental.

This monthly series of special programs dealing with human relations in the black communities of East Central Illinois explores the problems which blacks face in obtaining decent housing and a healthy environment in which to live. Principal objective of the series is to make white citizens aware of the feelings and qualities of black life, and to show why they should involve themselves in the struggle for human rights. Examples of program titles in the series: Black and Proud; Wanted; Supernigger; The Police (in which chiefs of police, a mayor, black militants, and ghetto residents give their viewpoints on the attitudes of the black community toward the police); The Legal System (an exploration of black attitudes toward an all-white judicial system).

Our People. Producer/Distributor: WTTWTV, 1969. Running time: 60 min. Rental.

A series with a magazine format which interviews prominent blacks from Chicago and across the nation; a "Buyer's Guide" in which experts from the black community tell viewers how to get the most from their dollar on purchases ranging from life insurance to children's shoes; reports on job-training for young people; interviews with such prominent members of local university faculties as John Hope Franklin, Charles Hamilton, and with Jesse Jackson about "Operation Breadbasket."

Project Understanding. Producer/Distributor: WMVSTV, 1969. Running Time: 30 min. Rental.

Evolving from a community effort to combat racial and religious prejudice, this program consists of two half-hour segments. The first segment is a film documentary or a discussion on a given subject, covering an area inflicted by prejudice. An hour later after viewing groups or individual have had an opportunity to discuss and/or phone in questions to the studio, a panel discusses the questions and comments which have been phoned in.

The Nature of Prejudice Films taken in Milwaukee that portray the effects of prejudice shown to the background of Tom Lehrer's satirical talk-song, "Brotherhood."

The Courses of Citizen Action Film clips of open housing marches, police brutality, etc. to the background of the Mormon Tabernacle Choir singing "This is My Country."

Racism in America. Producer/Distributor: SSC, 1969. Running Time: 60 min., each. Rental: $50. each. Purchase: $50, each.

This series consists of tapes made of informal in-studio panel discussions with principal speakers in a symposium held at Sacramento State on racism in America. Among the participants were Dr. Price Cobbs, co-author of *Black Rage;* Harry Edwards, the man behind the Olympic Boycott; Eldridge Cleaver, author of *Soul on Ice,* Dr. Benjamin Spock, pediatrician and war critic, and Kenneth Goode, author of *From Africa to the United States* and *Them.* The series covers nine separate programs.

Program I Guest: Ronald Dellus, City Councilman from Berkeley, California. Host: Lenard Starke, Student Body President at Sacramento State College. Panelists: Dr. Darryl Enos, Director of Community Study and Service Center at Sacramento State College; Jack Livingston, Professor of Government, Sacramento State College.

Program II Guest: Victor Comerchero, Professor of English at Sacramento State College. Host: Richard Snead, graduate student in Business Administration, Sacramento State College. Panelists: Rev. Cyrus Keller, pastor of St. Andrews African Methodist Episcopal Church; Jim Paz, Project Director of the Sacramento Neighborhood Youth Corps.

Program III Guest: Kenneth Goode, Administrative Assistant to the Executive Vice Chancellor, University of California at Berkeley. Host: Gregg Campbell, Assistant Professor of History at Sacramento State College. Panelists: Marion Woods, Chief of Manpower Training in Sacramento; Richard Reynolds, student instructor at Sacramento State College; Irving Jackson, Assistant to the Sacramento City Unified Schools Superintendent for Intergroup Relations, Frances Catlett, Assistant Professor of Social Work at Sacramento State College.

Program IV Guest: Octavio Ramano, Professor of Behavioral Sciences at the University of California at Berkeley. Host: Clark Taylor, Assistant Professor of Anthropology at Sacramento State College. Panelists: Manuel Alonzo, Mexican-American education specialist; Sue-Ellen Jacobs, Assistant Professor of Anthropology at Sacramento State College.

Program V Guest: Dr. Benjamin Spock, noted peace advocate and pediatrician. Host: William Dillon, Professor of Government at Sacramento State College. Panelists: Richard D. Hughes, Professor of Government at Sacramento State College, Peter Shattuck, Professor of Government at Sacramento State College; Phil Simmons, consultant in community development.

Program VI Guest: Eldridge Cleaver, Minister of Information for the Black Panthers, and Peace and Freedom Party presidential candidate. Host: Bill Mitchell, President of the Black Students Union at Sacramento State College. Panelists: Gene Taylor, Parliamentarian for the Black Student Union at Sacramento State College; Dean Dorn, Professor of Sociology at Sacramento State College.

Program VII Guest: Price Cobbs, co-author of *Black Rage* and Assistant Professor of Psychiatry at U.C. Medical Center in San Francisco. Host: Jack Livingston, Professor of Government at Sacramento State College. Panelists: Carolyn Jacobs, student at Sacramento State College; William Fowler, Superintendent of Schools, Del Paso District; Joseph Heller, Professor of Psychology at Sacrament State College.

Program VIII Guest: Father James Groppi, Roman Catholic priest, spokesman for Milwaukee's black activists. Host: Robert Thompson, Professor of Government at Sacramento State College. Panelists: James Dodd, Board of Regents, Junior Colleges of Califorina; R. Lee Page, Community Welfare Council.

Program IX Guest: Harry Edwards, black rightist, Professor of Sociology at San Jose State College, and chief advocate of the black boycott of the 1968 Olympics. Host: Donald Sturtevant, Professor of English at Sacramento State College. Panelists: Alan O'Leary, Activities Advisor at Sacramento State College; Willie Jones, student at Sacramento State College; Lawrence Lopes, Vice President of the Black Students Union; Adolphis McGee, athlete and coach.

Say, Brother. Producer/Distributor: WGBHTV, 1969. Color. Rental.

A series of programs produced by the black staff members of WGBH and members of the black community directed to the black community. Centered around local people and local issues such as the student takeover at Brandeis University, theater in the black community, the local school situation, the programs sometimes include national figures such as Bill Cosby, Jesse Jackson, Eldridge Cleaver, Stokely Carmichael, and Gladys Knight.

Shades of Black. Producer/Distributor: WTHSTV, 1969. Running Time: 60 min. Rental.

An experimental show with host-producer, Joe Powell, Shades of Black is a program aimed at black youth in hopes of providing them the opportunity to gain in self-pride and self-appreciation. The program seeks through forthright dialogue to open the lines of communication between old and young. The host-producer keeps the program flexible, as to choice of guest panelists, ideas, etc.

Soul! Producer/Distributor: WNDTTV, 1969. Running Time: 60 min. Color. Rental.

A series of one-hour programs, Soul deals with the social, cultural, and artistic aspects of the black community in New York City. Designed in the format of the late-night, talk-entertainment programs, this program features one interview per program with someone of interest to the black community and gives air time to new talent. Among guests featured have been Betty Shabazz, widow of Malcolm X; Julius Lester, writer-folksinger-author; James Finney and Conrad Lynn, black attorneys involved in the civil rights movement; Le Roi Jones, and Mrs. Shirley Chisholm.

Soul Talk. Producer/Distributor: WQEDTV, 1969. Grade Level: Adult. Running Time: 60 min. B&W. Rental.
A series exploring the development of the Black Arts in the areas of Music, Literature, Fine Arts, and Drama. The aim of the series of programs is to help the black man discover his self-identity. Examples of Programs: Black Sounds and Images: An exploration of the Music and Dance of the Black Man; Jitney or Red (introduces several of Pittsburgh's black painters and sculptors); A Pause of Silence (an investigation into the poetry of four black poets).

Spirit of Blackness. Producer/Distributor: KERATV. Running Time: 30 min. Rental.
A local half-hour program shown twice a month for about three months was conceived and produced by blacks for the purpose of helping to break down the communications barrier between blacks and non-blacks, exposing erroneous mythologies that stigmatized blacks; the program was also used as a means to highlight successful black citizens in the community. Examples of programs: The Success of Dr. Paul Freeman; The Role of the Black News Media; The Militant Movement in Dallas.

A Tribute to Martin Luther King, Jr. Producer/Distributor: WNYETV, 1970. Grade Level: All ages. Running Time: 28.30. B&W. Rental.

We Have a Dream. Producer/Distributor: WNYETV, 1970. Grade Level: Elementary. Running Time: 28:30. B&W. Rental.
A special program produced in honor of Martin Luther King, Jr.

Where It's At. Producer/Distributor: WETATV, 1969. Grade Level: Adult. Running Time: 59 min. Color. Rental.
A community Show, "Where It's At" springs from and is directed toward low-income ghetto people. The entertainers are from the inner city; its participative audience come into the studio from the surrounding neighborhoods. In addition to its live entertainment, the show invites guests to discuss broad aspects of social and vocational rehabilitation.

TELECOURSES

Americans From Africa. Producer/Distributor: CVETV/GPITVL, 1968. Grade Level: Sr. H.S. through Adult. Running Time: 30 min. Rental: $55, each.
This series of thirty 30-minute lessons is aimed at developing better understanding among students by increasing their awareness of the part that all Americans have played in the making of this nation. By emphasizing the historical role of the American Negro, generally omitted from school textbooks, the

series seeks to contribute to an easing of the tensions and an understanding of the present-day crises. Television teacher for the series is Dr. Edgar Allan Toppin, Professor of History at Virginia State College in Petersburg. Available only as a series.

The American Negro: What Must Be Done. Producer/Distributor: KUON, 1969. Grade Level: College, Adult. Running Time: 30 min. B&W. Rental: $60.

This program records a conversation between James Farmer, Assistant Secretary, U.S. Department of Health, Education, and Welfare, and Kenton Williams, Chief of Children and Family Services for the State of Nebraska Department of Welfare.

Approaching Poetry: An Introductory Program for Classroom Teachers. Producer/Distributor: WNDTTV/GPITVL, 1968. Grade Level: Sr. H.S. Running Time: 30 min. B&W. Rental.

This thirty minute teaching-training introductory program uses Gwendolyn Brooks, prize-winning poet, as the on-camera guest. The entire series is made up of fifteen 20-minute lessons with Bruce Cutler, poet and Professor of English at Wichita State University, as television teacher. Available only as a series.

Approaching Poetry—The Whole Poem: Channel to Action. Producer/Distributor: WNDTTV/GPITVL, 1968. Grade Level: Jr. & Sr. H.S. Running Time: 20 min. B&W. Rental.

This telecourse lesson which is a continuation of the discussion on the public functions of poetry by examination of the traditional role poetry has played in pointing out social problems calling for solutions. Pulitzer-prize-winning poet Gwendolyn Brooks is an on-camera guest. This lesson might be used in developing units on Negro poets and Negro poetry. Available only as a series.

Black Music. Producer/Distributor: LRC, 1970. Code No. M.V.-A-22 & 24. Running Time: 95 min. Purchase.

An organ recital. A selection of Creole folk songs is also offered.

Trio (Black Music). Producer/Distributor: LRC, 1970. Code No. M.V. A-21. Running Time: 51 min. Purchase. B&W.

D. Antoinette Handy-Miller offers a performance using three basic instruments—flute, base violin, and piano.

Browne, McGee & Soney Teary Concert (Black Music Seminar). Producer/Distributor: LRC, 1970. Code No. M.V. A-14.15. Running Time: 60 min. Purchase. B&W.

This folk concert presents two basic folk instruments: the guitar and harmonica. The music is basically the "down home" type, with a blues background. The artists have presented concerts in many foreign countries.

Cultural Understanding. Producer/Distributor: KRMATV/GPITVL, 1968. Grade Level: Elementary. Running Time: 30 min. B&W. Rental.

This series is designed to increase understanding of the cultural heritage, attitudes and contributions of four ethnic groups, Asian American, American Indian, Spanish American, and American Negro, and the contributions of each of the minority groups. Among the general concepts developed in Cultural Understandings are: 1) Every racial or ethnic group represented within the United States has made important historic contributions to the development of the country; 2) Customs practiced by peaple as part of a culture are slow to change; the need for change must outweigh an old belief before changes occur; 3) Prejudice is a barrier to understanding; accurate knowledge may help eliminate this barrier. Three of the programs deal specifically with the Negro:

Patriots and Western Pioneers A recounting of the important contributions made by American Negro patriots and pioneers in our history—in wartime as soldiers and in the early American West as cattlemen and other important roles. **America—Culturally Speaking** This lesson deals with the important contributions American Negroes have made in broad fields of cultural heritage—in art, music, literature, the theater, sports, motion pictures and dance. **American Negroes In Our City And Nation** "Where am I going?" "What is in my future?" "What type of work will I be doing?" This lesson attempts to answer in part these kinds of questions, particularly as they pertain to Negro boys and girls. Highlight of the program: renowned Negro actor Sidney Poitier speaks of his early life in the Bahamas and the difficulties he overcame in order to become one of our greatest contemporary actors. Available only as a series.

The History of American Civilization by Its Interpreters. Producer/Distributor: KLRNTV/GPITVL, 1965. Grade Level: College & Adult. Running Time: 30 min. Rental. B&W.
    John Hope Franklin on the Negro in American History Dr. Franklin gave two lectures in this series: The Negro in American History; The Militant South and Reconstruction. **Ralph Bunche on Twentieth Century Collective Security** This program is also useful for the study of Negro statesmen.

Kay Concert (Black Music Seminar). Producer/Distributor: LRC, 1970. Code No. M.V. A-11. Running Time: 60 min. Purchase. B&W.
    D. Antionette Handy-Miller's Suite for Flute in B minor, accompanied by Mr. Gatlin, piano; and Vivian Cannon, violin.

Rev. Gary Davis and the Sea Island Singers (Black Music Seminar). Producer/ Distributor: LRC, 1970. Grade Level: Elementary through Adult. Code No. M.V. A-16-17-18-19-20. Running Time: 120 min. Purchase. B&W.
    Rev. Gary Davis and his group originate from Sea Island, Georgia. Their basic repertoire consists of Negro spirituals. Along with their musical entertainment, Rev. Davis delights the audience with his amusing anecdotes of early life. He will often invite members of the audience on stage to participate in the program.

KINESCOPES

America in the 70's: The Critical Issues—Black America. Producer/Distributor: ETS/IU. B&W.
    Black America is one of a series of television programs now available on 16mm films.

The Economic Straightjacket The problems of Negro unemployment are discussed by Herbert Hill, National Labor Secretary of the NAACP, in which he analyzes problems and offers some solutions. Professor Albert Wheeler of the University of Michigan is the interviewer.

Is Justice Color Blind? Negro-Police relations, legal representation, bail, and judge and jury problems are considered by the Honorable Wade H. McCree, U.S. District Court, Eastern Michigan, and Professor Joseph R. Julin of the University of Michigan Law School as they view the question as to whether the Negro American gets a "fair shake" in the American scheme of justice.

Sanctuary and Spear: The Church in the Revolution The Reverend Louis Johnson, Pastor of Friendship Baptist Church in Detroit, describes with the aid of pictures the story of the Negro Church, refuge in the Nineteenth and early Twentieth Century, which has now become the church militant. The Reverend Gordon Jones of St. Andrews Episcopal Church in Ann Arbor describes the role of white churches in the civil rights movement. Both men discuss the ecumenical side effects of the Negro revolution.

A Sense of the Future Featuring Dr. Charles Stewart, Assistant Director of the Human Relations Commission of the Detroit Public Schools, this program takes us into the classrooms where we learn why Negro drop out rates are disproportionately high and what school and community can do about it.

The Struggle at Hand The Deputy Director of the 1963 March on Washington, Bayard Rustin, discusses with University of Michigan Professor Albert Wheeler why the Negro must choose nonviolence rather than violence in the current revolution.

Third Chance Professor Dwight L. Dumond, prize winning University of Michigan historian, considers the Negro American's African heritage and searches out why the Negro failed to achieve freedom after the American Revolution and the Civil War.

We Shall Overcome On the panel of civil rights leaders are Mr. Damon J. Keith, Co-Chairman of the Michigan Civil Rights Commission, Mrs. Gloria Brown, head of Detroit CORE, Professor Beuleah Whitby, chairman of the Department of Sociology at Mercy College in Detroit, and Mr. Charles Wells, psychiatric social worker and former NAACP official. Professor Albert Wheeler of the University of Michigan moderates the panel, which looks into the future of the Negro revolution.

Where Shall We Live? With the aid of pictures and drawings, Melvin Ravitz, Common Councilman and Wayne State University Professor of Sociology, analyzes the problem of housing as a race question.

White Guilt; Black Shame Dr. James Comer of the U.S. Public Health Service, a specialist in preventive mental health, describes the psychological barriers to brotherhood and what he feels can be done about them.

Who Am I? Dr. James Comer deals with the Negro child's search for identity and what a lack of identity means to every child.

Hey, Mister. Producer/Distributor: KETCTV, 1969. Grade Level: Sr. H.S. & College. Running Time: 15 min. B&W. Rental: $75. Purchase: $200.
Reviews the attitudes of the ghetto resident to job training programs.

Breakthru: New Neighbors. Producer/Distributor: KETCTV, 1969. Grade Level: Elementary & Jr. H.S. Running Time: 20 min. B&W. Rental: $100.
A view of relationships and causes of attitudes among white middle class Americans regarding those who are "different."

TV Typing. Producer/Distributor: KETCTV, 1969. Grade Level: Elementary through College. Running Time: 30 min. B&W. Rental.

Host is a prominent black entertainer who points up many black-only hints for motivation for learning new job skill. Thirty-two programs.

What's Black? Producer/Distributor: KETCTV, 1969. Grade Level: Sr. H.S. & College. Running Time: 58 min. B&W. Rental: $100. Purchase: $250.

Role-playing drama in which Negro youth take roles of two contrasting views of what it means to be black in 1969.

100 selected paperbound books

ART

Porter, James A. *Modern Negro Art.* Arno Press, 1969. $2.95.

An historical account of the Negro's contribution to art in America from pre-Civil War days to 1943. Comprehensive and scholarly, but very readable. The book is well documented, has copious footnotes, and an excellent bibliography.

BIBLIOGRAPHY

Jackson, Miles M. Jr., ed. *Bibliography of Negro History and Culture for Young Readers.* University of Pittsburgh Press. $2.50.

This bibliography's purpose is to provide teachers and librarians with a buying guide for materials by and about Negro Americans suitable for young adults and children. Complete bibliographic information and annotations are given.

Miller, Elizabeth W. *Negro in America: A Bibliography.* Harvard University Press, 1965. $2.95.

An excellent bibliography with background notes at the beginning of each chapter. Material covers the period from 1954–1965 and describes adequately each bibliographical notation.

National Education Association, Center for Human Relations. *The Negro American in Paperback: A Selected List of Paperbound Books Compiled and Annotated for Secondary School Students.* National Education Association, 1968. $.50.

An annotated bibliography of paperbound books that can be used in black studies courses on the secondary level.

Rollins, Charlemae Hill, ed. *We Build Together.* National Council of Teachers of English. $1.50.

The purposes of this pamphlet are: (1) to present the underlying principles in guiding teachers and librarians in choosing books for young people; (2) to list the many books now available that depict Negro life honestly and accurately and to annotate some which should be balanced by others that round out the portrait of Negro life as it is lived in America today.

Salk, Erwin A. *A Layman's Guide to Negro History*. McGraw-Hill, 1967. $5.95.

A comprehensive bibliography of books and teaching aids dealing with the history of the black man in the United States. The book contains categories on Negro achievements, organizations, and history.

BIOGRAPHY

Adams, Russell L. *Great Negroes, Past and Present*. 2nd ed. Afro-American Press, 1964. $2.95.

The publication of this book is a culmination of searching inquiry into the need for a popular rendering of historical source material on the American Negro. The text is documented. Source notes at the end of each biographical sketch guide the reader to additional information on the subject in the text. An extensive bibliography is included. Introductions to the chapters provide background information and place the sketches in their historical perspective.

Baldwin, James. *Notes of a Native Son*. Beacon Press, 1967. $1.95.

Commentaries on literature and the performing arts in addition to biographical essays which tell of the author's childhood and life in Harlem.

Bradford, Sarah. *Harriet Tubman: The Moses of Her People*. Corinth Books, 1961. $1.50.

The adventures and accomplishments of the anti-slavery movement during the Civil War. The biography reveals the history of the underground railroad taken directly from the recollections of Harriet Tubman, who was one of the most daring conductors of the railroad.

Broderick, Francis L. *W. E. B. Dubois: Negro Leader in a Time of Crisis*. Stanford University Press, 1959. $2.95.

A scholarly evaluation of one of the most extraordinary figures of modern times, who for many years was one of the chief spokesman of the Negro race. Although the work is controversial, Broderick cites DuBois' contributions, his fight for Negro freedom, his encouragement of young Negroes to lead intellectual lives, and his great years as editor of *Crisis*.

Brown, Claude. *Manchild in the Promised Land*. New American Library, 1966. $.95.

Brown describes his life as a Negro youth in Harlem in the post-World War II period. Yielding to and then resisting a life of crime, habituation to drugs, and numerous other such temptations, he performed the impossible and emerged an independent, mature man. Although this is the story of one man, it is also the story of millions of slum-imprisoned Negroes.

Cronon, E. David. *Black Moses: The Story of Marcus Garvey and the Universal Negro Improvement Association*. University of Wisconsin Press, 1955. $1.95.

Black Moses is a study of Marcus Garvey, the Jamaica–born Negro leader and his Back to Africa Movement which stressed pride in blackness and the desire to change the policies of colonialism with an Africa for the Africans assertion. Garvey was one of the most controversial figures of the twenties, and the author has portrayed the strength of his appeal and his hold on the Negro masses in a book that makes a contribution to the literature of the period.

Dobler, Lavinia & Edgar A. Toppin. *Pioneers and Patriots: The Lives of Six Negroes of the Revolutionary Era.* Doubleday, 1965. $1.45.
Brief biographical accounts of the accomplishments of Negroes during the Revolutionary War. The sketches include Peter Salem, Jean Baptiste de Sable, Phillis Wheatley, Benjamin Banneker, Paul Cuffee and John Chavis.

Douglass, Frederick. *Narrative of the Life of Frederick Douglass, an American Slave.* Harvard University Press, 1960. $1.45.
This autobiography of an escaped slave is an account of his life as a slave, the sufferings he endured, and his eventual escape to freedom. He wrote this book for the purpose of "throwing light on the American slave system, and hastening the glad day of deliverance to the millions of my brethren in bonds."

Graham, Shirley. *Story of Phillis Wheatley, Poetess of the American Revolution.* Simon & Schuster, 1969. $.50.
Recounts the life of the first American Negro to gain recognition as a poet.

Gregory, Dick. *Nigger.* Pocket Books, 1964. $.75.
Autobiography of the famous Negro entertainer who tells in detail what it is like to have grown up black in America.

Holt, Rackham. *George Washington Carver.* Abingdon, 1963. $2.75.
A biography of the great Negro scientist which was originally published shortly after his death. The story chronicles his early beginning with scientific experiments and discoveries until he received world recognition years later.

Hughes, Langston. *Famous American Negroes.* Apollo Editions, 1954. $1.75.
Seventeen biographical sketches of famous Negroes from various fields of American life are included in this volume. It is particularly recommended for children's and young adult collections.

Quarles, Benjamin, ed. *Frederick Douglass.* Atheneum, 1948. $3.25.
A vivid biographical account of Frederick Douglass presented in his own words. The editor has carefully selected material which express Douglass' views on the horrors of the institution of slavery as well as his concerns on prejudice and job discrimination—topics as relevant now as when they were written.

Washington, Booker T. *Up From Slavery.* Dell. $.45.
This is the autobiography of a slave who became a prominent American Negro educator and social reformer. The book is the outgrowth of a series of articles dealing with incidents in his life, that Mr. Washington wrote for the magazine, *Outlook.* He tells a simple, straightforward story and woven into the story are statements of his thoughts in regard to the American Negro's place in society and his potential.

White, Walter. *A Man Called White.* Arno Press, 1948. $3.25.

Autobiography of the famous general secretary of the National Association for the Advancement of Colored People who devoted his life to achieve equal opportunities for members of his race. The book is more than a personal narrative, it is the history of the Negro in the first half of the Twentieth Century.

CIVIL RIGHTS

Booker, Simeon. *Black Man's America.* Prentice-Hall, 1964.

The author, a Negro reporter, describes the various aspects of the Negro's fight for equality. Included are Booker's personal views on the attitudes of prominent government leaders and the influence of various Negro civil rights leaders.

King, Martin Luther. *Why We Can't Wait.* New American Library. $.75.

Dr. King explains the reasons for Negro demonstrations, the reason for their impatience. This is the story of the Birmingham demonstrations, the March on Washington, and the Negro Revolution.

Wright, Nathan. *Black Power and Urban Unrest: The Creative Possibilities.* Hawtharn, 1967. $1.95.

An analysis of the meaning and goals of Black Power. The author feels that the movement is essential to the growth and development of the entire nation. Some of the material originally appeared in periodicals.

Young, Whitney M. Jr. *To Be Equal.* McGraw-Hill. $1.95.

The Executive Director of the National Urban League proposes comprehensive program for black employment, education, housing, health and leadership. The program Mr. Young outlines is a practical alternative to continuous racial conflict and strife. He challenges American leadership to use their resources to alleviate the problem.

EDUCATION

Ashmore, Harry S. *The Negro and the Schools.* University of North Carolina Press, 1954. $1.50.

In this extremely readable and informative book, Ashmore has edited the contributions of 45 scholars to build a true story of the legal and social struggle of Negroes and whites who have believed either that the doctrine of "separate and equal" education was a myth or that it should be denied and abolished. It is an historical record of more than 100 years of dual education which has drained the strength of the South's educational system.

Bouma, Donald H. & James Hoffman. *The Dynamics of School Integration.* Eerdmans, 1968. $2.25.

Community X is a middle-sized midwest city noted for its typicalness. It was thus an excellent city for the study of a problem existing today in other cities: de facto segregation in schools. The authors analyze how Community X saw and actively confronted this problem; and they describe citizen reaction. All elements of the problem are treated. Also included are an extensive bibliography and complete indexes.

Bullock, Henry A. *A History of Negro Education in the South: From 1619 to the Present.* Harvard University Press, 1967. $3.45.

After a brief introduction dealing with Negro education before 1870, Bullock describes the emergence of a public school system for both races during Reconstruction, and the rise of legal segregation in the following years. The heart of the book is a discussion of the contributions of the Southern Education Board and the Slater, Jeanes, and Rosenwald funds to the development of a Negro school system that emphasized agricultural and vocational training. Bullock's central thesis is that the system contained within it the seeds of its own destruction.

Crain, Robert L. *Politics of School Desegregation.* Doubleday, 1969. $1.95.

Brief case studies of political activities in both northern and southern cities during the process of school desegregation. The events in the city of New Orleans, where integration was peacefully instituted, are compared with six other cities. Studies show methods used to make school policy and community decisions, also the attitudes of school boards and city officials. The book proves the existence of the political process in the decisions made for schools in the North and South.

Kozol, Jonathan. *Death at an Early Age.* Bantam, 1967. $.95.

The story of the "destruction of the hearts and minds of Negro children in the Boston public schools" by a young teacher who was fired because he used a poem by Langston Hughes which was not on the prescribed list of reading materials. Kozol tells what happened when he entered the system in 1964 until his dismissal the following spring. This is a picture of American education as it exists in the ghettos of a major northern city.

McGrath, Earl James. *Predominantly Negro Colleges and Universities in Transition.* Teachers College Press, 1965. $2.75.

This study of 123 predominantly Negro colleges and universities is indispensable for the understanding of the problems of higher education for Negroes. McGrath concludes that although the colleges vary in character and quality, they will still provide the main educational opportunity for Negro youth and they need the support of private and public agencies.

Passow, A. Harry, ed. *Education in Depressed Areas.* Teachers College Press, 1963. $3.25.

The papers in this volume were given at a conference of educators, psychologists and sociologists interested in the problems of educating lower class children in an urban environment. The book makes plain the fact that schools in depressed areas are usually inferior to those outside the slums and maintains that the shape of American education will be determined by what is done to make the schools responsive to the needs of all citizens.

Robinson, Armstead L., ed. *Black Studies in the University: A Symposium.* Yale University Press, 1969. $1.75.

Proceedings of a symposium sponsored by the Black Student Alliance at Yale University for the purpose of implementing a program of black studies. Though no solution was found to the problems, the study represents an inquiry into the many facets of a black studies curriculum.

Trubowitz, Sidney. *A Handbook for Teaching in the Ghetto School.* Quadrangle, 1968. $4.95.

This book is designed to "increase a teacher's familiarity with ghetto elementary schools. . . .". It attempts to acquaint teachers of low socio-economic area children with some of the problems they will encounter and suggests teaching methods that can be used. The material was gathered through interviews with teachers who have achieved success in the public schools of Harlem.

U.S. Commission on Civil Rights. *Civil Rights U.S.A.: Public Schools, Cities in the North and West.* U.S. Gov't. Printing Office, 1962. $2.00.

Protest of racial segregation in northern and western states has mounted since the New Rochelle case of 1961. Success of this case stimulated Negro citizens in other cities to protest the segregation of their children in public schools. The Commission has collected data on the problems involved in desegregation of schools in Highland Park, Michigan, New Rochelle, N.Y., Philadelphia, Chicago and St. Louis. In each case the developments studied represented a denial of equal protection of the laws according to the Constitution.

HISTORY

Bennett, Lerone Jr. *Before the Mayflower: A History of the Negro in America, 1619–1964.* Penguin, 1962. $2.45.

A popular history of the American Negro. The Negro's heritage is traced from his African beginning to the admission of James Meredith to the University of Mississippi. The book is well documented and refutes some popular notions that slaves accepted their lot meekly or that Negro politicians during Reconstruction were more corrupt or illiterate than white ones. Excellent illustrations.

DuBois, W. E. B. *Black Reconstruction in America, 1860–1880.* Atheneum, 1969. $4.95.

The book seeks to tell and interpret the 20 years of history when Negroes were freed and the attempt to reconstruct the basis of democracy. The book contains a lengthy discussion of the black man's transition from slave to worker. The whole history of Reconstruction, its challenge to democracy, and its contribution to America's economic history and social development is portrayed in this classic of Negro history.

DuBois, W. E. B. *The Souls of Black Folk; Essays and Sketches.* Fawcett, 1969. $.75.

A history of the Negro written at the dawn of the Twentieth Century. The problem then as now was the problem of the color line—the relation of the darker to the lighter races of men in Asia, Africa and America. The book deals with Emancipation, its aftermath and meaning to the Negro. Several chapters have appeared in the *Atlantic Monthly, New World,* and other publications.

Durham, Philip & Everett Jones. *Adventures of the Negro Cowboys.* Bantam, 1966. $.75.

The role of the Negro cowboy is chronicled in this book from the early, post-Civil War trial herds to the more recent, great wild west shows. This set of unrelated stories and legends is interspersed with solid facts and figures. Tales of bulldogging Bill Pickett; conniving Ben Hodges; outlaw Issac Dart; and Jesse Stahl, "the best wild horse rider in the West", provide excellent wild west reading.

Franklin, John Hope. *From Slavery to Freedom.* 3rd ed. Random House, 1967. $2.95.

This book is an attempt to bring together the essential facts in the history of the American Negro from his ancient African beginnings to the present time. A conscious effort was made to write the history of the Negro in America with due regard for the forces at work which have affected his development; the main stream of American history, dominant Negro leaders, and the American environment. The book has numerous "Bibliographical Notes" and it is indexed.

Hoover, Dwight W., ed. *Understanding Negro History.* Quadrangle, 1968. $2.95.

"This book considers the major problems in studying and writing Negro history . . . so that both laymen and historians . . . can categorize the rapidly increasing data". The selections are drawn predominantly from journals, particularly the *Journal of Negro History* and the *Journal of Southern History.*

Katz, William L. *Eyewitness: the Negro in American History.* Pitman, 1967. $5.25.

An illustrated collection of extracts from documents, political speeches, and letters which are eyewitness accounts of events and episodes in the history of the Negro in America. The accounts are divided into nineteen groups which are prefaced by a self-contained narrative. Copious illustrations correspond to the units of a social studies curriculum. Material was prepared by an American History teacher to provide material to supplement and correct the omissions and distortions pertaining to the Negro in textbooks.

Meier, August & Elliott M. Rudwick. *From Plantation to Ghetto: An Interpretative History of American Negroes.* Hill & Wang, 1966. $1.85.

A scholarly history of the Negro in America beginning with a description of West African culture and analyzing the life of Negores in the United States to the present. The authors, one a historian, the other a sociologist, have given their interpretation of today's problems and their evaluation of the various civil rights activities.

Meier, August & Elliot M. Rudwick, eds. *The Making of Black America.* 2 vols. Atheneum, 1969. $3.95 each.

This collection of essays is divided into two parts. Vol. 1 traces the origins of black Americans from Africa through Reconstruction. Vol. 2 deals with the foundations of the 20th Century black community and "The New Militancy and the Enduring Ghetto." The second volume is more comprehensive although both have excellent selections from such noted historians as John Hope Franklin and Benjamin Quarles. Most of the essays have previously appeared in periodical literature. Stylistically, they are intended for a scholarly audience and will be useful to college students as secondary source material.

Osofsky, Gilbert. *Burden of Race: A Documentary History of Negro-White Relations in America.* Harper & Row, 1967. $3.75.

The author has assembled a fascinating array of documents that trace relations between Negroes and whites from the pseudo-scientists who justified slavery as "natural" to today's racists, black and white. Osofsky lets the extremists handle themselves with their own shoddy rhetoric and has unearthed some new and rare documents. The weak choices from the Reconstruction and modern periods are more than balanced by superb selections from the post-Reconstruction and New Deal eras. A valuable contribution to an understanding of the historic roots of our racial crisis.

Parsons, Talcott & Kenneth B. Clark, eds. *The Negro American.* Beacon Press, 1966. $3.95.

Consisting of thirty penetrating essays, *The Negro American* is the most comprehensive survey of the problems and status of the Negro in American society since *An American Dilemma* by Myrdal in 1944. Each essay is by a different author and deals with a different facet of race relations problems. An expanded and revised collection of articles that first appeared in *Daedalus*, this book is destined to be a basic documentary of the evolving patterns of race relations in the sixties.

Quarles, Benjamin. *The Negro in the American Revolution.* University of North Carolina Press, 1967. $1.95.

This book fills a long time gap in the history of the Revolution and the Negro's participation in it. There are ten well documented chapters plus an excellent bibliography.

Wish, Harvey. *The Negro Since Emancipation.* Prentice-Hall, 1964. $1.95.

One of the books in the Eyewitness Accounts of American History Series. The author presents excerpts from Booker T. Washington to Elijah Muhammed to show the pattern and changes in Negro thought. Biographical sketches are provided for each contributor.

LITERATURE

Bone, Robert A. *The Negro Novel in America.* Yale University Press, 1958. $2.25.

This book represents a point of view which is sensitive to literary values as well as to social movements. Bone carefully plots the development of the Negro struggle in the United States, and relates the various literary tendencies to this movement. The history of the Negro novel is divided into four periods and the novels of each period are analyzed. The book is useful as a reference tool.

Bontemps, Arna, ed. *American Negro Poetry.* Hill & Wang, 1963. $1.55.

A collection of the works of 56 poets, including such noted authors as James Weldon Johnson, Paul Laurence Dunbar, Langston Hughes and Countee Cullen. An interesting and absorbing anthology which includes many poetic forms to lend variety and interest to the volume.

Brooks, Gwendolyn. *Selected Poems.* Harper & Row, 1963. $1.65.

A selection of poems by the noted author and Pulitzer Prize winner. Selections from "A Street in Bronzeville", "Annie Allen" and the "Bean Eaters", plus new poems. Poems deal with Negro life and contemporary problems.

Brown, Sterling. *Negro Poetry and Drama and the Negro in American Fiction.*
Atheneum, 1969. $3.45.

A survey of the Negro in American poetry and drama designed to show
the development of attitudes toward Negro life in American thinking. Seven
chapters are devoted to poetry, and three to drama. The drama section traces
the Negro character from the earliest subsidiary roles to the present major one.
An important review of the Negro's literary life and its influence on American
literature.

Cleaver, Eldridge. *Soul on Ice.* Dell, 1968. $1.95.

After a series of religious experiences in prison, young Cleaver became a
Muslim convert, then a Muslim preacher of extraordinary eloquence and conviction and a firm follower of Malcolm X. From this point began the remarkable
process of self-analysis, self-education and self-expression described in the pages
of this book which introduces to the reading public a major writer on the
American scene.

Cook, Mercer & S. E. Henderson. *The Militant Black Writer in Africa and the
United States.* University of Wisconsin Press, 1969. $1.95.

This volume consists of two essays which were enlarged from their original
versions given at a symposium. Cook presents a brief but introspective survey of
revolutionary African literature; Henderson discusses American black writing
with numerous illustrative samples. Both men explore the concepts of "negritude" or "soul" as it is expressed by black writers—African and American.
Henderson sees the writings of blacks as an integral part of "the Black Consciousness Movement."

Duberman, Martin B. *In White America: A Documentary Play.* New American
Library, 1964. $.60.

The social problem of the Negro presented in dramatic form. Duberman
chronicles the deprivation that has led to the militancy of Negroes.

Dunbar, Paul Laurence. *Complete Poems of Paul Laurence Dunbar.* Apollo
Editions, 1913. $1.95.

The first complete collection of Dunbar's poems, comprising the "Lyrics
of Lowly Life," "Lyrics of the Hearth-ride," "Lyrics of Love and Laughter,"
"Lyrics of Sunshine and Shadow," and a number of poems heretofore un-
published.

Gross, Seymour L. & John Edward Hardy. *Images of the Negro in American
Literature.* University of Chicago Press, 1966. $2.95.

A history of the Negro as author and subject in American literature. The
study indicates that he has been depicted more as a stereotype than as a human
being.

Haslam, Gerald. *Forgotten Pages of American Literature.* Houghton-Mifflin,
1970. $3.25.

An anthology designed to be used in "ethnic" literature courses. Consists
of selections from Asian-American, Latin-American, American Indian and
American Negro writings.

Hill, Herbert, ed. *Anger and Beyond: The Negro Writer in the United States.*
Harper & Row, 1966. $1.45.
This collection of essays traces the development of American Negro
writing from a literature of suppressed anger to one of open confrontation
between black and white. Writers on historical perspective include Saunders
Redding, Horace Cayton and Nat Hentoff. The book concludes with a symposium on Richard Wright.

Hughes, Langston, ed. *Best Short Stories by Negro Writers: An Anthology from
1899 to the Present.* Little, Brown, 1967. $2.95.
A collection of 47 stories ranging from the American Reconstruction to
the 1960s and in locale from the Caribbean to Chicago and New York. Selections
are based on literary styles as well as merit. Writers included are Chesnutt, Dunbar and such contemporaries as Baldwin, Yerby, and Ellison.

Hughes, Langston, ed. *New Negro Poets, U.S.A.* Indiana University Press, 1964.
$1.95.
Selection of poems by 37 Negro poets. Collection consists of five parts:
lyrical, protest, personal, general descriptions and personal reflective statements.
The poems have been called "a metrical sociology of the Negro heart".

Littlejohn, David. *Black on White: A Critical Survey of Writing by American
Negroes.* Viking Press, 1969. $1.45.
This is the only book-length survey of Negro writing since Bone's *The
Negro Novel in America.* The work is mainly a literary survey dealing with
works (chiefly fiction) written since 1940, although one chapter is devoted to
works before then. The book is well written with the central theme that Negro
literature is chiefly of the race war variety and cannot be judged from a strictly
aesthetic viewpoint.

Wright, Richard. *Native Son.* Harper & Row, 1940. $.95.
Often compared with Dreiser's *American Tragedy*, this novel is a moving
study of Negro life—brutal, frank and sordid. This is the story of a Negro boy's
crimes, of what part society played in those crimes, and of how the boy paid the
penalty.

MUSIC

Carawan, Guy & Candie. *Ain't You Got a Right to the Tree of Life?* Simon &
Schuster, 1966. $3.95.
Photos, songs, and tape recorded statements comprise a moving documentary of the life and traditions of this special Negro community inhabited
chiefly by the descendants of plantation slaves.

Charters, Samuel B. *Jazz: New Orleans: 1885–1963.* Oak Publications, 1963.
$2.95.
A study of the New Orleans musical environment, supplying brief biog-
raphies of musicians and musical groups. The historical information on New
Orleans music gives the reader an insight into the development of American
Negro music.

Johnson, James Weldon & Rosamond. *The Book of American Negro Spirituals.* Viking Press, 1969. $3.95.

A comprehensive collection of Negro spirituals, containing lyrics and music. Originally published in two volumes, it has been combined and reproduced in the original form. The preface to each book contains a history of the Negro in American music.

Jones, Leroi. *Black Music.* Apollo Editions, 1969. $1.95.

Collection of magazine articles, record reviews, and album notes written between 1959 and 1967 about such leading black jazz artists as John Coltrane, Ornette Coleman and Sonny Rollins. Provides a picture of the modern Negro community both musically and socially.

Jones, Leroi. *Blues People: Negro Music in White America.* Apollo Editions, 1963. $1.95.

An attempt to place black music in this country in the context of American cultural history. Chapters include: The Negro as Non-American; American Slaves: Their Music; Primitive Blues and Primitive Jazz; The Blues.

Ulanov, Barry. *Handbook of Jazz.* Viking Press, 1957. $1.45.

A good introduction to jazz for the novice jazz enthusiast. There are chapters on jazz history and instruments, as well as biographical sketches of jazz musicians. There is an excellent section on the chronology of jazz in the Twentieth Century.

POLITICS

Carmichael, Stokely & Charles Hamilton. *Black Power: The Politics of Liberation in America.* Random House, 1968. $1.95.

The book presents the case for Black Power and does not attempt to win, or pacify whites. The authors' analysis of Negro history in America leads them to conclude that racism still stifles Negroes, who must look to their own protection without considering coalitions with whites. They urge pride in race and political and economic unity as the methods of securing civil rights, with a few illustrations of the effectiveness of Black Power as well as some suggested courses of action.

Kalven, Harry, Jr. *The Negro and the First Amendment.* University of Chicago Press, 1966. $2.45.

Professor Kalven focuses on a by-product of recent divil rights activities: their impact on judicial formulations regarding the guarantees of free speech and freedom of association under the First Amendment. He uses three sets of cases to support his analysis.

RACE RELATIONS

Boyle, Sarah Patton. *The Desegregated Heart: A Virginian's Stand in Time of Transition.* Morrow, 1967. $2.95.

A personal narrative by a white southerner who took a stand with Negroes against the white South despite opposition by members of her community. The southern integration struggle is the background of this story.

Kitano, Harry L. *American Racism.* University of California Press, 1970. $1.95.

A theoretical model of race relations validated by historical materials. An insight into understanding American racism is provided through examination of the California experience, the essential simularity among target groups, the phenomenon of inter- and intra-ground hostility, and the negative effects of a parisa status are emphasized.

Muse, Benjamin. *American Negro Revolution: From Non-violence to Black Power, 1963–1967.* Citadel Press, 1968. $2.95.

A comprehensive account of the nonviolent campaigns of 1963 and 1964 to the nationwide riots of 1967. The principal Negro organizations from the NAACP to Black Muslims are described as well as school boycotts, marches, and demonstrations. Muse discusses the role of federal, state and local agencies and the development of integration through the courts as well as on the local level. The final chapter summarizes the report of the 1968 National Advisory Commission on Civil Disorders.

Woodward, C. Vann. *The Strange Case of Jim Crow.* Oxford University Press, 1966. $1.75.

Revised edition of a book recognized as a landmark in the history of American race relations. Extensive information is provided on developments and changes in the past decade including civil rights legislation, the non-violence resistance movement, racial strife, and problems in the North.

Wright, Nathan. *Let's Work Together.* Hawthorn, 1968. $1.95.

The chairman of the 1967 National Conference on Black Power appraises the movement and urges whites to help the Negro in his struggle for equal opportunity. He points out many of the areas of problems and discrimination and notes that power is also lacking to the lower class whites.

RELIGION

Essien-Udom, E. V. *Black Nationalism: A Search for an Identity in America.* Dell, 1964. $.75.

A searching and exhaustive sociological study of a Negro movement which originated as a result of the Negro's desire to seek his identity within the American scene. The author describes the origins of black nationalism, its organization and activities and attempts to explain the meaning and significance of the movement. The book is well documented and has a bibliography.

Frazier, Edward Franklin. *The Negro Church in America.* Schocken Books, 1964. $1.75.

An enlargement of a lecture given by the author at the University of Liverpool in 1953. Published as a tribute to Dr. Frazier, this work traces the evolution of the Negro church in America from its beginning to the present.

King, Martin Luther, Jr. *The Strength to Love.* Pocket Books, 1963. $.75.

A collection of seventeen sermons by the noted civil rights leader. The sermons are built on a theme of Christian love and we are reminded that "it does take strength to love."

Lincoln, C. Eric. *The Black Muslims in America*. Beacon Press, 1961. $1.95.

A description of the Black Muslim movement in the United States, its activities and goals. The story of the rise of the pseudo-Islamic movement describes one of the ways Negroes have used to fight back at white racial injustice.

Mays, Benjamin. *Negro's God as Reflected in His Literature*. Atheneum, 1968. $2.75.

Mays' purpose is to trace the development of the idea of God in Negro literature from 1760 to 1937. The types of literature included in the survey are spirituals, sermons, poetry, and fiction.

Washington, Joseph R. *Black Religion: The Negro and Christianity in the United States*. Beacon Press, 1964. $2.45.

Are American Negro churches Christian? The author, a Negro college chaplain and professor of religion, answers "no" in four essays written from a theologian's viewpoint. He states that Negro church life has centered, not on Christ, but on the drive for freedom, rights, opportunity.

SOCIAL AND ECONOMIC CONDITIONS

Ames, William C., ed. *The Negro Struggle for Equality in the Twentieth Century*. Heath, 1965. $1.84.

This book is listed with others as one that "can be used profitably as supplementary reading or unit in courses in history, geography, and international relations".

Boyton, James A. *Tension in the Cities: Three Programs for Survival*. Chilton Books, 1969. $3.95.

A thoughtful analysis of America's urban problems. The author concentrates his investigation on three cities: New York, Atlanta, and Washington, D.C., and concludes that none of these cities have adequately comprehensive programs to deal with their problems. Instead of workable solutions, motivated projects are piled upon each other, solving no fundamental ills. The author ends the book on a pessimistic note, questioning the existence of public concern and support for urban affairs.

Clark, Kenneth B. *Dark Ghetto: Dilemmas of Social Power*. Harper & Row, 1965. $1.75.

Based on reports prepared by Dr. Clark while he served as chief consultant to Harlem Youth Opportunities Unlimited; analyzes the poverty, crime, low aspirations, family instability and exploitations of people living in the dark ghetto of Harlem. Questions are raised about effectiveness of social service agencies in dealing with problems of the ghetto.

Conot, Robert E. *Rivers of Blood, Years of Darkness*. Bantam, 1967. $.95.

Detailed account of the events that took place before, during, and after the 1965 Watts Riot in Los Angeles.

Davis, Arthur & John Dollard. *Children of Bondage: The Personality Development of Negro Youth in the Urban South*. Harper & Row, 1964. $2.25.

A report in a series of studies made by the American Youth Commission on Negro Youth. Its aim is "to determine what forces are at work in training a child to participate in social life and what variables operate when the attempt is to re-socialize, that is, to alter the habits of adults."

Franklin, John Hope & Isidore Starr, eds. *The Negro in Twentieth Century America.* Random House, 1967. $2.45.

A kaleidoscope of opinion bearing on a variety of subjects relating to the Negro's struggle for civil rights in 20th Century America. It shows the dark side of human nature with its bigotry, hatred, and violence as well as the bright side of American decency, respect, and peaceful resolution of conflict. The purpose in presenting such a collection of conflicting opinions—in the words of the editors—"to understand the complexity of the problems of the Negro is the first step in the search for solutions." The opinions appear in various forms—documents, cartoons, charts, poems and selections from books, magazines and newspapers.

Frazier, Edward Franklin. *Black Bourgeoisie: The Rise of a New Middle Class in the United States.* Collier Books, 1962. $.95.

The primary purpose of this study is to make a sociological analysis of the behavior, attitudes, and values of the "black bourgeoisie." This segment of the Negro population came into existence because of racial discrimination and racial segregation. This book deals with the frustrations experienced by these people who try to conform to white standards, but who are rejected by the white world.

Frazier, Edward Franklin. *The Negro Family in the United States.* University of Chicago Press, 1966. $2.45.

A classic work written during the golden age of American sociology. Frazier relates the realities of Negro family life. Family patterns of the Negro American were established under slavery and were subjected to oppression and disruption. With this background, the family which evolved became increasingly more disorganized. The author is optimistic, feeling that full employment, proper housing, increased incomes, and a compassionate society will provide conditions to change the image of the Negro family.

Ginzberg, Eli, et al. *Middle-Class Negro in the White Man's World.* Columbia University Press, 1967. $2.25.

This "study is based on 120 interviews with middle-class Negro young men in Atlanta and New York City, high school seniors, college sophomores, and college seniors." The purpose of the study was to discover how middle-class Negro youth respond to their new opportunities. The findings are optimistic in view of the present gloom that is evident among Negroes today.

Ginzberg, Eli, ed. *The Negro Challenge to the Business Community.* McGraw-Hill, 1964. $1.65.

A collection of representative papers of a 1964 meeting of members of the American industrial and business community held at Arden House by the Graduate School of Business of Columbia University. The primary purpose of the meeting was to expose ways for the Negro to enter and mingle in the business community.

Herskovits, Melville J. *The American Negro: A Study in Racial Crossing.* Indiana University Press, 1964. $1.85.

Herskovits has centered his attention upon biological rather than sociological problems. The study begins with the observation that the Negro in this country is a new kind of Negro, a physical type that exists nowhere else. He defends his position by use of statistical procedure to show that this is a result of crossing between the Negro, the American Indian, and the white stock of this country. He explains how certain social standards have made the lighter Negro the privileged one and, thus, influenced biological changes. Guarded and cautious, this work deals with controversial topics without a trace of emotion. It deals with the necessary statistical concepts with great clarity.

Johnson, Charles S. *Growing Up in the Black Belt: Negro Youth in the Rural South.* Schocken Books, 1967. $2.45.

This study, sponsored by the American Youth Commission, analyzes the problems of 2000 Negro youths in eight counties in the Black Belt. The material is presented through case studies, is well organized, and gives statistical as well as factual data.

Locke, Alain, ed. *The New Negro.* Atheneum, 1968. $4.25.

"The New Negro, first published in 1925, was the definitive presentation of the artistic and social goals of the New Negro movement." The New Negro movement was also known as the Harlem Renaissance and the Negro Renaissance. It was the beginning of new racial attitudes and ideals of race consciousness and race pride. The anthology includes examples of Negro fiction, poetry, drama, music and essays. The bibliography includes most of the early notable books by Negroes.

Rainwater, Lee & William Yancey. *The Moynihan Report and the Politics of Controversy: A Transaction Social Science and Public Policy Report.* M.I.T. Press, 1967. $3.95.

A critique on the controversial Moynihan Report on the Negro family. Includes a portion of the report as well as working papers of the conference and serial accounts of the report. Valuable document for sociological research or courses in sociology and government.

Spero, Sterling D. & Abram L. Harris. *The Black Worker: The Negro and the Labor Movement.* Atheneum, 1968. $3.75.

This book is "an effort to set forth descriptively and analytically the results of a study of the American labor movement in one of its most important aspects, namely, the relation of the dominant section of the working class to the segregated, circumscribed, and restricted Negro minority."

Weaver, Robert C. *The Dilemmas of Urban America.* Atheneum, 1967. $1.95.

"The Administrator of the U.S. Housing and Home Finance Agency considers in this book the housing problems arising from the metropolitan population explosion." Chief focus is on building decent housing for Negroes and Puerto Ricans. The author points out the problems encountered in providing low and middle income housing and the conflicts with integration.

THEATRE

Marshall, Herbert & Mildred Stock. *Ira Aldridge: The Negro Tragedian.* Southern Illinois University Press, 1968. $2.85.

Biography of the famous Negro actor of the 19th Century who was one of the most celebrated Shakesperian actors of the time. This biography makes a unique contribution to the history of the Negro in the theatre.

Mitchell, Loften. *Black Drama: The Story of the American Negro in the Theatre.* Hawthorn, 1967. $3.95.

This book gives a historical review of the Negro in the American theatre. The years from 1820 to 1966 are described; authors, actors, and producers are discussed.

PART THREE: MULTIMEDIA MATERIALS IN THIS SECTION ARE DESIGNED TO PROVIDE AN UNDERSTANDING AND APPECIATION OF THE PEOPLES OF AFRICA, THEIR CULTURES, AND CONTRIBUTIONS TO MANKIND

Films (16mm)

Africa. Producer/Distributor: USNAC, 1961. Running Time: 35 min. B&W.
Joseph C. Satterthwaite, Assistant Secretary of State for African Affairs, appraises the history and basic problems facing the new Africa.

Africa Astir. Producer/Distributor: GORH, 1961. Running Time: 25 min. Color.
This overview of Africa shows contrasting life in several villages and illustrates the variety in types of people and ways of living in mountain, desert, and river communities along the Niger River.

Africa, Change and Challenge. Producer/Distributor: AIMS, 1968. Grade Level: Elementary through Sr. H.S. Running Time: 19 min. Purchase: $240. Color.
This film is different in spirit and context from the usual geographical approach to the study of Africa. The treatment used can add depth to that study by developing student understanding of the peoples of Africa south of the Sahara, and of the impact and problems of change.

Africa: Chopi Village Life. Producer/Distributor: AIMS, 1969. Grade Level: Elementary through Sr. H.S. Running Time: 16½ min. Purchase: $190. Color.
This story stresses the daily lives of the Chopi, a primitive tribe of Southeast Africa.

Africa: East African Aristocrats (Masai). Producer/Distributor: WSU, 1964. Grade Level: Primary through Adult. Running Time: 29 min. B&W & Color.
This film depicts the environment, customs and daily life of the Masai, and points out some of the problems of introducing changes into the African society and culture.

Africa: East and West. Producer/Distributor: TRIBU. Running Time: 28 min. Color.
The European influence is seen in East Africa in the supermarkets, modern cities and industries. In West Africa there are mosques and other Eastern influences. The film shows African tribal customs and dances, and its wildlife.

Africa, Giant with a Future. Producer/Distributor: EDS, 1957. Grade Level: Sr. H.S. through Adult. Running Time: 30 min. Rental: $10. Purchase: $195. Color.

This film presents a study of the people of Africa and their needs in the areas of health, education and a stable economy. It contrasts the centuries of old Africa with today's Africa of modern skyscrapers and inside plumbing, and gives a panoramic view of 16 countries south and east of the Sahara. The film shows how the governments of many countries and Protestant and Catholic missionaries are cooperating in the fight against ignorance and disease.

Africa Goes to School. Producer/Distributor: CFD, 1962. Grade Level: Intermediate through Jr. H.S. Running Time: 10 min. Color.

This film is an introduction to Africa which highlights the educational system and its relationship to job opportunities. The film depicts a cross-section of features, from modern cities to primitive jungle areas.

Africa: An Introduction. Producer/Distributor: FA, 1967. Grade Level: Elementary through Jr. H.S. Running Time: 18 min. Rental: $12.50. Purchase: Color, $200; B&W, $120.

This film is an overview of the geography of Africa and the many different people who make up its population. The major differences between the desert, grassland, and the tropics are shown, and the film explains how and why the lives of the people of Africa differ from one area to another.

Africa Is My Home (*Nigeria*). Producer/Distributor: DOUBLE. Grade Level: Elementary through Sr. H.S. Running Time: 22 min. Purchase: $200.

Many of the most important problems facing a changing Africa are conveyed through this story of a West African woman from birth through marriage. First-person narration offers insights into the problems of tradition versus modernization, Christianity versus Islam, and colonialism versus independence.

Africa—Jet Safari. Producer/Distributor: ALITIA. Running Time: 14 min. Color.

The film pictures a jet safari to the African countries of Ghana, Nigeria, South Africa, the Rhodesias and Kenya. It includes views of the Wankie Game Reserve, Victoria Falls, ceremonial dances and the treetops located deep in the jungle.

Africa—Land of Contrasts. Producer/Distributor: AIMS. Running Time: 17 min. Color.

This film shows why Africa is the continent experiencing the most changes in recent years, and illustrates contrasts between the back country and the major cities, with emphasis on the people.

Africa on the Bridge. Producer/Distributor: WWP, 1960. Running Time: 90 min. Color.

This film shows evangelist Billy Graham's 17,000 mile tour of Africa, including many of the new nations.

Africa Speaks. Producer/Distributor: BRAN, 1961. Grade Level: Sr. H.S. through College. Running Time: 18 min. Rental: $7.50. Purchase: $90.

This film recording made in Paris presents an exchange of opinions and facts by five African university students. Among the subjects they discuss are an evaluation of present African leaders, the role of the student in Africa and chances for African unity. Later, an American student leads the discussion into a consideration of the black man in the United States.

African Birdlife. Producer/Distributor: BFA, 1963. Running Time: 11 min. Color.
This film shows the birds of the tropical lakes and marshland streams of Central Africa in their natural habitat.

African Continent: An Introduction. Producer/Distributor: CORF, 1962. Grade Level: Intermediate through Jr. H.S. Running Time: 16 min. Purchase: Color, $195; B&W, $97.50.
This film shows major land formations, climatic regions, natural resources and land use, emphasizing Africa's vast wealth and its growing importance.

African Continent: Northern Region. Producer/Distributor: CORF, 1962. Grade Level: Intermediate through Jr. H.S. Running Time: 13½ min. B&W & Color.
North Africa is an old, yet rapidly changing part of a vast continent. The huge Sahara extends into the countries of North Africa. Most of these countries face the Mediterranean Sea. These are primarily Arab lands; there is a shortage of water; and there have long been European influences here.

African Continent: Southern Region. Producer/Distributor: CORF, 1962. Grade Level: Intermediate through Jr. H.S. Running Time: 11 min. B&W & Color.
In this area live many different people—farmers, miners, and villagers. The history of the peoples of Southern Africa is a story of great waves of migration and immigration. The descendants of these different groups are the people of Southern Africa today.

African Continent: Tropical Region. Producer/Distributor: CORF, 1962. Grade Level: Intermediate through Jr. H.S. Running Time: 13½ min. B&W & Color.
This film depicts tropical Africa, emerging from old to new ways, as an area containing vast resources—some developed, some still untouched.

African Cousins. Producer/Distributor: BAFC. Running Time: 14 min. Color.
This film emphasizes that all people are similar in their work, play and physical needs.

African Culture and Civilization. Producer/Distributor: CI. Grade Level: Sr. H.S. Running Time: 40 min. Purchase: $55. B&W.
This film recreates in photos and drawings the lives, activities, and cultures of the black people in Africa. Audio tape accompanies film.

African Dances. Producer/Distributor: MGH. Running Time: 28 min. Rental: $12.50. Purchase: $260. Color.
This film presents a performance in the General Assembly Hall at United

Nations headquarters of Les Ballets Africains, a group described by Clive Barnes in The *New York Times* as ". . . the most distinguished and sophisticated of all African dance companies." A United Nations Film.

The African Elephant. Producer/Distributor: MCHRIS, 1967. Running Time: 8 min. Color.
    This film presents a brief history of the elephant, showing wild elephants and their behavior in their natural habitat.

African Fauna. Producer/Distributor: BFA, 1957. Running Time: 11 min. Color.
    This film shows scenes of such animals as waterbuck, impala, cheeta, crocodile, elephant, zebra, lion, giraffe and hippopotamus, photographed in Kenya, Uganda and the Congo. From the Far Places Series.

African Girl—Malobi. Producer/Distributor: ATLAP, 1960. Grade Level: Elementary. Running Time: 11 min. Purchase: $120. Color.
    This film shows life in a native village; the work of the parents, marketing, rebuilding mud houses and other activities. A young girl tells how her life is changing and of her yearning for an education.

African Harvest. Producer/Distributor: FMETHC, 1959. Running Time: 43 min. B&W.
    This film describes the various installations and educational, medical and evangelistic programs of the African Missions operated by the General Mission Board of the Free Methodist Church.

African Horse Sickness. Producer/Distributor: USNAC, 1962. Grade Level: Sr. H.S. through Adult. Running Time: 29 min. Color.
    This film presents a photographic record of the progress of African horse sickness from infection to death, and describes the development, manufacturing and administration of preventive vaccines.

African Journey. Producer/Distributor: STOC, 1953. Grade Level: Intermediate through Adult. Running Time: 30 min. Color.
    This film pictures much of East Africa, including its principal cities, diamond and gold mines, the wild animals of Kenya and Tanganyika (Tanzania) and native dances of the Zulus, the Watussi tribe and the Wakamba tribe.

The African Locusts. Producer/Distributor: FLEET. Running Time: 10 min. Color.
    This film portrays the fight of African animals against the swarms of locusts that attack them. From Wonders of Wildlife Series.

African Musicians. Producer/Distributor: BRAN, 1957. Grade Level: Jr. H.S. through College. Running Time: 14½ min. Rental: $7.50. Purchase: $90. B&W.
    This film of the individual man and his tribe presents the ancient music of the tom-tom, calabash, twin xylophones and primitive horns. In sculpture as

well as song and ritual dance we learn how music plays its part "in harmony with the breathing of the world."

African Storyteller. Producer/Distributor: IFB, 1964. Grade Level: Intermediate through Adult. Running Time: 15 min. Color.

Life in Africa today is compared with that of 50 years ago. The film illustrates the life and death struggles of both animal and man.

African Tribes. Producer/Distributor: BFA, 1942. Running Time: 11 min. Color.

The film shows four tribes—Bamburi, saucer-lipped people of the Lake Albert District; Ifi pygmies of the Ituri Forest; long-headed Mangbettu of the Central Congo; and the Rendilli, strange nomads of the Kaisut Desert, Kenya.

African Trypanosomiasis. Producer/Distributor: USNAC, 1953. Running Time: 16 min. Color.

This film explains the etiology, epidemiology, symptomatology, diagnosis, treatment, prognosis, prevention and control of African Trypanosomiasis (sleeping sickness).

African Village. Producer/Distributor: PSU-TAD, 1960. Grade Level: Elementary through Jr. H.S. Running Time: 17 min. Rental: $6. Color.

This film depicts life in mid-tropical Africa, showing crude methods of cooking, washing, weaving, planting, harvesting, and visits to market. The film shows people becoming aware of the Twentieth Century, keeping old rituals in connection with planting while using modern tools.

African Wildlife Sanctuary. Producer/Distributor: BFA, 1957. Running Time: 11 min. Color.

A trip through Kruger National Park is portrayed with views of the rest camps and roads. Wild animals encountered include lions, elephants, hippos, elands, impalas and monkeys. From the Far Places Series.

African Writers of Today. Producer/Distributor: IU, 1964. Grade Level: Sr. H.S. through Adult. Running Time: 30 min. B&W.

A five-part series which includes: **Walter Allen, Amos Tutuola, Ulli Beier** Presents interviews with English literary critic Walter Allen, Nigerian author Amos Tutuola and Ulli Beier, German-born editor of the Nigerian Literary Magazine *Black Orpheus*. **Ezekiel Mphahlele** Presents an interview with exiled South African essayist and short story writer Ezekiel Mphahlele, who discusses the advantages of a writer in exile. Describes Mphahlele's autobiography and the impact of emerging African literature. **Chinua Achebe** Focuses on the craft and works of Chinua Achebe, questioning whether he deliberately avoids passing moral judgment. Discusses the influences which have shaped his artistic life and recounts experiences from visits to the United States. Examines the traditional novel and a possible new African novel form. **William Abraham** Presents an interview with Ghanan William Abraham, philosopher and author of the "Mind of Africa." Focuses on the function of the writer in Africa. **David Rubadiri** Presents an interview with poet and educator David Rubardiri of Nyasaland and Kenyan poet Joseph Kariuki. Discusses Rubadiri's personal struggle as a creative writer in an emerging nation, the general state of contemporary African literature, the native tradition involved in writing and the teaching of literature in the schools.

Africans All. Producer/Distributor: IFF, 1963. Grade Level: Elementary. Running Time: 22 min. Rental: $8.20. Purchase: $250. Color.

Julien Bryan's introduction to all Africa begins with Philip Stapp's lively animation, which parodies popular misconceptions about the contient and its peoples. Live action footage follows, showing the real Africa in all its diversity and color. Designed for elementary grades, this film has enchanted and informed audiences of all ages. Authentic African music and sounds recorded on location by Sam Bryan. Part of the African Village Life Series.

Africa's Future. Producer/Distributor: IU, 1959. Running Time: 29 min. B&W.

This film shows teenagers from Ceylon, Ethiopia, Ghana, and the Union of South Africa discussing African independence. The film tells of the necessity of foreign aid, where aid comes from, and how aid is best administered. The prospects for African independence and the effects of education in the realization of Africa's future are discussed. From the Young World Series.

Africa's Vanishing Wildlife. Producer/Distributor: BARR, 1967. Running Time: 15 min. Color.

This film depicts Africa's remaining wildlife regions, showing antelope, elephant, giraffe, baboon, crocodile, rhinoceros, hippopotamus and water birds. The presentation shows how the growing native population and their increasing herds are taking over the natural habitats of this wildlife.

Afro-American Music, Its Heritage. Producer/Distributor: CGW, 1969. Grade Level: Elementary through Sr. H.S. Running Time: 16 min. Purchase: $185.

The film begins with the primitive drums of West Africa leading into a similar rhythmic beat of a contemporary jazz quartet. From a Yoruba tribe work chant and the Talking Drum to the plantation life in America, we explore the evolution of the spiritual, the blues, ragtime, and dixieland jazz. Then up the Mississippi River to other parts of the country and on to New York for the Big Band or Swing Era of the thirties and forties. The African influence on South American music is also depicted by the Afro-Cuban beat. We conclude with rhythm and blues, or soul music.

The Ancient Africans. Producer/Distributor: IFF. Running Time: 27 min. Purchase: $325. Color.

In this survey of early African civilizations, imaginative maps by Philip Stapp set the scene for live photography of the ancient kingdoms of Kush, Axum, Ghana, Mali, Songhay, and the dramatic stone ruins of Zimbabwe. The exciting art of Benin and Ashanti allow the viewer to compare ancient Africa with life today. Archaeologists at work help raise questions about who the ancient Africans were and how they lived. Consultant, Richard Ford, Professor of African History, Clark University. Directed and photographed by Sam Bryan. Part of the African Village Life Series.

Ancient Phoenicia and Her Contributions. Producer/Distributor: ATLAP, 1968. Grade Level: Elementary through Sr. H.S. Running Time: 13½ min. Purchase: $150. Color.

Some of the first and most important contributions to the Western World occurred in the ancient Middle East. The significance of Phoenicia comes alive in this film. The Phoenicians were among the first people to use the open seas as a highway for trade and commerce. They colonized the Mediterranean shores, discovered the Atlantic and were the first to sail around Africa, over 3,000 years ago.

Animals of Africa. Producer/Distributor: MGH, 1968. Grade Level: Sr. H.S.
    through College. Running Time: 14 min. Code No. 634052. Rental: $15.
    Purchase: $210. Color.
    This film seeks to show some of Africa's fast-vanishing wildlife in its natural habitat. Also, it shows how conservationists are now at work in order to preserve the remaining animals from extinction. Part of the Documentary on Africa Series.

Annual Festival of the Dead: Dogon People. Producer/Distributor: IFF, 1967.
    Grade Level: Elementary through College. Running Time: 14 min. Pur-
    chase: $165. Color.
    The Dogon tribe devotes its most important annual festival to a commemoration of those who died in the past year. The villagers put on sham attacks and perform war games in the village square. With dance movements, the warriors enact the accomplishments, or what might have been accomplishments, of their departed comrades. Woman bring offerings for the relatives of the departed. The men, massed together, parade to the houses of those who departed within the past year. The festival concludes with the men drinking millet beer and the women dancing. Part of the African Village Life Series.

Arts and Crafts in West Africa. Producer/Distributor: BFA. Grade Level: Ele-
    mentary through Sr. H.S. Running Time: 10½ min. Rental: $6.50. Pur-
    chase: $135. Color.
    The arts and crafts of West Africa have an ancient heritage. They reflect not only the artistic sense of the people, but also the practical way in which they meet everyday needs with materials supplied by their environment. West African artists and craftsmen of today create goods from leather, cloth, metal, clay, gourds, and rattan. They observe many of the ancient traditions. Even the most simple and utilitarian object may be decorated by the craftsmen through the use of color, design, or texture.

A Backward Civilization: The Berbers of South Africa. Producer/Distributor:
    EBEC, 1937. Grade Level: Intermediate through Sr. H.S. Running Time:
    22 min. Rental: $3. Purchase: $135. B&W.
    This film presents a survey of life among the Berbers of North Africa. Their crude handicrafts, their primitive agricultural methods and their customs and superstitions, form a background for contrast with contemporary life in a modern age.

Bakuba—People of the Congo. Producer/Distributor: BRAN, 1957. Grade
    Level: Sr. H.S. through Adult. Running Time: 19 min. Rental: $7.50.
    Purchase: $90. B&W.
    This film shows crafts and decorations—woven mats, velvets, embroideries, ceremonial costumes, ritual tools and drums, statuary and carvings of the

heads of ancient kings, symbols in tattooing. Also shown are a session of the royal court, and dancing following a period of mourning.

The Bewildering Africa. Producer/Distributor: HURTE, 1961. Running Time: 30 min. Color.
This film shows the Tema Harbor and Volta River projects. Includes views of modern churches, hospitals, school buildings, homes, dancing at the Kumasi Festival and Africans engaged in actual building operations and industry. Shows the towns of Lagos, Ibadan, Kano and Accra.

Black Genesis. Producer/Distributor: PFP, 1970. Grade Level: Kindergarten through College. Running Time: 5 min. Rental: $10. Purchase: $100. Color.
This film depicts the art and sculpture of tribal Africa.

Black and White in South Africa. Producer/Distributor: MGH, 1957. Grade Level: Sr. H.S. through Adult. Running Time: 27 min. Rental: $5.50. B&W.
This film depicts interracial problems as they affect one of the largest members of the Commonwealth—a country of 14 million people where only one out of every 5 is white. The film presents a dispassionate appraisal of the motivations behind the policy of apartheid and the practice of segregation.

Bozo Daily Life: Mali. Producer/Distributor: IFF, 1967. Grade Level: Elementary through College. Running Time: 16 min. Purchase: $175. Color.
Between Mopti and Timbuktu the members of the Bozo tribe meet the demands of their environment through a classic division of labor determined in large part by the annual fluctuations of the Niger River. These black Africans are shown as they fish, weave, cook, and mill rice—the activities which form the backbone of their daily lives. This film presents a colorful overview of the Bozo culture and prepares the viewer for the shorter single concept films which complete the series. Part of the African Village Life Series.

Building a Boat: Bozo People. Producer/Distributor: IFF, 1967. Grade Level: Elementary through College. Running Time: 8 min. Purchase: $90. Color.
The vital craft of boat-building, fundamental to the existence of all river peoples, is the work of a group of specially skilled Bozo men. The hard timber, brought from the coastal rain forests many miles away, is skillfully converted into the long, narrow boats in which the Bozos fish, trade, and even move their families, as the seasons change. Careful camera work details how glue, nails, strips of cloth and even mud are used to make the boat watertight. Part of the African Village Life Series.

Building a House: Bozo People. Producer/Distributor: IFF, 1967. Grade Level: Elementary through College. Running Time: 7 min. Purchase: $90. Color.
The construction of a sturdy storage house suggests many aspects of the Bozo culture—the division of labor between men and boys; the artistry of the simple construction, using materials yielded by the river; the joy and harmony of working to fulfill a common need. Reeds are soaked and twisted into rope; poles form the framework; woven reed matting forms the floor and walls; thatch forms the roof. Part of the African Village Life Series.

Buma. Producer/Distributor: EBEC, 1954. Grade Level: Jr. H.S. through Adult. Running Time: 9 min. Rental: $4. Purchase: $135. Color.

This film shows Central and West African sculpture, wood statues and masks by means of which native Africans seek protection from the dangers of everyday living, and freedom from fear of the unknown. Striking lighting effects are used, with native music recorded in Africa.

Buma—African Sculpture Speaks. Producer/Distributor: EBEC, 1952. Grade Level: Jr. H.S. through College. Running Time: 9 min. Purchase: $135. Color.

Native music and pictures of carved masks and statues are used to portray the life of the natives of West and Central Africa and to reflect their fundamental fears and emotions.

Bushmen of the Kalahari. Producer/Distributor: MGH, 1968. Grade Level: Sr. H.S. through College. Running Time: 12 min. Code No. 634053. Rental: $12.50. Purchase: $175. Color.

The Bushmen of the Kalahari desert in central and southern Botswana are the subject of the film. The narrator, Dr. George Silberbauer, an anthropologist, discusses their way of life—how they get their food, educate their children, limit the size of their families, and cooperate with each other. Part of the Documentary on Africa Series.

The Calypso Singer. Producer/Distributor: MGH/CON. Running Time: 4 min. Rental: $10. Purchase: $100. Color.

This film depicts the trials and tribulations of a winsome little calypso singer and his hip bongo-playing accompanist. Animated figures are set to Stan Freberg's sound track (his parody of Harry Belafonte's "Day-O"). Winner of Golden Eagle Award.

Central Africa. Producer/Distributor: MGH, 1968. Grade Level: Jr. H.S. through College. Running Time: 20 min. Code No. 634060. Rental: $15. Purchase: $285. Color.

This film tells the story of modern Central Africa: Portuguese Angola and Mozambique; Northern and Southern Rhodesia; and the former Belgian Congo. Of all these essentially black African countries, only Northern Rhodesia and the Congo are controlled by black governments. It is with the others, where white minorities rule, that the film begins. Part of the Documentary on Africa Series.

Central African Republic. Producer/Distributor: UEVA, 1970. Grade Level: Intermediate through Sr. H.S. Running Time: 15½ min. Rental: $7. Purchase: $104. B&W.

Though rich in natural and human resources, the Central African Republic lacks technology. This film examines the role of capital investment and technology in a nation's attempt to reach her fullest potential. Particular emphasis is placed on the interdependence of nations—especially that of a former colony upon its mother country. Also featured are close-ups of people at work and some of the conflicts between an ancient tribal culture and the new technology.

Coffee Planters Near Kilimanjaro. Producer/Distributor: FI, 1969. Grade Level: Intermediate through College. Running Time: 14 min. Code No. 106-0020. Rental: $12. Purchase: $170. Color.

Naftali is a farmer and a member of the Tachago tribe. He and his two wives live near Kilimanjaro in Tanzania. Naftali raises coffee plants and the ripe coffee beans are sold through a cooperative. His son, Robert, goes to a modern school which owes its existence to the Native Cooperative Union. When the coffee beans ripen, they are picked by hand. The harvest is weighed and each picker is paid through the cooperative. We see how the beans are washed and dried in the sun on long belts, roasted, ground and brewed. Blacks and whites sit together on the coffee "Board." They evaluate the coffee by taking tiny gulps without swallowing the liquid. The two races have learned to work together harmoniously to ensure that the vastly improved living conditions and educational opportunities evident in the film continue to benefit the nation and the common good. Produced by the Institut fur Film und Bild. Part of Man and His World Series.

Come Back, Africa. Producer/Distributor: ROGOSN. Running Time: 83 min. Rental: $150.

This piece of cinema journalism presents a matter-of-fact, horrifying study of life in the black depths of South African society. Filmed in secret by moviemaker Lionel Rogosin, who worked in constant danger of arrest and deportation, this presentation is necessarily crude in craftsmanship. But Rogosin's camera looks deep into the private nightmare and social desperation of a man and a people.

Command 52. Producer/Distributor: ADF. Grade Level: Sr. H.S. through Adult. Running Time: 60 min. Rental: $50. B&W.

White mercenaries fight for colonial powers against the National Liberation Movements in Guinea, Mozambique, Angola and the Congo. This sequel to *The Laughing Man* includes portraits of 7 mercenaries, each of whom talks about his background and why he came to the Congo. In every case they came from the Nazi army or white South Africa. The camera follows them in village skirmishes, in which they indiscriminately kill scores of innocent villagers. Members of the Liberation Army discuss how they feel about the mercenaries and what they do to counter them. Civic and social probrams of the Liberation Army are shown.

Contemporary Africa. Producer/Distributor: CMSLS.

95555 In Search of Myself. $102. **95556** Education: Africa's Road to the Future. $96. **95557** Congo Doctor. $96. **95558** The New and the Old. $102. **95559** The Sun Serves Niger. $210. **95560** The Talking Drums. $180. **95561** Spreading the Word. $91. **95562** Congo: The Way Ahead. $86. **95563** Mali: The Desert and the River. $85. **95564** Visit to a Small Village. $144. **95565** Ethiopia. $98.

The Continent of Africa. Producer/Distributor: MGH, 1966. Grade Level: Intermediate through Sr. H.S. Running Time: 15 min. Rental: $15. Purchase: $205. Color.

Africa is a land of many contrasts and cultures, a continent in ferment. In big cities, doctors perform a difficult operation in a modern hospital; yet in a nearby village, witch doctors try to cure by magic. New highways circle many large African cities; but not far away, donkeys are the only means of transportation. This film provides full coverage of the four major regions of Africa—the dry North, the forests of the West, the industrial South, and the highlands of the East. Part of the Africa series.

Cotton Growing and Spinning: Dogon People. Producer/Distributor: IFF, 1967. Grade Level: Elementary through College. Running Time: 6 min. Purchase: $90. Color.

In small fields bounded by protective thorn fences, the Dogon tribe grows its cotton. A tribesman harvests the cotton and brings it back to his village hut, and a weathered Dogon woman prepares the cotton fibre before spinning the thread. Part of the African Village Life Series.

Country of Islam. Producer/Distributor: CF, 1957. Grade Level: Jr. H.S. through Adult. Running Time: 16 min. Rental: $3.70. Purchase: Color, $180; B&W, $90.

This film presents a picture of Morocco as seen through the eyes of Mustafa, a boy who leaves his village home and journeys to a city to seek an education. There is a farewell to the scenes of Mustafa's childhood, the adventure of acquaintances on the road, the uncertainty of a boy coming to a strange city, and finally his acceptance into a new life, into new homes, new friends, new school. This story is the vehicle for a consideration of the country's economy, culture and the religion of Islam.

Crisis at Suez. Producer/Distributor: MGH, 1962. Grade Level: Elementary through Adult. Running Time: 27 min. Rental: $5.50. B&W.

This film presents a short history of the Suez canal up to 1956. Discussed are the events leading to the attack on Egypt by England, France, and Israel, the reaction in England to the use of military force against Egypt, the truce, and U.N. soldiers enforcing the truce.

Crossroads Africa—Pilot for a Peace Corps. Producer/Distributor: MGH, 1961. Grade Level: College, Adult. Running Time: 54 min. Rental: $10.50. B&W.

This film is a report of an experiment in shoulder-to-shoulder diplomacy made by 14 American college students in the Republic of Guinea during the summer of 1960. The aim and methods used in this project are similar to those proposed by President Kennedy for the Peace Corps.

Daybreak in Udi. Producer/Distributor: BIS, 1949. Grade Level: Sr. H.S. through Adult. Running Time: 45 min. Rental: $8.70. B&W.

This film explores the political awakening of a Nigerian village during the building of a maternity house. It shows the opposition to local tradition and the encouragement of the British Colonial officer, concluding with a celebration of the completion of the home and the beginning of other locally-initiated projects.

Decolonization in Africa. Producer/Distributor: MGH, 1969. Running Time: 18 min. Code No. 408177. Rental: $10. Purchase: $130. B&W.

This report covers the meetings and discussions held with various leaders and groups interested in decolonization in the cities of Kinshasa, Kitwe, and Dar es Salaam by the Special Committee of Twenty-four established by the United Nations to discuss the ending of colonization in Africa.

Desert Nomads (French Morocco). Producer/Distributor: UEVA, 1949. Grade Level: Elementary through Adult. Running Time: 20 min. Rental: $4.50. B&W.

This film depicts the life of people who wander in search of pasture but return to oases to exchange their products for agricultural crops. Nomads are shown in hot, dry lands, moving about for food and water, raising goats and camels and making animal-hair products to sell.

Diamond Mining in East Africa. Producer/Distributor: FI, 1970. Grade Level: Intermediate through College. Running Time: 9 min. Code No. 106-0036. Rental: $10. Purchase: $120. Color.

Just south of Lake Victoria is "diamond country." The mine site looks like a well-protected industrial plant. Barbed wire, police and trained dogs guard the company from its worst enemy, the diamond smuggler. Huge trucks deliver the stones to a breaker plant where the stones are mechanically split. Inside the plant, there is constant surveillance of every process. Armed policemen watch the worker to forestall any attempt at stealing the precious stones. Outside the plant is a modern housing project where the diamond workers live. Produced by the Institut fur Film und Bild. Part of Man and His World Series.

Discovering the Music of Africa. Producer/Distributor: BFA, 1967. Grade Level: Elementary through College. Running Time: 22 min. Rental: $15. Purchase: $250. Color.

African music has developed over many centuries and, in its own way, is as complex as the music we hear in concert halls. Mr. Robert Ayitee, a master drummer of Ghana, and several associates demonstrate the complex rhythmical music of the bells, the rattles, and the drums. They describe how they are used today in Africa both as musical instruments and, in the case of the drums, as a means of communication.

East Africa. Producer/Distributor: EBEC, 1962. Grade Level: Intermediate through College. Running Time: 21 min. Rental: $4.50. Purchase: $135. B&W.

This film depicts the variety and natural beauty of the region's physical features; shows the influences of topography on settlement and economic development; examines the contrasting ways of life of the different peoples—Africans, Asians, Europeans, and Arabs—and discusses their respective activities, problems, and achievements in a period of transition.

East Africa: Tropical Highlands. Producer/Distributor: MGH, 1966. Grade Level: Intermediate through Sr. H.S. Running Time: 15 min. Code No. 402262. Rental: $15. Purchase: $205. Color.

This film discusses the rapidly developing states of Kenya, Tanzania, Uganda, Rwanda and Burundi, and points out the stark contrasts of the area they occupy. Part of the Africa series.

The Economy of Africa. Producer/Distributor: MGH, 1966. Grade Level: Intermediate through Sr. H.S. Running Time: 13 min. Rental: $15. Purchase: $185. Color.

This film traces the expanding African economy from its status in the colonial days through its development in the newly independent countries. The presentation points out the enormous problems facing these new nations as they struggle for economic well-being. Part of the Africa series.

An Egyptian Village. Producer/Distributor: FA, 1960. Grade Level: Upper Elementary through Sr. H.S. Running Time: 18½ min. Rental: $12.50. Purchase: Color, $200; B&W, $110.

Two-thirds of the population of Egypt today still live in small farming villages along the Nile. This film shows the everyday life of a farmer and his family as they work the fields, prepare and eat their meals, meet with other villagers, and arrange for a wedding. Strong religious traditions and lack of contact with the outside world have enabled the farmers of Egypt to continue their centuries-old way of life.

Ethiopia. Producer/Distributor: EBEC, 1956. Running Time: 24 min. B&W.

This review of the political events of the last 50 years includes the activities of Mussolini, the war with Italy and the role of Haile Selassie.

Ethiopia—Africa's Ancient Kingdom. Producer/Distributor: BFA, 1961. Running Time: 17 min. Rental: $10. Purchase: $170. Color.

This general overview of the principal characteristics of the country and the people makes brief reference to the history, influence and present status of the Italian occupation. The film includes scenes of tribal chiefs, farmers, religious leaders and Emperor Haile Selassie.

Ethiopia—Empire on the Mountain. Producer/Distributor: SF, 1966. Grade Level: Elementary through Jr. H.S. Running Time: 20 min. Purchase: $225. Color.

This film shows Ethiopia as a country of paradox: though it was the first African state to achieve independence, its modern growth is hindered by ancient customs, transportation problems and poor education.

Family of Ghana. Producer/Distributor: MGH, 1958. Grade Level: Elementary through Sr. H.S. Running Time: 27 min. Rental: $14. Purchase: $210. B&W.

This film provides a picture of the people and the way of life in a fishing village on the coast of Ghana. Produced by the National Film Board of Canada.

First World Festival of Negro Arts, Dakar, 1966. Producer/Distributor: MGH, 1966. Grade Level: Jr. H.S. through Adult. Running Time: 20 min. Rental: $8.50. Purchase: $180. Color.

This film shows impressions of the First World Festival of Negro Arts, held at Dakar in 1966, depicting music, dance, sculpture, painting, and the reciprocal influence of Negro art and culture in relation to the modern Western world. A co-production between UNESCO, the Alesandru Shaia Studio (Bucharest) and the Romanian National Commission for Unesco.

Fishing on the Niger River: Bozo People. Producer/Distributor: IFF, 1967. Grade Level: Elementary through College. Running Time: 18 min. Purchase: $195. Color.

For the Bozo tribe, fishing is particularly important, since the fish which thrive in the river Niger provide the only abundance in an otherwise parched and hostile environment. In beautiful detail, this film studies each of the Bozo's ingenious methods of catching fish—some requiring the finesse and skill of a single person; some requiring the combined efforts of small groups; and others, the unity and cooperation of the entire village community working a variety of nets. The fish are smoked for preservation and taken down river to market at Mopti in Mali. Part of the African Village Life Series.

Gentle Winds of Change. Producer/Distributor: CMC, 1961. Grade Level: College, Adult. Running Time: 33 min. Rental: $11.20. Purchase: $396. Color.

This examination of the pace and effects of westernization taking place throughout Africa today documents conditions of life among the Banyankole, a tribe living in Uganda, and focuses on the dialectic of accepted traditions and modern influences. Whereas to an outsider the "winds of change" appear to be of gale force, this film suggests a less dramatic characterization of the changes occurring in Africa—one which emphasizes the gradual readjustment by individual Banyankole to the demands of an increasingly complex society.

Ghana. Producer/Distributor: MGH, 1968. Grade Level: Jr. H.S. through College. Running Time: 14 min. Code No. 634057. Rental: $15. Purchase: $210. Color.

This film examines the problems which Kwame Nkrumah's one-man rule created and the measures taken by the Ghanaian military to alter the situation. Part of the Documentary on Africa Series.

A Giant People: The Watusi. Producer/Distributor: EBEC, 1939. Grade Level: Jr. H.S. through Adult. Running Time: 11 min. Rental: $2.50. B&W.

This film depicts the activities, customs, and traditions of people characterized by advanced culture. Scenes include the ruling prince and royal family; activities in the royal household including weaving, decorating, cooking, and churning. The prince is shown inspecting his cattle and leading a hunt; his young son is shown presiding over a ceremonial dance.

Growing up in Tunis. Producer/Distributor: UEVA, 1970. Grade Level: Intermediate through Sr. H.S. Running Time: 14 min. Color.

This film chronicles the joys and difficulties of growing into one's teens in a country on the coast of Africa that still retains its European cultural heritage.

The Hausas of Niger Smelt Iron. Producer/Distributor: LMEM. Running Time: 18 min. Rental: $20. Purchase: $240. Color.

This film shows iron-making as a craft, a tradition, and a ritual.

Health and Education: Keys to African Development. Producer/Distributor: MGH, 1968. Grade Level: Jr. H.S. through College. Running Time: 14 min. Code No. 634056. Rental: $15. Purchase: $210. Color.

This film deals with two aspects of modernization in present-day Africa: the improvement of the general health and the raising of the standards of education. The battles against disease and illiteracy are at present the most important to Africa's future. Part of the Documentary on Africa Series.

The Heart of Apartheid. Producer/Distributor: ROBECK, 1969. Grade Level: Jr. H.S. through College. Running Time: 39 min. Rental: $30. Purchase: $300. B&W.

In this film, the case of the non-white people is dramatically presented.

Herding Cattle: Peul People. Producer/Distributor: IFF, 1967. Grade Level: Elementary through College. Running Time: 7 min. Purchase: $90. Color.

These black nomads of the Peul (or Fulani) tribe wander with their cattle from one grazing ground to another. The viewer joins the Peul as they drive their cattle across the Niger—he hears the grunts and snorts of the struggling swimming beasts, the shouts of the willowy, graceful drovers, and the lapping of the water about the boats of the hired rivermen, who carry young calves and pick up stragglers. Part of the African Village Life Series.

A Hidden Africa . . . The Kapsikie. Producer/Distributor: AEF, 1969. Grade Level: Jr. H.S. through Adult. Running Time: 26 min. Rental: $25. Purchase: $260. Color.

Cut off from the North by the Sahara, surrounded by the Equatorial landscape, the Kapsikie live their lives out with ritualistic simplicity. Their future, the weather, marriage, life and death are told by an elder schooled in reading the movements of a crab in a pot.

The Hunters. Producer/Distributor: MGH. Running Time: 73 min. Rental: $12. Purchase: $500. Color.

This study of the life and culture of primitive African Bushmen is portrayed through the experiences of four aborigines and the giraffe which they hunt on the Kalahari Desert.

Hunting Wild Doves: Dogon People. Producer/Distributor: IFF, 1967. Grade Level: Elementary through College. Running Time: 8 min. Purchase: $90. Color.

A film for the study of the daring, skill, and bravery of the young men of the Dogon tribe. The agile young men of this black African culture scale the steep, sheer cliffs in search of the doves which nest in the craggy pockets. Their lives are dramatically suspended high above their onlooking elders by the strength of the rope handwoven from the bark of the Baobab tree by a fellow tribesman. Part of the African Village Life Series.

In Search of Myself. Producer/Distributor: MGH, 1966. Running Time: 30 min. Code No. 406725. Rental: $8. Purchase: $130. B&W.

Various facets of life in an emerging African nation are discussed by writers and artists; cultural heritage, writing, fine arts, crafts, and the language problem are dealt with.

The Islamic Republic of Mauritania. Producer/Distributor: UEVA, 1967. Grade Level: Intermediate through Sr. H.S. Running Time: 20 min. Rental: $7. Purchase: $137. B&W.

This film view of one of the least known countries of Africa shows Mauritania to be too dry and stony for much agriculture. While its proximity to the Atlantic Ocean brings much wealth from the sea, its future development depends in large part on the exploitation of large deposits of iron ore, copper and rock salt.

Journey to Magic Valley. Producer/Distributor: ROBECK. Grade Level: Jr. H.S. through College. Running Time: 25 min. Rental: $25. Purchase: $300.

This film depicts the Bushmen of Kalahari as a persevering people whose lives are one long struggle for survival against the evil spirits that can invade their souls. Next to the primitive Bushmen, the Matakam seem to have an almost luxurious existence, but they, too, are controlled by magic forces. Their "magicians" are of a royal class set apart from the other tribesmen, and their autonomy is almost complete.

Kenya: The Multi-Racial Experiment. Producer/Distributor: MGH, 1968. Grade Level: Jr. H.S. through College. Running Time: 19 min. Code No. 634059. Rental: $15. Purchase: $245. Color.

Part of the Documentary on Africa Series.

The Laughing Man. Producer/Distributor: ADF. Grade Level: College, Adult. Running Time: 60 min. Rental: $50. B&W.

This portrait of "Congo" Mueller, ex-Nazi officer and leader of a mercenary force of soldiers fighting for the U.N. forces in the Congo, presents him as a suave, debonair man, with a winning smile and manicured hands, talking glibly about massacres and atrocities committed by mercenaries. The mercenaries, it is pointed out, come from the armies of the Nazis or South Africa. The horror they perpetrate, led by the cosmopolitan Mueller, is made clear in camera shots of their actions.

Life in Hot, Wet Lands—The Congo Basin. Producer/Distributor: CORF, 1949. Grade Level: Intermediate. Running Time: 11 min. Rental: $2. Purchase: Color, $135; B&W, $65.

This film of native life in the Congo Basin was planned for social studies units to accompany a textbook. It shows how life is influenced by climate. Attention is focused on a village in the Congo Basin on the shores of the Ubangi River.

Life in the Sahara. Producer/Distributor: EBEC, 1932. Grade Level: Elementary through Sr. H.S. Running Time: 15 min. Rental: $6. Purchase: $167.50. Color.

This film reviews important aspects of the life, habits and customs of people living in the great Sahara Desert region of Africa. It portrays typical vegetation and topography of the desert, directing attention to water and transportation problems and emphasizing the contribution made by the camel to desert life.

Lobola. Producer/Distributor: MGH, 1966. Running Time: 26 min. Code No. 406889. Rental: $12.50. Purchase: $170. B&W.

This film shows the social problems of millions of South African natives and offers glimpses of the daily life in a primitive tribal village.

Magicians of the Black Hills. Producer/Distributor: ROBECK, 1965. Grade Level: Jr. H.S. through College. Running Time: 25 min. Rental: $25. Purchase: $300. Color.

This film presents the Matakam, who live in the valleys of the Mandara

Mountains in Cameroon. Only a privileged few know the secret of smelting iron, which to the Matakam is magic. To protect their power over the rest of the tribe, these blacksmiths hand the ancient rites down to their sons—sons who must marry the daughters of other blacksmiths.

Magic Rites: Divination by Animal Tracks: Dogon People. Producer/Distributor: IFF, 1967. Grade Level: Elementary through College. Running Time: 7 min. Purchase: $90. Color.

For the purpose of giving an initial understanding of Dogon religious practice, this film shows a common method of divining. A shaman, the Dogon soothsayer, an elder of the village, enters the sacred ground. Responding to questions posed earlier by members of his village, he uses a symbolic language to draw a representation of the village in the sand. He then drops peanuts at strategic places to lure the night jackals into the field. The following morning the shaman returns to prophesy the future from the tracks left by the jackal in the sand. Part of the African Village Life Series.

Magic Rites: Divination by Chicken Sacrifice: Dogon People. Producer/Distributor: IFF, 1967. Grade Level: Elementary through College. Running Time: 7 min. Purchase: $90. Color.

This film studies the role of religion in the life of an African tribe. The Dogon religion requires a steady practice of living animal sacrifice to insure a good relationship with the divine forces. This film details the most common sacrifice—the ritual execution and devouring of the chicken. Part of the African Village Life Series.

Masai in Tanzania. Producer/Distributor: FI, 1970. Grade Level: Intermediate through College. Running Time: 14 min. Code No. 106-0019. Rental: $12. Purchase: $160. Color.

This film presents a look at the famed African warrior tribe, the Masai. The tribesmen wear robes but some of the younger men wear European coats. The women are decorated with native jewelry—colored beads, metal bracelets. Cattle are prized possessions of the Masai. The young shepherds take the stance peculiar to the Masai—that of standing on one leg with the other foot pressed against the knee. Close-up shots show them drinking fresh blood from the cattle—their chief nourishment. The Masai now trade peacefully with neighboring tribes, but before the prohibition of carrying of weapons in the market place, the Masai provoked bloody battles at trading sites. Produced by the Institut fur Film und Bild. Part of Man and His World Series.

Masked Dances (Dogon). Producer/Distributor: IFF, 1967. Grade Level: Elementary through College. Running Time: 7 min. Purchase: $90. Color.
Part of the African Village Life Series.

Medicine Men of Africa. Producer/Distributor: NET/IU, 1967. Grade Level: Sr. H.S. through Adult. Running Time: 30 min. B&W.
Part I Introduces Dr. Stephen Block, an English psychiatrist, investigating the efficaciousness of the Nigerian medicine-men through interviews with medicine-men, their patients and Nigerian physicians. Shows diagnostic methods and treatments of the medicine-men. Discusses and illustrates their commercialism. From the Spectrum Series.

Part II Dr. Stephen Block, an English psychiatrist, investigates the effectiveness of the practices of Nigerian medicine men and finds that their mass psychotherapy is occasionally helpful. Dr. Block interviews Nigerians, describes religious rituals, pagan and Christian, and demonstrates the trance produced in some participants, which is shown to be hypnotic. From the Spectrum Series.

Mediterranean Africa. Producer/Distributor: EBEC, 1952. Grade Level: Sr. H.S. through Adult. Running Time: 12 min. Rental: $5. Color.

This geographical and historical survey shows the many-cultured aspects of this ancient invasion route and describes its continuing role as Europe's breadbasket and as a crossroads of culture.

Modern Africa: Sport and Entertainment. Producer/Distributor: MGH, 1968. Code No. 634058. Running Time: 14 min. Rental: $15. Purchase: $210. Color.

Part of the Documentary on Africa Series.

Modern East African Wood Carver. Producer/Distributor: MH, 1969. Running Time: 8 min. Code No. 699146. Rental: $10. Purchase: $105. Color.

This film focuses on the economic development involved in turning a handicraft—Makonde wood carving—into a viable business to benefit the nation of Tanzania. The film touches on a few of the misunderstandings that for centuries have perpetuated Western myths about Africa.

Modern Egypt. Producer/Distributor: MGH, 1966. Grade Level: Intermediate & Jr. H.S. Running Time: 18 min. Code No. 622130. Rental: $12.50. Purchase: Color, $240; B&W, $120.

Egypt, known today as the United Arab Republic, occupies the northeastern corner of the African continent. This film, which focuses on the climate of the country, dramatically shows how Egypt, in a few short years, has taken its place in the modern world.

Morocco—Chaoui Faces His Future. Producer/Distributor: UEVA, 1969. Grade Level: Intermediate through Sr. H.S. Running Time: 20 min. Rental: $9. Purchase: $264. Color.

This film shows how Morocco is changing and today's youth cannot afford to stand still. They must act now or else be prepared to watch the world pass by. Education is the doorway to the future; Morocco has been given the key.

Music of Africa. Producer/Distributor: IU, 1964. Running Time: 30 min. Rental: $7.25. Purchase: $150. B&W.

Fela Sowande of Nigeria—a leading African musicologist, composer, and organist—with a group of Nigerian musicians, shows how contemporary African music has mingled traditional African and Western idioms to create new forms.

Mussolini vs. Selassie. Producer/Distributor: FI, 1964. Grade Level: Sr. H.S. through Adult. Running Time: 25 min. Code No. 96-0018. Rental: $12. Purchase: $135. B&W.

Doggedly resisting France's collusion with Italy over East Africa, Ethiopian emperor Haile Selassie leads his untrained tribesmen, armed with primitive weapons, in a futile attempt to stop Benito Mussolini's modern armies and Italian mass air raids on Adowa and Addis Ababa in 1936. Produced by Metromedia Producers Corporation.

Negro Kingdoms of Africa's Golden Age. Producer/Distributor: ATLAP, 1968. Grade Level: Elementary through Sr. H.S. Running Time: 17 min. Purchase: $150. Color.

This film develops the main contributions of Phoenicia, constantly pointing out its relevance to the modern world. The Phoenicians were among the first people to use the open seas as a highway for trade and commerce. They colonized the Mediterranean shores, discovered the Atlantic and were the first to sail around Africa, over three thousand years ago.

The New Africa: Peoples and Leaders. Producer/Distributor: MGH, 1968. Grade Level: Jr. H.S. through College. Running Time: 15 min. Code No. 634051. Rental: $15. Purchase: $215. Color.

The film introduces the problem of nation-building in African states and explores how some African leaders handle this problem: specifically, how much these leaders are willing to accept outside help, and from whom, how much influence they allow these helpers in their policies, and how these leaders emphasize helping themselves. Part of the Documentary on Africa Series.

The New North Africa. Producer/Distributor: DOUBLE. Grade Level: Elementary through Sr. H.S. Running Time: 16 min. Purchase: $9.

This film explores the geography, history, government and cultural heritage of the Republic of Tunisia, presenting a picture of Africa's emerging nations.

Niger: Iron Making, The Old Way. Producer/Distributor: TEXF, 1969. Grade Level: Jr. H.S. through College. Running Time: 18 min. Rental: $20. Purchase: $240. Color.

This film shows in detail a traditional process involving a simple blast furnace. The work process blends music, design and ritual in an integrated world, and is rapidly disappearing.

Niger: Water on the Savanna. Producer/Distributor: TEXF, 1969. Grade Level: Jr. H.S. through College. Running Time: 20 min. Rental: $20. Purchase: $260. Color.

This film is about the Tuaregs and the Peuhls, herdsmen who live in the Savanna—in one of the greatest cattle-raising areas of black Africa. They are nomads, traditionally on the move and in search of water. The government of Niger has constructed deep, modern wells, equipped with electric pumps. For the first time, enough water is available for the herds and the herdsmen. The film shows how their lives are changing as villages begin to form around the wells.

Nigeria—Giant in Africa. Producer/Distributor: MGH, 1961. Grade Level: College, Adult. Running Time: 52 min. Rental: $25. Purchase: $275. B&W.

This film shows Nigeria's history and culture as a background to the study of changing times. Topics include the new federation of ancient tribes;

geography and topography; varied peoples; religions; British rule; forms of government; transportation; development of natural resources; place in world trade; products; free universal education; political leaders in their campaigns for election to the new independent Nigerian government formed in 1960. Two parts.

Nigeria—New Nation. Producer/Distributor: CON, 1959. Running Time: 28 min. Color.
　　Personalities in various walks of life are interviewed and the strides made in health, education, industry, and the democratic government are shown.

Nigeria: Problems of Nation Building. Producer/Distributor: ATLAP, 1967. Running Time: 22 min. Purchase: $220. Color.
　　This film provides a realistic appraisal of nationalism in Africa, particularly in Nigeria. It is a useful tool for the understanding of the underlying forces in Tropical Africa. Major sequences include: geography and climate of West Africa; development of prosperous medieval African empires; navigation along the Niger River; economy, education and religion. The Nigerian civil war is treated in historical perspective as a conflict between rival tribal loyalties.

The Nile Valley and its People. Producer/Distributor: EBEC, 1962. Grade Level: Intermediate through Sr. H.S. Running Time: 15 min. Purchase: $200. Color.
　　This film shows the route of the river from Lake Victoria to the Mediterranean and methods used for its control. Also shown are important cities on or near the Nile in Uganda, Sudan and Egypt, and their principal industries.

Nomads of the Jungle (Malaya). Producer/Distributor: UEVA, 1948. Grade Level: Elementary through Adult. Running Time: 20 min. Rental: $4.50. Purchase: $132. B&W.
　　This film shows the life of people who do not farm or build permanent dwellings, but live off wild plants and animals of the tropical rain forest.

Northern Africa: Water and Man. Producer/Distributor: MGH, 1966. Grade Level: Intermediate through Sr. H.S. Running Time: 16 min. Rental: $15. Purchase: $210. B&W & Color.
　　Northern Africa lies between the Mediterranean and the Sahara, where little grows and few people live, except where water can be obtained. The struggle to bring water to the dry land is an everlasting problem. In 1902, a major dam was built on the Nile at Aswan. With controlled irrigation, Egyptian farmers can now produce three crops a year, instead of only one. This film shows why this area has been slow to develop. Part of the Africa series.

Oasis in the Sahara. Producer/Distributor: FI, 1970. Grade Level: Intermediate through College. Running Time: 16 min. Code No. 106-0052. Rental: $12. Purchase: $190.
　　The Sahara is a hot country in which it gets very cold; a country in which one can walk for miles without a trace of vegetation, but in which there are also trees in a valley or plateau; a country so arid one must take along water, enough for a week, yet a country in which there are sections with so many lakes one is reminded of Finland. The immense natural forces which play upon the Sahara

add up to a journey dominated by the unpredictable. The route leads through the Tanesfuft (Land Without Fear) a desert within a desert. It is divided by the Tropic of Cancer, separated by rains from the Northern desert during the winter, buffeted by winds partly from the northwest, and partly from the southwest coast of Guinea, and faced with floods during the summer months. Along this route, students see a land of contrast; the "power" of the desert is made clear. Produced by the Institut fur Film und Bild. Part of Man and His World Series.

Oasis of the Sahara. Producer/Distributor: MGH, 1966. Running Time: 8 min. Code No. 658210. Rental: $10. Purchase: Color, $500; B&W, $100.

This film describes the customs of the people who live in the largest desert in the world.

The Old Africa and the New: Ethiopia and Botswana. Producer/Distributor: MGH, 1968. Grade Level: Sr. H.S. through College. Running Time: 17 min. Code No. 634054. Rental: $15. Purchase: $245. Color.

Part of the Documentary on Africa Series.

Omowale—The Child Returns Home. Producer/Distributor: IU. Running Time: 30 min. Rental: $2.40. Purchase: $125.

This film pictures John Williams, Mississippi-born Negro, on an odyssey to Africa to explore his ancestral roots. Williams explores the relationship of the American Negro to Africa and the Africans. The film emphasizes that the Negro in the United States is several generations removed from the African Negro, both culturally and economically. A film in the History of the Negro People Series.

Onion Farming: Dogon People. Producer/Distributor: IFF, 1967. Grade Level: Elementary through College. Running Time: 7 min. Purchase: $90. Color.

This film documents the division of labor, the unity of the tribal group at work, and the order, grace, and dignity of a black African people. Each step is shown as the Dogons process their onion crop. Women harvest the onions, and men pound them and squeeze out the fluid to preserve them in the torrid heat. The compressed balls are then dried and stored for use in flavoring food or for trade with nearby tribes. Part of the African Village Life Series.

People of the Congo: The Mangbetu. Producer/Distributor: EBEC, 1939. Grade Level: Intermediate through Adult. Running Time: 11 min. Rental: $2.50. Purchase: $70. B&W.

This film depicts the activities and traditions of a tribe clinging to such customs as head-binding and facial tatooing but having appreciation for neat, well-built homes and carefully prepared food. Barter, ivory carving, home decorating, construction of musical instruments, and native dances are shown.

The Peoples of Africa. Producer/Distributor: MGH, 1966. Grade Level: Intermediate through Sr. H.S. Running Time: 16 min. Code No. 402266. Rental: $15. Purchase: $215. B&W & Color.

This film shows Africa as a continent of many nations and cultures, and reveals how the people of Africa earn their living. Part of the Africa Series.

Pompo. Producer/Distributor: LMEM. Running Time: 20 min. Rental: $20. Purchase: $260. Color.

This film depicts the life of nomadic tribes in the Niger desert and the profound effect of a modern water system on their lives.

The Problem of Nigerian Unity. Producer/Distributor: MGH, 1968. Grade Level: Sr. H.S. through College. Running Time: 19 min. Code No. 634055. Rental: $15. Purchase: $275. Color.

This film explores the great diversity within Nigeria, showing the geographical differences, which cause variations in the agricultural production, and the many different life styles of the people. Part of the Documentary on Africa Series.

Problems of Emerging Nations. Producer/Distributor: AVED, 1962. Grade Level: Elementary through Adult. Running Time: 11 min. Rental: $8, daily; $16, weekly. Purchase: $125. Color.

This film explores the social and economic problems of the emerging African nations, such as communication, education, national unity, cultural conflict and poverty.

Pygmies of Africa. Producer/Distributor: EBEC, 1938. Grade Level: Intermediate through Adult. Running Time: 20 min. Rental: $5. Purchase: $135. B&W.

This film depicts the life of the pygmies, showing shelter construction, root digging, bow and arrow making, spear practice, techniques of hunting, food preparation, eating habits, basket making, wild honey harvesting, bark fabric preparation and dyeing, and ivory collecting.

Rainy Season in West Africa. Producer/Distributor: FI, 1970. Grade Level: Intermediate through College. Running Time: 14 min. Code No. 106-0054. Rental: $12. Purchase: $170. Color.

For months now, it hasn't rained and the African earth is parched. The villagers anxiously await the rainy season. They still cling to superstitious beliefs. A boy watches the rainmaker as he sacrifices a chicken. As though in answer to his incantations, thunder is heard and the first storm deluges the village. Within a few days the ground has softened and the villagers plant corn and millet. The rains turn the roads into liquid mud and communication between villages and cities ceases. As the season progresses, the crops begin to mature and the formerly parched earth is now a lush green paradise. But the cycle will repeat when the sun and lack of rain will again parch the earth. The elements and centuries-old beliefs have to be conquered before a modern economy can be established in this country. Produced by the Institut fur Film und Bild. Part of Man and His World Series.

Remnants of a Race. Producer/Distributor: EBEC, 1953. Grade Level: Intermediate through Adult. Running Time: 18 min. Rental: $6. Purchase: $167.50. Color.

This film shows the life of the Bushmen in the Kalahari desert in Bechuanaland, describing the unceasing hunt for food, sketches and paintings on ostrich egg, utensils, clicking manner of speech, and religious dances.

The Republic of Chad. Producer/Distributor: UEVA, 1967. Grade Level: Intermediate through Sr. H.S. Running Time: 20 min. Rental: $7. Purchase: $137. B&W.

This landlocked republic in north central Africa is depicted as primitive, but struggling to improve its way of life. Vivid sequences show how the people have just begun to make economic and social changes. The development of water resources, the stabilization of the meat-packing industry and improved health standards are helping move Chad into the world of today.

The Republic of the Ivory Coast. Producer/Distributor: UEVA, 1970. Grade Level: Intermediate through Sr. H.S. Running Time: 20 min. Rental: $7. Purchase: $137. B&W.

This film captures a thriving nation whose well-managed economy is based on a successful combination of ancient traditions and modern innovations. With the help of the government and foreign investments, the people of the Ivory Coast can look forward to an even more prosperous future.

Republic of Niger. Producer/Distributor: UEVA, 1967. Grade Level: Intermediate through Sr. H.S. Running Time: 20 min. Rental: $7. Purchase: $137. B&W.

The constant search for water and a life conditioned almost entirely by its shortage is vividly depicted in this film focused on Niger, on the southern edge of the Sahara desert. The film points out the active interest the government is taking by embarking on large-scale irrigation projects and pesticide programs.

The Republic of Senegal. Producer/Distributor: UEVA, 1970. Grade Level: Intermediate through Sr. H.S. Running Time: 16 min. Rental: $6. Purchase: $99. B&W.

Senegal's attempt to take its place in the modern world is depicted in this film. Gallantly the Senegales strive to develop the resources of this former French colony. Life in modern, urban Dakar is contrasted with a more primitive existence in the hinterlands to dramatize the fact that rich resources, burgeoning industry, and technological advances do not automatically enhance the lives of the people as a whole.

The Republic of South Africa—Its Land and Its People. Producer/Distributor: EBEC, 1956. Grade Level: Intermediate through College. Running Time: 17 min. Purchase: Color, $200; B&W, $102.50.

This revised version of *The Union of South Africa* studies the ways of life of native groups in South Africa—tribesmen on the reserves, workers on the Boer farms, miners and workers in the cities. The film describes the varying environments and cultures.

Riches of the Veld (South Africa). Producer/Distributor: UEVA, 1948. Grade Level: Elementary through Adult. Running Time: 20 min. Rental: $7. Purchase: $132. B&W.

This film depicts English family life in Johannesffiurg, and shows a trip through the mines and diamond houses. The native problem is not treated.

River Journey on the Upper Nile. Producer/Distributor: FI, 1969. Grade Level:
   Intermediate through College. Running Time: 18 min. Code No. 106-0028.
   Rental: $14. Purchase: $210. Color.

This trip to Juba, in the Sudan, unfolds a panorama of flora and fauna
native to this area. The White Nile drains what appears to be a continually
moving swamp and the small riverboats have difficulty in navigating the shifting
channel. Where there is dry open land, there is usually a village inhabited by
primitive farmers. As the boats and their passengers near Juba, the swampland
begins to disappear and elephants and hippos can be seen on the banks of the
river. The south Sudan, where Juba is located, is a poor section, but the government is working at developing the area. Priority is given to education and new
schools, many of which teach technical skills. Produced by the Institut fur Film
und Bild. Part of Man and His World Series.

River Nile. Producer/Distributor: MGH, 1964. Grade Level: Sr. H.S. through
   Adult. Running Time: 54 min. Code No. 606129. Rental: $18.70. Pur-
   chase: Color, $360; B&W, $180.

This exploration of the historic course of the Nile, its strange cultures
and remnants of past civilizations, shows archeological treasures of Egypt,
including the pyramids, the Sphinx, and the temples of Abu Simbel. Featured
also is the Aswan Dam. Narrated by James Mason. In two parts.

River People of Chad. Producer/Distributor: FI, 1969. Grade Level: Intermediate through College. Running Time: 20 min. Code No. 106-0030. Rental:
   $14. Purchase: $240. Color.

In the new African country of Chad, people in small villages still live as
they have for generations. Family and group interrelationships depict culture
traits dating back to earlier centuries. Their existence depends upon everyone—
men, women, and children—working together. The film visits the Kotoko tribe
for a day and night, showing how they farm, fish, cook, make tools and pots, and
live by primitive means, using the resources around them. There are no schools
for the children in this village. Contrasting with this existence is the capital city
of Fort Lamy, a modern city with hotels, department stores and airports. Produced by the Institut fur Film und Bild. Part of Man and His World Series.

She Shall be Called Woman. Producer/Distributor: BRAN, 1954. Grade Level:
   Jr. & Sr. H.S. Running Time: 14 min. Rental: $7.50. Purchase: $75.

This film depicts the woman's place in the old African society through
sculpture. As in other cultures in their early stages, Africa assigned specific roles
and duties to its women. Although many of these roles are dying out now as
Africa becomes more modern, many other female traditions are still maintained
in African society.

South Africa. Producer/Distributor: MGH, 1968. Grade Level: Jr. & Sr. H.S.
   Running Time: 27 min. Code No. 634061. Rental: $18. Purchase: $375.
   Color.

The most industrialized and Europeanized country on the African continent, South Africa is also, due to its special approach to the problem of race, the
most controversial. The purpose of this film is to give reasons why South Africa
has developed as it has, and to show what life is like there today. Part of the
Documentary on Africa Series.

South African Essay, Part I: Fruit of Fear. Producer/Distributor: IU. Running
Time: 60 min. B&W.
This film reports on the South African dual standards of living, from the
lavish white sections to the black ghettos. It includes interviews with such
people as Nobel Peace Prize winner Chief Albert Luthuli, Frank Waring and
author Alan Paton as to their attitudes toward their condition. From the Changing World Series.

South African Essay, Part II: One Nation, Two Nationalisms. Producer/Dis-
tributor: IU. Running Time: 60 min. B&W.
This film examines the political machinery which enforces apartheid, and
presents views of African spokesmen, whites and blacks, who support or oppose
this policy. The presentation focuses on the power of the white nationalist party.
From the Changing World Series.

Southern Africa: Industry and Agriculture. Producer/Distributor: MGH, 1966.
Grade Level: Intermediate through Sr. H.S. Running Time: 15 min. Code
No. 402264. Rental: $15. Purchase: $205. Color.
This film depicts diverse people working together to determine the future
of Southern Africa, and shows why this area is the continent's most highly developed industrial region. Scenes include the diamond mines, steel mills, fishing
industries, and coffee plantations of Southern Africa. Part of the Africa series.

Tanzania: Progress Through Self-Reliance. Producer/Distributor: MGH, 1969.
Running Time: 20 min. Code No. 699145. Rental: $12.50. Purchase: $260.
Color.
This film shows Tanzania's approach to the building of a nation and the
economic problems characteristic of all developing nations. The idea of African
socialism as a response to the challenge of development is discussed in terms of
the pressures under which newly emerging nations labor. The strength of people
working together for benefit of their nation is emphasized throughout the film.

Tanzania, The Quiet Revolution. Producer/Distributor: IU. Running Time: 60
min. Rental: $9. B&W.
This film depicts the geography and peoples of Tanzania, revealing
problems of poverty, illiteracy and racism. President Nyerere explains his policy
of nonalignment. From the Changing World Series.

Three Apprentices. Producer/Distributor: MGH, 1963. Grade Level: Sr. H.S.
through Adult. Running Time: 28 min. Rental: $6. B&W.
Patrick Ughe is an apprentice shipwright in the big seaport city of Lagos,
Nigeria; Ken Box, a journeyman pipefitter in the Canadian National Railway
shops near Winnipeg; Alaiso Barata is a skilled craftsman in a Rio de Janeiro
furniture factory. This film is a comparison of their lives, as they live, work,
play, and prepare for the responsibilities of manhood.

Three Grandmothers. Producer/Distributor: MGH, 1963. Grade Level: Sr. H.S.
through Adult. Running Time: 28 min. Rental: $14. Purchase: $200.
B&W.
This film shows glimpses into the lives of three grandmothers in widely
different parts of the world—in a city in Brazil, a rural community in Mani-

toba, and a village compound in Lagos, Nigeria. These three comparisons go to the very core of life in three countries and show how universal is the role of the grandmother. Despite differences in the pattern of family life, the grandmother has the same function of protecting the young, guiding the newlyweds, and enjoying her freedom to help. Produced by the National Film Board of Canada.

Tribal Dances of West Africa. Producer/Distributor: UMINN. Running Time: 27½ min. Rental: $25. Purchase: $250. Color.
    This film shows dances performed by The Dance Ensemble at the Institute of African Studies, University of Ghana, in authentic costumes and using authentic musical instruments.

Tropical Africa. Producer/Distributor: IFF. Running Time: 30 min. Purchase: $325. Color.
    This film is an introduction to three quarters of the great African continent—an area in political revolution and undergoing great social change. Primitive society is portrayed, but only as it relates to the new life. The great movement is to the cities, to the new factories and mines. The struggle for self-government, the effort to establish schools, universities, and hospitals—all these are shown, as well as the rapidly changing relationship between black and white Africans. Part of the African Village Life Series.

Tropical Forest Village (Congo Basin). Producer/Distributor: UEVA, 1950. Grade Level: Jr. & Sr. H.S. Running Time: 10 min. B&W.
    This film shows native jungle life in the hot, wet Congo Basin, where people live almost entirely out of doors, and men hunt large game while the women and children gather plants and small animals.

Upsurge of Nationalism. Producer/Distributor: MGH, 1964. Grade Level: Sr. H.S. through Adult. Running Time: 26 min. Rental: $5.50. Purchase: $155. B&W.
    This film shows the results of Western influence in North Africa and the Middle East, depicting the growth of technology as revolutionary leaders such as Bourguiba, Nasser, and Kassem reorganize feudal society and restore the pride of the people and the fertility of their soil.

Union of South Africa—Its Land and Its People. Producer/Distributor: EBEC, 1956. Grade Level: Elementary through Sr. H.S. Running Time: 17 min. Rental: $3.70. B&W.
    This film shows the geography, history, agriculture, and peoples of South Africa. It includes a visit to the family of N'Gana in Bantu, and to the farm of Jan Van Niekerk in the Transvaal. It also shows a view of Johannesburg gold and diamond industries.

Wanderers of the Desert. Producer/Distributor: EBEC, 1954. Grade Level: Elementary through Jr. H.S. Running Time: 10 min. Rental: $4. Color.
    This film depicts the nomadic life of the Bedouins and the work of a desert patrol which guards against smuggling, slavery, and other illegal activities. Scenes include a desert caravan putting up tents, preparing food, and dancing and singing at the end of the day.

West Africa: Another Vietnam? Producer/Distributor: ADF, 1968. Grade
Level: College, Adult. Running Time: 40 min. Rental: $50. Purchase:
$225. B&W.

The people of Portuguese Guinea are engaged in guerrilla warfare—
fighting and building for a new life. Portuguese colonialists are bombing the
country daily with napalm in an effort to maintain colonial rule. This film
documents this war on a day to day level. The camera records the actions of one
guerrilla unit and shows within its men the embryo of the world they are
fighting to create. They understand that national liberation can only come as the
culmination of many small victories, including the setting up of hospitals,
schools and providing food in the areas controlled by the guerrillas—now nearly
two-thirds of the country. Providing meaning and insight into the action of the
film are periodic flashbacks to an interview with their political leader, Amilcar
Cabral.

West Africa (Nigeria). Producer/Distributor: EBEC, 1963. Grade Level: Intermediate through College. Running Time: 22 min. Purchase: $265. Color.

This film reveals what Nigerians are doing to create unity out of the
diversity of tribal, religious and economic traditions. The film shows the great
geographical differences in this region. The problems of the new nations of West
Africa are likened to those of Nigeria. From the Africa in Change Series.

West Africa (Tropical Lowlands). Producer/Distributor: MGH, 1966. Grade
Level: Intermediate through Sr. H.S. Running Time: 15 min. Code No.
402263. Rental: $15. Purchase: $205. Color.

This film reveals West Africa as a land of new nations with many problems, and provides an understanding of the great changes that are sweeping this
area. Part of the Africa series.

Where the Brides Do the Choosing. Producer/Distributor: ROBECK, 1965.
Grade Level: Jr. H.S. through College. Running Time: 25 min. Rental:
$25. Purchase: $300. Color.

Deep in the Atlas Mountains of Morocco, thousands of tents are pitched
in the valley sacred to matrimony. Here the brides look over the bachelors,
much as their mothers inspect the chickens in the market place. The rejects are
solaced by an evening of entertainment and hopes that next year, their luck may
be better.

White Africa. Producer/Distributor: ROBECK, 1969. Grade Level: Sr. H.S.
through College. Running Time: 40 min. Rental: $30. Purchase: $300.
B&W.

This film makes an attempt to enter the mind of the white South African
and to allow him to speak for himself. The film questions the white minority
claim that it knows best what is good for its own country. Should they, it asks,
be left alone to work out their problems when it is certain that the decision will
always be to keep the black people separate?

Wind of Change. Producer/Distributor: MCDDC. Running Time: 28 min.
Purchase: $198. Color.

Apace with the emergence of new nations and a new way of life for many
of the people of Africa, is the development of commercial air travel to and

within the formerly "dark" continent. This concerns itself with the similarity between present day Africa and much that is deemed cosmopolitan in other regions of the world.

The Witch Doctor. Producer/Distributor: ROBECK, 1968. Grade Level: Sr. H.S. through College. Running Time: 35 min. Rental: $30. Purchase: $300. B&W.

Are African witch doctors more witch than doctor? Do they use magic or do they use science? The social and cultural environment in which these witch doctors, both men and women, practice their profession is examined in this film. Various case histories of "cures" by witch doctors are shown.

Worcester, Life in a South African Town. Producer/Distributor: FON, 1947. Grade Level: Sr. H.S. through Adult. Running Time: 10 min. Rental: $2.50. B&W.

This film depicts a typical Cape Province town, showing advances made in the fields of education, industry, and social service.

Films (8mm)

Africa. Producer/Distributor: USNAC, 1961. Running Time: 35 min. B&W.

Joseph C. Satterthwaite, Assistant Secretary of State for African Affairs, appraises the history and basic problems facing the new Africa.

Africa. Producer/Distributor: ABC, 1967. Running Time: 60 min. Color.

This film presents a study of the land, the people, the culture, history, and present day political and economic issues of Africa.

Africa: An Introduction. Producer/Distributor: BFA, 1968. Grade Level: Elementary through Jr. H.S. Running Time: 18 min. B&W & Color.

This overview of the geography of Africa and the many different people who make up its population shows the major differences between the desert, grassland and the tropics, and explains how and why the lives of the people of Africa differ from one area to another.

Africa: City Life. Producer/Distributor: ICF, 1965. Grade Level: Elementary through Adult. Running Time: 3 min. Color.

This film presents scenes of African urban life through views of Northern

Rhodesia, Southern Rhodesia, Ghana and Kenya. It pictures white collar workers, a mission school, and living and working conditions in a typical mining compound.

Africa: Cultural Groups. Producer/Distributor: ICF, 1964. Grade Level: Elementary through Adult. Running Time: 4 min. Color.
This film follows the different stages in man's evolution through cultural groups in tropical Africa, presenting four comparatively distinct groups: hunters and food gatherers; nomadic herdsmen; semi-nomadic farmers and settled farmers.

Africa Is My Home: Nigeria. Producer/Distributor: ICF, 1969. Grade Level: Elementary through Sr. H.S. Running Time: 22 min. B&W.
This film uses the story of a West African woman to explore the problems of the emerging nations. It describes the conflict between Islamic and Christian cultures, tradition and progress, independence and colonialism, and discusses the problems of economic reconstruction.

Africa: Tropical Products. Producer/Distributor: ICF, 1964. Grade Level: Elementary through Adult. Running Time: 4 min. Color.
This film presents a number of products from tropical Africa, such as tea, sisal, coffee, sugar cane, cotton, pyrethrum, pineapples, cocoa and copper.

Africa: Village Life. Producer/Distributor: ICF, 1965. Grade Level: Elementary through Adult. Running Time: 4 min. Color.
This film presents a composite impression of village life in Northern Rhodesia and Bechuanaland, including sequences on farming, herding, well-digging, building, dancing and relaxing.

Africa: Wild Life. Producer/Distributor: ICF, 1965. Grade Level: Elementary through Adult. Running Time: 3 min. Color.
Part I Pictures the lion, gazelle, giraffe, zebra, elephant and rhinoceros in their natural environments.
Part II Pictures the flamingo, vulture, crocodile, boomslant (or tree snake), cobra, millipede and chameleon in their natural environments.

African Animals in Drought. Producer/Distributor: EALING, 1967. Grade Level: Kindergarten through Adult. Running Time: 4 min. Color.
This film shows elephants digging for water in a dry stream bed, a rhinoceros trapped in a mudhole and a mass migration of many animals as dust storms threaten.

African Birdlife. Producer/Distributor: BFA, 1967. Running Time: 11 min. Color.
This film shows the birds of the tropical lakes and marshland streams of Central Africa in their natural habitat.

African Birds. Producer/Distributor: EALING, 1967. Grade Level: Kindergarten through Adult. Running Time: 3 min. Color.
This film pictures the crowned crane in flight and shows the great bustard, secretary bird and the courser as they hunt for food.

African Fauna. Producer/Distributor: BFA, 1957. Running Time: 11 min. Color.

This film shows scenes of such animals as waterbuck, impala, cheeta, crocodile, elephant, zebra, lion, giraffe and hippopotamus, photographed in Kenya, Uganda and the Congo.

African Horse Sickness. Producer/Distributor: USNAC, 1942. Grade Level: Sr. H.S. through Adult. Running Time: 29 min. Color.

This film presents a photographic record of the progress of African horse sickness from infection to death, and describes the development, manufacture and administration of preventive vaccines.

African Tribes. Producer/Distributor: BFA, 1942. Running Time: 11 min. Color.

This film shows four tribes—Bamburi, saucer-lipped people of the Lake Albert District; Ifi pigmies of the Ituri Forest; long-headed Mangbettu of the Central Congo; and the Rendilli, strange nomads of the Kaisut desert, Kenya.

African Trypanosomiasis. Producer/Distributor: USNAC, 1953. Running Time: 16 min. Color.

This film explains the etiology, epidemiology, symptomatology, diagnosis, treatment, prognosis, prevention and control of African Trypanosomiasis (sleeping sickness).

African Wildlife Sanctuary. Producer/Distributor: BFA, 1957. Running Time: 11 min. Color.

A trip through Kruger National Park is portrayed with views of the rest camps and roads. Wild animals encountered include lions, elephants, hippos, elands, impalas and monkeys.

Africans of the River Niger: Building a Boat. Producer/Distributor: EALING, 1968. Grade Level: Elementary through Adult. Running Time: 4 min. Color.

An adaptation from the feature film *Building a Boat*, this film shows African craftsmen as they build a boat—including the shaping of a mahogany plane to fit the curve of the boat, application of glue and strips of cloth to make the grain watertight, roping together the two valves of the boat with fibrous string, plugging with grass and clay and adding thwarts to give rigidity.

Africans of the River Niger: Building a House. Producer/Distributor: EALING, 1968. Grade Level: Elementary through Adult. Running Time: 4 min. Color.

An adaptation from the feature film *Building a House*, this film illustrates the construction of storage houses needed to protect the family possessions from the heavy floods of the river. The film includes scenes of sticks and branches lashed together with reed rope and shows thatching with thick bundles of reed.

Africans of the River Niger: Fishing. Producer/Distributor: EALING, 1968. Grade Level: Elementary through Adult. Running Time: 4 min. Color.

An adaptation from the feature film *Fishing on the Niger River*, this film illustrates various methods of fishing used by the Bozo tribe, beginning with individual fishermen using hand nets. The whole community cooperates in laying half a mile of net in a huge semi-circle from two points on the same bank, pulling the ends until all the trapped fish are brought ashore.

Africans of the River Niger: Preparing a Meal. Producer/Distributor: EALING, 1968. Grade Level: Elementary through Adult. Running Time: 4 min. Color.

An adaptation from the feature film *Daily Life of the Bozo*, this film describes a Bozo woman preparing a meal of rice and fish, including pounding, boiling and seasoning of the rice. The film points out that the meal is served first to men and boys according to Moslem custom.

Africans of the River Niger: Trading Smoked Fish. Producer/Distributor: EALING, 1968. Grade Level: Elementary through Adult. Running Time: 4 min. Color.

An adaptation from the feature film *Fishing on the Niger River*, this film describes the smoking of fish in preparation for taking it to market, boats with mats, where the fish is unloaded and sold to a government cooperative which controls the sale of fish.

Africa's Vanishing Wildlife. Producer/Distributor: ICF, 1967. Grade Level: Elementary through Sr. H.S. Running Time: 15 min. Color.

This film depicts Africa's remaining wildlife regions, showing antelope, elephant, giraffe, baboon, crocodile, rhinoceros, hippopotamus and water birds. The presentation shows how the growing native population and their increasing herds are taking over the natural habitats of this wildlife.

Agriculture in West Africa. Producer/Distributor: DOUBLE, 1968. Grade Level: Intermediate through Sr. H.S. Running Time: 4 min. Purchase: $19.50, super; $16, standard.

The harvesting of crops and livestock herding are shown in both wet and dry areas of West Africa. Air shots of farms are seen, as well as methods of irrigation. This film may be used to illustrate both the products and the problems of farming in West Africa.

City Life in West Africa. Producer/Distributor: DOUBLE, 1968. Grade Level: Intermediate through Sr. H.S. Running Time: 4 min. Purchase: $19.50, super; $16, standard.

Lagos, the capital of Nigeria, is seen from the air and from the busy streets in this sequence which demonstrates the formation of large urban centers in emerging Africa. From skyscraper to shantytown, students get an objective view of both the advantages and disadvantages of rapid urbanization typical of many developing nations throughout the world.

Dinner in West Africa. Producer/Distributor: DOUBLE, 1968. Grade Level: Intermediate through Sr. H.S. Running Time: 4 min. Purchase: $19.50, super; $16, standard.

Students accompany a Nigerian housewife as she bargains for different foods in an open market and returns to her middle-class home to prepare and serve dinner. The sequence introduces students to the foods, kitchen appliances, and sanitation practices of city and town people in tropical West Africa, as distinguished from the more commonly available films which emphasize village customs.

Home in Africa. Producer/Distributor: DOUBLE, 1968. Grade Level: Intermediate through Sr. H.S. Running Time: 4 min. Purchase: $19.50, super; $6, standard.
Many examples of urban and rural homes throughout different climatic regions of Africa are seen in this film. Aerial photography takes students on jaunts to different parts of the continent where strong Islamic and European influences are seen as well as purely indigenous styles.

Labor in West Africa. Producer/Distributor: DOUBLE, 1968. Grade Level: Intermediate through Sr. H.S. Running Time: 4 min. Purchase: $19.50, super; $16, standard.
Men, women, and children are seen at various types of skilled and unskilled labor. Workers are shown constructing bridges and houses, surveying roads and packing nuts. This film is useful in illustrating the variety of common labor available to the West African.

Markets in West Africa. Producer/Distributor: DOUBLE, 1968. Grade Level: Intermediate through Sr. H.S. Running Time: 4 min. Purchase: $19.50, super; $16, standard.
Market scenes of all types, from downtown department stores to calabash gourd vendors, are seen in this panorama of West African goods and sales techniques. Students are introduced to the many types of goods available in West Africa and to their influence upon the standard of living of a given people.

Negro Kingdoms of Africa's Golden Age. Producer/Distributor: ASAHIA/ICF, 1969. Grade Level: Elementary through Sr. H.S. Running Time: 17 min. Color.
This presentation of the history of the three major African empires which flourished more than 700 years ago uses little-known museum pieces, artists' recreations and on-location photography.

Peanuts—Important Product of West Africa. Producer/Distributor: DOUBLE, 1968. Grade Level: Intermediate through Sr. H.S. Running Time: 4 min. Purchase: $19, super; $16, standard.
Peanut production from harvesting to exportation is seen through a presentation of women harvesting "ground nuts," which are then shelled by hand-operated machines, bagged and hauled by donkeys to storage mounds for export. Filmed in Northern Nigeria, this sequence is useful for introducing the products and climate of the inland wet savanna as opposed to the coastal tropical rain forest and swamps of West Africa.

People of Africa. Producer/Distributor: DOUBLE, 1968. Grade Level: Intermediate through Sr. H.S. Running Time: 4 min. Purchase: $19.50, super; $16, standard.
Traditional peoples of North, West and East Africa are emphasized in

this sequence, which may be used to stress the relationship of man with his environment. Examples of people shown range from turbaned Moroccans to Masai chiefs and from palace guards to village dancers.

Progress in West Africa. Producer/Distributor: DOUBLE, 1968. Grade Level: Intermediate through Sr. H.S. Running Time: 4 min. Purchase: $19.50, super; $16, standard.

Effects are shown of modern technology upon rural areas and cities in West Africa. Among many things seen are highways traversing rain forests, rural health centers, newly developing factories and modern bridge construction.

Rubber Plantation in West Africa. Producer/Distributor: DOUBLE, 1968. Grade Level: Intermediate through Sr. H.S. Running Time: 4 min. Purchase: $19.50, super; $16, standard.

On the plantation and in the processing plant the production of raw rubber is viewed step by step from latex tapping to the shipment of bulk elastic blocks overseas. Filmed in Liberia, the sequence introduces students to the climatic conditions favorable to production of this important material in tropical regions of the world.

Rural Life in Arid West Africa. Producer/Distributor: DOUBLE, 1968. Grade Level: Intermediate through Sr. H.S. Running Time: 4 min. Purchase: $19, super; $16, standard.

Arid regions of the West African savanna zone are visited in this film which takes students through farmlands and into villages typical of this region. Agriculture and livestock form the basis of the economy here. The influence of Islam is seen in classes where children learn the Koran.

Semi-Nomadic Life in Dry West Africa. Producer/Distributor: DOUBLE, 1968. Grade Level: Intermediate through Sr. H.S. Running Time: 4 min. Purchase: $19, super; $16, standard.

From the air a small group of temporary huts appears and later is visited to introduce students to the activities of semi-nomadic cattle herders. Both work and recreation are seen, with parents and children sharing the activities of cattle herding.

Town Life in West Africa. Producer/Distributor: DOUBLE, 1968. Running Time: 4 min. Purchase: $19.50, super; $16, standard.

Surrounded by tropical vegetation, a Western Nigerian town and the activities of its people are shown. Dressed gracefully and colorfully in long skirts, blouses, and robes, people work, prepare food, attend church, and enjoy the recreation of dancing in this cross section of small town life in coastal West Africa.

Transportation in West Africa. Producer/Distributor: DOUBLE, 1968. Grade Level: Intermediate through Sr. H.S. Running Time: 4 min. Purchase: $19.50, super; $16, standard.

Many methods of moving people and materials are shown: carrying loads on the head, pushing hand carts, using donkeys, camels, canoes, cars, trucks, ships, and even jet airplanes.

Audiotapes

Early African Literature: Its Political Source and Commitment. Producer/Distributor: MGH, 1968. Code No. 75465. Running Time: 20 min. Purchase: $10.

This tape traces the development of early African writing from its first expressions of indigenous thought and culture to the post-independence period of nationalism following World War II.

Emerging Africa in the Light of the Past (Unit 1). Producer/Distributor: CHRI, 1969. Grade Level: Jr. & Sr. H.S. 7.5 IPS. Purchase: $46.57.

This tape outlines the cultural history of sub-Saharan Africa from the beginning to the arrival of the first Europeans in the 15th century. Includes selections on geography, environment, physical types, arts, music, Arab invasions, agricultural change and migrations, the arrival of the Portuguese. Text, notes, study outlines are included.

Emerging Africa in the Light af its Past (Unit 2). Producer/Distributor: CHRI, 1969. Grade Level: Jr. & Sr. H.S. 7.5 IPS. Purchase: $46.57.

Outlines the history of sub-Saharan Africa from the landing of the Europeans in the 1400's to today. Includes selections covering Benin and arts, European trading posts and the slave trade with the West, Stanley and Livingstone and the opening of the interior, the British and French invasions, Liberia, colonialism, effects of the World Wars, independence and its problems. Texts, notes, study outlines are included.

Modern African Literature: Its Challenge and Changing Direction. Producer/Distributor: MGH, 1968. Code No. 75466. Running Time: 22 min. Purchase: $10.

Mr. Wauthier analyzes the contribution of native South African writers to the gradual evolution of African nations. Beginning with the period directly after World War II, he depicts, through the voices of African writers, the rise of the anti-colonial movement, and weighs the impact of Western civilization on African religion, politics, and culture.

Population Pressures in Africa. Producer/Distributor: MGH, 1968. Code No. 75461. Running Time: 24 min. Purchase: $10.

The causes and consequences of Africa's population growth are considered, and the need for population control is suggested. Family planning prospects are then appraised in the light of recent research in sub-Saharan Africa.

This is my Country—Africa. Producer/Distributor: WILSNH, 1968. Grade
Level: Elementary through Sr. H.S. Code No. S4-T(2). Running Time: 18
min. 3¾ IPS. Purchase: 4 Tapes, $15.80.
Students interviewed are from Ethopia, Sudan, Zambia and Nigeria.
These interviews of people from other countries increase student understanding
of the various life-ways of mankind—and show that there are other ways of
solving common human problems. Each interview ends with an open-ended
question.

Filmstrips
(silent)

Africa. Producer/Distributor: SSSS. Grade Level: Jr. & Sr. H.S. Purchase: $7.50
each; $70 set. Color.
1. Life Among the Arabs, 1951; 25 frames. 2. Berbers of the Atlas Mts.,
1951; 25 frames. 3. Copper Belt of C. Africa, 1951; 27 frames. 4. East Africa:
People, Crops, and Cattle, 1951; 25 frames. 5. East Africa: Regional Survey,
1951; 26 frames. 6. South African Gold Fields, 1951; 30 frames. 7. Ghana, 1951;
28 frames. 8. Village Life in N. Nigeria, 1951; 25 frames. 9. A Journey Down the
Nile, 1951; 30 frames. 10. New Developments in the Sahara, 1951; 26 frames. 11.
Morocco. 12. Ports of West Africa.

Africa. Producer/Distributor: HULP. Single Strip. 44 frames.
Describes products of plant and animal origin and the mineral products
of North, West, Central, East and South Africa.

Africa. Producer/Distributor: POPSCI, 1963. Single Strip. 43 frames.
Discusses the three parts of Africa—North, Tropical, and South. Explains
why men are reluctant to penetrate the interior and why the exploration of
Africa was a relatively modern occurrence.

Africa—Climate and Vegetation. Producer/Distributor: EGH, 1963. Grade
Level: Elementary through Jr. H.S. Single Strip. 43 frames.
Explains the physical aspects of various continental areas and the effect
of natural environment on the activities of man.

Africa—Developing Continent. Producer/Distributor: BFA, 1966. Grade Level:
Elementary through Jr. H.S. 5 in series.
Uses a cross-section approach by subject area to examine Africa as a

whole, stressing its great variety both in natural and human resources and development. Includes maps. Includes: 1. African Transportation. 2. Culture in Africa. 3. Geography of Africa. 4. How the Africans Live. 5. What Africans Do For a Living.

Africa: Developing Continent. Producer/Distributor: AVMC. Grade Level: Elementary through Jr. H.S. 5 in series. Purchase: $7.25 each; $35 set.

Africa is recognized as a land of enormous potential. The geography, the peoples, how they live, their culture, their communications and transportation are described in this overview of modern Africa. The series provides an introduction to names, places, and characteristics of the country as a beginning reference springboard to further study or as a useful "main points" summary. Each strip ends with a list of "things to remember." Produced by Anne Marie Rambo.

Africa—Equatorial and Central. Producer/Distributor: Elkins, 1957. Grade Level: Elementary through Jr. H.S. 7 in series.

Depicts family life and villages in modern equatorial and Central Africa and shows methods of development. 1. An African Home Near the Equator. 2. The African Village Near the Equator. 3. Children of Equatorial Africa. 4. Farming in Equatorial Africa. 5. Modern Living Through Education in Africa. 6. Occupations in Equatorial Africa. 7. Transportation in Equatorial Africa.

Africa—Explosive Continent. Producer/Distributor: NYT, 1958. Single Strip. 60 frames.

Emphasizes the fact that Africa is a crucial area in the struggle between democracy and communism.

Africa: The French Community. Producer/Distributor: CAF, 1961. Grade Level: Jr. H.S. through College. 41 frames. Purchase: $4. B&W.

This filmstrip is one in a series dealing with contemporary affairs. Today, when the pressing problems of Africa command international attention, the concept of the community may serve in the future to inspire greater cooperation among other newly independent African states.

Africa in Ferment. Producer/Distributor: NYT, 1968. Grade Level: Jr. H.S. through College. 70 frames. B&W. Purchase: $9.

A filmstrip showing sub-Saharan Africa today, where tribalism confronts nationalism. Shows how new nations are facing their difficulties in entering the modern world, the role of the military and the involvement of the major powers.

Africa, the Land of Developing Countries. Producer/Distributor: SVE, 1965. Grade Level: Elementary through Sr. H.S. 6 in series.

Explores modern-day Africa, showing the chief cities and main industries. Pictures people of many nationalities in their daily routines. 1. The Congo Basin. 2. The Eastern Highlands. 3. The Nile Valley. 4. Northwest Africa and the Sahara. 5. Southern Africa. 6. The West Central Lowlands.

Africa: Land, People, and History. Producer/Distributor: CHRI.

This first of two comprehensive units outlines the cultural history of sub-

Saharan Africa from its beginnings to the arrival of the first Europeans 500 years ago. Subjects include: geography and environment; cultural diversity among the Bushmen, Hottentots, Pygmies, Bantu and Nilotic peoples; Arab invasions from the North; the Ancient Empire of Ghana; population expansion; the Arab slave trade; the giant Watusi and cultural domination of the Eastern grasslands; origins of the Hottentots; flight of the Bushmen into the Kalahari Desert; Henry the Navigator and the arrival of the Portuguese. *Africa: From Exploration to Independence.* This concluding introductory unit shows African history continuing to unfold in the interior and the early European influence. Subjects include: the Bakongo Kingdom; the Empire of Ghana; the discovery of America and the launching of slave trade; the Dutch in South Africa; the British and the Great Trek; slavery outlawed; Africa partitioned; consequences in the 1960's; Liberia and Ethiopia as the only free states; colonial development; independence for the Gold Coast; African independence for a look at problems today.

Africa: Regional Geography. Producer/Distributor: MGH, 1967. Grade Level: Elementary through Sr. H.S. 6 in series.

Presents the regional structure and economic development of Africa. Shows how and why the people of various areas differ. Demonstrates that the ways of making a living in Africa are closely related to differences in climate and landforms. 1. The Continent of Africa. 2. East Africa. 3. The Economy of Africa. 4. Northern Africa. 5. Southern Africa. 6. West Africa.

Africa—Rift Valley, Volcano, and Gorge. Producer/Distributor: CARMAN, 1966. Single Strip. 28 frames.

Describes the Rift Valley of Eastern Africa, Mount Kilimanjaro and the Blue Nile Gorge. Discusses rift valleys, volcanoes, vegetational changes as related to altitude, and river erosion through volcanic, sedimentary and igneous rocks.

Africa: Sahara to Capetown. Producer/Distributor: EBEC, 1961. Grade Level: Elementary & Jr. H.S. Purchase: $6 set.

This series shows how Africa is slowly changing and depicts the curious blend of old and new in today's Africa. Self-sufficiency as well as interdependency of each region is pointed out, and clear maps locate the regions under study. 1. Life Along the Nile. 2. Oasis in Libya. 3. Contrasts in Nigeria. 4. Life Along the Congo River. 5. Highlands of Kenya. 6. The Bantu in South Africa.

Africa—Tanganyika, Kenya, Uganda. Producer/Distributor: EBEC, 1952. Grade Level: Elementary & Jr. H.S. 4 in series.

Portrays geographical and social concepts of East Central Africa. 1. Animals and Birds. 2. Native Tribes. 3. Plants and Flowers. 4. The Region.

African Life in a Bechuanaland Town. Producer/Distributor: HULP. Single Strip. 34 frames.

Shows life in a Bechuanaland town, describing the need for water and viewing how the women prepare food. Includes views of sports, the school, the church and other points of interest.

Africa Today, Pt. I. Producer/Distributor: AFRICA, 1968. Single Strip. 53 frames.

Contrasts modern and ancient aspects of life in Africa and points out changes in various forms of government and economic conditions.

Africa Today, Pt. II. Producer/Distributor: AFRICA, 1968. Single Strip. 56 frames.

Describes principal industries and products in various parts of Africa and points out the different types of medical care, education, religion, arts, and recreation of different African groups.

African ABC. Producer/Distributor: TA, 1969. Grade Level: Elementary. 33 frames. Purchase: $6.

A lively, entertaining, alphabetical introduction to Africa's people, places and animals. Children learn the alphabet and gain insight into the African way of life.

African Cultural Backgrounds. Producer/Distributor: POPSCI. Grade Level: Jr. & Sr. H.S. Single Strip. 42 frames.

Traces ancient African history. Focuses on Egypt and the Western Sudan to show the origins of the diverse cultural patterns in Africa. Demonstrates the permanency of art forms which have survived in Africa and in other parts of the world.

African Folk Tales. Producer/Distributor: IBC, 1969. Grade Level: Primary. 6 in series.

Shows the cultural heritage of the African people. 1. The Children Who Lived in a Tree. 2. The Magic Drum. 3. The Singing Drum. 4. The Strong Man Who Boasted Too Much. 5. Three Tasks of Mizano. 6. Why the Bush-Fowl Calls at Dawn.

African Lion. Producer/Distributor: EBEC, 1955. Grade Level: Elementary & Jr. H.S. 6 in series.

Adapted from the motion picture of the same name, presents the lion and many other African animals in their native habitat. 1. Antelopes and Smaller African Animals. 2. Elephants in Africa. 3. King of Beasts. 4. The King's Realm. 5. Larger Animals of Africa. 6. Life and Death on the African Plain.

Central Africa: Focus on Liberia and Ghana. Producer/Distributor: CAF, 1957. Grade Level: Jr. H.S. through College. 41 frames. Purchase: $4. B&W.

This is a filmstrip dealing with contemporary affairs. Its purpose is to examine the cultural and political development of the two independent Negro states in predominantly colonial Central Africa. Both Liberia and Ghana are quite similar in climate, geographic environment, and cultural traditions. The filmstrip shows the gradual transition towards self-government on the Gold Coast of Africa, and contrasts the early settlement of Liberia in 1790 by free Negroes from the United States and the circumstances under which Ghana was granted her independence from Great Britain.

Central Africa and World Affairs. Producer/Distributor: CAF, 1965. Grade Level: Jr. H.S. through College. 45 frames. Purchase: $4. B&W.

This filmstrip is one in a series dealing with contemporary affairs. Today there are 30 independent states in the sprawling area of Central Africa. Most of these new countries, however, are confronted with momentous problems: they lack time-tested experience in self-government and suffer from internal unrest. Their quest for national unity is hampered by ingrained tribal traditions.

The Commonwealth: Focus on Australia and Nigeria. Producer/Distributor: CAF, 1961. Grade Level: Jr. H.S. through College. 40 frames. Purchase: $4.

This filmstrip is one in a series dealing with contemporary affairs. The example of two diverse countries—Australia and Nigeria—belonging to the Commonwealth of Nations stresses the fact that this voluntary association of sovereign states may have found a partial answer to the coexistence of different political and economic systems. Discusses how membership in the Commonwealth has contributed to the economic, educational, political, and scientific development of Australia and Nigeria.

Continent of Africa: The Children of Africa. Producer/Distributor: EGH, 1969. Grade Level: Primary & Intermediate. Code No. 160. Purchase: $5.25 each; $42.50 set.

A close-up of the various children from different regions of the continent. An introductory visit to a land of many Africas reflected by its children—primitive, urban, rural, desert, jungle, non-white and Moslem—demonstrating many surprising variations of custom and manner.

160A Babies of Africa, 42 frames **160B** Faces of African Children, 41 frames **160C** Moslem Children in Africa, 43 frames **160D** Children of Non-African Origin, 41 frames **160E** Children of Urban Africa, 42 frames **160F** Children of Rural Africa, 40 frames **160G** African Farm Children, 36 frames **160H** Children of the African Desert **160I** African Children at School, 41 frames.

Continent of Africa: The Countries of the Congo Basin. Producer/Distributor: EGH, 1969. Grade Level: Intermediate & Jr. H.S. Code No. 154. Purchase: $5.25 each; $42.50 set. Color.

Presents the geography and history, major cities, and chief ethnic groups in the Congo Basin. Highlights recent developments in educational, medical, mechanical and industrial self-sufficiency. Angola: Land, People, and Industries. Angola: Important Cities. The Republic of Cameroun. The Congo Republic. The Republic of the Congo: The Land. The Republic of the Congo: The People. The Republic of the Congo: The Cities. Federation of Rhodesia and Nyasaland. The Gabon Republic.

If You Were Born in Nigeria. Producer/Distributor: TA, 1969. Grade Level: Elementary. 42 frames. Purchase: $6.

A young Yoruba farmboy goes to Lagos with his father and meets a mysterious stranger. At the end of the day, Azeke is more than happy to return home. Nigerian history and culture are interwoven in the fabric of the story.

South Africa: The Price of Inequality. Producer/Distributor: CAF, 1970. Purchase: $7.50 each.

West Africa: Patterns of Traditional Culture. Producer/Distributor: CHRI.

First in a two-unit study of West Africa. Subjects include: Sudanese social organization, technology, agriculture, crafts, material culture, religion and kingdoms; the technological basis of life in the forest zone: resources, crafts and material; social, political, and economic organization in the Guinea forest; secret societies and their meaning; the Ashanti as a forest kingdom; religion and the forces of nature; early Europeans and the slave trade; the West African cultural heritage in the New World; the outlawing of the international slave trade and the rise of new interests in West Africa.

Filmstrips (sound)

Africa Past. Producer/Distributor: LIBFSC, 1969. Grade Level: Jr. H.S. through College. Single Strip. 50 frames.

Summarizes Africa's antiquity, discussing items isolated by archeological discoveries reflecting the old kingdom's technologies and the daily lives of the people.

Africa—The West Central Lowlands. Producer/Distributor: SVE. Grade Level: Elementary through Sr. H.S. 61 frames.

Points out the important resources of the West Central Lowlands of Africa—rubber, fishing, palm oil—and the Volta River Project.

African Art and Culture. Producer/Distributor: SCHLAT, 1968. Grade Level: Elementary through Sr. H.S. Single strip. 61–68 frames. 3 in series. 33⅓ RPM. Automatic changer. Purchase: $48.60; $148 with discs; $57 with cassettes. Color.

Documents the progress of Africa's many early societies, from the very cradle of mankind to the first days of the white man's colonizations of the Dark Continent. Includes accounts of ancient civilizations at Benin, Timbuktu and Zimbawe and the flourishing empires of Egypt, the Sudan and Ethiopia. Traces African art from the early colonial period and reveals much about the traditions, religions, livelihoods and tribal customs of African nations. Shows influence of African works on noted Western artists. Accompanied by a teacher's guide.

African Folktales. Producer/Distributor: CORF. Grade Level: Elementary & Jr. H.S. 6 in series. Purchase: $47.50.

This film presents 6 authentic, but little-known legends of African tribal folklore. These legends relate the culture of Africa to the basic universals of life and morality—the coming of man on earth, the importance of friendship, the appreciation of cleverness, and the dislike of such vices as greed and pride. Each filmstrip is delightfully illustrated in imaginative artwork with authentic African music and sound effects to enhance their charm.

The titles of the separate filmstrips are: The Creation of Man (45 frames, 12 min.) ; The Man Who Owned the Moon (45 frames, 12 min.) ; Kintu and the Law of Love (45 frames, 13 min.) ; The Queen and the Pool (45 frames, 12 min.) ; Kinneneh and the Gorilla (45 frames, 11 min.) ; The City of the Elephants (45 frames, 11 min.).

Africa: Sahara to Capetown. Producer/Distributor: BOW, 1965. Grade Level: Jr. H.S. 46 frames. 6 in series. Purchase: $6 each; $36 set. Color.

Presents economic and social changes occurring in the six regions of the continent. Shows topography, resources, people, agriculture, industries, and the strong contrasts of the new with the old. 1. Life Along the Nile. 2. Oses in Libya. 3. Contrasts in Nigeria. 4. Life Along the Congo River. 5. Highlands of Kenya. 6. The Bantu in South Africa.

African Heritage Set. Producer/Distributor: PPC, 1970. Grade Level: Elementary through Sr. H.S. 74 & 95 frames. 2 in series. 33⅓ RPM. Automatic changer. Purchase: $15. Color.

The roots of modern Afro-America are traced in this colorfully illustrated sound-filmstrip portraying the history and culture of Africa. Colored photographs, illustrations, dramatizations, authentic music and sounds beautifully illustrate the heritage that is Africa. Set contains student guide and teacher's manual, including scripts. Also: an LP record with narration by James Earl Jones.

African Stories and Legends. Producer/Distributor: UEVA, 1969. Grade Level: Elementary through Sr. H.S. 30 frames. Purchase: $85 set; $60 filmstrips only; $6 each (filmstrips) ; $5 each (record or cassettes).

A series offering a collection of authentic African tales for children. Each of these stories begins with a realistic scene of children being told the story in the African locale where it originated. These stories and legends are similar in some respects to Aesop's Fables and other classic children's lore of Europe.

Continent of Africa: The Countries of East Africa. Producer/Distributor: EGH. Purchase: $5.25 each; $42.50 set.

Presents the geography, historical background and government of the area. Highlights the strong physical contrasts of the nation, the educational opportunities, industries and new developments in transportation and communication in both cities and villages. Kenya: Land and People. Kenya: Industries and Products. Kenya: Principal Cities. Malagasy: Republic. Tanganyika: Land and People. Tanganyika: Industries, Products, Cities. Uganda: Land and People. Uganda: Industries, Products, Cities.

Continent of Africa: The Countries of North Africa. Producer/Distributor: EGH, 1969. Grade Level: Intermediate & Jr. H.S. Code No. 159. 10 in series. Purchase: $5.25 each; $47.25 set. Color.

Highlights the geographic features, major agricultural products, transportation and sports of the countries. Emphasizes how people in cities and villages dress, live and work. Algeria, 50 frames. Central African Republic, Republic of Chad, and Somali Republic, 58 frames. Ethiopia and Eritrea, 49 frames. United Kingdom of Libya, Republic of Tunisia, 52 frames. Islamic Republic of Mauritania, 47 frames. Kingdom of Morocco, 50 frames. Republic of the Niger, 48 frames. Republic of Sudan, 48 frames. Spanish African Territories, 48 frames. Republic of Mali, 47 frames.

Contrasts in Nigeria. Producer/Distributor: EGH. Single Strip. Automatic changer. Purchase: $5.25 each; $42.50 set.
Presents a picture story of people and places in Nigeria. Highlights the strong physical contrasts of the nation: the dry lands of the north and the rainy lands of the south; the old cities and the new cities; the old ways and the new modes of living and working.

Ethiopia: Emerging Nation (Parts I & II). Producer/Distributor: AVMC. Grade Level: Elementary through College. Purchase: $24.
Ethiopia has a unique variety of climate, topography and people. While Ethiopia is a highly agricultural nation, the farmers continue to use primitive tools and methods. The scenery and wild animals attract a growing number of tourists, but the economy still depends on its rich soil. Almost all manufactured goods are imported. Foreign capital and aid are helping to build new schools, dams, hospitals, roads, and industries. Two 12" LP records.

Eyewitness: Afro-American History Filmstrips. Producer/Distributor: PPC, 1970. Grade Level: Elementary through Sr. H.S. 8 in series. 33⅓ RPM. Automatic changer. Purchase: $60. Color.
The history of the Afro-American from earliest times in Africa to 1970 in the United States. Illustrated where possible. Contains two teacher's manuals, complete scripts, and a student guide. Narrated by James Earl Jones, Moses Gunn, and others. 1 & 2. African History, 74 & 95 frames. 3. Slavery Comes to America, 77 frames. 4. Freedom at Any Cost, 90 frames. 5. Voices for Freedom, 76 frames. 6. The Civil War, 71 frames. 7. New Hope, 79 frames. 8. Hard Time in the 20th Century, 96 frames.

The Living World of Black Africa. Producer/Distributor: TCP, 1969. Grade Level: Elementary through Sr. H.S. 12 in series. Purchase: $108.
Not only have these filmstrips captured the inherent beauty of the African landscape and its wildlife, they have also recorded the daily activities of its people. Each filmstrip provides a clear visual understanding of the many diverse ways of life led by black Africans. Students will see where the black African lives, how he lives, how he is affected by his surroundings and how technology and industrialization are creating a new way of life. 1. Black Africa: An Introduction. 2. The Living History of Black Africa. 3. The Living Art of Black Africa. 4. Life Along the Great River. 5. Lifeways of the Forest People. 6. Life in the Cities. 7. The Changing Economy of Black Africa. 8. Lifeways of the Masai, a People of East Africa. 9. Lifeways of the Rural Villages. 10. Lifeways in the Savanna. 11. Lifeways of the Nomads. 12. Kenya: A New Nation Faces its Future.

Nigeria. Producer/Distributor: BFA, 1966. Grade Level: Elementary & Jr. H.S. 33⅓ RPM. Automatic changer. Purchase: $24. Color.

Presents scenes of Nigeria which one would most likely see if he visited the country. Presents the Nigeria of today, emphasizing the contrast of the traditional life of the African with his expanding modernization.

Nigeria: What You'd See There (Parts I & II). Producer/Distributor: AVMC. Grade Level: Elementary & Jr. H.S. Purchase: $24.

Since gaining independence from Great Britain in 1960, Nigeria has been striving to raise her people's standard of living. These filmstrips show the changes that have taken place against the backdrop of the traditional ways of living. Part I is concerned with the home, school, clothing, and progress toward modernizing. Part II shows the traditional and modern marketplaces, fishing, transportation, community life, plus some of the unusual aspects of the Nigerian culture. Two 12″ LP recordings.

Southern Africa Today. Producer/Distributor: IIL. 6 in series. Purchase: $75.

Filmstrips deal with the wealth and the problems, the people and the important places of southern Africa (particularly South Africa, Rhodesia and South West Africa) and contain interviews with Africans of all races. 1. A First Look at Southern Africa. 2. Building Minds and Bodies in Southern Africa. 3. How Today's Africans Live. 4. Southern African Riches From Land and Sea. 5. Southern Africa's Cultural Heritage. 6. Water and Wildlife Conservation in Southern Africa.

Multimedia kits

African History (An Overview). Producer/Distributor: EDLACT. Media Kit Contents: 1 12″ LP record. 7 transparencies. Code No. Album EA 905. Purchase: $6.95.
1-12″ LP with guide.

By Dr. Josef ben-Jochannan, Master of African Studies at Harlem Preparatory School and Mr. Anthony Lewis, Head of the Social Studies Department at Harlem Preparatory School. Designed to stimulate discussion and interest in the neglected continent of Africa. In question-and-answer format, this record gives information on culture, tribal practices, religions, art, crafts, science, empires, etc. Suggestions for pre-listening orientation are made in the Teacher's Guide on the jacket, and a set of 7 transparencies (optional) facilitates focusing on the points discussed in the recording. An extensive bibliography with brief descriptions of the works listed is a valuable aid for further study by both teachers and students.

Merging Africa. Producer/Distributor: CHRI. Media Kit Contents: Tapes. Slides. Purchase: $37.50.

A new, basic survey of Africa south of the Sahara, past and present, in historical and cultural terms. Package includes 8 audio-visual units, each comprising printed text and documentation bibliography, study outline and research summary.

Recordings (discs)

African Folk Tales. Producer/Distributor: CMSR, 1968. Code No. Vol. I, CMS 547; Vol 88, CMS 550. Monaural. LP. 4 sides. 33⅓ RPM. Purchase: $5.95, each.

Vol I Umusha Mwaice, The Hunter & The Elephant, and How Beans Came to Have A Black Spot. Told by Bertha Parker. **Vol II** The Pigheaded Ruler, Legend of the Wandering Tribe, and A Giant On His Back. Told by Bertha Parker.

African Heritage. Producer/Distributor: FRSC.

This is a group of recorded programs dealing with the rich African heritage of the Negro people. **FW 8852 African Music** $5.79. With vocals and native instruments from French Sudan, Southern Nigeria, and British Cameroons. **FE 4503 Africa—South of Sahara** $13.58. Comprises music of Angola, Ruanda, the Congo, and Sudan; and of the Pantu, Watusi, Swazi, and Zulu. **FE 4500 Negro Folk Music of Africa and America** $13.58. Presents music of Negroes living in many parts of the world, highlighting the diversity of this musical heritage and illustrating a common bond, or perhaps a musical mother tongue. The drumbeats and native chants from the sound track of the movie *Naked Prey*, recorded in the villages of South Africa, are heard on the album **FS 3854 The Naked Prey** $5.79.

African Heritage Dances. Producer/Distributor: EDLACT. Grade Level: Intermediate through Sr. H.S. Code No. Alb. AR 36. 12″ LP. 1 side. 33⅓ RPM Purchase: $6.95.

Presents big drum rhythms and authentic simplified movements as characterized by folk dances of African origin. Modified by eliminating the most difficult steps, the easy-to-learn movements clearly reflect the area of their beginnings. Complete written instructions are printed on the album cover. By Mary Joyce Strahlendorf.

African Music from the French Colonies. Producer/Distributor: MLA.

This record presents African primitive music through 38 folk songs. Choral music and instrumental songs show the variety in native rhythms and the records reproduce the musical sounds of western Africa.

African Story-Songs. Producer/Distributor: UWASHP, 1969. Grade Level: Elementary through Sr. H.S. Monaural. 12″ LP. 2 sides. 33⅓ RPM. Purchase: $5.95.

This record presents eight story-songs commonly known by the Shona people who occupy about two-thirds of the present country of Rhodesia and part of Mozambique. The record illustrates the close relationships between music and the spoken word and between individual and group participation. The record makes it possible for these songs to be learned orally much as they would be taught in Africa, where visual reading of music is not part of the tradition. Told and sung by Abraham Dumisani Maraire.

Bantu Music from East Africa. Producer/Distributor: MLA.

The 32 examples of Bantu music in the album are of music of southern Africa, which has been found scattered over the greater part of the continent, south of the equator. The recordings reflect the movement of African life, composed and performed entirely for African satisfaction.

Folk Tales & Legends of Ethiopia (Vol. I & II). Producer/Distributor: CMSR, 1969. Code No. Vol. 1, CMS 572; Vol. 2, CMS 580. Monaural. LP. 4 sides. 33⅓ RPM. Purchase: $5.95 each.

Vol I Contains eight amusing, colorful and delightful stories. Told by Christine Price. **Vol II** Contains eight stories from Africa. Read by Christine Price.

Folk Tales from West Africa. Producer/Distributor: FRSC, 1969. Grade Level: Elementary & Jr. H.S. Code No. FC 7103. Monaural. 10″ LP. 2 sides. 33⅓ RPM. Purchase: $3.11.

A sampling of African folk literature for children.

Music of the Idoma of Nigeria. Producer/Distributor: PRSI, 1968. Grade Level: H.S. & College. Code No. AHM 4221. Monaural. 12″ LP. 2 sides. 33⅓ RPM Purchase: $7.95.

Recorded by Prof. Robert G. Armstrong with notes that include in special transcribed phonetics the words of each song with their English equivalents. Includes: Aleku Chants, Ichicha Songs, Onugbo and Oko, Ucholo Nehi (The Great Ceremony) of Oturkpo-Idoma, prayers. Sponsored by the Inst. of African Studies, Univ. of Ibadan, Nigeria, and UNESCO.

Yewe: Music of Ghana. Producer/Distributor: PRSI, 1968. Grade Level: Sr. H.S. & College. Code No. AHM 4226. Monaural. 12″ LP. 2 sides. 33⅓ RPM. Purchase: $7.95.

Recorded and edited by S. K. Ladzekpo, the discs contain music for the Yewe Cult Dance, Funeral Dirge, Kpegisu, Ga Dance, Gadzo Dance, Atsiagbek Dance, Brittania Hatsistsia, Adzida-Afawu, and Adzida.

Slides

Adventures in Africa's Big Game Country. Producer/Distributor: AVMC. 24 in set. Purchase: $5.

An excellent slide set containing shots of zebra and topi, buffalo, cheetah, hippopotamus, rhinoceros, lion, elephant, impala, giant bustard, Uganda kob ram, Grant's gazelle, Thompson's gazelle, and many others.

African Negro Art. Producer/Distributor: DBCP. 110 in set. Purchase: $82.50. Color.

An extensive selection of color slides on African art is pictured. They present the specimens from the country's leading museums and private collections, rounded out by valuable material from the loan exhibition, "African Negro Sculpture," in the De Young Museum, San Francisco, assembled by Dr. Paul S. Wingert. They stress the primitive's truth to material, his grand instinctive handling, and the three-dimensional conception of the African artist.

The collection includes slides of the following countries:
1. French Sudan
2. French Guinea
3. Liberia
4. Ivory and Gold Coast
5. Dahomey
6. British Nigeria
7. Cameroon
8. Gabun
9. French Congo
10. Belgian Congo
11. Tanganyika

Belgian Congo. Producer/Distributor: MMAL. Purchase: $1 each.

AF 86 Nusing woman on pedestal, Bakongo; wood; 12″ high. Brooklyn Museum. **AF 87** Nail fetish; Mangaka; wood studded with nails; 36″ high. Brooklyn Museum. **AF 88** Same; detail of head. **AF 89** Two fetish figures; Bateke; wood; 14″ and 12½″ high. Coll. George Rony, Los Angeles. **AF 90** Standing female figure; Bayaka; polychrome wood; 21″ high. Coll. Vincent Price, Beverly Hills. **AF 91** Mask; Bapende; wood, fiber, raffia; 13″ high. Coll. Edward Gans, New York. **AF 92** Ceremonial dance mask with square eyes; Bassongo Meno; polychrome wood, grass fringe; 26″ high. Peabody Museum, Harvard University. **AF 93** Large mask; Bakete; polychrome wood and raffia; 29″ high. American Museum of Natural History, New York. **AF 94** Carved cup with geometric design; Bushongo; wood; 6¾″ high. Buffalo. **AF 95** Two-headed vessel; Bakuba; wood; 6″ high. Peabody Museum, Harvard University. **AF 96** Ceremonial cup in the shape of a human head; Bakuba; wood inlaid with shell; 10″ high. Peabody Museum, Salem, Mass. **AF 97** Tufted cloth; detail; Bushongo; palm fiber; detail; 12″ × 18″. Brooklyn Museum. **AF 98** Ceremonial mask; Bena Lulua; polychrome wood with beads and cowrie shells; 14″ high. Peabody Museum, Harvard University. **AF 99** Round mask; Basonge; wood and hair; 17″ high. Buffalo Museum of Science. **AF 100** Standing figure with cowrie shell eyes; Basonge; wood and metal; 13″ high. New York Public Library, 136th Street. **AF 101** Standing female figure with gourd; Baluba; wood; 22″ high. Coll. Mr. & Mrs. Bernard J. Reis, New York. **AF 102** Same; side view. **AF 103** Stool with female figure as support; Baluba; wood; 22″ high. Mr. & Mrs. Bernard J. Reis, New York. **AF 104** Bow-rest with female figure as support; Baluba; wood; 36″ high. Buffalo Museum of Science. **AF 105** Figure holding bowl; Baluba; wood; 14½″ high. American Museum of Natural History, New York. **AF 106** Kneeling figure holding bowl; Baluba; wood; 14″ high. Peabody Museum, Harvard University. **AF 107** Neck rest with supporting female figure; Baluba; wood; 5½″ high. Peabody Museum, Harvard University. **AF 108** Horizontal drum carved as buffalo; Mangbetu; wood; 43″ long. American Museum of Natural History, New York. **AF 109** Effigy vessel; Mangbetu pottery; 16″ high. Brooklyn Museum.

African Safari. Producer/Distributor: AVMC. 26 in set. Purchase: $5.50.

Slides showing close-ups of black and white rhinos, hippos, elephants, lions, buffaloes, giraffes, zebras, ostriches, foxes, baboons, monkeys, wart hogs, wildebeest, impala, ankolis and kobs.

British Nigeria. Producer/Distributor: DBCP, 1940. Grade Level: All Ages. 110 in set. Purchase: $1 each. Color.

AF 34 Divination vessel; Yoruba; polychrome wood; 21″ high. Coll. William Moore, Los Angeles. **AF 35** Same; side view; left side with male figures. **AF 36** Same; detail; right side; female figures. **AF 38** Same; detail; face of large female figure; front view. **AF 39** Equestrian figure; Yoruba; wood; 11¾″ high. Newark Museum. **AF 40** Warrior on horseback; Yoruba; wood; 16″ high. Coll. Rene d' Harnoncourt, New York. **AF 41** Staff with mother and child group; Yoruba; wood; 16″ high. Coll. Rene d' Harnoncourt, New York. **AF 42** Same; detail of the two heads. **AF 43** Stool carved with two rows of figures; Yoruba; polychrome wood: 25″ high. Royal Ontario Museum of Archaeology, Toronto. **AF 44** Male head; Ife; bronze; 13½″ high. Coll. Prof. William R. Bascom, Evanston, Ill. **AF 45** Same; detail of face. **AF 46** Female head; Ife; bronze; 10″ high. Coll. Prof. William R. Bascom, Evanston, Ill. **AF 47** Same; side view. **AF 48** King's head; Benin; bronze; 12½″ high. Coll. William Moore, Los Angeles. **AF 50** Plaque with two figures in relief; Benin; bronze; 19″ high. Coll. William Moore, Los Angeles. **AF 51** Warrior on horseback; Benin; bronze; 7″ high. Peabody Museum, Harvard University. **AF 52** Staff surmounted by bird; Benin; bronze; 12¼″ high. Buffalo Museum of Science. **AF 53** Mother and child; Benin; ivory; 6″ high. Coll. William Moore, Los Angeles. **AF 54** Same; detail; suckling child. **AF 55** Same; detail; mother's head. **AF 56** Female figure; Benin; ivory; 14½″ high. Peabody Museum, Harvard University. **AF 57** Pierced carving with figures; Benin; ivory; 7¾″ high. Buffalo Museum of Science. **AF 58** Funerary mask; Ibo; polychrome wood; 11″ high. Coll. William Moore, Los Angeles. **AF 59** Seated male and female figures; Ibibio; wood; 28″ high. Coll. Helena Rubinstein, New York. **AF 60** Mask headpiece; Ijaw; wood and feathers; 21″ high. Peabody Museum, Salem, Mass. **AF 61** Same; detail of face.

Cameroon. Producer/Distributor: DBCP, 1940. Grade Level: All Ages. 110 in set. Purchase: $1 each. Color.

> **AF 62** Seated figure holding bowl; wood; 16¼″ high. Buffalo Museum of Science. **AF 63** Circular stool supported by human figures; Baendjo; 16″ high. Natural History Museum, Chicago. **AF 64** Stools supported by carved animals; wood, beaded surface; 16″ high. Natural History Museum, Chicago. **AF 65** Large antelope mask; polychrome wood; 26″ high. American Museum of Natural History, New York. **AF 66** Ceremonial mask; painted wood; 23½″ high. Peabody Museum, Harvard University. **AF 67** Same; side view. **AF 68** Head with crown of human figures; clay; 12″ high. Buffalo Museum of Science. **AF 60** Old ceremonial mask; Bamum; wood with grass fringe; 28″ high. Peabody Museum, Harvard University. **AF 71** Staff surmounted by human figure with leopard on back; side view; Bamum; cast brass; figures 11″ high. Peabody Museum, Harvard University. **AF 72** Same; front view. **AF 73** Pipe bowl; Bali; black clay; 7¾″ high. Coll. Dr. Fred Block, Hollywood.

Dahomey. Producer/Distributor: DBCP, 1940. Grade Level: All Ages. 110 in set. Purchase: $1 each. Color.

> **AF 31** Snake mask for serpent cult; Yoruba; polychrome wood; 18″ high. Coll. Vincent Price, Beverly Hills. **AF 32** Figure group; brass; 7″ high. Coll. Prof. Melville J. Herskovits, Evanston, Ill.

French Congo. Producer/Distributor: DBCP, 1940. Grade Level: All Ages. 110 in set. Purchase: $1 each.

> **AF 83** Spoon with carved handle; wood; 6½″ high. Coll. George Rony, Los Angeles. **AF 84** Dance head used in snake cult; Kuyu; polychrome wood; 14″ high. Coll. Ralph C. Altman, Los Angeles. **AF 85** Two seated figures; cast copper; 5¼″ high. Coll. George Rony, Los Angeles.

French Sudan. Producer/Distributor: DBCP. Purchase: $1 each. Color.

> **AF 2** Antelope head piece; Bambara; painted wood; 28″ high. Brooklyn Museum. **AF 3** Stylized bird headpiece; wood; 19¾″ high. Coll. Ralph C. Altman, Los Angeles. **AF 4** Same; detail of head. **AF 5** Standing female figure; Bambara; wood; 21½″ high. Brooklyn Museum. **AF 6** Standing female figure; Bambara; wood; 24¾″ high. Buffalo Museum of Science. **AF 7** Boy's secret society mask; Bambara; wood; 24″ high. Buffalo Museum of Science. **AF 8** Standing male figure; front view; probably Bobo; French Sudan and Ivory Coast; wood; 44″ high. Coll. Mr. & Mrs. Walter Arensberg, Hollywood.

Liberia. Producer/Distributor: DBCP. Purchase: $1 each.

> **AF 12** Female figure; wood with cowrie shell headband; 17″ high. Peabody Museum, Harvard University. **AF 13** Secret society mask (Poro); South Section; wood with leaves; 14″ high. Peabody Museum, Harvard University. **AF 14** Secret society mask (Poro); Gio; painted wood; 9″ high. Peabody Mu-

seum, Harvard University. **AF 15** Secret society mask (Poro); Mano; wood, metal and hair; 20¼″ high. Peabody Museum, Harvard University. **AF 16** Dance mask; Kaan; wood; 8½″ high. Coll. Ralph C. Altman, Los Angeles. **AF 17** Top of staff or rattle used by female secret society; Liberia-Western Ivory Coast; wood; 29″ high. Brooklyn Museum.

Tanganyika. Producer/Distributor: MMAL, 1940. Grade Level: All Ages. 110 in set. Purchase: $1 each. Color.
    AF 110 Mask; Makonde; wood; 16″ high. Buffalo Museum of Science.

Discovering the Art of Africa: African Dress and Design and *Treasures and Traditions of African Art.* Producer/Distributor: SVE. Purchase: $8.50 each. Color.
    Depicts great masterpieces of African art, dress and design. Included are sculpture, ceremonial objects, headdresses, textiles, masks of the Benin, Ashanti, Dogon and other ancient tribes.

East African Big Game Spectacular. Producer/Distributor: AVMC. 100 in set. Purchase: $21.
    Here is a comprehensive and spectacular coverage of the big game country of Kenya, Tanzania, and Uganda in East Africa. Shots include action and close-ups of such major species as crocodiles, elephants, giraffes, lions, leopards, black and white rhinos and other varieties such as baboons, flying bats, cheetahs, elands, coke's hartebeest, hybucks, wildebeest and zebras.

Egypt—Its Ancient Wonders. Producer/Distributor: AVMC. 31 in set. Purchase: $6.50. Color.
    This slide set takes in practically all of Egypt—the very heart of the country—ancient and modern.

Egypt—Land of the Pharaohs. Producer/Distributor: AVMC. 100 in set. Purchase: $21.
    A look at Egypt's heartland.

Equatorial Africa. Producer/Distributor: AVMC. 26 in set. Purchase: $5.50. Color.
    This slide set takes you deep into the heart of the jungle to adventures in East Africa, Kenya, Uganda, and the Congo. The set depicts cities and countryside, the people and their primitive way of life.

French Guinea. Producer/Distributor: MMAL, 1940. Grade Level: All Ages. 110 in set. Purchase: $1 each. Color.
    AF 10 Standing male figures; Baga; wood; 29″ high. Buffalo Museum of Science. **AF 11** Same; detail of head.

Gabun. Producer/Distributor: MMAL, 1940. Grade Level: All Ages. 110 in set. Purchase: $1 each. Color.
    AF 74 Seated male figure; Dan; wood; 25″ high. Coll. Jack Passer, Brooklyn. **AF 75** Figure of standing man; Pahouin; wood; 20½″ high. Coll. Mr. & Mrs. Walter C. Arensberg, Hollywood. **AF 76** Same; side view. **AF 77** Same;

detail of face; front view. **AF 78** Same; detail of head; side view. **AF 79** Female head; Pahouin; wood; 8″ high. Coll. Mr. & Mrs. Walter C. Arensberg, Hollywood. **AF 80** Same; side view. **AF 81** Ceremonial mask; painted wood; 20″ high. De Young Museum, San Francisco. **AF 82** Burial fetish; Bakota; copper over wood; 24½″ high. Brooklyn Museum.

Ivory and Gold Coast. Producer/Distributor: MMAL, 1940. Grade Level: All ages. 110 in set. Purchase: $1 each. Color.

   AF 19 Figure of standing female; Baoule; wood; 13¾″ high. Coll. William Moore. **AF 20** Same; rear view. **AF 21** Same; detail; side view of head. **AF 22** Figure of standing female; Baoule; wood; 14½″ high. Brooklyn Museum. **AF 23** Carved bobbin with horned human heads; Baoule; wood; 7″ high. Brooklyn Museum. **AF 24** Dance mask, gorilla type; Dan; wood and metal inlay teeth; 12″ high. Dr. George Altman, Theatrical Collection, Los Angeles. **AF 25** Dance mask; side view; Dan; wood; 8½″ high. Coll. William Moore, Los Angeles. **AF 26** Group of three figures; Senufo; wood; 13″, 8″, 12½″ high. Coll. William Moore, Los Angeles. **AF 27** Horned mask; Senufo; 15″ high; wood with traces of polychrome. Coll. Mr. & Mrs. Walter C. Arensberg, Hollywood. **AF 28** Five gold weights; Ashanti; bronze. Brooklyn Museum. **AF 29** Urn with animals on top; Ashanti; bronze, 9½″ high. Coll. William Moore, Los Angeles. **AF 30** Fertility figure; Ashanti; wood; 9″ high. Coll. Prof. William R. Bascom, Evanston, Ill.

Masks of Africa. Producer/Distributor: ACA. 32 in set. Purchase: $41.

   Slides of masks, photographed to show details of carving, color and character, from twenty-one tribes of west and central Africa.

Morocco—Oasis of North Africa. Producer/Distributor: AVMC. 30 in set. Purchase: $6.50. Color.

   Set includes views of Rabat, Meknes, Marrakech, Souk, Fez, SeFound, Erfoud, Moulay Idriss, the holy city, Ziz River, Targounit, the Kahbah of Tifoultout, native life and crafts, and panoramas of the countryside.

Study prints/pictures posters/graphics

African Heritage Chart. Producer/Distributor: PCET. 1 in set. 30″ x 40″. Purchase: $1.95.

   Through the use of maps, pictures and graphs, the chart shows artistic achievements in iron working and ivory, Benin City, the slave trade, the extent of European colonization, the trade routes within Africa, the movements of people from different sections of the continent, the extent of Islam, Kilwa trading city, the Berber Dynasties, Bantus, Cushites, Arabs, Mali, Songhai, Oyo Yoruba, Kongo, Mono-Matapa, Ashanti and the great civilizations of West Africa. A sweeping timeline traces and compares the historical developments in each section of Africa from 5,000 B.C., to the 20th century.

Transparencies

Africa. Producer/Distributor: EGH. Code No. 023.42. Purchase: $2.15. Single. 12″ x 9¾″. Color.
A two-color transparency from the series World History.

Africa: Political Geography and Nationalism. Producer/Distributor: VIMC, 1969. Grade Level: Jr. & Sr. H.S. Code No. AF-43. Purchase: $99. Series. Color.
A series of 13 transparencies with 44 overlays. Titles in the series include: Political Divisions as of 1968; Regional Organizations in Africa; United Nations' Role in the Independence of African Countries; Uhuru; Colonies to Independence; Politically Sovereign States of Africa; Nationalist Leaders of Black Africa; European Partition Agreements, 1884–1885 (Congress of Berlin); The Country of Nigeria; Republic of South Africa; Purposes and Aims of the OAU; Structure of the OAU.

The African Continent. Individual African Countries. Producer/Distributor: AMMAP, 1969. Grade Level: Elementary through Sr. H.S. Code No. T3001-T3017; T3018-T3056. Purchase: $198, set; $3.95, each. Series. 10″ x 10″. Color.
A set of 56 transparencies covering the African Continent scientifically, physically, and politically. Each transparency consists of one static and one clear acetate overlay. Thematic maps, based on research by John Bartholomew & Son Ltd., cover the following areas: politics, physiography, vegetation, rainfall, population, temperature, geology, structure and mineral resources, climatic regions and food potential, food producing areas, soil classification, major agriculture, languages, new nations. The transparencies for the individual countries show political outlines with physical features, shaded relief. The political maps also show place names.

Ancient Civilizations and Movements of People in Africa. Producer/Distributor: EGH. Code No. 023-43. Purchase: $3.90. Single. 12⅛″ x 9″. Color.
A four-color transparency showing civilizations and movements of African people (from the series World History).

Colonial Africa Before World War I. Producer/Distributor: EGH. Code No. 023-44. Purchase: $3.90. Single. 12⅛" x 9¾". Color.

A seven-color transparency from the series World History.

History and Culture of Africa. Producer/Distributor: AEVAC, 1969. Grade Level: Jr. H.S. through College. Code No. AF-44. Purchase: $118 set. Series. Color.

This set of 20 transparencies with 62 overlays examines the complex historical and cultural development of Africa, from the emergence of the tool-making man up to the present day. The transparency titles which follow indicate how the series traces the rise of empires, the accomplishments of their various civilizations, and the interaction of the European and African nations. The impact of Africa with its dynamic political leaders on the modern world is shown.

Part I Africa and the Origin of Man; The Beginnings of Organized Societies; Egypt, The Golden Age; The Rise of Kush; Ethiopia; Kush and Egypt—The End of the Golden Age; Africa and the Rise of Christianity; Africa and the Rise of Islam; The Rise of Ancient Ghana; The Rise of Mali.

Part II The Rise of Songhay; The Collapse of the Western Sudan; Consequences of the Collapse of the Western Sudan; The Coming of the Slave Trade; African Slavery and the Making of the New World; The African and the Exploration of the New World; The Colonial Era and the Nation-states of West Africa; Civilizations, Nations, and Kingdoms of East and Central Africa; Colonialism and Resistance in 19th Century Africa; Africa in the 20th Century.

Spectra Africa Transparencies. Producer/Distributor: KEC, 1968. Grade Level: Jr. & Sr. H.S. Code No. KEA 1-33. Purchase: $180. Series. Color.

Designed to serve as a core of materials basic to any in-depth study of Africa, this series of 33 transparencies includes introductory and background material and questions for class discussion. The topics were selected to give students a basic knowledge of Africa south of the Sahara. BASE MAPS: Africa: Outline; Africa: Political 1966; Africa: Population Distribution. INTRODUCTION: Africa in the World; Africa and the Continental U.S.; Regions of Africa: A Definition. GEOGRAPHY: Elevation Above Sea Level; Major Climatic Types; Major Vegetation Zones; Agriculture; Agricultural Products; Mineral Resources; Development of Basic Resources; Economic Development; Per Capita Income; Transportation. SOCIETY: Indigenous Races; Major Language Groups; Major Religions; Literacy; Patrilineal Family Structure; Area and Population. HISTORY: Major African Kingdoms; Exploring the Coast; Exploring the Interior; The Quest for the Niger; Search for the Sources of the Nile; Exploration of Southern and Central Africa; African Trade; European Settlements 1875; European Dependencies 1914; African Independence.

Video tapes/ telecourses/kinescopes

African Anthology. Producer/Distributor: WNYETV, 1968. Grade Level: Intermediate through Sr. H.S. Running Time: 18:30. B&W. Rental.

Children of Other Lands. Producer/Distributor: WNYETV, 1960. Grade Level: Elementary. Running Time: 18:30. B&W. Rental.
    From this Series, Kenya, Nigeria, Ethiopia, and United Arab Republic would be of interest in African studies.

TELECOURSES

African Music (Black Music Seminar). Producer/Distributor: LRC. Code No. M.V.A-1-5-7. Purchase.
    A demonstration of African music and instruments. The performing artists are from Howard University, Washington, D.C. They perform many of the dances that are customary of the different tribes in Africa.

Dr. Hall at Owens Hall (Black Music Seminar). Producer/Distributor: LRC, 1970. Grade Level: Elementary. Code No. M.V.A-9. Running Time: 60 min. Purchase. B&W.
    Dr. Hall talks with children about different musical experiences. He tells them of different songs from various African countries.

Dr. Vada Butcher (Black Music Seminar). Producer/Distributor: LRC, 1970. Code No. M.V. A-3. Running Time: 60 min. Purchase. B&W.
    A lecture on African music. Dr. Butcher uses tapes of the songs and music of Africa. The program includes a discussion of the history of rhythm and blues.

Olatungi Concert (Black Music Seminar). Producer/Distributor: LRC, 1970. Code No. M.V. A-13. Running Time: 60 min. Purchase. B&W.
    Olatungi and Company gives a performance in Virginia Hall. The company has put different and unusual instruments from Africa to use in presenting their program.

KINESCOPES

African Heritage. Producer/Distributor: KETCTV, 1970. Grade Level: Sr. H.S. & College. Running Time: 40 min. B&W. Rental.

Two views of Africa: History and Heritage. The first program features political, geographical, cultural backgrounds of Africa. The cultural program features native dances, art, and artifacts from Katherine Dunham Center, East St. Louis, Illinois. Two 20 minute programs.

Directory of producers and distributors

AAPC
Afro-American Publishing Co., Inc.
1727 Indiana Ave.
Chicago, Ill. 60616

ABC
American Broadcasting Company
Rockefeller Center
New York, N.Y. 10020

ACA
Art Council Aids
Box 641
Beverly Hills, Calif. 90213

ACI
ACI Productions
16 W. 46 St.
New York, N.Y. 10036

ADF
American Documentary Films Inc.
336 W. 84 St.
New York, N.Y. 10024

ADL
Anti-Defamation League
315 Lexington Ave.
New York, N.Y. 10016

AEF
American Educational Films
9878 Santa Monica Blvd.
Beverly Hills, Calif. 90212

AEVAC
AEVAC, Inc.
500 Fifth Ave.
New York, N.Y. 10036

AF
Association Films
347 Madison Ave.
New York, N..Y 10017

AFIC
American Foundation Institute of Corrections
1132 Phila. Nat. Bank Bldg.
Philadelphia, Pa. 19107

AHF
American History Filmstrips

AIM
Association Instructional Materials
600 Madison Ave.
New York, N.Y. 10022

AIMS
Aims Instructional Media Service, Inc.
Box 1010
Hollywood, Calif. 90028

AIRCO
AIRCO
150 East 42 St.
New York, N.Y. 10024

ALESCO
American Library and Educational
    Service Co.
404 Settle Dr.
Paramus, N.J. 07652

ALITIA
Alitalia Airlines
5670 Wilshire Blvd.
Los Angeles, Calif. 90036

AMMAP
American Map Co., Inc.
3 W. 61 St.
New York, N.Y. 10023

ARNO
Arno Press
330 Madison Ave.
New York, N.Y. 10017

ART
Artisan Productions
Box 1827
Los Angeles, Calif. 90028

ASAHIA
(See ICF)

ASSOC
Associated Publishers
1538 Ninth St., N.W.
Washington, D.C. 20001

ATLAP
Atlantis Productions, Inc.
894 Shefield Place
Thousand Oaks, Calif. 91360

AUDIOF
Audio Film Center
2138 E. 75 St.
Mount Vernon, N.Y. 10550

AVDC
Audio-Video Duplication Center
Dept. of Public Instruction
Commonwealth of Pennsylvania
Harrisburg, Pa. 17126

AVED
AV-Ed Films
7934 Santa Monica Blvd.
Hollywood, Calif. 90046

AVMC
Audio & Visual Methods Co.
49 N. Main St.
Homer, N.Y. 13077

BAFC
Broadcasting and Film Corporation of
Nat'l Council of Churches
475 Riverside Drive
New York, N.Y. 10027

BARR
Arthur Barr Productions
1029 N. Allen Ave.
Pasadena, Calif. 91104

BARKTB
Thomas B. Barker

BFA
Bailey Film Associates
11559 Santa Monica Blvd.
Los Angeles, Calif. 90025

BFI
Benchmark Films, Inc.
516 Fifth Ave.
New York, N.Y. 10036

BIS
British Information Service
845 Third Ave.
New York, N..Y 10022

BLC
Buckingham Learning Corporation
160-08 Jamaica Ave.
Jamaica, N.Y. 11432

BMIF
BMI Film Production, Inc.
4916 Main St.
Kansas City, Missouri 64112

BNA
BNA Films
Div. of the Bureau of Nat'l Affairs,
Inc.
5615 Fishers Lane
Rockville, Md. 20852

BOW
Stanley Bowmar Co.
12 Cleveland St.
Valhall, N.Y. 10595

BRAN
Brandon Films
221 W. 57 St.
New York, N.Y. 10019

CAF
Current Affairs Films
527 Madison Ave.
New York, N.Y. 10022

CAFM
Cathedral Film, Inc.
2921 W. Alameda Ave.
Burbank, Calif. 91905

CAROUF
Carousel Film, Inc.
1501 Broadway
New York, N.Y. 10036

CBS
Columbia Broadcasting System
485 Madison Ave.
New York, N.Y. 10022

CCUSF
Council for Civic Unity of San Francisco
40 First St.
San Francisco, Calif. 94105

CEF
Centron Educational Films
1255 Post St., Suite 625
San Francisco, Calif. 9409

CES
Civic Education Service
1733 K St., N.W.
Washington, D.C. 20006

CF
Churchill Films
662 N. Robertson Blvd.
Los Angeles, Calif. 90069

CFD
Classroom Film Distributors, Inc.
5620 Hollywood Blvd.
Los Angeles, Calif. 90028

CFS
Creative Film Society
14558 Valerino St.
Van Nuys, Calif. 91405

CGW
Communications Group West
6430 Sunset Blvd.
Hollywood, Calif. 90028

CHRI
Cultural History Research, Inc.
20 Purchase St.
Rye, N.Y. 10580

CI
Communications International
22 Oak Drive
New Hyde Park, N.Y. 11040

CMC
Center for Mass Communication
of Columbia University Press
440 W. 110 St.
New York, N.Y. 10025

CMSLS
Collier Macmillan School and Library
    Services
866 Third Ave.
New York, N.Y. 10022

CMSR
CMS Records, Inc.
14 Warren St.
New York, N.Y. 10007

COLBRN
John Colburn Assoc., Inc.
Box 236
Wilmette, Ill. 60091

COMMUN
Communicative Arts
Box 1107
San Diego, Calif. 92111

CON
Contemporary Films
330 W. 42 St.
New York, N.Y. 10036

CORF
Coronet Films
65 E. South Water St.
Coronet Bldg.
Chicago, Ill. 60601

CR
Columbia Records
51 W. 52 St.
New York, N.Y. 10020

CRI
Caedmon Records Inc.
505 Eighth Ave.
New York, N.Y. 10018

CSDI
Center for the Study
of Democratic Institutions
Box 4068
2056 Eucalyptus Hill Rd.
Santa Barbara, Calif. 93103

CURTAV
Curtis Audiovisual Materials
165 W. 46 St.
New York, N.Y. 10036

CVETV
Central Virginia ETV Corp.
1904 Old Farm Rd.
Richmond, Va. 23235

DBCP
Dr. Block Color Productions
1309 N. Genesee Ave.
Hollywood, Calif. 90046

DCAEP
DCA Educational Products, Inc.
4865 Stenton Ave.
Philadelphia, Pa. 19144

DCC
David C. Cook Publishing Company
School Products Division
Elgin, Ill. 60120

DEROCH
Louis deRochemont Associates
18 E. 48 St.
New York, N.Y. 10017

DESED
Designers for Education
3618 Superior Ave.
Cleveland, Ohio 44114

DIBIE
Dibie-Dash Productions
4949 Hollywood Bldg., Suite 217
Los Angeles, Calif. 90027

DIS
Robert Disraeli Films
Box 343, Cooper Station
New York, N.Y. 10003

DISNEY
Walt Disney Educational Materials
800 Sonara Ave.
Glendale, Calif. 91201

DOUBLE
Doubleday and Co., Inc.
501 Franklin Ave.
Garden City, N.Y. 11503

DPA
Documentary Photo Aids
Box 2620
Sarasota, Fla. 33578

DRI
Decca Records, Inc.
50 W. 57 St.
New York, N.Y. 10019

EA
Educational Associates
Ivy Place
Katonah, N.Y. 10536

EALING
Ealing Corporation
2225 Massachusetts Ave.
Cambridge, Mass. 02140

EAV
Educational Audiovisual
29 Marble Ave.
Pleasantville, N.Y. 10570

EBEC
Encyclopedia Britannica Educ. Corp.
425 N. Michigan Ave.
Chicago, Ill. 60611

EDLACT
Educational Activities, Inc.
Box 392
Freeport, N.Y. 11520

EDRS
Educational Reading Service, Inc.
Audiovisual Division
E. 64 Midland Ave.
Paramus, N.J. 07652

EDS
Educational Service, Inc.
1730 Eye St., N.W.
Washington, D.C. 20006

EEM
Educational Enrichment Materials
83 E. Ave.
Norwalk, Conn. 06851

EFLA
Educational Film Library Association
250 W. 57 St.
New York, N.Y. 10019

EGH
Eye-Gate House, Inc.
Subs. of Cenco Instrument Corp.
146-01 Archor Ave.
Jamaica, N.Y. 11435

ELAC
East Los Angeles College
East Los Angeles, Calif.

ELKINS
Herbert M. Elkins Co.
10031 Commerce Ave.
Tujunga, Calif. 91042

EMCC
EMC Corporation
Educational Materials Division
180 E. Sixth St.
St. Paul, Minn. 55101

EML
Educational Media Laboratories
20 First St.
Chicopee, Mass. 01014

ETM
Enrichment Teaching Materials, Inc.
246 Fifth Ave.
New York, N.Y. 10001

ETS
Educational Television Service
Indiana University
Bloomington, Ind. 47401

FA
Film Associates
11559 Santa Monica Blvd.
Los Angeles, Calif. 90025

FDI
Film Distributors International
2223 S. Olive St.
Los Angeles, Calif. 90007

FI
Films, Inc.
1150 Wilmette Ave.
Wilmette, Ill. 60091

FIP
Film Programs, Inc.
310 W. 53 St.
New York, N.Y. 10019

FL
Film Library
Collendale Campus
1455 E. Colvin St.
Syracuse, N.Y. 13210

FLEET
Fleetwood Films, Inc.
10 Fiske Place
Mount Vernon, N.Y. 10550

FMETHC
Free Methodist Church
General Missionary Board
Winona Lake, Ind. 46590

FON
Film of the Nations
5113 Sixteenth Ave.
Brooklyn, N.Y. 11204

FR
Fellowship of Reconciliation
Box 271
Nyack, N.Y. 10960

FRITH
Frith Films
Box 424
Carmel Valley, Calif. 93924

FRSC
Folkways Records
701 Seventh Ave.
New York, N.Y. 10036

GA
Guidance Associates
Harcourt, Brace & World
23 Washington Ave.
Pleasantville, N.Y. 10570

GEL
General Electronic Laboratories
Instructional Materials Dept.
1085 Commonwealth Ave.
Boston, Mass. 02215

GORH
Gertrude Purple Gorham Agency
291 S. La Cienaga
Beverly Hills, Calif. 90211

GPITVL
Great Plains Instructional TV Library
University of Nebraska
Lincoln, Neb. 68508

GROVE
Grove Press
Film Division
214 Mercer St.
New York, N.Y. 10012

GSF
Garden State/Novo, Inc.
630 Ninth Ave.
New York, N.Y. 10036

HAMMND
Hammond, Inc.
Educational Division
515 Valley St.
Maplewood, N.J. 07050

HANDY
Jam Handy Organization
2843 E. Grand Blvd.
Detroit, Mich. 48211

HBBB
Harlem Better Business Bureau
2090 Seventh Ave.
New York, N.Y. 10027

HBMP
Harlem Black Media Productions
Media Projects, Inc.
159 W. 53 St.
New York, N.Y. 10019

HDI
Human Development Institute
(*See* UM)

HRW
Holt, Rinehart & Winston, Inc.
383 Madison Ave.
New York, N.Y. 10017

HSPC
Hayes School Publishing Co.
321 Pennwood Ave.
Wilkensburg, Pa. 15221

HU
Howard University
Audiovisual Center
Washington, D.C. 20001

HUL
Hulton Press

HURTE
Leroy E. Hurte Productions
4477 W. Adams Blvd.
Los Angeles, Calif. 90016

HW
Haskel Wexler

IBC
International Book Corp.
7300 Biscayne Blvd.
Miami, Fla. 33138

IC
Instructo Corporation
Paoli, Pa. 19301

ICF
International Communications Films
1371 Reynolds Ave.
Santa Ana, Calif. 92705

IFB
International Film Bureau
332 S. Michigan Ave.
Chicago, Ill. 60604

IFF
International Film Foundation
475 Fifth Ave., Suite 916
New York, N.Y. 10017

IIL
Imperial International Learning
247 W. Court St.
Kankakee, Ill. 60901

IQF
IQ Films
689 Fifth Ave.
New York, N.Y. 10022

IU
Indiana University
Audiovisual Center
Bloomington, Ind. 47401

JACK
Jackdaw Kits

JAS
Jason Films
2621 Palisade Ave.
Riverdale, N.Y. 10463

JOU
Journal Films
909 W. Diversey Parkway
Chicago, Ill. 60614

KCETTV
KCET-TV Channel 28
Community TV of Southern California
1313 N. Vine St.
Los Angeles, Calif. 90028

KEC
Keuffel & Esser Co.
Educational AV Division
300 Adams St.
Hoboken, N.J. 07030

KERATV
KERA-TV Channel 13
Public TV Foundation for North
  Texas
3000 Harry Hines Blvd.
Dallas, Texas 75201

KETCTV
KETC-TV Channel 9
6996 Millbrook Blvd.
St. Louis, Mo. 63130

KLRNTV
KLRN-TV
University of Texas
Austin, Texas

KQED
KQED-TV
525 Fourth St.
San Francisco, Calif. 94107

KRMA-TV
414 Fourteenth St.
Denver, Colo. 80202

KTCATV
KTCA-TV Channel 12
Twin City Area Educational
  Television
1640 Como Ave.
St. Paul, Minn. 55108

KUHT
KUHT-TV
University of Houston
Cullen Bldg.
Houston, Tex. 77004

KUON
KUON-TV Channel 12
University of Nebraska
1600 R. St.
Lincoln, Neb. 68508

LA
Learning Arts
Box 917
Wichita, Kansas 67201

LACS
Los Angeles City Schools
450 N. Grand
Los Angeles, Calif. 90012

LEPI
Life Educational Productions, Inc.
262 E. 4 St.
St. Paul, Minn. 55101

LIBFSC
Library Filmstrip Center
3033 Aloma
Wichita, Kansas 67211

LIFE
Life Magazine
Filmstrip Division
9 Rockefeller Plaza
New York, N.Y. 10020

LIFERP
LIFE Educational Reprint Program
(See LIFE)

LIP
Leacock Pennebaker, Inc.
56 W. 45 St.
New York, N.Y. 10036

LLI
Listening Library, Inc.
1 Park Ave.
Greenwich, Conn. 06870

LMEM
Landmark Educational Media
1600 Broadway
New York, N.Y. 10019

LODGE
Arthur Lodge Productions
333 W. 52 St.
New York, N.Y. 10019

LPC
Lansford Publishing Company
2516 Lansford Ave.
San Jose, Calif. 95125

LRC
Learning Resources Center
Virginia State College
Petersburg, Va. 23803

LYCEUM
Lyceum Productions
Box 487
Altadena, Calif. 91001

MCDDC
McDonnell Douglas Corporation
Film & Television Communication
300 Ocean Park Blvd.
Santa Monica, Calif. 90406

MCHRIS
Machris Productions

MF
Mott Foundation
Flint, Mich. 48502

MFL
Materials for Learning

MGH
McGraw-Hill Films
330 W. 42 St.
New York, N.Y. 10036

MLA
Modern Learning Aids
16 Spear St.
San Francisco, Calif. 94105

MMAL
Museum of Modern Art Library
11 W. 53 St.
New York, N.Y. 10019

MMM
Mass Media Ministries
2116 N. Charles St.
Baltimore, Md. 21218

3M
Minnesota Mining and Manuf. Co.
Medical Film Library
2501 Hudson Road
St. Paul, Minn. 55071

MMPI
Multi-Media Production, Inc.
144 E. 30 St.
New York, N.Y. 10016

MSU
Michigan State University
Audiovisual Center
East Lansing, Mich. 48824

MTP
Modern Talking Picture Service
1212 Avenue of the Americas
New York, N.Y. 10036

MYI
Mobilization for Youth, Inc.
214 E. 2 St.
New York, N.Y. 10009

NARI
Newberry Award Records, Inc.
342 Madison Ave.
Norwalk, Conn. 06851

NBC
National Broadcasting Company
30 Rockefeller Center
New York, N.Y. 10020

NCC
National Council of Churches
475 Riverside Drive
New York, N.Y. 10027

NCF
North Carolina Fund
Public Relations Dept.
Box 687
Durham, N.C. 27702

NEA
National Education Association
1201 Sixteenth St., N..
Washington, D.C. 20036

NEFA
Narcotic Educational Foundation of
America
5055 Sunset Blvd.
Los Angeles, Calif. 90027

NET
National Educational TV, Inc.
2715 Packard Rd.
Ann Arbor, Mich. 48104

NEW
Henk Newenhouse, Inc.
1017 Longaker Road
Northbrook, Ill. 60062

NFBC
National Film Board of Canada
680 Fifth Ave.
New York, N.Y. 10019

NTAAC
New Thing Art and Architecture
Center
2335 Eighteenth St.
Washington, D.C. 20009

NTR
National Tape Repository
Stadium Building, Room 348
University of Colorado
Boulder, Colorado 80302

NYSTRO
A. J. Nystram & Co.
3333 Elston Ave.
Chicago, Ill. 60618

NYT
New York Times
Office of Educational Activities
229 W. 43 St.
New York, N.Y. 10036

OF
Osti Films
264 Third St.
Cambridge, Mass. 02142

PCET
Pictorial Charts Educational Trust
London, England

PEPI
Pepsico Inc.
300 Park Ave.
New York, N.Y. 10022

PFP
Pyramid Film Producers
Div. of Adams Production
Box 1048
Santa Monica, Calif. 90406

PIC
Pictura Films Distribution Corp.
4 W. 16 St.
New York, N.Y. 10011

POPSCI
Popular Science Publishing Co.
239 W. Fairview Blvd.
Inglewood, Calif. 90302

PPC
Pitman Publishing Corp.
6 E. 43 St.
Detroit, Mich. 48211

PRSI
Pioneer Record Sales, Inc.
701 Seventh Ave.
New York, N.Y. 10036

PSU-TAD
Pennsylvania State University
Theatre Arts Dept.
Schwab Auditorium
University Park, Pa. 16802

PTL
Pacifica Tape Library
2217 Shattuck Ave.
Berkeley, Calif. 94704

QED
QED Productions
(See CAFM)

RCA
Radio Corporation of America
RCA Service Co.
Camden, N.J. 08108

REYP
Stuart Reynolds Productions
9465 Wilshire Blvd.
Beverly Hills, Calif. 90212

RMIF
RMI Film Productions, Inc.
4916 Main St.
Kansas City, Missouri 64112

ROBECK
Peter M. Robeck . Co., Inc.
230 Park Ave.
New York, N.Y. 10017

ROGOSN
Rogosin Films
144 Bleecker St.
New York, N.Y. 10012

RTBL
Roundtable Films, Inc.
321 S. Beverly Drive
Beverly Hills, Calif. 90212

SAC
Spoken Arts Company
59 Locust Ave.
New Rochelle, N.Y. 10801

SAND
Sandak, Inc.
4 E. 48 St.
New York, N.Y. 10017

SAUDEK
Robert Saudek, Assoc., Inc.
(See IQF)

SC
Sonocraft Corp.
115 W. 45 St.
New York, N.Y. 10056

SCHLAT
Warren Schloat Productions, Inc.
Palmer Lane West
Pleasantville, N.Y. 10570

SCOTT
Scott Education Division
Scott Paper Co. Production Center
20 First St.
Chicopee, Mass. 01020

SE
Special Education
(See EGH)

SEEPS
Southern Educational Film
Production Service
(See IU)

SF
Sterling Educational Films
Box 8297
Universal City
Los Angeles, Calif. 91608

SFN
San Francisco Newsreel
450 Alabama St.
San Francsco, Calif. 94110

SILBUR
Silver Burdett Company
Park & Colombia Rd.
Morristown, N.J. 07960

SSC
Sacramento State College
Sacramento, Calif. 95819

SSSS
Social Studies School Service
4455 Lennox Blvd.
Inglewood, Calif. 90304

STOC
Standard Oil of Calif.
Public Relations Dept.
225 Bush St.
San Francisco, Calif. 94120

SVE
Society for Visual Education, Inc.
1345 Diversey Parkway
Chicago, Ill. 60614

SYRCU
Syracuse University
Collendale Campus
1455 Cleveland St.
Syracuse, N.Y. 13210

TA
Troll Associates
(See EDRS)

TDI
Tripod Distribution, Inc.
101 W. 55 St.
New York, N.Y. 10019

TECED
Tecnifax Education Division
(See TECVIS)

TECVIS
Tecnifax/Viscom
20 First Ave.
Chicopee, Mass. 01020

TEXF
Texture Films, Inc.
Room 200
1600 Broadway
New York, N.Y. 10019

TF
Target Films

TFC
Teaching Film Custodians
25 W. 43 St.
New York, N.Y. 10036

TIMELI
Time-Life, Inc.
Time & Life Building
Rockefeller Center
New York, N.Y. 10020

TPC
Teachers Publishing Corp.
23 Leroy Ave.
Darien, Conn. 06820

TRIBU
Tribune Films, Inc.
141 E. 44 St.
New York, N.Y. 10017

TU
Tapes Unlimited
Div. Education Unlimited Corp.
13113 Puritan
Detroit, Mich. 48227

UB
University of Buffalo
Buffalo N.Y. 14214

UC
University of California
2223 Fulton St.
Berkeley, Calif. 94720

UCLA
University of California at Los Angeles
405 Hilgard Ave.
Los Angeles, Calif. 90024

UEVA
Universal Educationan Visual Arts
221 Park Ave. S.
New York, N.Y. 10003

UM
University of Michigan
720 E. Huron St.
Ann Arbor, Mich. 48104

UMAVC
University of Michigan
Audiovisual Center
416 Fourth St.
Ann Arbor, Mich. 48104

UMC
Board of Admissions of the
United Methodist Church
Audiovisual Service
475 Riverside Dr.
New York, N.Y. 10027

UMINN
University of Minnesota
Motion Picture Production Division
55 Wesbrook Hall
Minneapolis, Minn. 55455

UMTVC
University of Michigan
720 E. Huron St.
Ann Arbor, Mich. 48104

USC
University of Southern California
Dept. of Cinema
University Park
Los Angeles, Calif. 90007

USNAC
U.S. National Audio-Visual Center
National Archives and Records Serv.
Washington, D.C. 20409

UVA
University of Virginia
Audiovisual Center
Charlottesville, Va. 22903

UWASHP
University of Washington Press
1416 N.E. 41 St.
Seattle, Wash. 98105

VDEF
Visual Dynamics Company

VIGNET
Vignette Films
981 S. Western Ave.
Los Angeles, Calif. 90006

VIMC
Valiant I.M.C.
237 Washington Ave.
Hackensack, N.J. 07602

VSC
Virginia State College
(See LRC)

WABC
(See ABC)

WCAUTV
WCAU-TV
City and Monument Ave.
Philadelphia, Pa. 19131

WCNYTV
WCNY-TV Channel 24
Old Liverpool Road
Liverpool, N.Y. 13088

WETATV
WETA-TV Channel 26
Greater Washington ETV Assn., Inc.
2600 Fourth St., N.W.
Washington, D.C. 20001

WFILTV
WFIL-TV
4100 City Line Ave.
Philadelphia, Pa. 19131

WGBHTV
WGBH Channel 12
WGBH Educational Foundations
125 Western Ave.
Boston, Mass. 02134

WHYYTV
WHYY-TV Channel 12
WHYY, Inc.
4548 Market St.
Philadelphia, Pa. 19139

WILLTV
WILL-TV Channel 12
University of Illinois
1010 S. Wright
Urbana, Ill. 61801

WILSNH
H. Wilson Crop.
555 W. Taft Drive
South Holland, Ill. 60473

WMSBTV
WMSB-TV Channel 10
Michigan State University
600 Kalamazoo St.
East Lansing, Mich. 48823

WMVSTV
WMVS-TV Channel 10
1015 N. Sixth St.
Milwaukee, Wis. 53203

WNDTTV
WNDT-TV Channel 13
Educational Broadcasting Corp.
304 W. 59 St.
New York, N.Y. 10019

WNYET
WNYE-TV Channel 25
112 Tillary St.
Brooklyn, N.Y. 11201

WPSXTV
WPSX-TV Channel 3
Pennsylvania State University
201 Wagner
University Park, Pa. 16802

WQEDTV
WQED-TV Channel 13
4337 Fifth Ave.
Pittsburgh, Pa. 15213

WSU
Wayne State University
680 Putnam
Detroit, Mich. 48202

WT
Washington Tapes
(See NTR)

WTHSTV
WTHS-TV
1410 N.E. Second Ave.
Miami, Fla. 33132

WTTWTV
WTTW-TV Channel 11
5400 N. St. Louis Ave.
Chicago, Ill. 60625

WUCMTV
WUCM-TV Channel 19
Delta College
University Center, Mich. 48701

WVIATV
WVIA-TV Channel 44
Northeastern Pennsylvania Box 4444
Educational Television Association
Scranton, Pa. 18509

WVIZTV
WVIZ-TV
Educational Television Assn.
   of Metropolitan Cleveland
4300 Brook Park Road
Cleveland, Ohio 44134

WWP
World Wide Pictures
Box 1368
Burbank, Calif. 90213

WYESTV
WYES-TV Channel I
Greater New Orleans Educational Tele.
   Foundation
916 Navarre Ave.
New Orleans, La. 70124

YU
Yale University
New Haven, Conn. 06520

ZP
Zenger Productions

Publishers of paperbound books

Abingdon Press
Nashville, Tenn. 37202

Afro-Am Publishing Co., Inc.
1130 W. Adams St.
Chicago, Ill. 60607

Apollo Editions, Inc.
201 Park Ave. S.
New York, N.Y. 10003

Arno Press
330 Madison Ave.
New York, N.Y. 10017

Atheneum Publishers
122 E. 42 St.
New York, N.Y. 10017

Bantam Books, Inc.
271 Madison Ave.
New York, N.Y. 10016

Beacon Press, Inc.
25 Beacon St.
Boston, Mass. 02108

Chilton Book Company
401 Walnut St.
Philadelphia, Pa. 19106

Citadel Press
222 Park Ave. South
New York, N.Y. 10003

Collier Books
(*See* Macmillan Company)

Corinth Books
(Orders to Citadel Press)
222 Park Ave. South
New York, N.Y. 10003

Dell Publishing Company
750 Third Ave.
New York, N.Y. 10017

Doubleday & Company, Inc.
501 Franklin Ave.
Garden City, N.Y. 11530

William B. Eerdmans Publishing Co.
255 Jefferson St., S.E.
Grand Rapids, Mich. 49502

Fawcett Publications, Inc.
Fawcett Place
Greenwich, Conn. 06830

Harper & Row Publishers, Inc.
49 E. 33 St.
New York, N.Y. 10016

Harvard University Press
79 Garden St.
Cambridge, Mass. 02138

Hawthorn Books, Inc.
70 Fifth Ave.
New York, N.Y. 10011

D. C. Heath & Company
2700 N. Richard Ave.
Indianapolis, Ind. 46219

Hill &Wang,Inc.
72 Fifth Ave.
New York, N.Y. 10011

Houghton Mifflin Co.
53 W. 43 St.
New York, N.Y. 10036

Indiana University Press
10th & Morton Sts.
Bloomington, Ind. 47401

Little, Brown & Co.
34 Beacon St.
Boston, Mass. 02106

M.I.T. Press
Massachusetts Institute of Technology
Cambridge, Mass. 02142

McGraw-Hill Book Company
330 W. 42 St.
New York, N.Y. 10036

Macmillan Company
866 Third Ave.
New York, N.Y. 10022

William Morrow & Company, Inc.
788 Bloomfield Ave.
Clifton, N.J. 07012

National Council of Teachers of English
508 S. 6 St.
Champaign, Ill. 61820

National Education Association of the United States
Publication-Sales Section
1201 Sixteenth St., N.W.
Washington, D.C. 20036

New American Library, Inc.
1301 Avenue of the Americas
New York, N.Y. 10019

Oak Publications
33 W. 60 St.
New York, N.Y. 10023

Oxford University Press
1600 Pollitt Dr.
Fair Lawn, N.J. 07410

Penguin Books, Inc.
7110 Ambassador Rd.
Baltimore, Md. 21207

Pitman Publishing Corporation
6 E. 43 St.
New York, N.Y. 10017

Pocket Books, Inc.
1 W. 39 St.
New York, N.Y. 10018

Prentice-Hall, Inc.
Englewood Cliffs, N.J. 07632

Quadrangle Books, Inc.
12 E. Delaware Place
Chicago, Ill. 60611

Random House
201 E. 50 St.
New York, N.Y. 10022

Schocken Books, Inc.
67 Park Ave.
New York, N.Y. 10016

Simon & Schuster, Inc.
1 W. 39 St.
New York, N.Y. 10018

Southern Illinois University Press
Carbondale, Ill. 62901

Stanford University Press
Stanford, Calif. 94305

Teachers College Press
Columbia University
1234 Amsterdam Ave.
New York, N.Y. 10027

United States Government Printing Office
Division of Public Documents
Washington, D.C. 20402

University of California Press
2223 Fulton St.
Berkeley, Calif. 94720

University of Chicago Press
5750 Ellis Ave.
Chicago, Ill. 60637

University of North Carolina Press
Box 510
Chapel Hill, N.C. 27514

University of Pittsburgh Press
3309 Cathedral of Learning
Pittsburgh, Pa. 15213

University of Wisconsin Press
Box 1379
Madison, Wis. 53701

Viking Press, Inc.
625 Madison Ave.
New York, N.Y. 10022

Yale University Press
149 York St.
New Haven, Conn. 06511

Index

Aaron, Chester, 193

Abbott, Robert, 191, 234

Abernathy, Ralph, 103, 184

Abolition, 109, 205, 220

Abraham, William, 273

Achebe, Chinua, 273

Adams, Russell L., 252

African ancestry, 115, 187, 199, 211, 213, 237

African art, 120, 275, 276, 277, 281, 286, 308, 309, 314, 317

African animals and big game, 271, 272, 273, 274, 275, 297, 298, 299, 306, 310, 314, 315, 317

African civilization, 89, 180, 271, 274, 275, 280, 281, 282, 283, 284, 286, 287, 289, 290, 291, 293, 294, 295, 297, 299, 301, 302, 303, 305, 306, 307, 308, 309, 311, 312, 317, 319, 320

African continent, 270, 271, 273, 277, 278, 279, 280, 281, 283, 286, 287, 288, 289, 290, 292, 294, 295, 296, 303, 304, 305, 306, 307, 308, 309, 310, 317, 318, 319

African dances, 95, 269, 271, 285, 294

African dress, 301, 317

African folk tales, 208, 306, 309, 312, 313

African history, 287, 294, 296, 300, 301, 304, 305, 306, 309, 310, 311, 312, 319, 320, 322

African life, 269, 270, 272, 273, 274, 275, 276, 277, 278, 279, 280, 281, 282, 283, 284, 285, 286, 287, 288, 290, 291, 292, 293, 294, 295, 296, 297, 299, 300, 301, 302, 304, 308, 317, 321

African music, 274, 280, 286, 313, 321

African people, 269, 270, 271, 272, 273, 275, 276, 278, 279, 280, 281, 282, 283, 284, 285, 286, 287, 288, 289, 290, 291, 292, 293, 294, 295, 298, 299, 300, 301, 305, 310, 311, 317, 318, 319, 321

African story-songs, 313

Afro-American art, 200, 229, 314

Afro-American history, 97, 102, 179, 180, 195, 201, 205, 216, 289, 310

Afro-American literature, 208

Afro-American music, 95

Afro-American studies, 74

Aiken, Michael, 53

Aldridge, Ira, 66, 190, 235, 236, 239, 240

Alexis, Marcus, 55

Ali, Noble Drew, 181

Alinsky, Saul, 149, 157, 241

Allen, Richard, 65, 230, 240

Allen, Walter, 273

Allen, William F., 55

Alonzo, Manuel, 245

Alston, Charles, 229

American Council on Education, 70

American Federation of Teachers, 69

American Revolution, 97, 127, 200, 213

Ames, William C., 263

Amos, William E., 51

Doddy, Hurley H., 51

Dodson, Dan W., 51

Dodson, Jacob, 190

Dollard, John, 263

Donald, Jon, 181

Dorn, Dean, 246

Douglas, Stephen A., 140

Douglass, Frederick, 65, 69, 121, 141, 160, 181, 182, 190, 193, 194, 196, 200, 202, 204, 206, 207, 208, 214, 219, 221, 223, 227, 230, 231, 232, 234, 235, 237, 239, 240, 253

Drake, St. Clair, 187

Drew, Charles R. (Dr.), 66, 130, 179, 190, 201, 207, 221, 230, 231, 236, 240

Dropouts, 116, 121, 130, 157, 158, 173, 178, 250

Drug abuse, 113, 116, 128, 129, 138, 143, 149, 157, 238, 241

Duberman, Martin B., 259

DuBois, William E. B., 53, 55, 65, 79, 121, 184, 190, 206, 207, 213, 221, 231, 232, 235, 236, 239, 256

Dumas, Alexander, 235, 236

Dumond, Dwight L., 166, 250

Dunbar, Paul Lawrence, 66, 150, 181, 219, 232, 235, 236, 259

Duncanson, Robert, 229

Dunham, Katherine, 190, 233

Durham, Philip, 256

Dwyer, Robert J., 52, 53

Early childhood curriculum, 61, 63

Eddington, Neil, 192

Edmonds, Ronald, 102

Edwards, G. Franklin, 51

Edwards, Harry, 53, 55, 105, 146, 245, 246

Eichmann trial, 170

Ellington, Duke, 65, 190, 191, 222, 233, 240

Elliot, Robert B., 205, 232, 235

Ellison, Ralph, 145, 191, 240

Emancipation Proclamation, 109, 202, 213

Employment, 100, 111, 122, 138, 140

Engler, David, 18, 24

Enos, Darryl (Dr.), 245

Epton, Bill, 98

Essien-Udom, Essien, V., 53, 262

Evans, Lee, 105, 146

Evers, Charles, 231

Evers, Medgar, 211

Fair Labor Standards Act of 1938, 111

Family living, 119, 144, 150, 155, 165, 188, 211, 233

Far West Laboratory for Educational Research and Development, 70

Farmer, James, 190 , 248

Father Divine, 231, 239

Faubus, Orville, 211

Faulkner, William, 175

Fauset, Arthur H., 54, 85

Faust, Albert B., 88

Fetchit, Stepin, 184

Fifteenth Amendment, 237

Finn, James D., 19

Finney, James, 247

Finney, Joseph C., 54

Fisher, Miles M., 55

Multimedia Materials for Afro-American Studies

Gunn, Moses, 221

Gustafson, Lucille, 54

Guzman, Jessie P., 51

Hager, Don J., 54

Hall, George Cleveland, 80

Hall, Prince, 66

Hamer, Fannie Lou, 98

Hamilton, Charles V., 23, 24, 245

Hamilton, Homer, 54

Hamilton, Thomas, 79

Handlin, Oscar, 53, 56

Handy, William C., 66, 170, 190, 231

Handy-Miller, D. A., 248, 249

Hansberry, Lorraine, 154, 191, 201

Hardy, John Edward, 259

Harlem, New York City, 112, 115, 125, 179, 204, 205, 221, 227

Harper, Frances, 226, 233

Harris, Abram L., 265

Harris, Edward E., 52

Harris, Patricia H., 232

Harris, Patricia R., 216, 231

Harris, Sydney, 241

Harrison, E. C., 54

Harrison, Richard, 190

Hartgrove, W. B., 80

Hartman, Lou, 181

Haslam, Gerald, 259

Hatcher, Richard, 191, 211

Havighurst, Robert J., 17, 18, 24

Hayes, Al Stacey, 96

Hayes, Charles F., 54

Hayes, Roland, 66, 190, 232, 235

Head Start, 108, 125

Health education, 128, 145, 161, 193, 205, 215

Healy, James A., 230

Heath, Gordon, 220

Heller, Joseph, 246

Henderson, A. D., 56

Henderson, S. E., 259

Henderson, Vivian W., 56

Henry, Hayward, 186

Henry, John, 197

Henson, Josiah, 231

Henson, Matthew A., 66, 221, 231

Henson, Matthew M., 190, 207

Heredity, 106, 110, 126

Herndon, Angelo, 51

Hernton, Calvin C., 226

Herskovits, Melville J., 265

Hieroglyphics, 96

Higgins, George, 167

Hill, Beatrice M., 54

Hill, Herbert, 97, 250, 260

Hilliard, David, 114

Hine, Ralph H., 52

Hines, Jim, 105, 146

Hinton, William A., 66

Hodges, Edward III, 167

Hoffman, Marvin, 51

Holiday, Billie, 105, 146

Holmes, Eugene C., 54

Holt, Rackham, 253

Hoover, Dwight, 257

Hope, John, 56, 230

Kalven, Harry, Jr., 261

Kariuki, Joseph, 273

Katz, Irwin, 56

Katz, William Loren, 257

Kaunda, Kenneth, 189

Keckley, Elizabeth (Madam), 233

Keith, Damon J., 171, 250

Keller, Cyrus (Rev.), 245

Kelly, William, 228

Kennedy, Flo, 191

Kennedy, John F., 153, 211

Kenyatta, Jomo, 192

Kerner Report, 38, 39, 40, 109, 207

Killian, Lewis, 56

King, Coretta Scott, 103

King, Martin Luther, Jr., 69, 103, 109, 130, 137, 139, 141, 166, 181, 183, 185, 190, 193, 194, 198, 200, 201, 207, 209, 210, 211, 214, 217, 221, 223, 228, 230, 231, 240, 244, 247, 254, 262

Kitano, Harry H. L. (Dr.), 262

Kitt, Eartha, 221

Koenig, Fredrick W., 52

Kozol, Jonathan, 255

Kramer, Stanley, 128

Ku Klux Klan, 110, 136, 181, 206, 207, 214

Kumata, Hideya, 19

Kutchins, Herb, 190

Kwapong, Alex (Dr.), 146

Labor unions, 100, 111, 169

Lacy, Leslie A., 56

La Forge, Peter, 226

Laine, Cleo, 220

Lalime, Arthur W., 14, 15, 24

Lammer, Paul, 132

Lane, Russel A., 56

Langston, John Mercer, 233, 236

Language communication, 5, 63, 114, 115, 117, 123, 129, 164, 183, 198

Languages, 114, 164

Latimer, Lewis Howard, 231, 235, 239

Laurents, Arthur, 128

Law, 95, 117, 135, 153, 168, 170, 173, 175

Law and order, 112, 131, 136, 179, 197

Lawrence, Jacob, 229

Leakey, Louis (Dr.), 115, 205

Le Corbusier, 109

Lee, Canada, 113, 190

Lee, Frank F., 54

Lee, Harold F., 56

Lee, Wallace, 54

Lee-Smith, Hughie, 229

Legislature, 137, 238

Lennon, Florence Baker, 190

Lester, Julius, 247

Levittown, Pennsylvania, 112

Lewis, Anthony, 311

Lewis, Henry, 231

Lewis, John, 98

Lewis, R. H., 79

Lincoln, Abraham, 140, 232

Lincoln, C. Eric, 182, 263

Little Rock, Arkansas, 214

Littlejohn, David, 260

Litwack, Leon, 189

Trotter, James M., 232

Trotter, William Monroe, 214

Trubowitz, Sidney, 46, 47, 256

Truth, Sojourner, 190, 193, 200, 226, 231, 236, 239, 240

Tubman, Harriet, 65, 125, 184, 190, 193, 195, 196, 200, 202, 206, 208, 215, 219, 223, 230, 231, 237, 239, 240

Turner, Bishop, 212

Turner, Charles H. (Dr.), 65

Turner, Henry McNeal, 233

Turner, Nat, 69, 166, 184, 194, 198, 202, 206, 214, 227, 231, 234, 239

Turner, Ralph H., 55

Tuskegee Institute, 105, 176

Tutola, Amos, 273

UNESCO Constitution, 84

U.S. Commission on Civil Rights, 82, 256

Ulanov, Barry, 261

Unemployment, 33, 35, 97, 109, 118, 151, 173, 250

United Nations, 108

Urban education, 127, 165

Urban rehabilitation, 115, 168, 169

Urban renewal, 107, 115, 165, 169, 173, 190

Valien, Preston, 56

Vandalism, 169, 170

Vann, Robert, 191

Venereal disease, 4, 126, 144, 199

Vesey, Denmark, 69, 206, 214

Vincent, Ted, 190

Vinter, Robert (Prof.), 104

Vittenson, Lillian K., 53

Vocational education, 173

Vontress, Clemmont E., 55

Voting procedures, 170, 189

Walker, David, 69, 206

Walker, C. J. (Madame), 191, 236

Walker, Jack L., 56

Walker, Maggie, 234

Walker, Margaret, 219

Wallace, Mike, 179

Waller, Fats, 227

Ward, S. R., 236

Ware, Gilbert, 55

Washington, Booker T., 65, 105, 120, 121, 141, 182, 188, 190, 193, 200, 206, 207, 212, 213, 221, 222, 227, 231, 232, 235, 239, 253

Washington, Gertrude J., 233

Washington, Joseph R., 263

Waters, Ethel, 227

Watson, Tom, 214

Watts, Daniel H., 98, 114

Watts, Los Angeles, 147, 164, 171, 204

Weaver, Robert C., 29, 56, 187, 191, 216, 232, 240, 265

Webb, H. C., 235

Weinburg, Carl, 53

Weir, Olga, 182

Weld, Theodore, 69

Wells, Charles, 172, 250

Wells, Ida B., 232, 233, 236, 239

Wells, Warren, 143

Welsh, Erwin K., 57

Weltfish, Jean, 106